F.F. BRUCE

F.F. BRUCE

A Life

Tim Grass

Paternoster:
thinking faith

This edition first published 2011 by Paternoster
Paternoster is an imprint of Authentic Media Limited
Presley Way, Crownhill, Milton Keynes, MK8 0ES
www.authenticmedia.co.uk

British Library Cataloguing in Publication Data

A catalogue record for this book is available from the
British Library

ISBN-13: 978-1-84227-737-9

Unless otherwise stated Scripture Quotations are taken from the
Authorised Version of the Bible

Cover design by David McNeill
Printed and bound in the UK by Bell and Bain, Glasgow

Contents

Contents

List of Illustrations

Thanks are due to the following for supplying copies, allowing me to make scans, or granting permission to reproduce pictures: Pam Bruce for nos 4 and 5; Pam Harris for nos 3, 10 and 11; Roger Holden for no. 13; David Humphries for no. 12; Sheila Lukabyo for nos 6, 9 and 16; David Payne for no. 7; The University of Sheffield for no. 15. Every effort was made to trace the copyright holder of no. 14, but without success; I should be happy to rectify this in subsequent editions of the book.

Abbreviations

BibSac: Bibliotheca Sacra
BJRL: Bulletin of the John Rylands Library (vols 1–50; vols 51–4: *Bulletin of the John Rylands Library of Manchester;* vol. 55 on: *Bulletin of the John Rylands University Library of Manchester)*
BM: The Believer's Magazine
BRC: Biblical Research Committee
CBA: Christian Brethren Archive, John Rylands University Library
CPF: Cambridge Prayer Fellowship
CBR: Christian Brethren Review (continuation of *Journal of the Christian Brethren Research Fellowship)*
CBRF: Christian Brethren Research Fellowship
CG: Christian Graduate
CT: Christianity Today
EQ: Evangelical Quarterly
ExT: Expository Times
FT: Faith and Thought (continuation of the *Journal of the Transactions of the Victoria Institute)*
H: The Harvester (continued by *Aware)*
IR: F.F. Bruce, *In Retrospect: Remembrance of Things Past* (London: Marshall Pickering, rev. edn, 1993)
IVF: Inter-Varsity Fellowship
IVP: Inter-Varsity Press
*JCBRF: Journal of the Christian Brethren Research Fellowshi*p (continued by *Christian Brethren Review)*
JSS: Journal of Semitic Studies
JTVI: Journal of the Transactions of the Victoria Institute (continued by *Faith and Thought)*
LBC: London Bible College
LST: London School of Theology
n.d.: no date

NICNT: New International Commentary on the New Testament
NIGTC: New International Greek Testament Commentary
NLCNT: New London Commentary on the New Testament
n.p.: no publisher given
n.pl.: no place of publication given
ns: new series
os: old series
PEQ: Palestine Exploration Quarterly
publ.: published
Q.: Question (referring to answers he provided to questions submitted by readers in *The Harvester* and elsewhere)
repr.: reprinted
SNTS: Society for New Testament Studies
SOTS: Society for Old Testament Studies
TB: Tyndale Bulletin
TF: Tyndale Fellowship
UCCF: Universities and Colleges Christian Fellowship
W: The Witness

Introduction

Having completed four years of work on a history of the Christians known in Britain as Open Brethren or Christian Brethren, *Gathering to His Name*, I wondered whether I would ever undertake further research on that community of Christian believers. Soon after it was published in 2006, I happened to mention to Jeremy Mudditt, who had overseen its publication, the need for a biography of F.F. Bruce, as he had helped to shape the thinking of many post-war Brethren in the English-speaking world. Jeremy's ready and decided approval took me by surprise, but as before he offered all needed help; family members also expressed warm interest, and it was decided that a book should appear for the centenary of Bruce's birth on 12 October 2010 (as things turned out, this proved impossible for a variety of reasons but, like the prospect of imminent execution, it did at least concentrate our thinking).

No previous biography has appeared because Betty, Fred Bruce's widow, had been reluctant for one to be written. She felt that his autobiography, *In Retrospect: Remembrance of Things Past*, had said all that should be said. Yet he enjoyed ten further productive years after it was published; moreover, the series of articles on which it was based had themselves been written several years earlier, for the Brethren monthly *The Witness*; a great deal of it was not about himself and his work but about the books he had acquired and the people he had encountered; and of course a biographer's perspective is always going to be different from that of the writer of an autobiography. Several valuable articles have surveyed his work from an academic perspective,[1] but there was a need to relate this to his background and

---

[1] See, e.g., David J.A. Clines, 'Frederick Fyvie Bruce, 1910–1990: In Memoriam', *CBRF Journal*, no. 123 (August 1991): pp. 53–4 http://www.shef.ac.uk/bibs/ DJACcurrres/Bruce.html (accessed 7 January 2008); I. Howard Marshall, 'Bruce,

religious affiliation as a lifelong member of the Open Brethren community. The issues raised by Bruce's life and thought remain pertinent, and a sense of urgency has been imparted to my work by the deaths of some who had contributed during earlier stages of research.

I have written as a historian, and it may be that on occasion I have not picked up the significance of certain remarks or positions in ongoing debate among biblical scholars, but I have tried to place Bruce in the constantly changing settings of twentieth-century Brethren and of English-speaking evangelicalism. In time others will wish to undertake extended analysis of particular aspects of his thought, and so I have concentrated on offering an overview of his life and main writings. What I have sought to avoid, however, is duplicating accounts of people and places which he offered in his own reminiscences.

But why write a biography of such a man? Indeed, given that so much of his life was about thought rather than action, is the enterprise even possible? This book represents my answer to such questions. Inevitably, it is something of an intellectual biography in that it focuses on exploring his thought and his impact, but I have tried to ground this in an understanding of Bruce as a human being. For a succinct assessment of Bruce as a person, we may look to J.I. Packer:

> Bruce was a very Scottish Scotsman, in whom tough independence of mind was married to a sensitive common-touch courtesy, warmth of heart went with verbal coolness, and an exquisite dry humour, genially deflationary, reflected robust common sense. Blessed with a stellar memory, superb academic instincts, energy and versatility of mind, an easy, limpid fluency on paper, and a huge capacity for work, he wrote more than forty books . . . plus nearly two thousand articles and reviews . . . A gentle, modest Christian humanist, an intelligent, quizzical man of letters, and a lover of good men and good causes . . . a great man, who under God accomplished a great deal.
>
> No Christian was ever more free of narrow bigotry, prejudice and eccentricity in the views he held and the way he held them; no man ever did more to demonstrate how evangelical faith and total academic integrity may walk hand in hand . . . [2]

Frederick Fyvie (1910–1990)', in *Oxford Dictionary of National Biography* [online edition] http://www.oxforddnb.com (accessed 14 April 2008); idem, 'Frederick Fyvie Bruce 1910–1990', *Proceedings of the British Academy* 80 (1991): pp. 245–60; A.R. Millard, 'Frederick Fyvie Bruce 1910–1990', *JSS* 36 (1991): pp. 1–6; Peter Oakes, 'F.F. Bruce and the Development of Evangelical Biblical Scholarship', *BJRL* 86/3 (Autumn 2004): pp. 99–124.

[2] J.I. Packer, foreword to *In Retrospect: Remembrance of Things Past*, by F.F. Bruce (London: Marshall Pickering, rev. edn, 1993), pp. xi–xiii [hereafter cited as *IR*].

A reserved and self-effacing man, Bruce rarely talked about himself or put himself forward, and he could therefore seem even more private than he actually was. But it is going too far to describe him, as one obituary did, as a 'dour Scot'. He was a Scot, certainly, and to the end of his life he remained proud of his identity; but he was not dour. Sober, perhaps; often dressed in a suit and tie, and with decidedly modest and often traditional tastes in everything from food to worship; but those who knew the man testify to a vein of wry humour which was never far below the surface.

Because Bruce was a private individual, little of his correspondence has survived apart from letters found between pages of his books when they were given away after his death. However, a number of people have kindly provided me with copies of letters in their possession, and about ninety items have survived in various files of the Christian Brethren Archive in Manchester. There has also been an overwhelming response to requests for information, recollections and materials, from people in various parts of the world, and family members have been most helpful and supportive. Photographs have emerged, and even recordings of him lecturing or preaching. The greatest logistical problem has been locating and reading what he wrote. The fifty books were not too difficult, but some of the periodicals ultimately proved elusive, and I have not even tried to read all his two thousand-plus book reviews.

The reactions to my inquiries indicate that here was a man who attracted a great degree of loyalty from an unusually wide range of people. When I put out appeals for information in various quarters, I did not expect the volume – or the warmth – of response which I received. It made me wonder what kind of person could evoke such feelings almost twenty years after their death; this book attempts to answer that question.[3] Of course, there is a risk that what I have written could seem hagiographic; I hope that readers will not put it down with that as their concluding assessment, for I have tried to indicate where a measure of critical evaluation might be in order. Like Bruce in his handling of Scripture, however, I have preferred to adopt an inductive approach, letting the story tell itself before engaging in too much analysis or evaluation. And in listening to the evidence, I have often been surprised by what I heard.

There are many acknowledgements to be made, for this work is to a significant degree the product of many minds and hearts. In particular,

---

[3] Oakes noted that he still received visits and inquiries from those who revered Bruce's memory: 'Bruce', p. 124.

let me express my gratitude for the willing assistance afforded by members of Bruce's extended family. Secondly, I wish to thank those who responded to my appeals for information and recollections. Some answered questions; some allowed me to interview them by telephone or in person; and some wrote down their recollections for me. They did so from many countries, testimony to the international scope of Bruce's influence. Were I to list all of them by name here, the list would be inordinately long; many are cited in the footnotes, while others preferred to remain anonymous, but I want all to know how grateful I am for their willingness to help. Thirdly, there are those who kindly lent or gave me books, manuscript materials, photocopies of letters, recordings and photographs. I am also grateful to those who provided welcoming hospitality on my trips to North East Scotland and to North America. The J.W. Laing Trust provided a generous grant to cover the costs incurred in my research: I hope the trustees will feel that this book contributes, as Bruce did, to the advancement of evangelical Christianity. Unpublished material is used by kind permission of the institutions where it is held; in particular, material from the archives and special collections of the University of Manchester is reproduced by courtesy of the University Librarian and Director, The John Rylands University Library, The University of Manchester; material from the archives of Tyndale House and the Tyndale Fellowship (including the Bible Research Committee) is used by permission of the Warden of Tyndale House. Finally, I wish to express my great indebtedness to two people, no longer among the saints on earth, without whom this book might never have been written: Jeremy Mudditt, who commissioned it and encouraged me in various ways, and my father, who until his death, to use the words of one of Bruce's dedications, 'kept me at it'.

Tim Grass
September 2010

1

Background and Early Life (1910–21)

Our story begins in north-eastern Scotland. East of Inverness a strip of fertile farmland runs along the sandy coast for about 45 miles. The market town of Elgin lies towards the further end of this, 5 miles inland from the port of Lossiemouth. The fertility and the surprisingly mild climate combine to make this an excellent area for growing barley, essential for the distilleries populating the north-east of Scotland. To the south, the land rises steadily towards the Cairngorms, which, with the Grampians further east, long presented a natural barrier to communication with central and southern Scotland. Along the whole coast, towards Fraserburgh at the north-east's tip, are a string of small ports and fishing villages. Seventy miles to the south-east of Elgin lies the city of Aberdeen, whose university has for centuries received the sons and daughters of many local families.

Elgin itself has a long history, having been the county town of Morayshire from the thirteenth century until late twentieth-century reorganization. Its spectacular ruined cathedral, 'the lantern of the north', also dates from the thirteenth century. The nineteenth century saw the foundations laid for the town's more recent prosperity: Elgin Academy was founded in 1801, although its roots go back to the medieval period, and Highland gentry found the town an attractive place to spend the winter, more accessible than Edinburgh but with something of the capital's cultural life and neo-classical style. Significantly, the first railway to reach Elgin (in 1852) was not initially connected with the rest of the national network, but ran to Lossiemouth; for the local economy it was evidently more important to ensure easy access to shipping facilities than to Aberdeen or Inverness, although a railway linking Elgin with them followed. By the beginning of the twentieth century the town's population was about twenty thousand, and it has continued to grow since.[1]

[1] Anon., 'Undiscovered Scotland: Elgin' http://www.undiscoveredscotland.co.uk/elgin/elgin/index.html (accessed 17 November 2009).

The relative isolation of the north-east from the centres of power further south has meant that it has always manifested a degree of independence in religious matters. In the seventeenth century, when Covenanting fervour swept much of the nation, relatively little impact was made on this area, and even now it has a higher proportion of local people belonging to the Episcopal Church than other parts of Scotland. To add to the mix, Roman Catholicism has retained a presence, and a variety of more recent evangelical traditions – Methodist, Baptist and Brethren – have also established themselves. To a considerable extent this was the fruit of revival from 1858 onwards and of subsequent vigorous outreach.[2] One of the best-known figures in this movement was the gentleman Brownlow North (1810–75), whose residence lay at Bishopmill, just to the north of the town. His conversion in 1855 saw him becoming an itinerant lay evangelist; unusually, and in spite of his being from an Episcopalian rather than Presbyterian background, he received official recognition from the Free Church of Scotland in 1859. The revivalist ethos was one of warm, even enthusiastic, spirituality, and lay people tended to play more prominent roles in such traditions than in the Presbyterian denominations. A link has often been seen between this type of spirituality and the insecurity of life for many in the fishing communities, for whom the loss of boats at sea was all too common. Revivalism certainly remained part of the spiritual outlook of these communities, in some cases until the present.

Local Brethren had their roots in this revival, rather than in earlier gatherings at Dublin or Plymouth which have traditionally been seen as the movement's beginning.[3] It begat a wave of activism which issued among other things in the formation of the North-East Coast

---

[2] On revivals in the region, see Donald E. Meek, '"Fishers of Men": The 1921 Religious Revival, its Cause, Content and Transmission', in *After Columba – After Calvin: Religious Community in North-East Scotland*, Elphinstone Institute Occasional Publications 1 (ed. James Porter; Aberdeen: Elphinstone Institute, 1999), pp. 135–42; Kenneth S. Jeffrey, *When the Lord Walked the Land: The 1858–62 Revival in the North East of Scotland* (Carlisle: Paternoster, 2002).

[3] *IR*, pp. 2–6. This was a fairly standard (and historically justified) local argument, enabling Brethren to stand apart from the Open-Exclusive division which racked Brethren everywhere from 1848: since the pioneers in the north-east did not come out to join an entity known as 'Brethren' they could hardly be held responsible for that entity's earlier history. Cf. *Donald Ross, Pioneer Evangelist of the North of Scotland and the United States of America* (ed. C.W. R[oss]; Kilmarnock: John Ritchie, n.d.), p. 169, citing John Ritchie, *'The Way Which They Call Heresy.' Remarks on Mr. W. Blair Neatby's Book, 'A History of the Plymouth Brethren'* [Kilmarnock: John Ritchie,

Mission in 1860. During the 1860s Donald Ross (1824–1903) and other evangelists associated with him in these agencies came into conflict with the Free Church of Scotland, to which they belonged, because their way of working was not amenable to control by a denominational leadership; furthermore, they were outspokenly critical of the fact that many communicant members of the Free Church were unconverted. The evangelists accordingly withdrew from the NECM and founded another agency, the Northern Evangelistic Society, in 1870, to work in inland areas. Thereafter they gradually adopted views on church order and believer's baptism which paralleled those of the Brethren, leading to the formation of several dozen assemblies (as Open Brethren congregations were called) in the region as converts found it impossible to remain in existing churches. Only once this process had begun did significant contact develop with Brethren elsewhere. Exclusive Brethren also established a strong presence in the region, likewise largely independent at first of what was happening elsewhere in Britain.[4] Further growth came through awakenings in the 1880s, the mid-1890s and 1921; intervening contraction was due to heavy emigration to Aberdeen and overseas.[5] In 1893–4 along the Moray Firth 1,600 were converted, 300 of them in the fishing village of Hopeman, a few miles north-west of Elgin. Another outbreak of

n.d.], p. 100; H.A. Ironside, *A Historical Sketch of the Brethren Movement* (Grand Rapids, MI: Zondervan, 1942), pp. 70–73; Neil Dickson, 'Open and Closed: Brethren and Their Origins in the North East', in Porter, ed., *After Columba – After Calvin*, pp. 151–70; idem, *Brethren in Scotland 1838–2000: A Social Study of an Evangelical Movement* (Carlisle: Paternoster, 2002), pp. 92–9; Tim Grass, *Gathering to His Name: The Story of Brethren in Britain and Ireland* (Milton Keynes: Paternoster, 2006), pp. 124–5. Ritchie was from Inverurie, 15 miles north-west of Aberdeen; Ironside also came from Aberdeenshire.

[4] Dickson, 'Open and Closed', pp. 154–5. Brethren divided into Open and Exclusive wings from 1848, the main issues between them being related at first to the question of the local assembly's responsibilities in dealing with perceived doctrinal error. Open Brethren asserted that each assembly was autonomous, whereas Exclusive Brethren argued that assemblies had a duty to act together; the latter also tended to stress separation from evil as the basis for Christian unity. For a very brief overview, see my article, 'A Brief History of the Brethren' http://www.brethren-history.org/?pageid=809 (first publ. in *Grace* Magazine, July 2008, pp. 18–19).

[5] Dickson, 'Open and Closed', p. 159. This emigration helped to fuel the rise of Open Brethren in the United States, since several Scottish evangelists decided to cross the Atlantic, including Ross and Munro: Robert H. Baylis, *My People: The Story of Those Christians Sometimes Called Plymouth Brethren* (Port Colborne, ON: Gospel Folio Press, repr. 2006), pp. 117–22.

revival occurred in 1921–2, connected with Jock Troup of Wick and spreading as far as Lowestoft through the movements of workers in the fishing industry.[6] Brethren shared fully in reaping the harvest at such times.

It should be stressed that solid theology was by no means regarded as inimical to such vigorous growth. The seventeenth-century Westminster Shorter Catechism was one of the foundational documents of all Presbyterian denominations in Scotland, and at this time every child would have learned it at school. Ross had received a thorough grounding in its theology, to the extent that he was nicknamed 'the walking Shorter Catechism'.[7] But he combined this with a stress on salvation as a gift which could be received in an instant (contrasting with the prevalent belief that the road to Christ was long and often agonizing as the sinner's heart was laid bare by the terrors of God's law), and on assurance as the normal experience of the believer (again, a contrast with the widespread belief that it was given only to those who had progressed far in the Christian life). He founded several magazines, most of which failed, but one, the *Northern Intelligencer*, would develop into *The Witness*, a respected British Brethren monthly. The motto of the *Northern Intelligencer* included these two emphases on instant salvation and assurance, and the combination of these with moderate Calvinistic theology marked many Scottish assemblies, both locally and further afield. Bruce described the Brethren circles in which he had been brought up as moderate ones which saw limited atonement (the doctrine that Christ died for the elect only, and not for all) and double predestination (the idea that God predestined some individuals to be saved, and others to be lost) as extreme.[8] Their Calvinism, then, differed somewhat from that of the Westminster Confession and Catechisms; but it reflected the fact that these had come under increasingly critical scrutiny in Presbyterian circles from 1830 onwards.

We have noted that the revival ethos sat lightly to the order and polity of more established churches; the activity of the Spirit was held to justify departures from the norm. One such was the countenancing

---

[6] [Sandy Stewart], 'A Record of Gospel Work. Christian Brethren. Moray and Nairn' (file, in private hands).

[7] R[oss]., ed., *Donald Ross*, p. 130; the epithet could justifiably have been applied to Bruce.

[8] Madrid, Comisión de Biblioteca y Archivos, Centro Evangélico de Formación Bíblica en Madrid, Bruce to Ernest H. Trenchard, 5 October 1964.

of women's preaching. Women played a prominent role in some local assemblies at a time when this was almost universally disapproved of in other parts of Britain. That at Rhynie in Aberdeenshire continued to allow women to preach, to the extent that one Brethren publisher, Henry Pickering (1858–1941), allegedly considered publishing a manuscript written against its practice.[9] And Bruce himself remembered meeting as a boy the widow of an evangelist, Mrs Lundin-Brown (1829–1924), who had herself been a preacher in revival times and who still used to participate audibly in prayer in local assemblies as a regular visitor.[10]

The new gatherings experienced ferocious opposition, especially from other evangelicals such as those in the Free Church of Scotland, and Brethren accordingly adopted quite a strongly separatist outlook, something which has persisted in most assemblies in the region. As Bruce explained, many of them had come out of churches which they considered to be hindered by human tradition from obeying the Scriptures fully and they had no desire to develop a tradition of their own; yet, paradoxically, that is exactly what they did.[11] Such tradition, however, did not always align with that developed by assemblies 'down south'; there was a degree of robust independence of mind at work. This did not only relate to attitudes towards early Brethren history (which these assemblies did not see as part of their history); it related to a range of practices, most notably for Bruce their handling of the Scriptures. As he put it (referring to himself), 'no north-eastern Scot would change his opinion just because a respected authority held a different opinion!'[12] And the graciousness for which Bruce became known in the academic world may have been the result of a deliberate attempt to counter 'the more abrasive individualisms that would pass unnoticed in my home territory'.[13]

Nevertheless, for the most part this individualism only manifested itself on minor issues; local Brethren tended to follow the same

[9] Dickson, *Brethren in Scotland*, p. 151; Grass, *Gathering*, pp. 181–2. Bruce described Rhynie as an example of 'the priesthood of all believers (and not, in effect, of only 50% or less)': Manchester, CBA, Box 323/4/1/3, Bruce to Neil Dickson, 26 April 1987.

[10] F.F. Bruce, 'Women in the Church: A Biblical Survey', *CBR* 33 (1982): pp. 7–14, at pp. 13–14; Dickson, *Brethren in Scotland*, pp. 153, 493.

[11] *IR*, p. 7.

[12] *IR*, p. 10.

[13] Ibid.

approach to interpreting the Bible as their co-religionists elsewhere. This has become known as 'dispensationalism', and it teaches that God's dealings with humanity may be divided into a series of eras or ages; in each, salvation is by divine grace, and in each the professing people of God descend into failure and ruin. The believer's hope is to be 'raptured', caught up secretly to heaven to be with Christ; those left behind are to suffer a brief period of unparalleled tribulation during which the full extent of human opposition to God and its satanic inspiration is revealed, before Christ returns visibly with his saints to execute judgement and inaugurate the millennium, a thousand-year period of unimaginable blessing and prosperity. Such a scheme of interpretation served to shield its adherents from the inroads of critical thought on traditional belief; it also encouraged the belief that Christians should have as little as possible to do with the world around them. Attempts at 'world improvement' were seen as misdirected, since only God could 'improve' the life of a person by converting them, and doomed to failure because of the innate sinfulness of human beings. Brethren thus tended to be culturally conservative rather than open to change. Education was regarded with suspicion; politics was taboo; and life centred on the regular round of meetings in the assembly. The most important of these was the Sunday morning communion or 'breaking of bread', an unstructured service at which any male believer might pray, give out a hymn, or read and comment on a Bible passage. Sunday afternoons were often devoted to 'ministry meetings', at which extended teaching from the Bible would take place; in the evenings there would be a gospel service designed to provide an opportunity for unconverted people to hear the Christian message and respond. During the week there would be gatherings for prayer, for Bible study, and for evangelism directed at particular groups such as mothers or children. Each Open Brethren assembly was self-governing, but they enjoyed close fellowship with others in their area through such means as Saturday conferences, gatherings for ministry with a break for tea which provided an ideal opportunity for socializing.

Assemblies provided ideal opportunities for individuals to be active in Christian work; evangelism took a high place in their priorities, and British Brethren supported dozens of full-time evangelists who travelled from place to place, holding series of meetings in tents or borrowed halls and seeking to plant new congregations. It was through their labours that many assemblies came into being, especially during the late nineteenth century and the first third of the twentieth.[14] Furthermore, evangelism overseas lay close to the heart of many Brethren, and from the 1870s onwards British assemblies sent hundreds of missionaries to all parts of the world. But Bible study was also prominent in assembly life, and many who had left school as soon as they could later became remarkable for their self-taught depth of insight into the teaching of Scripture, as well as their ability to communicate it, often in intricate detail. It was by no means unknown for them even to teach themselves the biblical languages of Hebrew and Greek. Brethren were suspicious of worldly education, but they found alternative forms of intellectual stimulation which satisfied many. This world was the one into which F.F. Bruce was to be born.

◆　　◆　　◆

Bruce's father, Peter Fyvie Bruce (1874–1955), was born at Ellon, a small town about twenty miles north of Aberdeen.[15] The sixth of a family of twelve, he became a farm worker as his father had been, that part of the region being good farming country; the farm where he worked was Netherleask, near Ellon.[16] His mother was a Fyvie, with roots in the village of that name which lay some miles to the west. Peter's course of life was to change, however, as the result of his conversion at the age of 16: in discussion with a friend who was also spiritually concerned, he saw that it was simply by believing on Christ, whose work on the cross was complete and sufficient, that he could be saved. He joined an assembly in the nearby village of Newburgh which had begun through the work of Donald Ross, later transferring to one in Aberdeen (St Paul Street) when he found work in the city. Although he had left school at 11, he had a natural aptitude for study which he would pass on to several of his children. At the age of 24 he was asked to assist an itinerant evangelist for some weeks during the summer, so following the Brethren pattern of learning the ropes by spending time working alongside a more experienced colleague. Having more money at the end of the period than he had when he began, Peter Bruce felt he should continue evangelizing, which he did

---

[14] For such evangelists, see Grass, *Gathering*, pp. 131–46, 285–7.
[15] This and the following paragraphs draw on Bruce to Sandy Stewart, 15 July 1974, in [Stewart], 'Record of Gospel Work'; F.F. Bruce, 'My Father: Peter Fyvie Bruce (1874–1955)', *BM* 87 (1977): pp. 20–21; *IR*, chs 2–5.
[16] Phil Hill, in conversation, 4, 8 April 2009.

for fifty-six years, although from the 1930s he dropped tent work in favour of door-to-door visiting, which he did in virtually every county in Scotland, travelling often by bicycle. As a younger man, he would do seasonal farm work and then preach each evening, sometimes from a few headings jotted on the back of an envelope. He is recalled as having a good voice, but a rather monotone delivery. Nevertheless, his son reckoned that hundreds must have come to faith in Christ through his ministry. Fred sometimes commented that there was one ministry which he regarded even more highly than his own as a teacher, that of evangelist.[17] Shortly before his death, Peter was urged to take things more slowly, but his only response was 'He'll get all of me there is to give', and he died while conducting a young man's funeral at Huntly.[18]

Conducting a mission at Rosemarkie, a village on the Black Isle immediately north of Inverness, Peter met a young lady named Mary MacLennan (1883–1965). She was a nursemaid in the family of a doctor in Dingwall, and belonged to a newly formed assembly there. They were married on 26 November 1909 by another Brethren evangelist, Duncan McNab (with whom Peter had often worked), at the house where Mary had worked. They settled in Elgin, living in the first and second floors of a house in Rose Place; their part of the house had its own stair but, like most dwellings of that period, there was no electricity supply, neither was there a bathroom.[19] There Frederick Fyvie Bruce made his entrance into the world on 12 October 1910, the first of seven children.

As an evangelist, Peter Bruce had no guaranteed income; he, like missionaries and full-time Bible teachers among the Brethren, practised what was known as 'living by faith', depending on God to provide for their needs without making these known.[20] But his work as an itinerant preacher did not stop him from taking a full share in the domestic chores when at home. He kept a vegetable

---

[17] e.g. *IR*, p. 311.

[18] Sandy Stewart, interview, 22 August 2008; John L.M. Patterson to the author, 15 September 2008; Sheila Lukabyo, interview, 2 September 2009.

[19] Fred Evans to the author, 25 July 2008, 9 August 2010; Alastair Rossetter, interview, 23 August 2008; Sheila Lukabyo, interview, 2 September 2009.

[20] On 'living by faith', see Harold H. Rowdon, 'The Concept of Living by Faith', in *Mission and Meaning: Essays Presented to Peter Cotterell* (ed. Anthony Billington, Tony Lane and Max Turner; Carlisle: Paternoster, 1995), pp. 339–56; Timothy Larsen, '"Living by Faith": A Short History of Brethren Practice', *Brethren Archivists' and Historians' Network Review* 1/2 (Winter 1998): pp. 67–102.

garden and stocked up his woodshed, and was proficient at gutting rabbits, which would have provided an inexpensive source of meat. Each Saturday evening he would polish the family's shoes ready for the following day, the sanctity of which would have been observed with due rigour.[21] The ethos was one of 'plain living and high thinking',[22] and not untypical of evangelical homes in northern Scotland. In some of his books Fred used the story of John A. Mackay (1889–1983), president of Princeton Theological Seminary, who had been converted while reading Ephesians as a teenager; and lest he be thought unusual in his choice of reading, Bruce proudly informed his readers that Mackay was 'a Highland Scot, brought up to know what life's priorities were and to recognize excellence when he met it'.[23] For all the lack of excess money, books were a prominent feature of the Bruce home: classic fiction, an encyclopedia, missionary biographies, works on church history, and some idiosyncratic evangelical works such as Alexander Hislop's *The Two Babylons*, which purported to demonstrate that Roman Catholic worship was derived from Ancient Near Eastern idolatry. And since there were few children's books on the shelves, and Fred had an inquiring mind, he grew up reading such works.[24]

Peter Bruce developed a sturdily independent approach to the Scriptures, and his views on the Second Coming and associated events diverged from those normally advocated among Brethren, with the result that his ministry was not acceptable to some assemblies.[25] His eldest son was also to manifest this character trait, being quite prepared when the occasion was right to advocate views not generally accepted among evangelicals. Family tradition has it that

---

[21] Sheila Lukabyo, interview, 2 September 2009.

[22] *IR*, p. 14. The high thinking appears to have been matched by wide reading: Bruce referred to having read some of the volumes of the Bampton Lectures (given since 1780 at the University of Oxford on some aspect of Christian theology) as a teenager: *IR*, p. 17.

[23] F.F. Bruce, *The Message of the New Testament* (Exeter: Paternoster, 1972), p. 41.

[24] *IR*, ch. 4; Sheila Lukabyo, interview, 2 September 2009.

[25] Indeed, I have been informed that Brethren in the area conferred regarding Peter Bruce's independent views, possibly about the time Fred was a student, and that they were advised by a brother well known nationally, W.W. Fereday (1861–1959), to starve him out (personal information). This would have affected the financial support he received from assemblies. Expounding his views at one conference, Peter Bruce was contradicted in public: Dickson, *Brethren in Scotland*, p. 247.

Fred said that he never received a letter from his father without learning something new about the Scriptures.[26]

Mary Bruce seems to have been a more retiring figure; in later life she felt somewhat inferior, proud of her eldest son but not convinced that she had contributed anything to his development. The youngest two children were also boys, but the four in between them and Fred were girls. Fred's earliest memory was of seeing one of his siblings being given an injection.[27] Given that their father would have been absent for considerable periods each summer, Fred as the eldest would have helped look after the others (although he was prone to be so engrossed in his studies that he did not notice the others, with their friends, jumping from one piece of furniture to another in the living room!), and in later life family relationships remained extremely important to him. All the girls remained with the Brethren, and three began their working lives in the offices of local legal firms. Another sister and brother worked for a local grocer. Lena would marry a former missionary to China, Fred Rossetter. Ella, with her husband Athol Forbes, kept a post office and shop in the village of Clatt, near Huntly. Jim went to Cambridge and then worked for a shipping company in London; as a young man, he preached among assemblies.[28]

The Bruces were one of the two main families in the Brethren assembly in Elgin, which at that time met in the High Street. Having been founded in 1872 in a town which was a regional centre commercially and culturally, it would have been looked to for support for more recently established assemblies in smaller communities, and the young Fred appears to have accompanied his father on preaching engagements. (One informant recalled that Peter Bruce would take Fred with him when giving Bible readings and get him to read out the Scripture references, a practice which must have done much to familiarize him with the English Bible.) However, Fred recalled the other leading brothers as 'warm-hearted, God-fearing men, quite ungifted, who nevertheless carried on the services to the best of their ability'.[29]

---

[26] Peter Oakes, 'F.F. Bruce and the Development of Evangelical Biblical Scholarship', *BJRL* 86/3 (Autumn 2004): pp. 99–124, at p. 103; Alastair Rossetter, interview, 23 August 2008.

[27] John Drane to the author, 20 October 2009.

[28] Pam Harris, interview, 13 March 2008; Sandy Stewart, interview, 22 August 2008; Sheila Lukabyo, interview, 2 September 2009; Pam Harris to the author, 15 August 2010.

[29] *IR*, p. 15.

Among them was his Sunday School teacher, whose lessons were frequently drawn from the Acts of the Apostles, a book which Fred learned virtually by heart and which he would later come to make his own as a scholar.

From 1915 to 1921 Fred attended West End School in Elgin. The headmaster at the time, Peter Dow, had set very high standards and was rewarded by a corresponding rise in the school's reputation. However, the first few months of Fred's scholastic career were disrupted by the school's being requisitioned as an army billet, necessitating the removal of the infants and juniors to the Victoria School of Science and Art in Gordon Street. School life was strictly disciplined, classes could be as large as fifty, and poverty was an obstacle for many families.[30] Nevertheless, one aspect of his primary education which would shape his later development was the requirement to learn by heart the Shorter Catechism. Although he did not understand the words at the time, he would later come to regard it as one of the greatest statements of the Christian faith, quoting its definitions frequently as admirable doctrinal summaries. Throughout his life, he was to see himself as belonging to the Reformed tradition, which in his opinion was 'perhaps more logical and does more justice to the biblical revelation than any other way'.[31]

The education provided was of sufficient quality to enable Fred to go on to Elgin Academy rather than remaining at West End until the school leaving age. In the next chapter we shall see how this opened up to him new horizons.

---

[30] Gordon Barron, *West End School: A Celebration of 130 Years, 1875–2005* ([Elgin]: n.p., [2005]), pp. 15, 19, 22, 27.

[31] Ward and Laurel Gasque, 'F.F. Bruce – The Apostle Paul and the Evangelical Heritage', *H* 68/7 (July 1989): pp. 10–12, at p. 10.

2

Student at Elgin Academy (1921–8)

At this time, most children in Scotland stayed at their original school until leaving at 14, but those who showed academic promise were able to go to secondary schools at 11. Fred went up to Elgin Academy.[1] His mother told him not to read the swear-words in his school books, but she need not have worried. His classical studies proved far more interesting, for he was able to learn Latin and (from the age of 13) Greek as well as the usual subjects; he would later pay tribute to the high quality of the Greek teaching in particular, not least because it taught him to spell words with their accents.[2]

On several occasions he contributed poems or other pieces to the *Elgin Academy Magazine*. One, on 'The Antiquity of the Scottish Race', claimed that the Scots were descended from ancient Egyptians and Assyrians, and that the Stone of Scone, which from time immemorial had played a part in the coronation rituals of Scottish, English and finally British rulers, was none other than Jacob's pillow mentioned in Genesis 28.[3] Another, on a former pupil, Professor James Cooper (1846–1922), was a remarkably mature piece of writing, showing a sound grasp of recent Scottish ecclesiastical history and trends, as well as some sympathy for Cooper's quest for ecclesiastical reunion.[4]

---

[1] This section draws on *IR*, ch. 5. Incidentally, his nephew Alastair Rossetter served as deputy rector (the Scottish equivalent of the assistant or deputy headmaster in many English schools).

[2] Several informants recall him asserting the desirability of beginning to learn Greek while still at school.

[3] F.F. Bruce, 'The Antiquity of the Scottish Race', *Elgin Academy Magazine*, June 1925, p. 8. This was a traditional claim, apparently; the stone was said to have migrated via Egypt, coming to Ireland with the deposed Pharaoh Sheshonk.

[4] F.F. Bruce, 'School Celebrities. (Number 3.) The Very Reverend Professor James Cooper, M.A., D.D., Litt.D., D.C.L., Ll.D.', *Elgin Academy Magazine*, December 1927, pp. 14–15.

During the 1926–7 school year, he edited the magazine, thus obtaining a useful grounding in the basic technical aspects of editing.[5]
He was not a sporty boy, and did not play outside as most children would have done; it may be that he was already suffering from the asthma with which he was later diagnosed. Although he went to the baths each week, he never learned to swim. Nor was he mechanically minded; it was said in the family that it took him all his time to learn to ride a bicycle.[6] Given that this was his father's preferred mode of transport, one wonders what was said about this at home. Rather, he stayed indoors exploring the bookshelves and, according to a sister, compiling chronologies of the kings of Israel and Judah (no easy task, as generations of Old Testament scholars would testify).[7]

♦ ♦ ♦

A highlight of assembly life was the annual conference; each would attract visitors from other assemblies and churches. In the north-east the pre-eminent one was the three-day New Year conference held in Aberdeen.[8] This began in 1874, and Peter Bruce, who was a regular attender, first took his son along in 1923. It was perhaps by way of reaction, however, that Fred learned from these gatherings. Incomprehensibility, which was then deemed to be part of what made a good speaker in the minds of some, was the last thing which could be alleged of his own writing and lecturing. Furthermore, 'If I learned anything in those days, I learned not to inflict Greek on Greekless audiences!'[9]

At one point in his autobiography he implies that as a teenager he had some 'sorting out' to do in relation to the ideas and beliefs with which he had grown up among the Brethren. Help came to him from his English master, A.B. Simpson, a man who had been brought up among the Raven Exclusives (then the most introverted group among

---

[5]*IR*, p. 181.
[6]Bruce to Alan Millard, 4 December 1968; Alastair Rossetter, interview, 23 August 2008; Sheila Lukabyo, interview, 2 September 2009.
[7]W. Ward Gasque, 'Bruce, F(rederick) F(yvie) (1910–1991)', in *Dictionary of Major Biblical Interpreters* (ed. Donald K. McKim; Downers Grove, IL: IVP, 2007), pp. 237–42, at p. 238.
[8]On the Aberdeen Christian Conference, see [Matthew S.R. Brown, et al.], *Aberdeen Christian Conference Centenary 1874–1973* (Aberdeen: Alex P. Reid, 1972).
[9]*IR*, p. 25.

Exclusive Brethren) before finding his way out without losing his faith.[10] Another help was his father, 'my first and best teacher of theology',[11] who was not afraid to adopt a different line from the majority if led to do so by his study of Scripture.

> Among all the varieties of ministry to which I was thus exposed I was able to find my way by using the clue which my father recommended to me in my teens: never to accept anything offered in the way of Christian faith or practice unless I saw it clearly for myself in the Scriptures. This advice I have regularly passed on to others, warning them especially not to accept anything just because I have said it.[12]

And as Fred was to recall: 'I have never had to unlearn anything I learned from him.'[13] 'He had a tremendous influence on me, and wholly for good. I thank God on every remembrance of him.'[14] On his death, Fred wrote:

> I attached great value to his sound judgment, and subconsciously rather than consciously I habitually subjected what I wrote to what I

---

[10] *IR*, pp. 38–9. The Raven Brethren followed the teaching of F.E. Raven, who was condemned in 1890 for allegedly denying that Christ had a human soul (this denial had appeared in the fourth century, when it was known as Apollinarianism); they were also the most centralized of the various Exclusive groupings. For Bruce's lucid outline of how Brethren replicated the main errors of the early Church concerning the person of Christ, see F.F. Bruce, 'The Humanity of Jesus Christ', *JCBRF*, no. 24 (September 1973): pp. 5–15.

[11] J.D. Douglas, 'A Man of Unchanging Faith: An Interview with F.F. Bruce', *CT*, 10 October 1980, pp. 16–18, at p. 16.

[12] *IR*, p. 26. Bruce's daughter Sheila recalled her grandfather telling her not to believe anything just because her father did: Sheila Lukabyo, interview, 2 September 2009. One to whom Bruce passed on this advice was Charles Price, formerly principal of Capernwray College near Lancaster and now pastor of the People's Church, Toronto. 'When I began preaching I asked him if he had any advice to offer a young preacher. He looked at me and thought for a moment then said, "Never be afraid of your own conclusions." It was one of the best pieces of advice I ever received. He elaborated that many preachers consult the commentaries and books of systematic theology but don't actually think for themselves and come to conclusions of their own': Charles Price to the author, 27 January 2008.

[13] *IR*, p. 13.

[14] Bruce to Sandy Stewart, 1 June 1974, in [Sandy Stewart,] 'A Record of Gospel Work. Christian Brethren. Moray and Nairn'.

knew his judgment on it would be. We had very much in common, and agreed on most matters. I was still in my teens when he taught me never to accept anything that might be offered as the mind of God unless I saw it clearly for myself in the Scriptures. This was his own policy, and he maintained his intellectual flexibility in accordance with it to the end of his days.[15]

He also raided his father's bookshelves, finding 'highly instructive', though not always agreeing with, the works of the Brethren apologist Sir Robert Anderson (1841–1918).[16] A more surprising source of help, though it is not clear whether this was before or after he went to university, was a book by the Methodist scholar A.S. Peake (1865–1929), *The Bible: Its Origins, Its Significance and Its Abiding Worth* (1913).[17] Peake, who was to be the first occupant of the professorial chair at Manchester which Bruce would later fill, saw his life's work as being to mediate the fruits of higher critical study of the Scriptures to ordinary Christians, demonstrating the possibility of combining an acceptance of modern theories regarding the composition of the Pentateuch and other such matters with a warm evangelical faith. However, evangelicals at that time were fairly consistently and often vocally opposed to Peake's project. It is clear that Bruce's schooldays and university career saw the foundation laid for his openness to engaging with other viewpoints and his reasoned approach to matters of faith.

His first venture into print in the public arena came early in 1928. The local newspaper, the *Banffshire Journal*, had included in its correspondence columns letters defending infant baptism, signed 'Historicus'; these formed part of a lengthy and ill-tempered exchange which had been precipitated by reference made in a local presbytery of the Church of Scotland to 'the "unmoral religion" and "primitive theology" of one denomination along the Banffshire coast that excluded infant baptism from its tenets' (probably a reference to the Brethren, although most of the respondents appear to have been Baptists).[18] Fred decided to go one better and wrote a rejoinder

---

[15] G.C.D. Howley, 'Frederick Fyvie Bruce: An Appreciation', in *Apostolic History and the Gospel: Biblical and Historical Essays Presented to F.F. Bruce on His 60th Birthday* (ed. W. Ward Gasque and Ralph P. Martin; Exeter: Paternoster, 1970), pp. 15–19, at p. 17.
[16] 'Professor Bruce Asks', *H* 59/1 (January 1980): p. 7.
[17] *IR*, p. 59; F.F. Bruce, *The Canon of Scripture* (Glasgow: Chapter House, 1988), p. 317.
[18] *Banffshire Journal*, 20 March 1928, p. 5.

arguing for believer's baptism (even though he had not yet been baptized himself), signing it 'Apostolicus'. He asserted that 'A study of early ecclesiastical history has convinced me that the practice of infant baptism is largely due to the doctrine of original sin as formulated by St Augustine of Hippo, together with the various repulsive and unscriptural dogmas attached to it', and quoted a range of theologians belonging to churches which practised infant baptism, who all denied that there was any evidence for it in the New Testament.[19]

The date of his conversion to Christ is not known, however; when asked on one occasion how he had 'come to know the Lord', he replied: 'I suppose I imbibed it with my mother's milk.'[20] As he explained in an interview, 'I had little option in the matter of becoming a Christian. The truth of the gospel was the major premise of all thinking and living in the home into which I was born. When I came to years of discretion, I naturally had to make an independent and deliberate commitment to it. But it never occurred to me to do anything else.'[21] However, he must have given satisfactory evidence of having been converted since he was baptized (in the Brethren hall at Lossiemouth, as the Elgin assembly did not then have its own premises in which a baptistery could be installed) and admitted to membership in September 1928, a month before his departure for university in Aberdeen. But to the end of his days he retained a certain Calvinist reserve in speaking of personal spirituality. As he wrote in his own reminiscences:

> While some readers have observed that in these chapters I have said little about my domestic life, others have wondered why I have been so reticent about my religious experience. The reason is probably the same in both instances: I do not care to speak much – especially in public – about the things that mean most to me . . . it calls for quite exceptional qualities to be able to do this kind of thing without self-consciousness or self-deception. It is helpful at times to be able to draw on one's own spiritual experience in the privacy of personal counselling, or in a small

---

[19] 'Apostolicus', 'Infant Baptism', *Banffshire Journal*, 1 May 1928, p. 3; *IR*, p. 174.

[20] Vancouver, Regent College, faculty discussion, 8 April 2009. Such a pattern of experience is quite common in Calvinist traditions, and contrasts with the expectation of some Brethren evangelists of the period that every convert should be able to point to a certain day and hour when they came to Christ.

[21] Douglas, 'A Man of Unchanging Faith', pp. 16–17.

'sharing' group, but to expose it to indiscriminate publicity makes no appeal to me.[22]

Nevertheless, we shall see that as a university student his faith was central to his life and developing academic career, and that he was active in sharing that faith with others.

---

[22] *IR*, pp. 306–7. For a fuller discussion of Bruce's thinking about spiritual experience, see my article 'Called to Freedom: The Spirituality of F.F. Bruce', *Crux* 45/4 (Winter 2009): pp. 10–20.

3

Setting Out on an Academic Career: Aberdeen, Cambridge, Vienna and Edinburgh (1928–38)

In Scotland, even families of modest means looked to send intelligent sons and daughters to university, being prepared to sacrifice in order to do so. A university education was not the middle-class thing that it was in the England of the 1920s. Accordingly, the Bruces looked to see Fred go to university – quite a daunting prospect, financially speaking, given his father's lack of a settled income.[1] However, Fred was to solve that problem in a remarkable way – by winning first prize in a bursary competition. Indeed, one theologian who had entered Aberdeen at the same time believed that Bruce had obtained the highest ever mark in the entrance bursary competition.[2] His old school greeted the news warmly: 'As this success gained a holiday for the school, we would recommend Bruce's example as one to be followed by all school captains or other members of Class VI in the future, if they wish their memories to be treasured long after their departure!'[3]

Lest anyone should write off the Brethren as ignorant fundamentalists, here is his own recollection of how his success in becoming first bursar was greeted by them:

> Our brethren in the Open meetings in the north-east were second to none in their veneration of learning. When in 1928 I attained an

---

[1] On this section, see *IR*, chs 6–8.

[2] Charles S. Duthie, 'F.F. Bruce – Committed to the Substance of Scripture', *British Weekly*, 6 November 1970.

[3] *Elgin Academy Magazine*, December 1928, p. 12, cited by Murray J. Harris, 'Frederick Fyvie Bruce', in *Bible Interpreters of the 20th Century: A Selection of Evangelical Voices* (ed. Walter A. Elwell and J.D. Weaver; Grand Rapids, MI: Baker, 1999), pp. 216–27, at p. 216.

academic distinction much thought of in those parts, the acclaim with which they greeted the news was enough to turn my head; it was all the greater because I was the son of one of their own evangelists. One of our local weekly newspapers, in reporting it, improved the occasion by listing a number of men who had received this distinction from 1860 onwards; the list was headed by the name of William Robertson Smith (and this, I think, has left a lasting impression on me).[4]

When the Aberdeen New Year Conference of Brethren celebrated its centenary in 1973 by inviting Bruce to be one of the speakers, the advertising referred to his having been first bursar.[5] Visiting North-East Scotland in 2008, I found this acclaim still evident in the reactions of Brethren to the mention of Bruce's name, a respect which is the more noteworthy because most of the local assemblies would be of a decidedly traditional stamp. One brother, himself a retired academic, commented that Bruce was said to have been the most brilliant student of his generation.

Although his specialist subjects were to be Latin and Greek, he took courses in others, including English, Logic and Moral Philosophy. In the summer of 1929 he also undertook a crash course in Hebrew. Of his teachers, the one who had the most influence on him was

---

[4] *IR*, p. 40. William Robertson Smith (1846–94) was an Old Testament professor at the Free Church of Scotland's college in Aberdeen. Articles by him in the *Encyclopaedia Britannica* advanced views which were deemed incompatible with orthodox belief in biblical inspiration. He was accordingly tried for heresy and removed from his chair in 1881, taking up a post at Cambridge. The main advocate in Britain of the conclusions of contemporary German Old Testament criticism, he nevertheless claimed to subscribe *ex animo* to the Westminster Confession of Faith. Bruce 'was interested in Smith and had some sympathy for his problems, too, from the point of view of his Christian faith': Alan Millard to Prof. W. Johnstone, 16 November 1993. He would sometimes quote Smith's appeal to the inward witness of the Holy Spirit as being the reason why he received the Bible as the word of God and as the only perfect rule of faith and life: *Answer to the Form of Libel: Now before the Free Church Presbytery of Aberdeen*, p. 21, quoted in Richard Allen Riesen, *Criticism and Faith in Late Victorian Scotland: A.B. Davidson, William Robertson Smith and George Adam Smith* (Lanham, MD, and London: University Press of America, 1985), p. 209. Nevertheless, like the historian and essayist Thomas Carlyle (1795-1881), Bruce felt that Smith could not consistently combine the premises of unbelief with the conclusions of orthodoxy: *JTVI* 78 (1946): pp. 137–8.

[5] [Matthew S.R. Brown et al.], *Aberdeen Christian Conference Centenary 1874–1973* (Aberdeen: Alex P. Reid, 1972), p. 8.

Alexander Souter, Professor of Humanity (i.e. Latin). Souter was a devout Christian whom Bruce assisted in his editing of the *Oxford Latin Dictionary* between 1933 and 1936, and by proofreading the second edition of his Greek New Testament in the 1940s.[6]

To his bursarship Fred added the Linton Bursary, one of the most valuable at £70 per annum; this was awarded by competition and tenable throughout his course on condition of continued good character and academic progress.[7] On top of that came a whole string of prizes. In his first year (1928–9) his prize haul included the Earl of Buchan's Silver Pen, as well as money to be spent on books. The following year saw him carry off five prizes in Latin, Greek and Comparative Philosophy. In the third year, apart from the usual class prizes, he was awarded the Jenkyns Prize in Classical Philology (worth £9 10s.) and the Liddel Prize in Greek verse composition (for translating part of Shakespeare's *Julius Caesar*). And in his final year (1931–2) he was awarded the Seafield Gold Medal in Latin, the Simpson Greek Prize (worth £65) and the Robbie Gold Medal (he would also have been awarded the Dr Black Prize in Latin because he came first in the examination, but his winning the Simpson Prize rendered him ineligible).

Life was not all study, however: it appears to have been in 1929 that he first met his future wife, Annie Bertha (Betty) Davidson.[8] She was the eldest of four children of Anthony Bellett Davidson, a Brethren farmer from New Deer.[9] He had been an electrical engineer in Chicago, where Betty was born on 15 November 1910, but took up his brother's farm, Wardford, in the parish of Methlick, in 1913 after his brother was killed in an accident. His father, John Davidson, had baptized Donald Ross in 1871, and he and other members of the family were active preachers. Distant Brethren relations included Harry A.

---

[6] *IR*, p. 275; *Novum Testamentum Graece* (ed. A. Souter; Oxford: OUP, 2nd edn, 1947), p. vii.

[7] For this section, I am indebted to the *Aberdeen University Calendar* for the relevant years.

[8] Much later, he recalled: 'You ask how my wife survives. She manages to do so rather well, in fact: she has been at it for 48 years. Moreover, we had a seven-year courtship before our marriage, so she had a fairly good idea what kind of person she was undertaking to live with, and seemed to like the prospect': Bruce to Desmond and Gill Ford, 18 December 1984. Since they married in 1936, their courtship presumably began in 1929.

[9] The obituary in the *Daily Telegraph* (20 September 1990) was thus incorrect in stating that she was the daughter of A.B. Davidson, the Hebrew grammarian.

Ironside (1876-1951), who became pastor of the large fundamentalist Moody Memorial Church in Chicago and paid tribute to his origins in his history of the Brethren, and John McGaw, an itinerant evangelist whose son Andrew became a preacher in Australia.[10] So in Brethren eyes this was a good match – an evangelist's son marrying into a family of preachers.

On becoming president of the IVF in 1954–5, Fred alluded in his presidential address to the way in which so many Christian students met their marriage partner through its activities. ' "I was a student in Aberdeen. I was president of the CU. I was one of those presidents who didn't marry the vice-president." (Laughter.) "The secretary had her." (More laughter.) "He was welcome." (Bedlam!) "I married the vice-president who was vice-president the year after." '[11] But during his time at Aberdeen he was also active in evangelistic endeavours, participating in campaigns in various towns under the auspices of the Scottish Students' Campaign Movement, which was founded by D.P. Thomson in order to perpetuate the revival of the early 1920s. Within the university, he had a choice of Christian groups with which to identify: at a national level, a number of evangelical university groups had withdrawn from the Student Christian Movement (SCM) because of dissatisfaction at its lack of a clear evangelical stance; they were to form the nucleus of the Inter-Varsity Fellowship, established as a national body in 1928. Both were represented at Aberdeen, and Bruce joined both. The Christian Students' Fellowship (later the Christian Union) was the IVF-orientated body, and had been formed in 1922. In 1930–31 Bruce served as its president, and one student recollected that the standing in which he was held contributed to its official recognition by the university; he appears to have left the group in a much stronger condition than it had been when he arrived.[12] As for the SCM, its local group was (confusingly) known then as the

---

[10] Sheila Lukabyo and Lesley Young, interview, 2 September 2009; Lesley Young to the author, 26 September 2009, 9 August 2010. Ironside was a third cousin of the aunt of Betty Davidson (who became Bruce's wife) although there is no evidence that the connection was ever recognized; Andrew McGaw's daughters were Betty's cousins.

[11] Geraint Fielder, *Lord of the Years* (Leicester: IVP, 1988), p. 139. Bruce recalled Betty as having been vice-president in 1932–3 (her final year): Bruce to Alan Lukabyo, 11 October 1989.

[12] Ibid. p. 68. This date does not appear to be reconcilable with that given for Betty's vice-presidency above, and I have not traced any records for the Christian Union at Aberdeen which would enable me to confirm it.

Christian Union; the SCM laid great stress on the study of social and economic problems from a Christian perspective, and he was its study secretary for a year before becoming the CSF's president.[13]

Aberdeen had a concentration of Brethren assemblies, and on Sundays Fred attended the largest, Hebron Hall, in Thistle Street at the western end of the city centre. This had been founded in 1889 by members of an assembly then meeting in St Paul Street, and had a peripatetic existence until settling in a new building during 1911.[14] But his evangelical and Brethren allegiances did not hinder him from continuing to rethink his faith. One writer to whom he acknowledged his debt in this regard was the philosopher of religion W.R. Matthews:

> At a time when I was as skeptical as an undergraduate ought to be, a paper of his in the *Hibbert Journal* for January, 1930, on 'The Destiny of the Soul' showed me how I might understand and continue to accept *ex animo* the Christian doctrine of the resurrection of the body. About a year later his *God in Christian Thought and Experience* was my first textbook in the study of the philosophy of religion.[15]

Another was to be Karl Barth, about whom Bruce heard a lecture in the spring of 1930 by W.A. Visser t'Hooft (later to become the first general secretary of the World Council of Churches), followed the next year by a series of lectures on Barth's theology from G.T. Thomson, the professor of dogmatics. Bruce recalled that at that time many in Scottish universities (among whom he included himself), and their teachers, found that Barth sent them back to the Bible and the Reformed faith 'to rediscover something more satisfying than a theological liberalism that had outlived its apparent relevance'.[16] He

---

[13] By the end of his life, he could write to his grandson that 'the time has long since gone by when the S.C.M. could be called Christian in any distinctive sense'; even then, he recalled, it had been a very open fellowship of those desiring to understand the Christian faith and live the Christian life: Bruce to Alan Lukabyo, 9 March 1990.

[14] F. Cordiner, *Fragments from the Past: An Account of People and Events in the Assemblies of Northern Scotland* (London: Pickering & Inglis, 1961), pp. 61–2; Anon., 'Hebron Evangelical Church: Background' http://www.hebronchurch.org.uk (accessed 19 November 2009).

[15] *JTVI* 84 (1952): p. 129.

[16] *JTVI* 87 (1955): p. 140. He wrote this at a time when Barthian theology was coming under renewed and often very antagonistic evangelical scrutiny; see ch. 6 for Bruce's involvement in one particular case.

would later defend Barth as standing 'squarely within the Reformation tradition'.[17]

Aberdeen was influenced by the tradition established by William Ramsay of philological study closely linked to archaeology, and Bruce had read many books by scholars such as Ramsay and Adolf Deissmann before he went to university.[18] However, his researches deepened as his linguistic competence grew. His reading was fuelled by second-hand bookstalls which provided access to works from a variety of theological perspectives. As for periodicals, once he became financially independent he took out subscriptions to two Brethren monthlies, *The Harvester* and *The Believer's Magazine*, which he appears to have continued for the rest of his life.[19] But the most important was the *Evangelical Quarterly*, which he discovered with its second issue in April 1929: 'In our undergraduate eyes this new arrival in the field of theological literature was a most heartening sign; it was good indeed to know that scholars in various lands were so devoted to the cause of expounding and defending the faith once for all delivered to the saints.'[20] Already, then, he was reading and learning from a far wider circle of thinkers than was usual among even the most open-minded Brethren.

It may have been through his father that Fred came to write his first article on a Christian theme, 'The Proof of God's Love', an evangelistic message based on Romans 5:8 which appeared in the *Nairnshire Telegraph* for 3 May 1932. This was later reprinted as an evangelistic tract. His first scholarly article to find its way into print was a paper he read to the Classical Society at the university around 1929/30, which appeared in a Brethren periodical, *The Bible Student*.[21] This was one of a number of small-circulation titles providing material for Brethren who wished to dig deeper in their Bible study. The topic of

---

[17] *H* 36 (1957): p. 155: Q. 627.

[18] T.C. Mitchell, 'Professor Frederick Fyvie Bruce, D.D. F.B.A.', *FT* 117 (1991): pp. 2–5, at p. 2.

[19] 'Professor Bruce Asks', *H* 63/8 (August 1984): p. 7. On these, see Tim Grass, *Gathering to His Name: The Story of Open Brethren in Britain and Ireland* (Bletchley: Paternoster, 2006), pp. 311–14, 403–6.

[20] *EQ* 31 (1959): p. 1. When his library was disposed of after his death, it contained a complete run.

[21] F.F. Bruce, 'The Early Church in the Roman Empire', *Bible Student* (Bangalore) no. 56 (March–April 1933): pp. 30–32; no. 57 (May–June 1933): pp. 55–8; cf. *IR*, p. 174. One wonders how the editor, a Brethren missionary in India named A. McDonald Redwood, found out about the paper.

the paper, 'The Early Church in the Roman Empire', shows his interest in interpreting the New Testament against its classical background, something which was to be a prominent feature of his subsequent work.

◆   ◆   ◆

In 1932 Fred graduated MA with first-class honours in language and literature. He was advised to study for another classics degree at Cambridge, and so in December 1931 he entered England for the first time, to sit an entrance scholarship examination.[22] Once again, his studies were to be funded by scholarships and prizes. Aberdeen had awarded him a Fullerton, Moir and Gray scholarship in Classics and he entered Gonville and Caius College as a major scholar and college prize man in Greek verse composition and the Greek New Testament. In 1933 he secured a first in part I of the Classical Tripos, as well as the Ferguson scholarship in Classics (awarded to a student from any of the Scottish universities) and a Croom Robertson fellowship from Aberdeen, tenable for three years.[23]

For some, Cambridge offered a hectic round of parties and socializing. Fred, by contrast, was rarely to be seen because he was always at his studies, taking every opportunity to learn; he even attended lectures in Sanskrit.[24] In one seminar tutored by A.E. Housman, there was only one other student – the brilliant Enoch Powell, who became professor of classics in Sydney at the age of 25 and later returned to Britain, becoming a highly controversial politician.[25] Yet there is some

---

[22] On this section, see *IR*, chs 9–10.

[23] His dissertation for the latter was on 'The Latinity of Gaius Marius Victorinus Afer, with appendices on his Biblical text and on the vocabulary of Candidus the Arian': Aberdeen, Aberdeen University Library, Special Collections, MS 2975; cf. I. Howard Marshall, 'Frederick Fyvie Bruce 1910–1990', *Proceedings of the British Academy* 80 (1991): pp. 245–60, at p. 247. The university's manuscript catalogue dates it to 1935, but one source dates his fellowship to 1933–6: *Pauline Studies: Essays Presented to Professor F.F. Bruce on His 70th Birthday* (ed. Donald A. Hagner and Murray J. Harris; Exeter: Paternoster, 1980), p. xxxvii. In any case, it must have been completed by 1934, when he began postgraduate study in Vienna.

[24] Mitchell, 'Bruce', p. 2.

[25] Bruce was once asked about Powell, who by the 1960s had adopted some eccentric views regarding Christian origins; he replied only that 'He attends Holy Communion and thereby signifies his dependence on divine grace': Robert Gordon, interview, 6 August 2008; Gordon to the author, 9 August 2010.

evidence of a certain 'suppressed flamboyance'.[26] As a young man he would twirl his walking stick as he walked along, and when crossing the road would hold it out in front of him. He tried growing a moustache as a student, quickly removing it when, unlike his hair, it grew ginger. And he did apparently go punting on the river, although one wonders how he managed, given his non-mechanical turn of mind.[27]

Undergirding all this activity was a deepening Christian commitment in which his parents rejoiced. His father told a friend, 'We are so glad he takes such an interest in the Scriptures and in gospel work.' At the heart of that commitment was, once again, the local Brethren assembly. Founded in the late nineteenth century, it had just moved to a hall in Panton Street, located in an area of small houses between the centre and the railway station. It would have had a somewhat different feel from many assemblies, for Peter Bruce recorded that there were eighteen students, three doctors, and quite a few teachers.[28] It was through this assembly that Fred came to the notice of several leading lights among the Brethren. One was Frederick Tatford, then a civil servant with the Inland Revenue and from 1933 one of the editors of *The Harvester*, an outward-looking Brethren monthly for which Bruce would write a great deal. He recalled being struck on first meeting Bruce by 'the confident views of one who was surprisingly mature for his age and who obviously knew where he was going'.[29] Shortly after that, we find Bruce writing for *The Harvester*; the invitation probably came from Tatford, who had been impressed by his maturity of judgement.[30] Another who was similarly impressed was G.C.D. (Cecil) Howley, later to become a close friend as well as editor of *The Witness* (for which Bruce would also write a great deal), who was impressed by the way that he spoke plainly and intelligibly during a service, in a way that all present could grasp.[31]

---

[26] A phrase used by Laurel and Ward Gasque in an interview, 6 April 2009.

[27] Bruce to Alan Lukabyo, 11 October 1989; Sheila Lukabyo, interview, 2 September 2009.

[28] Peter F. Bruce to Mr Taylor, 16 December 1932.

[29] F.A. Tatford, 'An Outstanding Person I Have Met: Dr. Frederick A. Tatford Writes about Professor F.F. Bruce', pp. 2–3 (cutting from unidentified source).

[30] F.F. Bruce, 'The Chester Beatty Papyri', *H* 11 (1934): pp. 163–4; idem, 'The New Gospel', *H* 12 (1935): pp. 168–70. Brethren were keenly interested in archaeological and manuscript discoveries relating to the Bible.

[31] G.C.D. Howley, 'Frederick Fyvie Bruce: An Appreciation', in *Apostolic History and the Gospel: Biblical and Historical Essays Presented to F.F. Bruce on His 60th Birthday* (ed. W. Ward Gasque and Ralph P. Martin; Exeter: Paternoster, 1970), pp. 15–19, at p. 15.

After the more doctrinal cast of Scottish evangelicalism, which helped to shape Bruce and other evangelical students at Aberdeen, he appears to have found the Cambridge Inter-Collegiate Christian Union (CICCU) something of a shock to his system. It had been the first to separate from the SCM (in 1910), but its grasp of theology went little beyond the evangelical basics. At this time it was, like much student evangelicalism in England, fairly devotionally orientated and anti-intellectual, more interested in winning university sportsmen for Christ than in wrestling with the intellectual and doctrinal aspects of Christian faith in evangelism or teaching.[32] This, and the public school ethos, may explain why he was not too involved in it, although he did serve as college representative during his second year and he attended the CICCU sermon each Sunday evening, among other meetings; the fact that he had already begun to read theologians such as Barth would not have made things any easier for him. Those who graduated in 1934 formed the Cambridge Prayer Fellowship, keeping in touch through their contributions to a twice-yearly prayer letter, but it was only in 1970 that Bruce was asked to join. However, one student who came to reject the CICCU approach found Bruce's contributions at the Breaking of Bread in Panton Hall refreshing because they were different from so many others.[33] Bruce's ecumenical sympathies continued to be apparent too: 'he used to attend matins in the college chapel on Sunday mornings, where he served for a time as chapel clerk, just having time to disrobe and cycle down to the Panton Road Assembly for their morning meeting.[34] On occasion he even took communion at the early morning service held each weekday. And at the university sermon each Sunday afternoon in Great St Mary's Church he heard many of the best-known preachers of the day.

Vacations often saw him remaining in England, spending time in London undertaking research at what was then the Reading Room of the British Museum. He stayed frequently in the suburban homes of Henry Pickering and J.B. Watson, two successive editors of *The Witness*. This enabled him to get to know a number of assemblies and teachers among the Brethren, doubtless helping to pave the way for

---

[32] Fielder, *Lord of the Years*, p. 69. On the Christian Union during this period, see Oliver R. Barclay, *Whatever Happened to the Jesus Lane Lot?* (Leicester: IVP, 1977), ch. 7.

[33] Jack Earl, interview, 8 August 2008; cf. *H* 67/4 (April 1988): p. 5.

[34] John Capon, 'From Scotland with Scholarship', *Crusade*, April 1976 (transcript provided by author).

reception of his later writing. He both preached and sat under preachers (Brethren and others).

As a graduate, Bruce was able to take his degree in two years rather than the normal three, and in 1934 he duly graduated with first-class honours in Classics; indeed, in the part II examination which he took that year, he obtained a double distinction. News spread rapidly, and reference was made in Aberdeen to his success, at a meeting of the Senatus Academicus.[35] Peter Bruce also maintained a keen and proud interest in his son's accomplishments, although he was careful not to ignore those of the rest of the family. In a letter to his daughter Pat shortly after Fred had taken his Cambridge degree, he acknowledged that she might be receiving lots of congratulations on her brother's success but made a point of asking her to tell Winnie, Ian and Jim that he was very pleased to hear of theirs too, even if they were not as brilliant as Fred. That said, he asked Pat to save him any papers or cuttings which said anything about Fred's success.[36]

◆　　◆　　◆

It was clear by now that he was destined for an academic career, something which was then relatively unusual among Scottish Brethren.[37] For the year 1934–5, Cambridge awarded him a Sandys studentship, which helped to finance his postgraduate study.[38] With the Croom Robertson fellowship mentioned above, he had sufficient to support himself at the University of Vienna, where he went to do postgraduate research under Paul Kretschmer. Kretschmer was Professor of Indo-European Philology and an expert on the development of the Greek language. During his year Bruce studied Greek, Indo-European Philology and the Hittite language.[39] We should note at this point his mastery of a wide range of languages; apart from the expected command of Hebrew, Greek and Latin, as a book reviewer he later handled titles in Dutch, French, German, Italian and Spanish. And on one occasion during a Manchester faculty meeting, R.P.C. Hanson,

---

[35] 'Brilliant Scholar', *Aberdeen Press & Journal*, 19 June 1959; unidentified newspaper cuttings in family hands.
[36] Peter Bruce to Pat [Bruce], 29 June 1934.
[37] On this section, see chs 11–12.
[38] *Aberdeen University Review* 37 (1957–8): p. 176; Hagner and Harris, eds, *Pauline Studies*, p. xxxvii.
[39] Mitchell, 'Bruce', p. 2.

then Professor of Theology and an authority on St Patrick, was arguing that students did not need to know the biblical languages; in support of his case, he argued that although he taught a course on Patrick
he did not know Middle Irish. Bruce responded: 'Well, I do!'[40]

The atmosphere in the city was tense, the Austrian Chancellor having been assassinated that summer, and armed police were on per-
manent guard outside the university buildings. Bruce lived at a
Protestant *pension*, the Evangelisches Hospiz, Langegasse 15. He
found fellowship with a small group of Brethren, and his German
improved by leaps and bounds as he was expected to preach frequently. A letter to his father written soon after he arrived offers some
insight into attitudes among the evangelical community at that time.
One brother in the assembly was a cousin of Hitler; at a gathering in
the flat of some of the members, he was introduced to a visiting
German brother named Kähler who lectured in the Brethren Bible
school at Wiedenest. Kähler was delighted to meet this man, for he
was an ardent Nazi and would hear no criticism of Hitler, whom he
claimed was doing God's work in Germany. He assured the company
that the German 'Free Churches' (who met in the same manner as
Brethren) had every freedom because they gave the state no trouble,
unlike the Catholics and mainstream Protestants. Fred had his
doubts, and suggested that anti-Semitism had always injured those
nations which had adopted it, only to be told that Germany was not
anti-Semitic but simply treated Jews as foreigners.[41]

The location of Vienna made it easy for Bruce to visit Brethren in
Hungary and Czechoslovakia and occasionally to minister at their
conferences. His experience in Vienna and Central Europe of the economic legacy of the break-up of the Austro-Hungarian Empire in the
wake of the First World War would contribute to making him a strong
supporter of the Common Market, as it was to be known.[42] The depth

---

[40] Adrian Curtis, tribute at the Service of Thanksgiving, Brinnington Evangelical
Church, 27 October 1990; Philip Alexander, interview, 30 May 2008; Alexander to
the author, 1 August 2010. In confirmation of this, Alexander recalls going through
Bruce's books after his death and finding Irish grammars and dictionaries.

[41] Bruce to his father, 10 October 1934; this fills out the picture in *IR*, pp. 84–5.

[42] Peter Oakes, 'F.F. Bruce and the Development of Evangelical Biblical Scholarship',
BJRL 86/3 (Autumn 2004): pp. 99–124, at p. 106. He would assert that Christians
would do better to consider the evangelistic opportunities presented by the
prospect of Britain's joining than to consider how it was foretold in 'the toes of
Nebuchadnezzar's image': *H* 41 (1962): p. 90: *Q*. 1036.

of his conviction regarding this may be gauged from the fact that it was very rare for him to express any political opinion.

◆   ◆   ◆

Back in Britain during September 1935, he was surprised to receive a letter encouraging him to apply for a position as Assistant in Greek at the University of Edinburgh.[43] Taking it would mean abandoning his doctoral studies, but it presented an opportunity to get his foot on the academic ladder. The position was renewable annually, and could only be held for a maximum of three years; the salary was £250 a year, payable quarterly.[44] Nevertheless, he willingly accepted it. Since he was required to start on 15 October, he had time only for a hasty return to Vienna to collect his belongings, discontinue his studies and say goodbye to his friends. His year's study was not wasted, however; material from his researches appeared in two articles.[45] Apart from the academic incentive which the post presented, there was a financial and personal one. After Betty graduated from Aberdeen in 1933 she had become a primary school teacher at New Fryston, near Pontefract in West Yorkshire.[46] Marriage was out of the question until there was a prospect of his being able to support her, as she would have been required to leave teaching. This post would make that possible.

Settling in Edinburgh, Fred quickly made his home with a Brethren assembly. The one he joined had been founded in 1891, and met from 1919 in a former German Lutheran church in Rodney Street, to the north-east of the city centre in the direction of Leith; this had promptly been renamed Bellevue Chapel, one of the earliest instances of Brethren using the term 'chapel' to designate their buildings. I suspect that the congregation's willingness to take over such an ecclesiastical-looking building (it still has its spire) was an indicator that it was somewhat more open and outward-looking than many Scottish assemblies at the time. Almost immediately he was appointed to the eldership, sharing

[43] On this section, see *IR*, ch. 13.

[44] Letter of appointment from Edinburgh University, 20 July 1937.

[45] F.F. Bruce, 'Latin Participles as Slave Names', *Glotta* 25 (1936): pp. 42–50 (this was a *Festschrift* for his former professor); 'Some Roman Slave-Names', *Proceedings of the Leeds Philosophical Society: Literary and Historical Section* 5/1 (1938): pp. 44–60.

[46] John Mackintosh, comp., *Roll of the Graduates of the University of Aberdeen 1926–1955: With Supplement 1860–1925* (Aberdeen: University of Aberdeen, 1960), p. 204.

in secretarial and youth work.[47] Again, willingness to trust younger men in positions of responsibility indicates that this was quite a progressive assembly. Yet in some respects he was rather conservative in his views. This would have assisted his reception in the assemblies in which he preached throughout Edinburgh and the Borders.

Nothing is known about his duties while at Edinburgh, although we do know that he shared an office in Old College, an early nineteenth-century building off South Bridge. However, now that he had an income, the marriage could take place. As Aberdeen graduates, Fred and Betty were entitled to have their wedding at King's College Chapel, which they did on 19 August 1936. The ceremony was performed by Frank Innes, a minister from Bridge of Allan, near Stirling. Fred's best man was Dr William Thomson Walker. The two had met at Panton Hall, Walker then being an assistant in the medical practice of a leading member, Dr Archie Hanton, and studying in his spare time for a theology degree.[48] A newspaper photograph shows Fred and his father in top hat and tails; it could not have been a typical Brethren wedding![49] The reception was a six-course lunch in the Caledonian Hotel, and the honeymoon was spent revisiting Austria, Czechoslovakia and Hungary, renewing friendships with local Brethren. The marriage was very much a partnership, and it always gave Fred particular joy when Betty's contribution received due recognition.[50]

The couple set up home in 17 Learmonth Avenue, a quiet street of Georgian houses north-west of the centre, and the summer of 1937 saw the arrival of their first child, Iain Anthony Fyvie Bruce. What with family, work and church responsibilities, life must have been full for Fred, but he still found time to write a series of short articles on 'Early Translations of the Bible', which appeared in *The Harvester* intermittently from May 1936 to November 1938.

Since his post could only be held for three years, a move was required at the end of the 1937–8 academic year. Fred therefore applied for a post in South Africa and travelled to London at Easter 1938 for an interview. The successful candidate was from the

---

[47] Cf. *H* 48 (1969): p. 191: Q. 1673.

[48] *IR*, p. 77; L.R.T., 'William Thomson Walker', *British Homeopathic Journal* 72 (1983): pp. 87–9.

[49] 'Graduates Wed in Aberdeen', *Aberdeen Press & Journal*, 20 August 1936; photograph from *Bon Accord*, 21 August 1936.

[50] *IR*, p. 305.

University of Leeds, and on the sleeper northwards, an academic friend whom he met advised him to apply for the vacancy which would result there, promising to put in a word on his behalf with the Professor of Greek.[51] He did, was appointed, and would live in England for the rest of his life.

---

[51] *IR*, pp. 104–5.

4

From Classicist to Biblical Scholar: Leeds (1938–47)

In the autumn of 1938 Bruce took up his new appointment as Lecturer in Greek at the University of Leeds.[1] This was one of the so-called 'redbrick' universities, founded in the late nineteenth century and with an ethos which he found highly congenial. As well as teaching Greek, Bruce lectured each week on the history of the Latin language.

Paradoxically, at the same time as he was establishing himself as a classicist, indications began to appear of an imminent change in direction. Firstly, as a graduate of a Scottish university, he was eligible to sit for the Crombie Scholarship in biblical criticism, a sum of money which was awarded by competitive examination. He did so successfully at St Andrews in June 1939, as the only candidate. The examination required him to study parts of the Bible (as well as Pentateuchal introduction) in the original languages and at much greater depth than he had previously done.

Secondly, once war broke out, and the local Methodist college (Wesley) was closed for the duration, the university asked him to lecture on the Greek New Testament to remaining candidates for theological degrees. He was examined for military service (and would have served, since he was not a conscientious objector), but asthma meant that he was rejected as unfit. Instead, he combined his academic career with night-time stints as an air-raid warden and fire-watcher. When he was required to be on duty in a cinema, he would take a torch and a book with him to pass the time.[2] One informant

---

[1] On the following paragraphs, see *IR*, ch. 14.

[2] F.F. Bruce, 'Biblical Criticism', *Essential Christianity*, June 1963, p. 10; Pam Harris, interview, 13 March 2008; Sheila Lukabyo to author, undated; Sheila Lukabyo, interview, 2 September 2009. His brothers both served in the forces, although their

recalled being told by Bruce that he began writing his commentary on the Greek text of Acts (of which more below) in an air-raid shelter with his notebook and Greek New Testament.[3] He also studied Hebrew under Dr Simon Rawidowicz for the University Diploma, which he was awarded in 1943.[4] During his time at Leeds he developed firm friendships with members of the local Jewish community, on occasion attending the synagogue as a visitor; he recalled hearing his name announced in the same way that Brethren traditionally announce the names of visitors at the start of the Breaking of Bread. Whilst he claimed in *In Retrospect* that he was not overburdened with academic work, something of his capacity for profitable use of time is already evident.

Thirdly, he read the proofs of three of the four volumes of the *Expository Dictionary of New Testament Words*, compiled by W.E. Vine (1873–1949). Vine was another Brethren leader who was also a competent classicist, but after school teaching he had become an editor with the Brethren missionary agency Echoes of Service. His work soon established itself as a classic evangelical reference work and remains in print. Bruce read most of it in typescript and then in proof, a task which he described as 'a real education in New Testament usage', and wrote forewords to three of the four volumes.[5] Finally, he became involved in attempts by the Inter-Varsity Fellowship (IVF) to promote biblical research by evangelicals, of which more later in the chapter.

Apart from his academic duties, Bruce soon became involved with the Yorkshire Society for Celtic Studies, initially a staff club of the university, serving as its president from 1949 to 1951 after he had moved to Sheffield. This met several times a year to hear papers from a wide variety of disciplines. Several of the lectures came from Bruce, on themes such as 'The Evangelization of Scotland' (February 1940), 'Reformation and Counter-Reformation in the Highlands of Scotland'

---

father had been a conscientious objector during World War I, as had many Brethren: see Tim Grass, *Gathering to His Name: The Story of Open Brethren in Britain and Ireland* (Bletchley: Paternoster, 2006), pp. 324–32.

[3] J. Julius Scott Jr, telephone conversation, 11 June 2009.

[4] T.C. Mitchell, 'Professor Frederick Fyvie Bruce, D.D. F.B.A.', *FT* 117 (1991): pp. 2–5, at p. 3.

[5] Forewords to *Expository Dictionary of New Testament Words*, by W.E. Vine, vols 2–4 (London and Edinburgh: Oliphants, 1939–41); F.F. Bruce, 'W.E. Vine – The Theologian', in *W.E. Vine: His Life and Ministry* (ed. Percy O. Ruoff; London: Oliphants, 1951), pp. 69–85, at p. 71.

(November 1943) and 'St Patrick, Apostle of Ireland' (May 1952). The minutes summarize his answer to the perennial poser, 'Who Killed Lord Darnley?', delivered on 4 March 1948:

> His was a most lucid account of a most tortuous affair, with a sketch of the background of violence & intrigue against which it was played. The lecturer's very persuasive interpretation was that Darnley & his family had, with Balfour as chief agent, laid the plot to destroy the Queen & part of the Protestant nobility; an indiscrete [*sic*] confidence by Darnley to his servant had been passed to the intended victims & Bothwell had then lit the fuse to destroy Darnley, the latter had fled precipitously only to fall into the hands probably of the Hamiltons & Douglases with fatal results to himself.[6]

According to the vote of thanks, the audience found this 'a most interesting & convincing lecture', which may explain why the minutes departed from the hitherto normal practice of recording only the titles of lectures. From 1945 to 1957, when it effectively ceased publication, he also edited the society's journal, *Yorkshire Celtic Studies*, although this was not an onerous responsibility, as only three issues appeared during that time.[7] It was not long, either, before he was proving a major help to the Christian Union.[8] In each university where he taught he would do so, and he was also active in the IVF at a national level.

◆   ◆   ◆

Home was to be 11A Estcourt Avenue, Headingley, a suburb of Leeds. This rented house was one of a terrace, with a tiny front garden and back yard, and a cellar in which the family sometimes slept during air-raids. Fred and Betty's second child, Sheila, was born in November 1938. The family soon established a domestic routine, something which must have been indebted in part to the orderliness and disciplined nature which Fred had inherited from his father. Betty was the main disciplinarian in the home, though Fred was by no

---

[6] Leeds, Leeds University Archive, Staff: Clubs and Societies [Sta/005], Yorkshire Society for Celtic Studies, Box 1, Minute Book, 11 May 1928 – 8 February 1949.

[7] *IR*, pp. 181–2; Anon., 'Yorkshire Celtic Studies: Table of Contents' http://www.ucc.ie/locus/ycs.pdf (accessed 12 November 2009).

[8] Oliver Barclay, 'F.F. Bruce and the Inter-Varsity Fellowship', *JCBRF*, no. 22 (November 1971): p. 20.

means unconcerned about his children. He is recalled as loving to quote from children's writers such as Lewis Carroll, Edward Lear and Hilaire Belloc, and the children's comics were carefully 'vetted' – *Dandy* and *Beano*, and then as they grew up *Eagle* and *Girl*.[9] Spiritually, too, a foundation was established; each morning after breakfast there was a brief Bible reading and prayer,[10] while most Sundays saw the Bruces entertaining students; Betty was very much supportive of this, even when wartime rationing taxed her ingenuity to cope with unanticipated guests.

Fred and Betty joined Fenton Street Hall in Leeds, an assembly which had been founded about 1864 and therefore had had time to accumulate its own traditions.[11] In his reminiscences, Bruce suggested that its inertia was its downfall, as it failed to act promptly enough when plans to reconstruct the locality were first mooted, shortly before his arrival. There is also a hint of regret on his part that wartime bombs had missed the building in which the assembly's upstairs premises were located! Nevertheless, the family were made very welcome in the fellowship, and Fred found openings for ministry. Indeed, by 1944 he had agreed to commence a weekly Saturday afternoon lecture on systematic theology for local preachers.[12]

It was through one of the elders at Fenton Street, a Mr May, that Bruce first met G.H. Lang (1874–1958), an itinerant teacher and preacher associated with the Brethren, although they had corresponded before this. A former Exclusive brother, Lang was something of a loose cannon, having already earned considerable criticism as early as 1912 for advocating the view that only some (rather than all) believers will be caught up to heaven at the rapture. His belief was that the usual Brethren view, that all believers would be raptured, encouraged careless living rather than the pursuit of holiness.[13] Lang was also a vocal critic of anything savouring of a tendency to centralization among Brethren, whether in the context of defending conscientious objectors or that of mission support.[14] Their correspondence on critical and exegetical matters indicates that Bruce thought highly

---

[9] Sheila Lukabyo, interview, 2 September 2009; Sheila Lukabyo to the author, 29 November 2009.
[10] Howley, 'Appreciation', p. 16.
[11] For what follows, see *IR*, ch. 15.
[12] Leicester, UCCF archives, Bruce to Douglas Johnson, 16 October 1944.
[13] Grass, *Gathering*, pp. 168–9, 304.
[14] Ibid. pp. 328–9, 345–9.

of Lang as a scholarly exegete, and it is clear that Bruce approved of Lang's wish to engage with the text rather than merely follow a party line.

Beyond the local assembly, Bruce was always willing to visit small gospel halls to preach on a Sunday night or perhaps during the week. Many Yorkshire assemblies were traditional in outlook, but his ministry appears to have been fairly widely acceptable. As part of that, he became a frequent conference speaker. The main regional conference for ministry was held in Bradford each Whitsun, but each local assembly also held its own annual Saturday conference. He was fortunate in that Brethren had a unique appetite for solid teaching in the form of conference addresses, thus providing an ideal platform for his spoken ministry at a time when many other strands of British evangelicalism were somewhat wary of anything not 'devotional' in tone.[15] During this period he also received his first invitations to speak at two flagship gatherings, the Glasgow Half-Yearly Believers' Meetings (commenced in 1865) and the twice-yearly series of ministry meetings held by Brethren at Bloomsbury Central Baptist Church in London. The itinerant preachers who often spoke at such gatherings were usually self-taught in theology and biblical exegesis. Whilst Bruce exemplified this genre in certain respects, his academic studies and position enabled him to offer something distinctive; it is surprising, though, that more of his addresses at such gatherings were not published.

A special place in his affections, however, belonged to a young people's house party for North Midlands assemblies held each Easter in Glossop, about 20 miles east of Manchester, and later elsewhere. He was asked to speak at it in 1944, and so began thirty years' association with these gatherings as a host, speaker and committee member. Fred was obviously very active, giving Bible readings and so on; but Betty also attended for some years and made herself available for private interviews with the girls present.[16] Its purpose was to provide solid teaching, but also to stimulate consideration of vocational choices from a Christian perspective (which, for Brethren, entailed facing the challenge of missionary service overseas). In the wider evangelical

---

[15] Robert Gordon, interview, 6 August 2008.

[16] David and Vivienne Humphreys, interview, 27 March 2009. This may soon have ceased, as the Bruces' daughter, who attended these house parties during the 1950s, did not recall her mother acting in this capacity: Sheila Lukabyo, interview, 2 September 2009.

world, Bruce's interest in students meant that he accepted an invitation to become a vice-president of IVF; his name was listed as such from 1943 until 1968, when such lists ceased to be published.[17] It also meant that where appropriate he would commend the work of the IVF as worthy of support, and commend individuals going to university to the care of local Christian Unions. One such was drawn to Bruce's attention by friends in Gloucester; he commended the student to the care of the Christian Union at Oxford, and shortly afterwards the student was converted to faith in Christ at a Christian Union meeting. His name was James I. Packer, and he would later become a fellow worker with Bruce in the Tyndale Fellowship.[18]

Already Bruce's departures from traditional Brethren thinking were attracting notice: in 1941 C.F. Hogg, a Bible teacher of considerable repute among Brethren, wrote to J.B. Watson, then editor of *The Witness*: 'I am sorry to hear he has become a tribulation saint. He is a promising lad, I hope he may be kept on the right path to the end.'[19] At some point Watson rejected a manuscript which Bruce had submitted for publication in *The Witness* because its eschatological implications were not in agreement with the magazine's standard line.[20] He was evidently following in his father's footsteps. So what were his views? In a foreword to G.H. Lang's *The Revelation of Jesus Christ*, he expressed hearty agreement with Lang's assertion that the true interpretation of Revelation was the eschatological one, which saw the book as primarily about the end, and not an allegorical one which could not accept the idea of a literal millennium. Evidently, then, he was not an amillennialist, although he expressed hearty approval of William Hendriksen's classic amillennial exposition of Revelation, *More Than Conquerors*.[21] He also rejected the idea that Revelation portrayed the whole course of church history, an approach associated with the school known as

---

[17] *Inter-Varsity Magazine*, Michaelmas 1943, p. 21.

[18] UCCF archives, Bruce to Douglas Johnson, 27 October 1944, 11 November 1944, supplementing the account in Alister McGrath, *To Know and Serve God: A Biography of James I. Packer* (London: Hodder & Stoughton, 1997), ch. 2.

[19] Manchester, CBA, J.B. Watson papers, 'Letters from Friends', Hogg to Watson, 12 July 1941. Hogg may well have been referring to Bruce's article 'The End of the First Gospel', *EQ* 12 (1940): pp. 203–14, in which he rejected the idea of a pre-tribulation rapture.

[20] F.F. Bruce, 'His Writings', *W* 85 (1955): p. 199.

[21] F.F. Bruce, 'Eschatology and Apocalyptic', *Theological Notes*, July/October 1944, pp. 3–5, at p. 3.

historicist premillennialism.[22] It would appear, therefore, that if he was anything at this period (his exegetically orientated approach would later make him reluctant to identify with any systematic school of thought), he may have been a premillennialist of the variety later exemplified by the American scholar George Eldon Ladd (1911–82); Ladd would argue that Christ's Second Coming would be followed by a literal millennium, but he did not accept the popular view that these events were to be preceded by a rapture of the saints and a seven-year 'Great Tribulation'. This is confirmed by a later letter to Lang, in which Bruce advanced the view that 'if we read Paul's statement at Athens of the day in which God "will judge the world in righteousness", etc., in the light of its O.T. background, it must be interpreted premillennially. It is not the end of all things, but the beginning of a new era of blessedness on earth, that is in view in Ps. 96:13; 98:9.'[23]

◆   ◆   ◆

It was during his years in Leeds that Bruce's writing career began to take off. A succession of articles appeared, many in *Evangelical Quarterly* or *The Harvester*, on a range of exegetical topics, from the Philistines to Armageddon. In them, certain characteristic emphases were already appearing. One was his interest in the role and functions of women in church life and worship. A 1943 article on 'The Ministry of Women' gave a cautious welcome; whilst 1 Corinthians 14:33–36 was to be taken as meaning exactly what it said, he thought it could be argued that Paul was imposing a general principle in a particular context in a way which he would never do with reference to someone like Priscilla, who with her husband Aquila taught the newly converted Apollos the way of the Lord more perfectly. Since the Holy Spirit never contradicted himself (a principle he drew from the Scottish reformer John Knox), Bruce concluded that if the service of women for Christ was being blessed, it could be assumed that this did not contradict biblical principles. He also commended female founders of certain Brethren congregations in Europe, such as Toni von Blücher of Berlin, whose audible devotions were heard at the Lord's Supper.[24]

---

[22] F.F. Bruce, foreword to G.H. Lang, *The Revelation of Jesus Christ*, by (London and Edinburgh: Oliphants, 1945), pp. 9–10.

[23] CBA, Box 69, Bruce to Lang, 15 May 1957.

[24] F.F. Bruce, 'The Ministry of Women', *Supplement to the I.V.F. Graduates' Fellowship News-Letter*, no. 9 (April 1943). The previous year, he had written to Lang to thank

Wartime meant that the filing system which he began in connection with his biblical studies was a modest one: it comprised old cereal boxes arranged in biblical order from Genesis to Revelation.[25] While he later adopted proper office files, frugality continued to mark his administrative practice, old envelopes and unused pages from university examination books all being pressed into service. Some of his extant exegetical notes are made on the backs of letters to him, tied together with a tag. Betty recalled that 'he never threw a piece of paper away, for it might have had a useful note written on it'.[26]

Bruce's first book was to prove one of his most enduring: *Are the New Testament Documents Reliable?* (1943). The title was first suggested for a young people's meeting in Leeds at which he was to speak.[27] The book itself was a by-product of work on Acts for a commentary, which he had begun in 1939, and his approach was strongly influenced by the Aberdeen archaeologist Sir William Ramsay, who believed that a study of Acts in its wider historical and archaeological context would demonstrate its reliability.[28] In 1960 the title was changed to *The New Testament Documents: Are They Reliable?*, under which it was reprinted as recently as 2003, with a foreword by N.T. Wright, an internationally respected New Testament scholar and Anglican bishop who shares Bruce's concern to bridge the gap between the academic and church worlds. In 2006, the American evangelical periodical *Christianity Today* voted it one of the top fifty books which had shaped evangelicals. Precise sales figures cannot be compiled, but such as I have seen indicate that its sales so far go well into six figures. Long a bestseller among his works, it has been translated into various languages, including German, Spanish, Japanese, Korean, Portuguese, Swedish, Polish and Romanian.

---

him for sending a booklet on Toni von Blücher; 'I had heard a little of her story, and was glad to have this fuller account. It helps one to appreciate the truth about the ministry of women, to read the narrative of a woman's service so manifestly guided by the Holy Spirit': CBA, Box 69, Bruce to Lang, 18 June 1942.

[25] W. Ward Gasque, 'Bruce, F(rederick) F(yvie) (1910–1991)', in *Dictionary of Major Biblical Interpreters* (ed. Donald K. McKim, Downers Grove, IL: IVP, 2007), pp. 237–42, at pp. 239–40.

[26] Laurel and Ward Gasque, 'Frederick Fyvie Bruce: An Appreciation', *H* 69/11 (November 1990): pp. 1–6, at p. 2.

[27] F.F. Bruce, 'Of Making Many Books', *News from Paternoster* [undated publicity brochure from the mid-1970s], p. 2.

[28] Ward Gasque, *A History of the Criticism of the Acts of the Apostles* (Tübingen: J.C.B. Mohr [Paul Siebeck], 1975), p. 258; Mitchell, 'Bruce', p. 3.

The book's impact was due not only to what it said, but who was saying it – a scholar who was respected in the secular educational world.[29] Based on talks to young people (especially students) about the trustworthiness of the gospels and other New Testament documents, it was the first of several works in which Bruce made full use of his training as a classicist to offer a perspective on the Scriptures which contrasted somewhat with those on offer from professional biblical scholars. (It is worth noting that there were a number of 'believing classicists' who went into print on similar themes during the mid-twentieth century, among them E.M. Blaiklock and E.V. Rieu, and that a parallel phenomenon was observable among scholars of English literature, such as C.S. Lewis.) Diffident regarding the limitations of his book, he explained that he had 'written as a teacher of classics, with the purpose of showing that the grounds for accepting the New Testament as reliable compare very favourably with those on which the classical student accepts the authenticity and credibility of many ancient documents'.[30] His approach was to establish the general credibility of the documents rather than demanding an _a priori_ acceptance of their authority.[31] Not only would this serve an apologetic purpose, but also, he hoped, Christians would have their faith confirmed by such study and hence be better equipped to give a reason for their hope.[32]

When this little book appeared, there was very little for young Christians of a thoughtful turn of mind on the reliability of the Bible as a record of divine revelation, which helps to explain the epochal nature of its impact. Howard Marshall, a Methodist who became Professor of New Testament at Aberdeen, was one of many who were greatly helped by the way that Bruce showed in this book how it was possible to be an evangelical without being guilty of intellectual dishonesty, and demonstrated that the way to meet attacks on the Bible was not to ignore them but to respond with superior scholarship.[33] An American, Jim Nyquist, recalled reading the book as a turning point in his faith, bringing it into the historical arena. Quite a few in

---

[29] Peter Williams, in conversation, 26 July 2009.

[30] F.F. Bruce, _Are the New Testament Documents Reliable?_ (London: IVF, 2nd edn, 1946), p. iii.

[31] Ibid. p. 4.

[32] Ibid. p. 118.

[33] I. Howard Marshall, 'Afterword', in T.A. Noble, _Tyndale House and Fellowship: The First Sixty Years_ (Leicester: IVP, 2006), p. 276.

his constituency (the Inter-Varsity Christian Fellowship) had been helped by it, and it was usually to be found in the cases of books for sale which IVCF staff workers took with them on visits to student groups.[34] It was not long before Bruce was being asked to speak on the topic, and he continued to do so for many years, presenting a boiled-down version of his argument; one person I interviewed heard him address the Christian Union at Nottingham University in 1947,[35] and I have a recording of him speaking on it to a Canadian Brethren congregation in 1973. In the latter talk, which may safely be taken as typifying his approach since this did not change substantially over time, Bruce surveyed the documents which were included in the New Testament, considered why they had been written, how they had been selected to form part of a collection and how to test them for reliability. Such testing involved listening to see whether the documents possessed what the translator J.B. Phillips called 'the ring of truth', as well as examining them according to the canons of historical study. But no such tests could tell the reader whether Christ was indeed the Saviour; that (and here we see his evangelistic spirit) could only be proved in experience.

The book appears to have attracted fairly wide attention, even the atheist magazine *The Freethinker* offering an extended and vitriolic review over four issues of what it called 'one of the latest re-hashes of conventional and mostly quite out-of-date apologetics'.[36] More importantly, one reviewer, Christopher Evans of King's College, London, asked a simple but significant question regarding the title: 'reliable as what?' This stimulated Bruce to further reflection, and we shall see that the purpose of Scripture came to figure largely in his understanding of its authority and infallibility, to an extent that was not always the case in evangelical treatments.[37]

◆   ◆   ◆

In strategic terms, perhaps the most important development during this period was Bruce's involvement with the work of the Biblical

---

[34] Jim Nyquist, interview, 2 April 2009.

[35] Alan Dixon, telephone conversation, 5 October 2009.

[36] H. Cutner, in *The Freethinker*, 30 March 1947, p. 104.

[37] *IR*, p. 175; cf. F.F. Bruce, 'Are the New Testament Documents Still Reliable?', in *Evangelical Roots: A Tribute to Wilbur Smith* (ed. Kenneth S. Kantzer; Nashville, TN: Thomas Nelson, 1978), pp. 49–61, at pp. 49–50; for the review, see *Theology* 48 (1945): p. 17.

Research Committee (BRC). Between the wars, evangelicalism in Britain was far more pietistic than scholarly. For some decades, most of the best brains had been encouraged to go abroad as missionaries; few achieved positions of leadership in British denominations; and there was a suspicion of both the institutional church and intellectual study of the Scriptures. Such suspicions represented something of a reaction to the marginalization of all forms of conservative thought by liberal theologians; but they were also fed by a widespread premillennial pessimism (which foresaw only a continuing slide into apostasy for the institutional church) and by a debased form of evangelical spirituality which emphasized individual experience at the expense of engagement with theology, church structures, society or the cultural world. Even the IVF was not immune to this, certainly in England, as Bruce had found at Cambridge. Fundamentalism, which had mushroomed in the United States during the 1920s and now adopted a militantly anti-critical stance, had not secured a firm foothold in Britain, but the prevailing approach to Scripture among IVF students could barely be distinguished from it. However, a few visionary spirits believed that the lack of evangelical scholarship could and should be addressed, and in 1938 the IVF set up the BRC.[38]

To avoid overstating things, it is important to be aware that Bruce's role in the development of Tyndale House and Fellowship was not that of an initiator. He was early identified by the BRC as a man to watch, though it was not felt appropriate to invite him to join the committee at that stage. However, it had discussed the need for good commentaries (including some on the Greek texts) as part of a strategy to provide evangelical works on the Bible for ordinands and others, and his offer to write a commentary on the Greek text of Acts was discussed and accepted in May 1939.[39]

Bruce was present at a planning conference initiated by the BRC and held at Kingham Hill School (the wartime home in the Cotswolds of the Anglican Oak Hill College) in July 1941 which did much to lay the foundations for the post-war growth of IVF and the Tyndale Fellowship. The conference theme was 'Revival of Biblical Theology' and he had been asked to speak on the topic of the resources available in the field of biblical scholarship in terms of

---

[38] Essential reading on the development of evangelical scholarship in Britain is Noble, *Tyndale*, chs 1–2. The following section is much indebted to it.

[39] Noble, *Tyndale*, pp. 31–2. In the event, only two such commentaries were published, Bruce on Acts and E.K. Simpson on the Pastoral Epistles.

'senior men', those experienced in teaching and ministry who could assist students and ordinands. This implies that he was already seen as well connected, though we do not know whether this talk was actually given. It was just after this conference that Bruce and another member of the Brethren, W.J. Martin (a lecturer in Semitic languages at Liverpool University), were asked to prepare lists of articles and possible writers for a one-volume Bible dictionary, Bruce being responsible for the New Testament and Martin for the Old. The first invitations to contribute were sent out in 1942, and in time G.T. Thomson was invited to become the third editor, overseeing the field of systematic theology. Bruce was given final responsibility for editorial decisions, but by 1945 work was at a standstill, mainly because of Martin's absence overseas and the impossibility of getting any work out of him.[40] It seems probable that the project was abandoned after Westminster Press in the USA issued a one-volume Bible dictionary which was felt to cover the same ground and which was greeted warmly by Bruce in a review.[41]

It was not until 1953 that the American publisher William B. Eerdmans suggested a joint venture which would revise an existing publication, the *International Standard Bible Encyclopedia*. Eventually it was agreed with IVF that a smaller and entirely new work should be produced, and Bruce was appointed a consulting editor. From 1943 he was also an advisor for the IVF's projected one-volume Bible commentary, and the BRC that year gave a warm welcome to the proposal that he be invited to write a volume on the Synoptic Problem (the problem of the relationships between the first three gospels and the possible sources used in their compilation).[42]

Another development at the Kingham Hill conference was the acceptance by the BRC of the ownership of the *Evangelical Quarterly*.

---

[40] BRC minutes, 15 August 1941, 4 January 1945; BRC subcommittee minutes, 7–10 September 1942; 'Biblical Research Committee', 1944 memorandum. Overlapping sets of BRC minutes and records exist at Tyndale House (Cambridge) and in the UCCF archives (Leicester).

[41] BRC minutes, 8 September [1945]; F.F. Bruce, 'A One-Volume Bible Dictionary', *TB*, os, July 1946, p. 8. On the same page as the latter article appears the statement that the Tyndale Fellowship council had 'at one time' considered whether to produce such a volume, but that the need had now been met.

[42] Douglas Johnson, *Contending for the Faith: A History of the Evangelical Movement in the Universities and Colleges* (Leicester: IVP, 1979), pp. 211, 324–5; idem, 'The Origin and History of Tyndale House', fols 6, 14 (Cambridge, Tyndale House, Box 41); Noble, *Tyndale*, pp. 33, 40.

Its editor, Professor D.M. Maclean of the Free Church College in Edinburgh, insisted on handing over ownership 'and refused to take No for an answer'.[43] Looking back, Bruce thought it had been offered to the IVF not only to ensure a sound financial basis for its continuance but also to 'instruct the I.V.F. in the way of the Lord more perfectly' – in other words, in the Reformed faith.[44] Bruce, who had already contributed several articles, became an associate editor (with the Welsh minister of London's Westminster Chapel, Martyn Lloyd-Jones) in 1942, assistant editor the following year (to J.H.S. Burleigh, later to become Professor of Ecclesiastical History at New College, Edinburgh), and finally editor from 1950 until 1980.[45] As assistant editor it was his responsibility to deal with the proof pages of each quarter's issue, a task in which he would attain legendary competence.[46]

Even more importantly, it was at Kingham Hill that Martin put forward a proposal which he had been promoting in private for several years to create an institution and a library dedicated to biblical research, along the lines of St Deiniol's at Hawarden near Chester.[47] In due course recommendations were made to relevant committees of the IVF.[48] On a lighter note, the conference also witnessed a contest between Martin and Bruce: Martin asserted that a true Old Testament scholar ought to be able to translate from Hebrew to Greek (as had been done with the Septuagint) and back again without loss of accuracy, and Bruce challenged him to a competition; the result, apparently, was a dead heat![49]

Clearly, Bruce's contribution at Kingham Hill must have laid to rest any doubts about his gifts and scholarship, as he was asked to join the BRC afterwards. The following year he became its chairman, on the

---

[43] Bruce, in a book review in *EQ* 63 (1991): p. 69.

[44] *IR*, p. 184; cf. *EQ* 28 (1956): p. 2; 40 (1968): p. 194.

[45] *IR*, pp. 185–6.

[46] Johnson, 'Origin', fol. 12.

[47] Noble, *Tyndale*, pp. 36, 38; cf. Douglas Johnson, 'The History of Tyndale House', 1987 (Cambridge, Tyndale House, Box 41). St Deiniol's had been founded by W.E. Gladstone as a residential library, and has especially strong holdings in the areas of history and literature. The idea of making the proposed library a residential one appears to have been suggested to Martin by D. Broughton Knox (who as principal of Moore College, Sydney, would exercise a significant influence on Australian Anglicanism), after a stay at St Deiniol's in 1940.

[48] Johnson, 'History'.

[49] Johnson, 'Origin', fol. 9; Noble, *Tyndale*, p. 38 n. 47, citing John Marsh, 'On Not Watching the Wind', *Christian Arena*, November 1994, p. 16.

recommendation of the former missionary and senior evangelical statesman G.T. Manley; the appointment of a classicist rather than a biblical scholar is indicative of the serious weakness of evangelical biblical scholarship at that time, although Bruce was already meditating a change of discipline. Bruce and Martin tutored the first IVF summer school (at St Deiniol's) for theological students, in Greek and Hebrew respectively.[50] Bruce also gave the first annual Tyndale New Testament Lecture at Oxford in December 1942, during a joint conference of theological students and graduates. This was published the following year as *The Speeches in the Acts of the Apostles*.[51] He used it to argue for the authenticity of the speeches as condensed reports of what was actually said, in the mould of the Greek historian Thucydides; this contrasted with a tendency, especially in Germany, to regard them as invented by Luke, who put into the mouths of the speakers the message he himself wished to convey.[52] For several years he would be a regular speaker at summer schools and theological students' conferences organized by the IVF and the Tyndale Fellowship (on which see below). The variety of topics on which he was asked to lecture demonstrates how short IVF circles were of scholarly evangelicals on whom they could call: titles included 'Biblical Studies in 1944', 'Immortality and Eternal Life', 'The Parousia' and 'The New Approach to the Pentateuch'.[53] Doubtless drawing on these lectures, a

---

[50] Johnson, 'Origin', fols 11–12; Noble, *Tyndale*, pp. 41, 43; cf. BRC minutes, 7–10 September 1942. It was at this meeting that Bruce suggested translating two volumes on biblical theology by Erich Sauer, principal of the Brethren Bible school at Wiedenest in Germany, a courageous suggestion at that time. In the event, they *were translated by Lang and published by Paternoster in 1951 as The Dawn of World Redemption and The Triumph of the Crucified.*

[51] He would also give the Tyndale Old Testament Lecture for 1947, published by Tyndale Press as *The Hittites and the Old Testament*, and the Tyndale Lecture in Biblical Archaeology for 1956, *The Teacher of Righteousness in the Qumran Texts*. These and other works helped to bolster the new imprint's reputation as a publisher of scholarly work in the field of biblical studies. A number of other Brethren scholars have given Tyndale Lectures in the various fields of biblical studies, but none in Christian Doctrine, Historical Theology, or Ethics.

[52] He would update it, but without fundamental change, in 'The Speeches in Acts: Thirty Years After', in *Reconciliation and Hope: New Testament Essays on Atonement and Eschatology Presented to L.L. Morris on His 60th Birthday* (ed. Robert Banks; Exeter: Paternoster, 1974), pp. 53–68.

[53] UCCF archives, conference programmes for Tyndale Fellowship and Tyndale House.

steady stream of articles flowed from his typewriter for two periodicals aimed at theological students, *Theological Notes* and its successor the *Tyndale House Bulletin*, later the *Tyndale Bulletin*. Many offered concise summaries of current debates and trends or of major themes in biblical theology. As he explained to Douglas Johnson, the hard-working secretary of IVF, he was willing to offer articles in order to maintain a flow of good material in its publications.[54] Jointly with Alan Stibbs (1901–71), who taught at Oak Hill Theological College, he also took responsibility for *Theological Notes*. Its successor, the *Tyndale Bulletin*, is still the foremost evangelical periodical in the field of biblical studies.[55]

Martin's vision of a residential study centre soon began to become a reality, as a property in Cambridge was purchased in 1944. Bruce became part of a BRC subcommittee charged with seeking a librarian and preparing plans for the property's use; he then chaired the dedication service in January 1945, the act of dedication being conducted by Lloyd-Jones.[56] The subcommittee also recommended the formation of what became the Tyndale Fellowship for Biblical and Theological Research as an agency to bring together evangelical theologians and promote theological work by evangelicals at the academic level, asserting the importance of allowing free critical inquiry and not pre-determining acceptable conclusions in contentious areas. Bruce agreed to draft a publicity brochure outlining its aims. Once the fellowship was founded, with a doctrinal basis shared with the IVF, the BRC oversaw it, reporting to the IVF executive committee.[57]

Bruce and Martin between them played key roles in ensuring that the focus of the Tyndale Fellowship's activities remained on biblical research; theological work was undertaken, but it has never been as important a feature of the fellowship's activities in the way that Lloyd-Jones wanted it to be. Indeed, it has been suggested that Bruce and Lloyd-Jones each thought that the other was leading the Tyndale Fellowship in the wrong direction.[58] It might be surmised that the Brethren background of Bruce and Martin, with its tendency to downplay the significance of creeds,

---

[54] UCCF archives, Bruce to Douglas Johnson, 13 May 1944.
[55] Noble, Tyndale, p. 55.
[56] Ibid. pp. 49, 54, 58.
[57] Johnson, 'Origin', fol. 16; Noble, *Tyndale*, pp. 50–51, 56, 59–60.
[58] J.I. Packer, interview, 7 April 2009. Nevertheless, whenever Bruce commented on Lloyd-Jones's works in *EQ*, his tone was positive and respectful; cf. *EQ* 57 (1985): pp. 91-3; 63 (1991): p. 174, reviewing the two volumes of Murray's biography.

was at work here. It would be a misunderstanding to say that Brethren had no theological tradition through which the authority of Scripture was mediated; they did (it was, essentially, a combination of dispensational eschatology and lay-orientated primitivist ecclesiology), but these two did not share it – or at least, not its eschatology. Nevertheless, they agreed that the Bible functioned authoritatively, not as it was refracted through the prism of a particular doctrinal standard such as the Westminster Confession or the Thirty-Nine Articles, but as it was studied carefully and reverently.[59] In any case, correspondence between Bruce and Johnson during the mid-1940s demonstrates that it was Bruce who wanted to ensure that the constitution of the new Tyndale Fellowship made reference to historic confessions such as the Westminster Confession and the Thirty-Nine Articles of the Church of England. So a perceived aversion to systematic theology on Bruce's part should not be advanced as an explanation for the direction taken by the Tyndale Fellowship.

Perhaps more to the point was the need to concentrate scarce resources on doing one thing well – developing a network of productive evangelical biblical scholars – which meant that other objectives (such as the training of systematic theologians), however desirable in themselves, had to be held over. Given the foundational status of biblical authority in evangelical approaches to doctrinal formulation, the choice can be understood. And it should not be forgotten that evangelicals at this time were all too conscious that the issue of biblical inspiration and authority was an area of intense conflict between them and theologians of other traditions, and that they were pilloried for their views.

Bruce's vision for the Tyndale Fellowship was set out (against the backdrop of the needs of evangelicalism generally) in an article which appeared in the *Evangelical Quarterly* during 1947.[60] Summarizing developments to that date, he denied that its doctrinal basis prescribed the conclusions which researchers were to reach and argued that its members were free to engage in 'unfettered research'; in this it

---

[59] Noble, *Tyndale*, p. 68. Noble states that Bruce doubted whether a unified theological system could be derived from Scripture; in qualification, it should be noted that Bruce was and would remain happy to sign the doctrinal basis of the IVF, believing that it had helped to preserve the movement from the kind of shift which had affected the SCM.

[60] F.F. Bruce, 'The Tyndale Fellowship for Biblical Research', *EQ* 19 (1947): pp. 52–61, repr. in Noble, *Tyndale*, pp. 314–25.

contrasted with the Roman Catholic Church. (Bruce's insistence on 'unfettered research' should be understood against the background of Catholicism rather than Protestant liberalism.) Hence evangelical scholars could hold varying views on such matters as the process of codification of the Pentateuch, the composition of Isaiah, the date of Daniel, the sources of the gospels, or the authenticity of the pastoral epistles as Pauline; the examples he gives are significant, because at that time any evangelical scholars departing from accepted evangelical views would soon have found themselves in hot water. In any case, since all scholars had presuppositions, it was better to be open about them, an attitude which he contrasted with the implicit anti-supernaturalism of many contemporary critics. In addition, those who believed their position secure would surely welcome further light on the issues, from whatever source.

Alongside this openness on critical issues was a keen sensitivity to wider evangelical opinion; early in 1947 Bruce turned down an article (presumably for the *Evangelical Quarterly*) by his friend George Beasley-Murray, a New Testament scholar who later became principal of Spurgeon's College, because it proposed a late date for the book of Daniel. Bruce explained that, in the light of the 'hawks', it was not possible to take too many risks.[61]

As a committee member, Bruce appears to have had a good sense of what people could reasonably and realistically be asked to do, which was married with an unobtrusive and sensitive style of leadership. He was a tireless worker with a wide range of competence. His goal was not simply to see the Tyndale enterprises achieve academic respectability or to prosecute biblical studies for its own sake, but to promote godly Christian living and to equip those who sought to minister the word of God.[62] As part of this, he wanted his work to assist in raising the quality of preaching (in his reminiscences he often commented on the preaching under which he had sat in Brethren circles). He was not at all unusual among academics of the time in this concern: the 1940s and 1950s were the heyday of the 'Biblical Theology movement'; this had its roots in a reaction against liberal Protestantism in North America, and it sought to recover a sense of the unity of the Bible as a record of salvation-history and to adopt a

---

[61] Paul Beasley-Murray, *Fearless for Truth: A Personal Portrait of the Life of George Raymond Beasley-Murray* (Carlisle: Paternoster, 2002), pp. 44–5, citing a letter from Bruce to Beasley-Murray of 22 March 1947.

[62] J.I. Packer, interview, 7 April 2009.

more conservative approach to Scripture without reverting to fundamentalism. At the same time, a continental form of this reaction against liberalism, sometimes known as Neo-Orthodoxy, was reaching its high-water mark. Prominent in this was the Swiss theologian Karl Barth, who had spoken in Britain at various points in the 1930s and attracted a considerable degree of attention from some evangelicals, including Bruce and other members of the Brethren who kept abreast of current theological trends.[63] Two points about these movements are relevant here: firstly, they stressed the importance of preaching (indeed, Barth regarded it as one of the three forms of the word of God, alongside Christ and Scripture); secondly, their stress on the unity and divine authority of the Bible's message (which did not amount to a belief in verbal inspiration) made for an eminently preachable theology. The period saw something of a flowering of preaching, because there was a hunger for it. Even preachers such as Lloyd-Jones, who distanced himself from both these movements, were nevertheless influenced by the climate in which they ministered, one in which war was thought to have made many people more receptive to a message which claimed divine authority.

Given the extent and formative nature of Bruce's activity in the field of evangelical theological enterprise, it is not surprising that his career as a classicist languished somewhat. As late as 1944 he still entertained the hope of being awarded a DLitt for a thesis (on Marius Victorinus, the early Christian commentator on whom he had already written).[64] But in a tribute to his former head of department at Leeds, he wrote: 'his considerateness and tolerance towards his assistant will be a matter for personal gratitude, especially when the assistant spent a good deal of his time in those non-classical divagations which have at length turned him from a teacher of *litterae humaniores* into a teacher of *litterae sacrae*'.[65] In 1946 Bruce applied for the chair of Greek at Cardiff.[66] He was unsuccessful; the door was closing on his classical career, and his next post was to see him complete the transition to the field of biblical studies.

---

[63] Grass, *Gathering*, p. 299; Ian Randall and David Hilborn, *One Body in Christ: The History and Significance of the Evangelical Alliance* (Carlisle: Paternoster, 2001), pp. 202–7.

[64] UCCF archives, Bruce to Douglas Johnson, 13 May 1944; whether he ever produced such a thesis is doubtful.

[65] F.F. Bruce, 'Emeritus Professor Walter Manoel Edwards', *University of Leeds Review* 2/2 (December 1950): pp. 159–62, at p. 161.

[66] *IR*, p. 203.

5

Pioneering in Biblical Studies:
Sheffield (1947–59)

It was in the spring of 1947 that a colleague at Leeds drew Bruce's attention to an advertisement in the *Times Literary Supplement* for a lecturer to head up a new department of biblical studies at the University of Sheffield.[1] His attention to biblical topics could so easily have led to his falling between two stools, not properly qualified to take a university post in the field, but no longer carrying out the kind of research which would maintain his academic credibility as a classicist and hence his chances of obtaining another post in that discipline. This opening, however, was suited to him because it occurred not in the Faculty of Theology but in the Faculty of Arts, where his broader background would have stood him in good stead. It may well be that he would not have obtained such a good post in an established department; certainly he would not have been able to do so a few years later.

Towards the end of his career, Bruce could assert: 'I can think of no better foundation than a classical education for the professional cultivation of biblical studies.'[2] In his view, there could never be an excess

---

[1] For the following paragraphs, see also *IR*, ch. 18; David J.A. Clines, Stephen E. Fowl and Stanley E. Porter, eds, *The Bible in Three Dimensions: Essays in Celebration of Forty Years of Biblical Studies in the University of Sheffield*, JSOT Supplement Series 87 (Sheffield: Sheffield Academic Press, 1990), p. 13; John W. Rogerson, 'Biblical Studies at Sheffield', ibid. pp. 19–23; David J.A. Clines, 'The Sheffield Department of Biblical Studies: An Intellectual Biography', in idem and Stephen Moore, eds, *Auguries: The Jubilee Volume of the Sheffield Department of Biblical Studies*, JSOT Supplement Series 269 (Sheffield: Sheffield Academic Press, 1998), pp. 14–89, at p. 14; Peter Oakes, 'F.F. Bruce and the Development of Evangelical Biblical Scholarship', *BJRL* 86/3 (Autumn 2004): pp. 99–124, at p. 113.
[2] *IR*, p. 145.

of contributions to New Testament study from classical scholars.[3] His training as a classicist meant that he brought with him certain perspectives which became widely regarded as strengths in his work. One was his emphasis on the need for immersion in the biblical languages and the value of the close inductive study of the primary sources which that made possible. He was always aware of, and frequently engaged in, the scholarly debates of the day; but he was most at home studying the ancient writings themselves. This may explain why, although Ronald Inchley sought during the late 1940s to persuade him to write a New Testament introduction for the publishing house of the Inter-Varsity Fellowship (confusingly, both were known as IVF), he never did so.[4] With his preference for working with the primary sources, Bruce would have found the necessary discussion of scholarly theories regarding the origin, date and purpose of biblical books uncongenial. Similarly, although he did consider issues related to the methodology of biblical interpretation, he did not develop it in any significant way. He was an exegete rather than a theoretician, who 'preferred engaging in the exegetical task to discussing the principles of interpretation: playing the game was much more satisfying to him than discussing the rules'.[5]

Another legacy of his classical training was a greater readiness to entertain the essential historicity of the New Testament documents, and to contemplate testing them by the canons of historical investigation, than was often the case in biblical scholarship at that time. In his view, students (for whom he had written *New Testament Documents*):

> were readier to entertain seriously the claims of the gospel if they were persuaded that its documentary sources were (contrary to much popular prejudice) historically respectable. Writing in those days as a teacher of classics, I tried to show that the New Testament writings stood up impressively well to the canons of historical and literary criticism which students of Greek and Roman antiquity were accustomed to apply to the writings with which they dealt.[6]

---

[3] F.F. Bruce, 'New Testament Studies in 1960', *CT*, 13 February 1961, pp. 8–10, at p. 8.
[4] BRC minutes 1942–52.
[5] Murray J. Harris, 'Frederick Fyvie Bruce', in *Bible Interpreters of the 20th Century: A Selection of Evangelical Voices* (ed. Walter A. Elwell and J.D. Weaver; Grand Rapids, MI: Baker, 1999), pp. 216–27, at p. 223.
[6] *IR*, p. 175.

Uniquely for a British university, the department at Sheffield was founded as a 'Department of Biblical History and Literature' with no corresponding department of theology, thus excluding more narrowly theological study. It was the first in Britain to be located within an arts faculty rather than one of divinity or theology. During the 1930s William Temple, later to become Archbishop of Canterbury, had endorsed requests that the university should establish a department of theology, but the economic situation was cited as making it impossible to do so. In fact, Sheffield, like other universities founded in the late nineteenth and early twentieth centuries, was wary of confessional theology and the wrangling which it seemed to produce. However, the 1944 Education Act had given 'religious instruction' (often known then simply as 'Scripture') the status of a compulsory subject, thus stimulating a considerable rise in the numbers wishing to study biblical studies or theology at university level, and so it was agreed that a department of biblical studies was now needed. But this position was only reached, and the department founded, after what has been described as an 'unholy' row.[7] The Bishop of Sheffield, Leslie Hunter, wanted a department of theology to train Anglican ordinands; the Professor of Education wanted to train religious instruction teachers; others were opposed to any study of theology or biblical studies in a university setting. The Senate considered teaching theology too contentious but agreed that a department of biblical studies would be acceptable.

Another dispute ensued over interviews for the post of head of department; the bishop wanted a cleric, but most of the panel wanted Bruce, who was both a Nonconformist and a layman. Bruce was accordingly called for interview, along with two Presbyterian ministers, and was offered the post immediately. His classical background and objective approach would have commended him to the authorities and allayed the fears of some regarding the appropriateness of teaching biblical studies in the university.

Bruce seized the opening with both hands, later describing the opportunity to focus on biblical studies as 'enjoyable beyond words' because it allowed him to do something he loved and to be well paid for it.[8] The teaching was expected to be 'non-doctrinal', i.e. not committed to a particular confessional viewpoint, but he had no problems

---

[7] Helen Mathers, *Steel City Scholars: The Centenary History of the University of Sheffield* (London: James & James, 2005), p. 148.
[8] *IR*, p. 142.

with such a stipulation for he would not have dreamed of trying to teach in any other way; indeed, he stated that he took it for granted that the same methods were appropriate in approaching the Bible as he had used in teaching classics. Nevertheless, he was aware that many of his students were planning to teach in schools. This, he believed, held rich promise for the future of British Christianity, and schools themselves presented a fertile field for wise evangelism.[9]

For the first year he was the only member of staff in the department, and his only duties were to lecture to half a dozen students on the Bible in English, with special attention to Judges and Acts,[10] but soon it began to grow and its course offerings to develop. In addition to full-time courses there was also a two-year evening course mainly for teachers wishing to add a qualification in Scripture. Teaching a variety of students provided a good training in self-discipline, he acknowledged; for that and other reasons, it 'can be the most exhilarating and rewarding work in the world'.[11]

When he arrived it was only expected that the department would teach for the pass degree, but he worked to ensure that an honours school was inaugurated in 1949, requiring three years' study of Hebrew and Greek. The first year's intake comprised just one student, David Payne (1949–52), who recalls Bruce lecturing to him in his office, but he set the school on a firm footing, gaining a first-class hon-

---

[9] *JTVI* 80 (1948): pp. 100–01.

[10] F.F. Bruce, 'Biblical Studies at Sheffield: The Early Days', in Clines, Fowl and Porter, eds, *The Bible in Three Dimensions*, pp. 25–7, at p. 25. Bruce wrote the section on Judges in the *New Bible Commentary* (1953), and he later supposed that it and his other contributions on the Old Testament had been based on his lectures: Bruce to Alan Lukabyo, 11 October 1989. But he may have chosen it for a different reason; as he wrote in response to a review of the *New Bible Commentary* by Professor T.W. Manson, 'What you say about the O.T. conservatism of the work being more extreme than the N.T. conservatism is curious, but true. When Davidson [the editor] asked me, quite early on, to choose an O.T. book to comment on, I should have liked to explore Genesis. But I knew that, while Q, L and M in gospel criticism were likely to be just tolerated, JE, D and P in Pentateuchal criticism would be completely unacceptable. So I played for safety and chose Judges': Manchester, John Rylands University Library, Special Collections, Manson papers, E.I.235: Bruce to Manson, 24 November 1953. He might also have added that he did not hold to a creationist interpretation of Genesis 1 – 3, on which he argued that divergent views had co-existed for two thousand years: 'The Christian Faith and Genesis 1 – 3', *Senior Teacher's Magazine* 8 (1955): pp. 51–2, 63.

[11] F.F. Bruce, 'Religious Education: Bible Teaching in the Faculty of Arts', *ExT* 65 (1953–4): pp. 306–7.

ours degree and being awarded the Gibbons Prize for the most distinguished graduating student in the Faculty of Arts.[12] Immediately after his finals, Bruce gave him a week's crash course in Syriac – an example of how he always had time for people who needed it.[13] Throughout his time at Sheffield Bruce would use his office for teaching small groups; one student remembers how he would stand up when her Hebrew class entered the room and only sit down once they were settled.[14] Another student from a Brethren background recalled that 'we were encouraged to see the biblical characters as individuals and not just as studies for gospel addresses'.[15] In time Bruce secured approval from the university to accept students for postgraduate research degrees, and he was promoted to professor in 1955, a referee for the process being the Baptist Old Testament scholar H.H. Rowley (1890–1969).[16]

While still a classicist Bruce served as an internal examiner in Biblical Studies at Leeds from 1943, and until 1975 he acted as external examiner for a number of universities.[17] This was an accepted part of the duties of established academics, but it involved a considerable amount of work, ensuring that an institution's examination and marking were up to standard. On one occasion, a member of the Brethren whom Bruce knew was being examined in Biblical Studies at Leeds. Meeting him in a Brethren context, Bruce asked him how the examinations were going. Receiving the response 'I'll flannel my way through the Old Testament paper', Bruce responded, 'I don't think so; I'm the external examiner!' In later life, Bruce delighted to introduce him by telling this story, or would challenge him to recall it.[18]

Beyond the student world, he became a frequent lecturer on what were then known as extra-mural courses, giving series of evening classes for the benefit of the general public. Many of these courses

[12] *IR*, p. 230; David Payne to the author, 25 February 2008.

[13] Service of Thanksgiving, Brinnington Evangelical Church, 27 October 1990.

[14] Margaret Curtis to the author, 2 December 2009.

[15] Anthea Cousins, appreciation in *H* 69/11 (November 1990): p. 6.

[16] *IR*, pp. 142, 166; Ronald Clements, interview, 6 August 2008. Rowley also made a number of openings for Bruce to write or review: *IR*, pp. 165–6.

[17] Leeds 1943–7, 1957–60, 1967–9; Edinburgh 1949–52, 1958–60; Bristol 1958–60; Aberdeen 1959–61; London 1959–60; St Andrews 1961–4; Cambridge 1961–2; Wales 1965–8; Sheffield 1968–70; Newcastle 1969–71; Keele 1971–3; Dublin 1972–5: *Who's Who 1990* (London: A&C Black, 1990).

[18] Jean Angell, telephone conversation, 4 July 2008; Dennis Angell to the author, 15 July 2008.

were on the Dead Sea Scrolls or on other aspects of the historical background to the Bible, but he also taught a course on the Epistle to the Hebrews jointly with the Archdeacon of Sheffield, D.E.W. Harrison, in 1955–6.[19] He also lectured under the auspices of the Workers' Educational Association at Chesterfield Public Library in 1951.[20] Another body to which he lectured, and of which he become a joint-chairman, was the Sheffield Theological Society. Once again, this gave the wider population opportunities to hear the foremost contemporary biblical and theological scholars.[21]

Having changed discipline, Bruce lost no time in joining the Society for Old Testament Studies in 1947 and the Society for New Testament Studies in 1948, at the time the foremost academic bodies in their respective fields.[22] He became a regular attender at their annual conferences, so developing an extensive network of friends and colleagues. The SOTS was a British institution, which required of prospective members the ability to appreciate the Old Testament in Hebrew. Bruce testified to its helpfulness to him during his time at Sheffield, when he spent over half his time teaching the Old Testament. As early as 1951 he read a paper to its annual meeting, on 'Eschatology in the Prophets of the Persian Period'.[23] The SNTS was international in its membership, met in various countries, and required members to have the level of competence expected of university and college lecturers in the field.[24] At the same time he maintained his activity in promoting evangelical biblical scholarship. Although in 1950 he stepped down as chairman of the BRC to make way for 'someone more in touch with the centre', he took on the leadership of the Tyndale New Testament Study Group.[25] The study groups were the backbone of the fellowship's corporate life, holding regular conferences bringing together those working in that particular discipline.

---

[19] F.F. Bruce, *The Epistle to the Hebrews*, NLCNT (London: Marshall, Morgan & Scott, 1965), p. xii.

[20] Mrs R. Sawyer to the author, March 2008.

[21] *IR*, pp. 162–3.

[22] See *IR*, ch. 21.

[23] *IR*, p. 164. The paper was never published.

[24] *IR*, pp. 169–70, 190.

[25] T.A. Noble, *Tyndale House and Fellowship: The First Sixty Years* (Leicester: IVP, 2006), p. 65, citing BRC minutes, July 1950; it is noteworthy that two subsequent chairmen of the BRC, Donald Wiseman (1957–86) and Alan Millard (1986–96) also belonged to the Brethren: ibid. p. 282.

Wider recognition came surprisingly rapidly. In 1957, Bruce was delighted to receive an honorary DD from Aberdeen. In the citation, he was described as 'probably the finest scholar that Aberdeen has produced [in biblical studies] in the last forty years'.[26] In February 1957 he undertook his first overseas lecture trip, having been invited under a scheme organized by the British Council to lecture at the Free University of Amsterdam and elsewhere on the Dead Sea Scrolls. The lectures were published as *Biblical Exegesis in the Qumran Texts*.[27] Into the Easter vacation of 1958 he squeezed a hectic lecture tour to the United States, where among other engagements he gave the John A. McElwain lectures at Gordon Divinity School in Wenham (Massachusetts), and the Calvin Foundation lectures at Calvin College and Seminary, Grand Rapids (Michigan). The former were on Paul and the Old Testament, and all but one of the eight remained unpublished, although he had hoped to revise them for publication.[28] The latter were published in North America as *The Defense of the Gospel in the New Testament* and in Britain as *The Apostolic Defence of the Gospel*. Bruce's main aim in these lectures was to study New Testament apologetic practice in order to establish the lines on which contemporary Christians should defend the faith. Notably, he defended the use of arguments from prophecy and miracle,[29] and of the argument from Christ's resurrection he wrote that Christians 'may also emphasize the evidence for His resurrection as a most potent argument for the truth of Christianity; and their evidence will be the more effective if the power of His life is at work in their lives in such a way that others take note of it'.[30] Bruce might not have seen himself as an evangelist, but it is clear that he had inherited at least something of his father's passion to see people coming to faith in Christ. We find him outlining the evangelistic motivation of the would-be apologist:

> The twentieth-century apologist, in confronting contemporary paganism, especially in the western world, will find it necessary to expose

---

[26] *Aberdeen University Review* 37 (1957–8): p. 176.

[27] *IR*, pp. 193–4; F.F. Bruce, *Biblical Exegesis in the Qumran Texts*, Exegetica 3.1 (Den Haag: Van Keulen, 1959; Grand Rapids, MI: Eerdmans, rev. edn, [1959]/London: Tyndale Press, 1960).

[28] *IR*, pp. 194–9; Bruce to Leslie Allen, 20 December 1958.

[29] F.F. Bruce, *The Apostolic Defence of the Gospel: Christian Apologetic in the New Testament* (London: IVF, 1959), p. 12.

[30] Ibid. p. 18.

erroneous ideas for what they are. He must remove obstacles which lie in the way of people's accepting the truth – false beliefs about God, for example. He must not try to accommodate the gospel to them, for all his endeavour to present it in an idiom understood by his hearers or readers. He will, however, be vigilant to seize upon every appropriate point of contact. Anything that rings a bell in his hearers' minds may serve, for their minds are full of questions and aspirations – sometimes only half-consciously realized – to which the answer and fulfilment are provided by the gospel.

Like his first-century predecessors, the apologist of today must confront men with the truth about God – Creator, Provider, Lord of history, Judge of all – and His command to repent. He must confront them with the truth about man, and his moral bankruptcy in the sight of God. And above all he must confront them with Jesus Christ in His resurrection power, His authority to execute judgment, and His redeeming love by which He delivers men and women from their estrangement and rebellion and creates them anew in the knowledge of their Creator.[31]

We also see him striking what was to become a characteristic note in his insistence on the impossibility of being justified by any form of human achievement:

Some of the deviations with which they had to deal are still with us. The most perennially popular is that which imagines that we can win acceptance with God by our own works, or simply by our ordinary decent nature. What more could God want? I suppose several of us have had the experience of explaining justification by faith to someone in words of one syllable, so as to make it crystal-clear – only to be told at the end: 'Yes, that's what I always say: we must just do the best we can.' Man's bankruptcy before God, his utter indebtedness to God's free grace, the all-sufficiency of Christ – these foundations of the gospel need to be insisted upon today as much as they did when Paul wrote his Epistle to the Galatians.[32]

Uncompromisingly he asserted that 'Christianity will not come to terms with other religions, nor will it relax its exclusive claims so as to countenance or accommodate them. It presents itself, as it did in

---

[31] Ibid. pp. 41–2.
[32] Ibid. p. 76.

the first century, as God's final word to man; it proclaims Christ, as it did in the first century, to be the one Mediator between God and man.'[33]

◆ ◆ ◆

It was not long before the family moved to Sheffield, settling at 79 Bower Road, a detached property with a garage and a stable, above which was a loft and a room which could be used as an office.[34] The house was equipped with a telephone (under the stairs) and Fred had a good-sized study in the attic to accommodate his burgeoning book collection. Outside, the garden was mostly laid to grass, ideal for a young family. The domestic routine went like clockwork; an evening meal would be ready when Fred came in, something which would have been helpful if he had an evening speaking engagement, as he relied on public transport. When at home, Betty would whistle him down for meals or a cup of tea. Fred had his share of the chores, one being to clean out the grate for a new fire to be lit. Betty maintained a wide range of interests. She is remembered as a good teacher, with a passion for history; over time, she built up quite a library on her own account, including many historical novels. Like others of her generation, she was often knitting or making clothes. Both of them enjoyed listening to classical music on the wireless, which they acquired during the late 1940s, although they did not often go to concerts. While in Sheffield, Fred bought Betty a radiogram, and later he would buy her a record player. On occasion they could also make their own music: Fred could play hymn tunes by ear on the harmonium at home, while Betty could play the piano from memory, having had lessons as a child. They also enjoyed Scrabble, which first appeared around 1950, being very evenly matched at what can be an extremely competitive game.

Holidays would be spent in Scotland, two weeks with one set of parents and two with the other; this he later described as a manifestation of his 'homing instinct'.[35] Fred kept in touch with his Elgin roots and enjoyed good relations with his brothers and sisters, who would tell his children stories about him as a child. He would always give

---

[33] Ibid. p. 78.
[34] Besides the other sources cited, this section owes much to an interview with Sheila Lukabyo on 2 September 2009; cf. Sheila Lukabyo to the author, 29 November 2009.
[35] H 41 (1962): p.186: Q. 1078.

his mother the housekeeping money which he would have given Betty when at home. He usually took some work with him, but Sundays at Elgin were strictly observed. Sometimes the family would take Fred's parents on day trips by bus; Peter Bruce would insist on standing to say grace in the hotel at lunchtime, but his taste for ginger ale worried his wife, who thought that it looked like something alcoholic. At other times, the family might go to the beach at Lossiemouth; one such trip during the late 1940s resulted in them featuring on a postcard!

The children 'were encouraged to be original in thought and action',[36] but on Sundays they were not allowed out to play; meetings were a highlight of the day. Unlike some families, the Bruces appear to have attended the Breaking of Bread together. Sheila and her mother would wear hats, not because Fred believed this to be commanded by Scripture but in order not to cause 'weaker brethren' in the assembly, who did believe this to be commanded, to stumble in their faith.[37] In the afternoon, Sheila and Iain would attend the local Crusader class rather than the assembly's Sunday School.[38] As had been the case in Leeds, there would usually be visitors (mostly students) at lunch and tea, sometimes as many as twenty. During the afternoon, Fred would join in the conversation to the full, writing letters at the same time; one visitor recalls him producing over twenty letters in one such afternoon.[39]

Iain and Sheila thus grew up in an atmosphere in which Christian faith was integral to daily life. Sheila recalls that when she was about 12 years old, she asked her father about being baptized. In due course she and Iain were baptized as believers at the same time, Brethren often baptizing teenagers in this way.[40]

The assembly in which the family settled met at Cemetery Road Hall, and had once formed part of the Lowe Exclusive grouping.[41] A

---

[36] Anthea Cousins, appreciation in *H* 69/11 (November 1990): p.6.

[37] This, or his own experience as a child, may be behind a comment that some children actually found the unpredictable format of the service, in which no one part lasted too long, 'quite exceptionally fascinating': *H* 35 (1956): p. 43: Q. 444.

[38] Crusaders was founded as an interdenominational outreach to children in what was known as 'the grammar school stream': Tim Grass, *Gathering to His Name: The Story of Open Brethren in Britain and Ireland* (Bletchley: Paternoster, 2006), p. 283 n. 31.

[39] David and Jean Payne, interview, 2 May 2009.

[40] Sheila Lukabyo, interview, 2 September 2009.

[41] On what follows, see *IR*, ch. 19. For the Lowe Brethren, see Grass, *Gathering*, p. 205. H.L. Ellison once suggested that its meeting place would be better named 'Resurrection Hall': *The Household Church* (Exeter: Paternoster, 2nd edn, 1979), p. 20.

few relics of its past history remained; one was the presence of a number of members who had been baptized as infants (Open Brethren practised believer's baptism), and another was the use at the Breaking of Bread of an Exclusive Brethren compilation entitled *Hymns for the Little Flock*, a book which he considered was given to mangling the words of hymns in order to make them express Exclusive theology.

Bruce became joint-secretary of the assembly. Here and in other assemblies to which he belonged, he was called upon to conduct weddings and funerals, and to act as precentor at the Breaking of Bread, at which the singing was traditionally unaccompanied.[42] He was quite prepared to get involved in more menial ways, too: apart from giving out the hymnbooks on the door, he often stoked up the boiler on Sunday mornings to ensure that the hall would be warm for the meeting; on one occasion, a visiting speaker whom Bruce had been due to meet arrived for a conference, and found him at this task in his overalls; he required some convincing that this was the *Professor* Bruce whom he was expecting to meet. Similarly, he was happy to perform such tasks as sweeping up and setting out the chairs when the Brethren held a tent mission locally. He was not held in awe, therefore, and others felt free to disagree with him. But he was respected, and also appreciated; one student recalled her sense of relief when he stood up to speak at the Breaking of Bread. Apart from preaching at the gospel meeting, he took a full part in the midweek ministry meeting, at which it was the practice to give more extended Bible teaching. Considerable pastoral concern was evident in his attitudes to others; one distraught widower was grateful when on several occasions Bruce accompanied him to his wife's grave. Always looking for the best in others, he showed himself a keen but kindly observer of their failings, as when he described one brother's interminable prayers as 'like an aeroplane going round and round looking for somewhere to land'. What was less well known was his keen missionary interest (this would, of course, have been universally encouraged in Brethren circles); he supported many missionaries financially and corresponded with them.[43]

The many assemblies then existing in Yorkshire preferred to have their own conferences rather than join together, and so Bruce spent

---

[42] Alan Millard, 'F.F. Bruce (1910–90)', in *They Finished Their Course in the 90s* (comp. Robert Plant; Kilmarnock: John Ritchie, 2000), pp. 29–34, at p. 30.

[43] Jean Angell, telephone conversation, 4 July 2008; Dennis Angell to the author, 15 July 2008; David and Jean Payne, interview, 2 May 2009; Jack Green, interview, 3 June 2010.

many Saturday afternoons and evenings attending, and often speaking at, such gatherings.[44] Sometimes he was feted as an academic, but on one occasion at a conference in Grimsby he reacted with annoyance when the other speaker (it was a frequent practice to have two speakers at a conference session) was told to keep his contribution short and to allow Bruce the maximum amount of time; Bruce told his colleague to take whatever time he needed, as he had come to receive ministry as well as to give it.[45] In any case, he was not a long-winded speaker as was the manner of some; one informant remembered him asserting that if it could not be said in twenty minutes, it was not worth saying.[46]

He also preached frequently on Sunday evenings, and not only in Brethren circles; for several years in the late 1950s he was on one local Methodist circuit's preaching plan.[47] However, he got a shock when asked to preach at an Anglican church in Bakewell on 30 January 1951, the feast day of King Charles the Martyr. Apparently he indicated beforehand that he might not give the congregation what they were expecting; apologizing, the vicar explained that he did not realize Bruce was a 'Presbyterian', 'and would be able to give us a different angle on King Charles the 1st', and expressed the hope that he would come to preach another time when a less controversial subject would be possible.[48] Betty, too, would speak at least once to a women's meeting in a Sheffield Baptist church where one of Bruce's postgraduates was the minister.[49]

Because he did not drive a car, he often needed to be transported to preaching engagements. Jack Green, who often undertook this service, recalled how Bruce would always have a kiss for Betty at the door when he left, and that he liked to navigate, using a road map. Cheerful company in the car, he would become more serious as they

---

[44] *IR*, p. 152. For the following paragraphs, see *IR*, pp. 154–8.

[45] Personal information. It may have been for this conference at Grimsby that the advertising is recalled as having used bigger type for Bruce's name than for that of the other speaker: Jack Green, interview, 3 June 2010.

[46] Anne Russell, undated memorandum.

[47] *IR*, p. 152.

[48] P. Hadfield to Bruce, 15 January 1951. The vicar was his first doctoral student: *IR*, p. 155. Asking a Scot with strong Calvinist roots to preach at a service commemorating the *bête noire* of the Covenanters was bound to provoke a reaction, even from one so irenic as Bruce.

[49] Ronald Clements, interview, 6 August 2008. Clements was later to become well known as an Old Testament scholar.

approached their destination; he could even turn on a dour image for meetings if needed. Although he preached at certain Yorkshire assemblies, especially around Sheffield, the more traditional standpoint of many in the Leeds area meant that he was not always looked on with favour. Certainly he was not prepared to assert the perfection of the assemblies: when Sheffield assemblies organized a series of Saturday evening meetings on groups such as the Jehovah's Witnesses and Mormons, under the title 'What's wrong with . . .?', he suggested that the spare evening remaining could be filled by a meeting looking at 'What's wrong with us?' In addition, his style was not that of the usual gospel preacher; it was like his lecturing style, although more conversational. His sermons would have been largely bare of the kind of illustrative anecdotes beloved of many Brethren evangelists at that time, but his usual practice was to take a narrative, perhaps from the gospels, and to explain the meaning and significance of its key words, actions and setting, making it come alive for thoughtful listeners. He would then go on to explain what Christ had done to save human beings, inviting his hearers to get caught up in the drama of it.[50] In 1954, the BBC had asked him to broadcast an evening service at Christmas; having already accepted an invitation to preach in a gospel hall in Doncaster, he arranged that the broadcast should take place from there.[51]

Bruce saw no tension between teaching in the university and doing so in the church. For him there was no contradiction between critical study and Bible exposition; indeed, the former fed into the latter. Conversely, he believed that active church membership would help to earth academic theologians. In his view, the Open Brethren tradition made such a marriage natural, because it encouraged individuals to study the Scriptures for themselves and to reach their own conclusions.[52] He might have taken a different view if he had been associated with a more conservative assembly, and it is probable that he came to be allowed greater latitude by Brethren because of his eminence, even if they would have disapproved of some of his conclusions. Already he was being recognized as a leading light among the assemblies, and in

---

[50] Dennis Angell to the author, 15 July 2008; Jack Green, interview, 3 June 2010, and telephone conversation, 18 June 2010. Angell recalls that by listening carefully to Bruce's choice of words and phrases, the academically aware could infer which current theological views and fashions he accepted or rejected.

[51] Personal information.

[52] *IR*, p. 144.

1948 he was one of thirty-five such figures who commended an appeal to Brethren to recapture the vision of Christian unity.[53] As such, he was invited to speak on 30 October 1953 at the London Missionary Meetings, the foremost Brethren gathering in support of overseas mission; held annually, at this period they attracted large crowds.[54] His address was printed and shows his approach to overseas mission to be very much in line with traditional Brethren thinking, yet drawing on contemporary biblical scholarship to support it. Entitled 'The Apostolic Witness', it summarized the apostolic preaching and teaching in terms strongly reminiscent of the approach of C.H. Dodd's landmark book *The Apostolic Preaching and Its Developments*, and called for a focus on church planting. Schools, hospitals and other such institutions were auxiliaries to this and could be taken over by hostile governments for other purposes, as had recently happened in China, whereas churches could survive and perpetuate Christian witness. In support of his understanding of the missionary task, he called on the missiologists Roland Allen and David Paton, both of whom were being widely read at that time.[55] On similar lines was his address to the Bloomsbury meetings on 13 November 1954 on 'The Planting of Churches': based on 1 Corinthians 3:9, it argued that church planting was an essential aspect of mission.[56]

His involvement with the young people's house parties each Easter continued; for many, these were their first experience of ministry which expounded the biblical text in a systematic manner, and this did much to stimulate their appetite for serious Bible study. One who attended them from 1954 to 1965 recalled that Bruce always did the Bible readings and that he encouraged note-taking.[57] As part of this, he produced a series of paraphrases of Paul's epistles which were duplicated for attenders, the first being Galatians in 1955. Short of material for *Evangelical Quarterly* on one occasion, he inserted it to fill the gap. A paraphrase of Colossians prepared two years later also found its way there, and Howard Mudditt as publisher encouraged Bruce to continue, describing this as the most important work he had ever done. Over the next six years, therefore, the rest of Paul's epistles appeared in the same journal before being revised for publication in

[53] Montague Goodman, *An Urgent Call to Christian Unity* (London: Paternoster, 1948), p. 2.
[54] Grass, *Gathering*, p. 487.
[55] F.F. Bruce, 'The Apostolic Witness', *W* 83 (1953): pp. 209, 212.
[56] F.F. Bruce, 'The Planting of Churches', *W* 85 (1955): pp. 113–14.
[57] David Humphreys, interview, 27 March 2009.

book form.[58] *The Expanded Paraphrase of the Epistles of Paul* (1965) was dedicated to Howard Mudditt, 'who kept me at it'. Mudditt requested that the work appear with the text and critical references of the Revised Version set in parallel with the paraphrase, which may have made it appear more technical than it was intended to be. This may explain why, although the hardback sold well, a paperback reprint did not, even though by this time there was a rapidly growing market among evangelicals for modern-language versions.[59] While some considered that belief in biblical inspiration necessitated an exact translation of the God-breathed words, Bruce argued that 'the translator's business is, as far as possible, to produce the same effect on readers of the translation as the original text produced on those able to read it'.[60] He was adopting the approach known as 'dynamic equivalence', which underlies versions such as the Good News Bible and *The Message*. What he produced may not strike us as particularly arresting today, but to a generation reared on the Authorized Version, Bruce's dignified modern prose would have helped greatly towards a better understanding of the text. But even he could nod on occasion; it was for this work that he translated 1 Corinthians 15:44 using the expression 'pneumatic body', and Mudditt returned the manuscript with the annotation 'Shades of Dunlop!'[61]

Another annual residential conference began in 1956, the purpose of which was to instruct young men in assemblies in basic Bible teaching and homiletics.[62] A seven-year syllabus was devised in an attempt to rectify some perceived deficiencies in assembly life of the time, most notably the lack of solid expository preaching, an approach which was becoming very popular in other circles through the ministry of such men as Lloyd-Jones and John Stott and which was beginning to attract some away from assemblies. Bruce spoke at the first Young Men's Bible Teaching Conference in Weston-super-Mare, and at many subsequent ones (they were held in Oxford from 1957 until 1968 and then moved to Winchester, with attendances often over three hundred). His contributions ranged across much of the field of

---

[58] F.F. Bruce, *An Expanded Paraphrase of the Epistles of Paul* (Exeter: Paternoster, 1965), p. 9.

[59] Jeremy Mudditt, telephone conversation, 4 March 2009.

[60] Bruce, *Expanded Paraphrase*, pp. x–xi, quotation at p. xi.

[61] F.F. Bruce, *History of the Bible in English* (London: Lutterworth, 1979), p. 144 n. 1; Jeremy Mudditt, telephone conversation, 4 March 2009.

[62] See *IR*, pp. 158–9.

basic Christian doctrine; few if any were published as given, but his preparation would have contributed towards other published work, and would have helped to shape the thinking and teaching of a generation of Brethren preachers.[63] Bruce also joined the committee, where he sought to ensure that the original vision of a teaching conference was maintained.[64] Although committee wives usually attended the conferences (partly in order to cook for the crowds), Betty does not appear normally to have followed this custom.

In 1953 a conference was commenced for older Brethren who were already recognized leaders in assembly life. Apart from the first, these took place at High Leigh in Hertfordshire and later at Swanwick in Derbyshire. Bruce was invited to contribute on several occasions.[65] The first was in 1954, when he contributed a paper on 'The Local Church in the New Testament' which was read in absentia.[66] Already there were signs of his adopting a more flexible approach to matters of church order, his exposition of which was marked by a refusal to legislate where he felt that the New Testament did not do so.

---

[63] *W* 86 (1956): p. 169; cf. *W* 87 (1957): p. 112 (advertisements). On these conferences, see Grass, *Gathering*, p. 412. Topics on which Bruce spoke included: The Cross of Christ; Justification by Faith (both 1956); The Spirit of God and the Word of God; The Work of the Holy Spirit (both 1957); Revelation and Inspiration; The Authority of the Word (both 1958); The Exalted Servant (1959); The Church and Its Constitution (1960); The Content of the Gospel (1961); God's Purpose in Man (1963); The Certainty of Personal Faith and Tests of Assurance (1964); Perils of a False Literalism (on biblical interpretation; 1965); The Story of the Church (1967); God in Jesus Christ (1968); How to Expound the Bible (tutorial; 1969); God's Purposes for His Land and His People; and God's Purposes through Christ for His World (both 1973).

[64] In 1969 he added a postscript to a letter to Alan Millard: 'I should like the message to get through to the Exec. Committee that much more teaching should be included in the programme. This is essentially a teaching conference – a Bible teaching conference at that. Conferences which specialize in devotional appeals are two a penny, and the raison d'être of this conference is to provide something different. The fault lies not in the subjects chosen by the committee so much as in the failure of some of the speakers to give positive teaching on them . . . I have an idea that some of the men got more instruction by browsing around the bookroom than they did at the sessions': Bruce to Millard, 30 September 1969.

[65] *IR*, pp. 159–61; Manchester, CBA, Box 26, G.W. Robson to Bruce Winter, 30 January 1991. On the significance of these conferences and the reaction which they provoked, see Grass, *Gathering*, pp. 408–11.

[66] F.F. Bruce, 'The Local Church in the New Testament', in *The New Testament Church in the Present Day* (ed. P.O. Ruoff; n.pl.: n.p., 1954), pp. 24–41.

Assemblies should be interdependent but not federated; a combination of mutual help and local autonomy served as a protection both against sectarianism and against the possibility of takeover by a hostile state. In this he agreed with G.H. Lang, who had had wide experience in Central and Eastern Europe and who never spared those among British assemblies who he believed were seeking to introduce a greater degree of federation and centralization.

The following year he was present to read his paper on 'The Church and Its Ministers'.[67] In it he challenged two Brethren sacred cows. The first was peripatetic ministry (preachers criss-crossed the country to speak at gospel halls other than their own), against which he argued that it was better to speak to a congregation which the preacher knew. The second was the silence of women: not only did he now deny that 1 Corinthians 14:34 prohibited their praying in the assembly,[68] but he also contended that in distributing spiritual gifts, 'the Lord does not concentrate exclusively on one sex'.[69] However, he did not see any need to depart from traditional views regarding the appointment of elders; rather than adopting a democratic approach in which appointment was primarily a matter of congregational election, existing elders should look for younger men whom they could invite to join with them in the work of oversight.[70]

Bruce was not the only speaker whose opinions proved controversial, and several conservative Brethren went into print to express their disquiet and disapproval. He therefore defended the conferences in an article for *The Witness*. Such gatherings, he wrote, showed a welcome lack of complacency and a desire to confess faults and to seek God's direction for reformation (this was a period when Brethren were beginning to engage in some intensive self-examination, stimulated in

---

[67] F.F. Bruce, 'The Church and Its Ministers', in *A New Testament Church in 1955: High Leigh Conference of Brethren, September 16th to 19th, 1955* (Stanmore: T.I. Wilson, [1955]), pp. 44–51.

[68] Earlier he appears to have held that they might pray in a mixed prayer meeting but not 'lead in prayer' as this would contravene the hierarchical order laid down in 1 Cor. 11:3 and amount to exercising leadership or authority over men: *H* 32 (1953): p. 94: QQ. 130-31.

[69] Bruce, 'The Church and Its Ministers', p. 49. A little later he gave approval to the appointment of women as deacons, diplomatically hiding behind a widely respected Brethren teacher, E.W. Rogers: *H* 36 (1957): p. 123: Q. 607, citing *A Return to Simplicity: Conference of Brethren Held at 'High Leigh,' Hoddesdon from September 28th to October 1st, 1956* ([Stanmore: T.I. Wilson], n.d.), p. 28.

[70] Cf. *H* 34 (1955): p. 27: Q. 313.

part by a dawning awareness that God had been blessing other parts of the evangelical world through such phenomena as the Billy Graham crusades, in which many Brethren were wholeheartedly involved, but that the blessing appeared to have passed them by). Published reports enabled wider discussion, and published critiques helped too.[71] It all seems rather like the academic debate to which Bruce was accustomed, and in which it was (theoretically) possible to disagree vigorously without any diminution of mutual respect. But if that was his expectation, he was perhaps too sanguine, as the movement's subsequent history would show.

Another area in which Bruce's views were becoming more obviously divergent from Brethren concerned the interpretation of biblical prophecy. In 1957 Lang wrote to him of a drift to amillennialism among teachers in assemblies, a fruit of the post-war resurgence of interest in Reformed theology, and expressed the hope that Bruce would reverse the trend.[72] He was to be disappointed. Lang also appears to have felt that Bruce could have been a little more outspoken in the cause of truth, for he concluded one letter: 'The Lord make you as bold as you are discreet.'[73] But when Bruce wrote Lang's obituary for *The Witness*, he testified that many of his own generation who were engaged in public ministry had been deeply influenced by Lang, and that many who rejected his eschatology nevertheless valued his stress on holiness. Bruce had read and commented on the manuscripts of every book Lang wrote for twenty years, and he encouraged others to read them, not because he agreed with them but because they stimulated readers to closer study of the Scriptures.[74]

At some point Bruce had joined the Prophecy Investigation Society, an interdenominational body founded in 1842 and embracing representatives of various schools of interpretation, which met to hear papers on the topic. In April 1959 he gave a paper to the society on *Antichrist in the Early Church*, which was duly published. Rather than trying to identify him with some individual, office or trend in history,

---

[71] F.F. Bruce, 'High Leigh Again', W 87 (1957): p. 152.

[72] CBA, Box 69: Lang to Bruce, 13 May 1957.

[73] CBA, Box 68, Lang to Bruce, 6 December 1957.

[74] F.F. Bruce, 'George Henry Lang: Author and Teacher, 1874–1958', W 88 (1958): pp. 253–4. Some years later, Bruce wrote: 'his intelligence and insight were of exceptionally high quality, but at times he almost gave the impression that if a simple and a complicated explanation of some Scriptural issue were available, he would prefer the complicated one. He was a man of outstanding godliness': CBA, Box 26, Bruce to Mr [J.A.] Green, 27 March 1971.

Bruce asserted that Antichrist was at work externally whenever a ruler demanded that obedience which was due to Christ alone, or (more deadly, in his view) internally, the only safeguard against which was self-examination and submission to the lordship of Christ. In 1962 he agreed to become a vice-president of the society (Ellison was its president), and its last extant minutes record that he was due to give another paper, on the historical development of prophetic exposition of Scripture; we do not know whether he did so, or what happened to the society, and Bruce does not refer to it in his autobiography.[75]

By 1959, his publicly expressed views were developing along lines more commonly associated with postmillennialism. In a book review for the *Evangelical Quarterly*, he wrote that when Israel as a whole recognized Christ as the Messiah, 'the missionary force thus released will spread gospel blessings across the world on a scale unknown since apostolic days', and he looked forward to 'the integration of the people of God by the reunion of Church and Synagogue in a common allegiance to Him who is Lord and Saviour of both'.[76] All the same, a sense of fairness and fine judgement led him to defend dispensationalism on one occasion against the charge that it had contributed to the church's failure to spread the gospel.[77]

If not all Bruce's fellow Brethren approved of his views, his influence in the wider evangelical scene was growing. With Billy Graham's visits to Britain in 1954 and 1955, evangelism was in the news, and the *Methodist Recorder* commissioned three articles from Bruce on 'The Bible and Evangelism'. Aware that some readers might be critical of mass evangelism, he made clear his support for Billy Graham's message and methods, commending the stress on following up those who made a response to Graham's altar calls. Bruce found it significant that the renewed attention to evangelism should have coincided with the rediscovery in academic circles of the unity of the biblical message, as expounded by scholars such as the Methodist N.H. Snaith in his *Distinctive Ideas of the Old Testament*, a book to which Bruce acknowledged his debt (here, as so often, Bruce chose his examples and authorities to suit his audience). Examining

---

[75] Prophecy Investigation Society, minute book 1928–62.

[76] *EQ* 31 (1959): pp. 126–7; cf. *H* 41 (1962): p. 170: Q. 1069. His relationships with Jewish academics in the SOTS and elsewhere appear to have been good, and he would contribute extensively to the *Encyclopedia Judaica*.

[77] *EQ* 33 (1961): p. 153.

the apostolic proclamation of the gospel, Bruce argued that Christ was central to the apostles' message, that they struck the note of personal experience, that they adapted their presentation according to their audience, and that they laid equal stress on the objective and subjective aspects of their message, calling their hearers to respond in repentance and faith (which he carefully explained – perhaps with a sense of the evangelistic moment). Bruce's thinking about evangelism appears to have remained substantially unchanged thereafter: a recording of his lecture during the 1970s at Regent College, Vancouver, on 'Evangelism in New Testament Perspective' covers the same ground in the same manner and uses some of the same descriptive expressions, although by this time he was placing increasing emphasis on the need to build bridges with one's hearers and to use language they would understand – a reflection not only of his developing thinking but also of the declining familiarity of the population at large with basic Christian concepts.[78]

---

[78] F.F. Bruce, 'The Bible and Evangelism. 1: The Prime Purpose of Revelation', *Methodist Recorder*, 31 March 1955, p. 11; 'The Bible and Evangelism. 2: Lessons in Witness-Bearing', *Methodist Recorder*, 7 April 1955, p. 9; 'The Bible and Evangelism. 3: Faith and Repentance', *Methodist Recorder*, 14 April 1955, p. 9; cf. idem, 'Evangelism in New Testament Perspective', Regent College, Vancouver, (ref. 312), undated but possibly from 1976.

6

Developing His Written Ministry
(1947–59)

Bruce's books were to prove of particular and timely significance, coming as they did at a point when evangelical publishers in Britain and America were seeking to establish their lists as worthy of serious attention from the academic world. Mark Noll's analysis of American evangelicalism has noted its heavy dependence during this period on British scholarship, for models as well as content; the firm of William B. Eerdmans, who played a major role in the post-war resurgence of American evangelical publishing, signed up several major British authors.[1] Part of the attraction was that British evangelicals led the way in securing positions in secular universities,[2] and Bruce was something of a pioneer in this respect. This chapter looks at how his writing career developed in various ways during his time at Sheffield, examining certain significant books as well as reviewing his editorial work, his phenomenal output as a book reviewer and his ministry answering questions in Brethren periodicals.[3]

Almost twenty of his titles appeared with a small Brethren company which had been founded in London during 1935, Paternoster. Bruce probably knew the firm's founder, Howard Mudditt (1906–92), before he went into publishing; it was probably while still a student at Cambridge that he occasionally visited Mudditt's Brethren assembly, Folkestone Road Hall in the north-east London suburb of Walthamstow. Bruce and Mudditt got on extremely well, and would

---

[1] Mark A. Noll, *Between Faith and Criticism: Evangelicals, Scholarship, and the Bible* (Leicester: Apollos, 1991), pp. 8, 104–5, 120.

[2] Ibid. p. 138.

[3] For this chapter, see also *IR*, chs 22–23, and the bibliography at the end of this work, which offers an overview of how his writing career developed.

go to a hotel in Bloomsbury for lunch. But the relationship was, nonetheless, formal; Mudditt's son Jeremy, when he joined the business, was told to call Bruce 'Sir', and their correspondence did not adopt first-name terms until about 1985. The first of Bruce's books for the firm appeared in 1950 and the last in 1992, after his death; he stayed loyal to this publisher long after he could have moved to a larger concern. Indeed, his titles did much to help it establish a reputation for publishing thoughtful and open-minded evangelical works. Moreover, several of his scholarly colleagues also published with Paternoster, strengthening their lists still further. Howard Mudditt recalled visiting a chemist in Fort William whose shop doubled as a Christian bookshop; on being introduced to the company, one man responded: 'Fred Bruce made that firm!'[4] But it may be a surprise to learn that one of the motives for his taking up writing was economic necessity; he explained that he had two children whose school fees had to be paid and the £50 advance offered by Mudditt for his first Paternoster title was thus a great attraction.[5]

Some of his titles sold better than others; books based on series of lectures did not sell so well, perhaps because they lack something of the coherence and broad appeal of his other works, and until recently the only one to be reprinted was *The Apostolic Defence of the Gospel*. All the same, Howard Mudditt described Bruce as 'an author worth having'; the manuscript for *The Dawn of Christianity*, for example, arrived a day before the deadline, and like all subsequent manuscripts it was meticulously prepared and typed, it needed little editing and it was refreshingly free from idiosyncratic judgements.[6] Sales figures have not survived, but the average print run would have been around three thousand copies, decreasing somewhat by the 1980s.[7] New technology, by which titles can be made available on a 'print on demand' basis, has made it possible to keep a number of his titles in print.

---

[4] B. Howard Mudditt, 'The Paternoster Story (4): "The End of the Beginning" ', *H* 64/9 (September 1985): pp. 5–7, at p. 7.

[5] *IR*, p. 178; Oliver Barclay, 'F.F. Bruce and the Inter-Varsity Fellowship', *JCBRF*, no. 22 (November 1971): p. 20; Jeremy Mudditt, telephone conversation, 4 March 2009.

[6] As he would later comment, 'Being an editor of so many things for many years has taught me not to make things difficult for other editors!': Bruce to Alan Millard, 20 April 1971.

[7] B. Howard Mudditt, 'A Publishing Partnership', *JCBRF*, no. 22 (November 1971): pp.19–20; Jeremy Mudditt, telephone conversation, 4 March 2009.

Several further books appeared with another Brethren publisher, Pickering & Inglis, some after beginning life as series of magazine articles in periodicals such as *The Witness*, with which this publisher had a close link. Apart from some books written during the first half of his career for Inter-Varsity Fellowship (later Inter-Varsity Press), several other books were published in Britain as part of a series issued by Hodder & Stoughton, the 'Jesus Library', whose first titles appeared in the mid-1970s.

In North America, the great majority of Bruce's books appeared with Eerdmans, a company based in Grand Rapids and having strong roots in the Dutch Reformed tradition. According to its current senior editor, Jon Pott, it was through Ronald Inchley of IVF in Britain that the firm first signed Bruce up; Eerdmans, IVF and Paternoster collaborated closely for some decades. Whilst those in the Reformed tradition which formed Eerdmans' traditional customer base preferred to read continental European writers, plenty of other conservative Protestant streams in North America welcomed Bruce's writings, which were undoubtedly a factor in the broadening of the company's appeal. It always knew that a new work by him, or a reprint of one, would sell well. Bruce was also an easy author with whom to deal; he never tried to bargain with the company, but was happy to accept whatever they offered.[8] Indeed, my researches indicate that his works continue to sell, though it has been impossible to compile much more than partial sales figures for any of Bruce's books. During the 1980s some titles appeared with the American arm of Inter-Varsity Press, whose lists were not quite as conservative as those of its British counterpart; they appear to have been primarily works published in Britain by Hodder & Stoughton.

Bruce's Brethren background comes out most clearly in his writings on church history. In 1949 he contributed a chapter on 'Church History and Its Lessons' to a Brethren symposium on the church.[9] The chapter began with a lengthy quotation from the Anglican W.R. Inge to the effect that the real history of Christianity is of a spiritual tradition rather than an institution, a viewpoint which was less widespread then than it has since become, and one which paralleled Brethren thinking about the topic. Indeed, Bruce commended as an exposition of this interpretation *The Pilgrim Church*, by the Brethren

---

[8] Jon Pott, interview, 31 March 2009.
[9] F.F. Bruce, 'Church History and Its Lessons', in *The Church* (ed. J.B. Watson; London: Pickering & Inglis, 1949), pp. 178–95.

missionary E.H. Broadbent, which had first appeared in 1931.[10] Bruce's Scottishness is evident in the choice of examples made to back up his assertions, and his Brethrenism perhaps influenced him to write that 'if Church History teaches one thing more than another, it is that there is a constant tendency to deterioration'; however, unlike the nineteenth-century Brethren leader John Nelson Darby he did not consider this tendency irreversible: there was always the possibility of a return to the word of God under the guidance of the Holy Spirit.[11] Accordingly, he considered how such reformation worked out in the areas of the church's form and ministry, its relations with the state, and its mission in the world. Indeed, he expressed approval of the thesis of the American historian Kenneth Scott Latourette that church history was a succession of advances and recessions, each advance going further forward than previously and each recession taking the church less far back.[12] Such a hopeful perspective set Bruce apart from the dispensationalist pessimism which characterized much Brethren thinking: this saw church history as culminating in a catastrophic slide into apostasy, preparing the way for the rise of the Antichrist.

It was from extra-mural courses that Bruce's three books on early church history were developed: *The Dawn of Christianity* (1950), *The Growing Day* (1951) and *Light in the West* (1952). These appeared in Paternoster's 'Second Thoughts Library', intended as a counter to the

---

[10] Ibid. p. 178. Bruce wrote a foreword to a reprint of Broadbent's work, and while he took the point made by critical reviewers that the author had included some heterodox groupings in his succession of true believers, he defended the approach adopted, arguing that in most of them the tokens of true apostolic succession could be recognized, in their teaching and fellowship. 'If mainstream Christianity has accomplished what these "separated brethren" could not have achieved, it must be said that the "separated brethren" have at times borne a distinctive and indispensable testimony to essential aspects of Christian truth which, but for their faithfulness, might have been lost': E.H. Broadbent, *The Pilgrim Church* (repr. London: Pickering & Inglis, 1985), p. iv.

[11] Bruce, 'Church History', p. 179. Darby played a central role in the division of Brethren in the 1840s and his writings remained influential among Open as well as Exclusive Brethren. He taught that in each dispensation humanity was put on probation by God and failed the test; thus the body which was meant to embody and represent God's people (in this dispensation, the church) was bound to fall into ruin. It was not God's purpose to try to restore it; attempts to do so were like attempts to secure justification by one's own works.

[12] Ibid. pp. 192–5.

rationalist 'Thinker's Library'.[13] The three works were combined into
a one-volume edition under the title *The Spreading Flame* by Eerdmans
in 1953.[14] Bruce was convinced, as he later explained, that the reason
why many Christians found church history dull was that it was inad-
equately presented; but 'When it is treated as the history of a work of
God, that should kindle spiritual interest.'[15] That desire to communicate something which had fascinated him is fully evident in this tril-
ogy. One reason for its appearance (which also explains the choice of
title) was the desire of author and publisher to offer something better
than *The Rise of Christianity* (1948), by the liberal Bishop of
Birmingham, E.W. Barnes.[16] Bruce had written a review article on the
book for a short-lived Paternoster periodical, *Science and Religion*,
objecting to 'an arbitrary treatment of ancient documents and an attitude to historical evidence which, if justified, would go far to rendering the writing of ancient history altogether impossible',[17] and it may
be that this article stimulated Mudditt to offer him a commission. An
unusual feature is the inclusion of a chapter summarizing Jewish history from Abraham to John the Baptist, which would have surprised
Brethren readers but appealed to Reformed ones, Reformed theology
stressing the continuity of the people of God in Old and New
Testament eras. Bruce's sympathies appear to have lain with those
who would trace the history of a spiritual tradition rather than that of
an often fallible and corrupt institution, and he considered it 'more

---

[13] T.C. Mitchell, 'Professor Frederick Fyvie Bruce, D.D. F.B.A.', *FT* 117 (1991): pp. 2–5, at
p. 4.

[14] *IR*, pp. 156, 178–9. Although Paternoster did not follow suit until 1958, the edition
which they issued was thoroughly revised and updated: F.F. Bruce, *The Spreading
Flame: The Rise and Progress of Christianity from Its First Beginnings to the Conversion
of the English* (repr. Bletchley: Paternoster, 2005), p. 9.

[15] Manchester, CBA, Box 11(11g), Bruce to Ian S. Davidson, 22 August 1988. One rea-
son for Bruce's own fascination was his acquisition of a work by the historian F.J.
Foakes-Jackson, *A History of Church History: Studies of Some Historians of the Christian
Church* (1939).

[16] *IR*, p. 178; I. Howard Marshall, 'F.F. Bruce as a Biblical Scholar', *JCBRF*, no. 22
(November 1971): pp. 5–12, at p. 9, cf. Howard Mudditt, 'Publishing Partnership',
p. 19.

[17] F.F. Bruce, 'Bishop Barnes and "The Rise of Christianity" ', *Science and Religion* 1
(1947–8): pp. 108–13, at p. 109. In spite of his severe criticisms, Bruce's charity
showed itself in a concluding comment that 'the true state of the evidence for the
trustworthiness of these documents is such that Dr. Barnes's faith is better founded than he himself realizes': ibid. pp. 112–13.

important to trace the fortunes of the message than to enlarge on the misbehaviour of the messenger'.[18] As he explained to Lang, 'For the type of reader aimed at in The Second Thoughts Library I am concentrating on the spread of evangelization and not on lessons for church doctrine and practice.'[19] This was relevant history, with frequent application to contemporary life; moreover, he sometimes picked up parallels which would be of especial relevance to the Brethren.[20] A thematic approach means that at times it is hard for the reader to grasp the details of the course which church history took from one decade to the next, but it also allowed Bruce to offer enlightening discussions of issues such as apostolic succession (which he saw as grounded in continuity of doctrine rather than of ordained ministry), an issue on which he considered it hard to avoid being influenced by one's particular theological or ecclesiastical bias.[21] It was, according to one reviewer, 'the book on Church History for which we have been waiting'.[22] A slightly revised edition appeared in 1981, which was reprinted as recently as 2005 – testimony to the enduring value of this lucid overview.

A very different book, though equally accessible, was *The Books and the Parchments* (1950), which was partly based on a series of articles during 1946 in a small Scottish Brethren monthly, *The Believer's Pathway*. To them the book added articles and papers from various occasions, dealing with matters related to ancient writing, the biblical languages, the transmission and translation of the biblical text, the

---

[18] Bruce, *Spreading Flame*, p. 162.

[19] CBA, Box 64, Bruce to Lang, 21 July 1951.

[20] For example, Bruce, *Spreading Flame*, p. 213 n. 1 (quoting a comparison of the third-century Novatianists with the Brethren), pp. 216–17 (discussing the tensions which could arise between itinerant and settled ministers; Brethren venerated those who gave their whole time to itinerant evangelism and Bible teaching), p. 294 (excluding the possibility of 'contracting out' of a share of the responsibility for the scandals which had disfigured church history, something which groups like the Brethren who stressed the purity of the church were inclined to do), p. 310 (describing Apollinarianism, the denial that Christ possessed a human soul, as 'the heresy to which many Christians who think themselves orthodox are specially, though unconsciously, prone'). This feature of the work rebounded on Bruce when a review in the *Irish Evangelical* for September 1951 took issue with him for implying that independency (the idea that each local congregation was self-governing) was taught in the New Testament.

[21] Bruce, *Spreading Flame*, pp. 203, 209.

[22] Review by O.R. J[ohnston]., in *CG* 4 (1951–2): pp. 126–7, at p. 126.

relationship between Old and New Testaments, early versions, the formation of the canon, biblical authority and English translations. A number of these themes would receive fuller treatment elsewhere, but this work offered a way in to them for interested laypeople; Brethren, of course, numbered many such among their assemblies, often self-taught men who sought to equip themselves to minister and teach acceptably in their local settings. The work went through four editions, last being reprinted in 1991. In his foreword to the fourth edition, Bruce made clear that he did not see himself as one of those scholars who contented themselves with producing works of scholarship which nobody read or noticed; rather, his greatest reward was to see enthusiasm and interest being sparked in his readers as a result of his work.[23]

Bruce's most important works during this period, however, were two commentaries on Acts, which set the standard for works on the Greek and English text of Scripture respectively. The first was his commentary on the Greek text, published by Tyndale Press, which had been set up as an academic imprint of IVF (it was hoped that the different name would overcome the widespread academic prejudice against IVF titles). This book did much to help IVF's works to gain a measure of scholarly acceptance.[24] Its publication, though, was the end of a saga of delays, due doubtless in part to the impact of the war on printers and publishers. Bruce had been working on this project from 1939, when he had offered to write a commentary for the IVF (preferably on the Greek text rather than the English). It was ready for the intended publisher, James Clarke, by 1944, but in September 1945 it was reported that they 'were being held up by the question of text'. In 1946 they claimed that they could not publish it for at least two years, and so Ronald Inchley agreed that it could form one of a new series of commentaries on the Greek text; Tyndale Press was in any case Bruce's preferred publisher. By May 1947 it had finally gone to the printers but even then it was delayed; the preface was dated July 1949, and the book did not appear until 1951.[25] According to Howard Marshall, who would become a friend and associate of Bruce and Professor of New Testament at Aberdeen, its appearance marked a watershed in the

---

[23] F.F. Bruce, *The Books and the Parchments: How We Got Our English Bible* (Old Tappan, NJ: Fleming H. Revell, 4th edn, 1984), p. ix.
[24] Oliver Barclay to the author, 20 August 2009.
[25] BRC minutes, 11 May 1939, 8 September [1945], 5 April 1946, 3 May 1947; Leicester, UCCF archives, Bruce to Douglas Johnson, 26 April 1944.

revival and recognition of evangelical scholarship.[26] Although it was clearly the work of a classicist rather than a biblical scholar, and he was later somewhat embarrassed about what he regarded as its immaturity in certain respects, it was this commentary which was primarily responsible for his decision to switch from classics to biblical studies.[27]

The other commentary, on the English text, appeared in 1954 as part of what has become known as the New International Commentary on the New Testament.[28] The invitation to write it came while Bruce was still working on his Greek commentary, and he welcomed it as an opportunity to follow up certain trains of thought which lay outside the scope of the first work.[29] In this, his first commentary on the English text of the Bible, Bruce manifests a characteristic feature of his approach in later commentaries – the quotation of apposite hymns, often by the great eighteenth-century authors such as Isaac Watts and Charles Wesley.[30] Occasional flashes of humour also appear,[31] and he is capable of thoughtful pastoral application, as in his handling of the story of Ananias and Sapphira in Acts 5.[32] As well as engaging with the full range of contemporary scholarship, he takes time to interact with Brethren writers and ideas,[33] and his Brethren standpoint shows itself in occasional comments directed at high-church thinking on such matters as apostolic succession.[34] Not surprisingly, Marshall offered the opinion that Bruce was at his best in this series.[35] The work was warmly welcomed by reviewers of

---

[26] Marshall, 'Bruce', p. 12.

[27] F.F. Bruce, *The Acts of the Apostles: The Greek Text with Introduction and Commentary* (Leicester: Apollos / Grand Rapids, MI: Eerdmans, 3rd edn, 1990), p. xvi.

[28] As published in Britain, it went for some years under the series title of the New London Commentary on the New Testament.

[29] F.F. Bruce, *Commentary on the Book of the Acts: The English Text with Introduction, Exposition, and Notes*, NICNT (Grand Rapids, MI: Eerdmans, rev. edn, 1987), p. 7.

[30] F.F. Bruce, *Commentary on the Book of the Acts: The English Text with Introduction, Exposition, and Notes*, NLCNT (London: Marshall, Morgan & Scott, 1954), pp. 55, 60, 91, 151.

[31] Ibid. pp. 84, 288 n. 18.

[32] Ibid. pp. 113–15.

[33] e.g. ibid. p. 168 (on dispensational interpretations of 7:55–56), p. 415 n. 54 (on William Kelly's dispensationalist distinction between 'preaching the kingdom' and 'the gospel of God's grace' in 20:24–25).

[34] e.g. ibid. pp. 79 (on 2:41–42), 201 (on 9:17).

[35] Marshall, 'Bruce', p. 9. Bruce also contributed commentaries on Colossians (1957; bound with a commentary on Ephesians by E.K. Simpson), Hebrews (1965), and Ephesians (1984; bound with a revision of his work on Colossians).

many different persuasions. As the newly evangelical R.V.G. Tasker, then Professor of New Testament Exegesis at King's College, London, commented: 'When we remember how much the Book of Acts has suffered at the hands of subversive radical scholars, it is certainly most refreshing to find the historicity of the book vindicated on grounds of scholarship as well as of faith.'[36] From a more theologically liberal standpoint, William Barclay described Bruce's name as 'synonymous with the best conservative scholarship' and the commentary as 'a book for which there can be nothing but praise and nothing but gratitude'.[37] All the same, the former Strict Baptist Ernest F. Kevan, by now principal of London Bible College, wished that it had contained more theology,[38] a sentiment sometimes expressed by later reviewers.

One factor giving rise to such a criticism is that evangelicals have tended to approach Scripture in a different way from other ancient literary texts, expecting to hear a word from it for today; Bruce undoubtedly expected that too, but he insisted on approaching it in the same way as other ancient texts. In his handling of the text, he was prepared to distinguish between Scripture as divinely inspired and Scripture as a human production in a way which would not have commended itself to some evangelicals, especially if they were from traditions which placed great weight on systematic theology as a guide to biblical interpretation.

In the 1972 reissue of his English *Acts*, Bruce noted Barth's criticisms of commentaries which confined themselves to a certain (presumably technical) mode of textual interpretation and failed to overcome the barrier between the first century and the present, as being in reality but the first steps towards proper commentaries; he acknowledged that his work on the Greek text was such a book, and admitted that his second work had not overcome that barrier either.[39]

---

[36] Review in *CG* 8 (1955): pp. 72–3.

[37] Review in *British Weekly*, 25 November 1954. It is worth noting that British scholars tended to be more conservative regarding issues of historicity, and hence more likely to welcome Bruce's work, not least because they had been educated in a system which emphasized the study of the classics rather than of philosophy: Gerald Bray, *Biblical Interpretation Past and Present* (Leicester: Apollos, 1996), pp. 570–71, 577.

[38] Review in *The Christian*, 12 November 1954.

[39] Bruce, *Acts*, NICNT, rev. edn, pp. 8–9. This edition, while it included a replacement preface in which Bruce referred to a few significant continental works published since 1954, did not update the bibliographical references, although Bruce's own copy of the first edition (in private hands) is heavily annotated in this respect.

Clearly he was aware of the criticisms, but he did not do anything about them. This indicates a deliberate policy, one which is reflected in his other scholarly commentaries. It might be thought that this was from a desire to secure credibility with mainstream critical scholars (and Bruce would on occasion be accused of this), but in my view it was unquestionably a function of his classicist's approach to the text. It seems that Bruce's idea of what a scholarly commentary should do was shaped by prevailing notions about commentary-writing in the classical field, and the first of these commentaries was written just before opinions about commentary-writing in the theological sphere shifted and theology came to be emphasized as a primary component of such works.[40] Reviewing a later work on Acts, by the German scholar Hans Conzelmann, Bruce commented on what he discerned as the recent tendency for some to emphasize the theology of Acts at the expense of its historical value, and for others to do the opposite. 'If the reviewer falls into the second category (as he certainly does), perhaps Professor Conzelmann falls into the former.'[41] Perhaps he felt that his approach was needed as a counterbalance. It should also be noted that more overtly theological work appeared in the form of articles, of which there were usually several to accompany or follow one of his commentaries.[42]

Another perspective on the issue was offered by a reviewer of the revision of his commentary on the English text of Acts: the lack of application to the present day was 'not a weakness of the commentary, but rather an indication of the type of commentary it is'.[43] The

---

We may compare his comment in the course of reviewing Rudolf Bultmann's collected essays, that grammatico-historical study was adequate for a commentary on a classical writing, but was only the beginning for understanding the Bible, because of the dimension of existential encounter which Bultmann stressed: *Erasmus* 15/23–24 (25 December 1963): cols 711–13.

[40] I. Howard Marshall, 'Frederick Fyvie Bruce 1910–1990', *Proceedings of the British Academy* 80 (1991): pp. 245–60, at p. 255.

[41] *EQ* 36 (1964): p. 117.

[42] On Acts, for example, see F.F. Bruce, 'The Holy Spirit in the Acts of the Apostles', *Interpretation* 27 (1973): pp. 166–83; 'The Davidic Messiah in Luke-Acts', in *Biblical and Near Eastern Studies: Essays in Honor of William Sanford LaSor* (ed. Gary A. Tuttle; Grand Rapids, MI: Eerdmans, 1978), pp. 7–17; 'Paul's Apologetic and the Purpose of Acts', *BJRL* 69 (1986–7): pp. 379–93; 'Luke's Presentation of the Spirit in Acts', *Criswell Theological Review* 5 (1990): pp. 15–29; 'The Significance of the Speeches for Interpreting Acts', *Southwestern Journal of Theology* 33 (1990): pp. 20–28.

[43] Conrad Gempf, in *Themelios* 16/2 (January 1991): pp. 28–9, at p. 29.

type of commentary Bruce wrote varied according to (i) the objectives of the particular series, (ii) what he was trying to achieve, and (iii) changing views in the evangelical world, which appears to have placed increasing emphasis on the theological dimension. His Greek *Acts*, which he began writing as a classicist, was primarily a linguistic, geographical and cultural commentary, for example. It was, as a later reviewer wrote, 'basically what we would expect from a commentary on Thucydides'.[44] Given that he had a fairly clear and developed theological understanding, it seems to me that he chose to keep this in the background, because of his preference for working inductively from the text; theology should be derived from it rather than imposed on it.

If Bruce's commentaries on Acts established him among the fraternity of biblical scholars, his work on the Dead Sea Scrolls, first discovered at Qumran in 1947, did much to establish him in the wider intellectual world. Bruce was the main evangelical writer to deal with them, his first articles appearing during 1950,[45] and many more coming between 1956 and 1971.[46] He wrote for academics, for church

---

[44] Moises Silva, 'Betz and Bruce on Galatians', *Westminster Theological Journal* 45 (1983): pp. 371–85, at p. 378 n. 11.

[45] F.F. Bruce, 'The Dead Sea Scrolls', W 80 (1950): p.62, a brief account of what had so far been found and its importance. On 27 March 1950 he gave a paper on the same lines to the Victoria Institute: 'Recent Discoveries in Biblical Manuscripts', *JTVI* 82 (1950): pp. 131–44.

[46] Other notable writings on the subject by Bruce included: 'Qumran and Early Christianity', *New Testament Studies* 2 (1955–6): pp. 176–90; *Second Thoughts on the Dead Sea Scrolls* (London: Paternoster/Grand Rapids, MI: Eerdmans, 1956); *The Teacher of Righteousness in the Qumran Texts* (London: Tyndale Press, 1957); 'The Dead Sea Habakkuk Scroll', *The Annual of Leeds University Oriental Society* 1 (1958–9): pp. 5–24; 'Qumran and the New Testament', *FT* 90 (1958): pp. 92–102; 'Qumran and the Old Testament', *FT* 91 (1959–60): pp. 9–27; 'The Dead Sea Scrolls', *Modern Churchman* NS 4 (1960–61): pp. 45–54; 'The Dead Sea Scrolls and Early Christianity', *BJRL* 49 (1966–7): pp. 69–90; 'Holy Spirit in the Qumran Texts', *Annual of Leeds University Oriental Society* 6 (1966–8): pp. 49–55; 'The Book of Daniel and the Qumran Community', in *Neotestamentica et Semitica: Essays in Honour of Matthew Black* (ed. E.E. Ellis and M. Wilcox; Edinburgh: T&T Clark, 1969), pp. 221–35; 'Jesus and the Gospels in the Light of the Scrolls', in *The Scrolls and Christianity*, SPCK Theological Collections 11 (ed. M. Black; London: SPCK, 1969), pp. 70–82; 'The Qumran Discoveries and the Bible', *Ekklesiastikos Pharos* 51 (1952–69): pp. 49–59; 'Biblical Exposition at Qumran', in *Gospel Perspectives III: Studies in Midrash and Historiography* (ed. R.T. France and D. Wenham; Sheffield: JSOT Press, 1983), pp.

members, and on occasion for the wider public.[47] In every conceivable kind of venue, and to audiences of many different religious persuasions, Bruce lectured on the scrolls.[48] Yet it may be suggested that his interest in a nonconformist group which existed alongside mainstream Judaism owed something to his identity as a member of a twentieth-century Nonconformist group which existed alongside more mainstream churches. This comes out most clearly in an article from 1962, in which he drew on the mentality of Brethren interpreters of prophecy to illuminate the mindset which he believed to be operative among the Qumran community, and perhaps within the apostolic church too:

> Within the Christian church today (not to go farther afield) we sometimes come upon small pious communities of people who have very similar ideas about their own place in the divine scheme of things. They alone can interpret the Bible (particularly biblical prophecy and apocalyptic) properly, and they look with mingled pity and disapproval on theological professors and church leaders who, for all their learning and fame, have obviously had concealed from them those revelations which God in his wisdom has communicated to babes like themselves. Such an attitude commonly leads to a profound sense of humility before God, a deep appreciation of his grace in so dealing with them, all unworthy as they are, an unshakable conviction that they are right and all others wrong, and a sublime disregard for the criticisms of scholars who point out that their cherished interpretations of Holy Writ violate the canons of history, philology, and exegesis. If they do, so much the worse for those canons! If we have any acquaintance with members of such groups, we shall have some insight into the personal religion of the men of Qumran. And at the same time we may have some insight into the picture that the church of apostolic days must have presented to the religious leaders of Judaism or to the heads of philosophical schools in the Graeco-Roman world. For those early

---

77–98. His ability as an interpreter of the scrolls was also acknowledged by Jewish scholars, and he served as departmental editor for Dead Sea Scrolls for *Encyclopedia Judaica* (16 vols; ed. C. Roth and G. Wigoder; Jerusalem: Encyclopedia Judaica/ Macmillan, 1971), contributing a number of the articles himself.

[47] F.F. Bruce, 'The Significance of the Dead Sea Scrolls', *Times Literary Supplement*, 27 March 1961, pp. vi–vii; 'Dead Sea Scrolls', in *Man, Myth and Magic* (ed. R. Cavendish; London: B.P.C. Publishing, 1970), pp. 609–11.

[48] *IR*, p. 157.

Christians believed that to them, God's holy and elect people, had been revealed the secret of the divine kingdom which was hidden from the wise and prudent.[49]

Bruce also turned his position as a member of a religious community in which there was no caste of ordained clergy to good effect in the controversies which soon blew up concerning the implications of the Dead Sea Scrolls for Christian belief. In 1955, an American literary critic, Edmund Wilson, went into print with the claim that Jesus was not an original teacher but derived his ideas from the Essene community. Christian history, he asserted, would have to be rewritten. In addition, he made the sensational allegation that the scrolls were slow to be published because clergy scholars were unwilling to face the implications of their discoveries.[50] It was probably his articles which Eerdmans sent to Bruce, and which provided the inspiration for the latter's *Second Thoughts on the Dead Sea Scrolls* (1956).[51] Bruce dismissed Wilson's claim by appealing to his own lay status: 'Whether the following pages are the work of a scholar is for others to judge. But it cannot be argued against them that they are the work of a clergy man.'[52] And he saw the scrolls not as overturning, but as reinforcing, the views he had expressed in *The Dawn of Christianity*.[53] All the same, in an epilogue to the second edition (1961) outlining recent discoveries, he stressed the provisional nature of the book in the light of the probability that yet more discoveries would be made.[54] The work enjoyed a period of popularity for several years while the scrolls were in the public eye, a typical assessment of it being that of Bruce's friend Professor S.H. Hooke (1874–1968), who described it as 'excellent, sane and wholly scholarly'.[55]

---

[49] F.F. Bruce, 'Preparation in the Wilderness: At Qumran and in the New Testament', *Interpretation* 16 (1962): pp. 280–91, at p. 281.

[50] Stephen Neill and Tom Wright, *The Interpretation of the New Testament 1861–1986* (Oxford: OUP, 2nd edn, 1988), pp. 323–4.

[51] Jon Pott, interview, 31 March 2009.

[52] F.F. Bruce, *Second Thoughts on the Dead Sea Scrolls* (London: Paternoster, 1956), p. 9.

[53] Ibid. He saw the value of the scrolls as providing information regarding the Hebrew text of the Old Testament and light on the Jewish background to the New, as well as underlining the uniqueness of the Christian faith: *H* 35 (1956): p. 27: Q. 431.

[54] Bruce, *Second Thoughts* (London: Paternoster, 2nd edn, 1961), p. 156.

[55] *PEQ* 89 (1957): p. 147.

A convenient summary of his views on the relationship between Qumran and early Christianity is provided in a paper he gave to the SNTS conference at Bangor in September 1955 on 'Qumran and Early Christianity'. Both communities, he explained, believed that they were participants in the eschatological fulfilment of Old Testament prophecy. Qumranic interpretation of the Old Testament shows that the community associated the time of fulfilment of prophecy with three messianic figures, prophetic, priestly, and royal, a priestly 'Messiah of Aaron' taking primacy. By contrast, the one Christian Messiah's priesthood was necessarily based on grounds other than the Levitical descent which was a prerequisite for the Aaronic priesthood. Each tradition followed a coherent scheme of Old Testament interpretation, taught first by its founder, and involving the founder as a central figure in it. The parallelism of thought was, Bruce considered, most striking in their interpretation of the Servant Songs of Isaiah; Qumran associated these with Daniel's Son of Man figure, interpreting his activity in corporate terms and seeing the community as called to atone for the sins of others by piety and to judge the ungodly in the end-time. Differences between the two traditions appeared on the issues of priesthood, temple and sacrifice; warfare; and the Levitical organization and outlook which marked the Qumran sect. Doubtless the movements were historically linked, but the links were not so close as to establish the identity of the two movements or the direct dependence of one upon the other. The unique character of Christianity derived from the character, teaching and achievement of its founder Jesus Christ.[56]

The discoveries at Qumran and the varying interpretations of the evidence might, in spite of the sensational claims made, seem unrelated to Christian life and thought, but Bruce's comments on the community's handling of the Hebrew Scriptures – a topic on which he has been recognized internationally as an expert and a judicious commentator[57] – are anything but. The conclusion to his monograph on *Biblical Exegesis in the Qumran Texts* indicated his readiness to accept the idea that there was a fuller meaning in the biblical text of which the original writers and readers were unaware:

> Here, then, is the key to that distinctive interpretation of the Old Testament which we find in the New Testament. Jesus has fulfilled the

---

[56] Manchester, John Rylands University Library, Special Collections, Manson Papers, F.IV.15, duplicated synopsis.

[57] George Brooke to the author, e-mail, 1 April 2010.

ancient promises, and in fulfilling them He has given them a new meaning, in which their original meaning is not set aside but caught up into something more comprehensive and far-reaching than was foreseen before He came. In His own perfect way He has accomplished a ministry which involves the finishing of transgression, putting an end to sin, atoning for iniquity, bringing in everlasting righteousness, and setting the seal on vision and prophecy; and has thus vindicated His right to be hailed as the Lord's Anointed, the Holy One of God. And as we learn to interpret 'in all the scriptures the things concerning himself' (Luke xxiv. 27), we can best understand what He meant when He said of those scriptures: 'It is they that bear witness to me' (John v. 39).[58]

On similar lines was his presidential address to the IVF conference in 1955, *The Christian Approach to the Old Testament*. Old and New Testaments were related to each other as promise and fulfilment, and the canonical status of the Old Testament was secured by virtue of its function as witness to Christ: 'The Christian approach to the Old Testament is dictated by Christ's own approach to it.'[59] The Old Testament witnessed to Christ by showing how God prepared the way for the coming of the Saviour and by unfolding the principles of salvation which were fully revealed in Christ.[60] The careful expositor of Scripture therefore had no need to follow the practice common among evangelicals at that time of allegorizing parts of the Old Testament in order to make them speak of Christ, which was too liable to lead to reading into Scripture what people wanted to find there.[61] Bruce

---

[58] F.F. Bruce, *Biblical Exegesis in the Qumran Texts* (London: Tyndale Press, 1960), p. 88.

[59] F.F. Bruce, *The Christian Approach to the Old Testament* (London: IVF, 1955), pp. 4–6; quotation at p.6. Significantly, he quotes one of the 'believing critics', George Adam Smith, at this point.

[60] Ibid. pp. 6–7.

[61] Ibid. p. 15. In the nineteenth and earlier twentieth centuries, Brethren in particular were wedded to the practice of allegorical interpretation of material in the Old Testament, notably the regulations concerning the tabernacle and its worship; narrative was also treated in this way. Allegory was a way of interpreting Scripture which tended to see the primary meaning of such texts as hidden; they were vehicles of truth concerning Jesus Christ, rather than being (as a surface reading would suggest) primarily about Israel's worship or God's dealings with his people. It is not always easy to draw a clear distinction between allegory and typology, which gives due weight to the original setting and surface meaning of these texts but which seeks to discern recurrent patterns of divine action in human history; on this basis it is then possible to understand an Old Testament passage or event as prefiguring some aspect of Christ's work.

acknowledged the existence of recurring patterns of divine action and human response,[62] but his overall approach had far more in common with cautious Reformed exegesis than with the interpretations which were virtually normative among Brethren.

Bruce's approach also fitted well with the emphases of what was known as the Biblical Theology movement. According to one of its leading exponents, Brevard S. Childs, this movement, whose centre of gravity was North America, began around the end of World War II, and represented a rediscovery of the unity of the biblical message. Liberal theology of the time had largely abandoned any attempt to interpret the Scriptures as a coherent whole with an overarching theme, regarding them as a disparate collection of writings. The Biblical Theology movement was attractive because it presented itself as a middle way between the alternatives of fundamentalism (which rejected modern methods of critical study of the Bible) and modernism (which rejected or watered down the idea of divine revelation), and it saw itself as conducive to the recovery of a robust theology which was unashamed to confess traditionally fundamental truths. For theologians of this stamp, the Bible bore witness to God's saving acts in history, culminating in the coming of Christ. Biblical Theologians therefore anchored revelation in human history and stressed the distinctiveness of biblical ideas when considered against the backdrop of their ancient setting. With this movement came a renewed interest in the background and archaeology of the Bible. Evangelical scholars found it far easier to work with, and profit from, exponents of Biblical Theology than with liberal theologians, even if the Biblical Theologians did not usually go so far as to accept the verbal inspiration of Scripture. The movement enjoyed a brief period of popularity in ecumenical circles and was very influential in the early years of the World Council of Churches, which began its formal existence in 1948. It would, however, decline during the 1960s, thanks to a combination of scholarly critiques, internal weakness and cultural change (most obviously the serious onset of secularization and the decline of interest in the Bible on the part of society at large).[63] Thereafter, the emphasis among academic interpreters once again shifted to the diversity to be found in the biblical writings.

Neither in Britain nor in America were many of Bruce's books published by mainstream religious or secular firms. Yet his loyalty to

---

[62] Ibid. p. 19.

[63] Brevard S. Childs, *Biblical Theology in Crisis* (Philadelphia, PA: Westminster, 1970).

evangelical publishers does not appear to have hindered the impact of his books; it seems that he possessed sufficient academic credibility as a writer from his contributions to mainstream journals such as *The Expository Times, Interpretation,* and *New Testament Studies.* In evangelical circles, his contributions often featured in the *Evangelical Quarterly* and the *Journal of the Transactions of the Victoria Institute,* later renamed *Faith and Thought.*[64] Many of his articles in journals and magazines were written in response to requests from editors; at one point he had a reputation for answering frantic requests from hard-pressed editors let down by others, working into the night to produce articles by return of post.[65] Others had first been given as lectures. As well as writing for students and scholars, he wrote for ordinary church members. For example, a series of twenty-one short articles for a small periodical with Brethren roots, *Essential Christianity,* between 1958 and 1963 explained and demonstrated contemporary academic methods of interpreting Scripture in non-technical language, analyzing different types of psalm and outlining form-critical approaches to the gospels. He followed this with a series on Jesus during 1964–5. From 1949 to 1957, he was a regular contributor to the *Scripture Union Bible Study Notes,* and in the mid-1960s to *Daily Notes.* These were designed to assist Christians with their daily Bible reading, although Bruce's notes are remarkable for their lack of practical application.

◆   ◆   ◆

Bruce's services were also in demand as an editor. He was elected to the editorship of the *Journal of the Transactions of the Victoria Institute* in 1950, taking over from R.E.D. Clark when eye trouble forced him to give up the role, but was able on Clark's recovery to demit his charge in 1957 after taking on the editorship of the *Palestine Exploration Quarterly.* Bruce was never an archaeologist, and was not at his best when writing on archaeological themes, so it is surprising that he should have been invited to edit this prestigious journal, which

---

[64] The Victoria Institute was founded in London in 1865 to provide a forum in which Christians could engage with the issues of the day in science and philosophy in such a way as to uphold the credibility of traditional Christian belief. On its history, see T.C.F. Stunt, 'The Victoria Institute: The First Hundred Years', *FT* 94 (1965): pp. 162–81.

[65] Barclay, 'Bruce', p. 20; Peter Oakes, 'F.F. Bruce and the Development of Evangelical Biblical Scholarship', *BJRL* 86/3 (Autumn 2004): pp. 99–124, at p. 114.

appeared under the auspices of the Palestine Exploration Fund.[66] However, such were the claims of his friendship with the retiring editor, Professor S.H. Hooke, that he did not feel he could refuse Hooke's invitation to take over; nor could he lay down the responsibility until 1971, after Hooke had died. Although he was evidently well regarded as editor, Bruce did not usually attend the meetings of the executive committee.[67]

Like the Palestine Exploration Fund, the Victoria Institute refused to let go of him when he ceased to edit its journal; he was elected president in 1958 and remained in office until 1964, during which period he delivered several presidential addresses.[68] Evidently the institute was not deterred by his earlier critique of its tendency to have addresses on biblical subjects by non-specialists. Bruce had contended that they might have something to offer, but that the institute should not adopt the view that expertise disqualified someone from speaking on such topics. He acknowledged that it was a mixed body whose members represented many professions and academic disciplines, and was convinced that each discipline could contribute something of value, brought together as they were by a shared faith. Nevertheless, these disciplines would be most useful if theology were to be given its rightful and traditional place as queen of the sciences.[69]

His primary editorial role, however, was with the *Evangelical Quarterly*. Looking back over his tenure of this office, he considered that the main feature of his editorship had been a shift towards exegetical articles and away from more narrowly theological ones: 'Every editor, I suppose, imparts something of his own character and

---

[66] Anon., 'R.E.D. Clark: Memories and Appreciations', *FT* 112 (1986): p. 127.

[67] *IR*, pp. 182–4; London, Palestine Exploration Fund, Minute Book 9, 1935–66; Minute Book 10, 1965–90. After submitting his resignation as editor, he was appointed to the executive committee as a representative of the membership, retiring in 1974. On Hooke, whose roots were among Exclusive Brethren, see *IR*, pp. 150, 167–9, and the obituary by Bruce, 'Samuel Henry Hooke (1874–1968)', *W* 98 (1968): pp. 101, 107.

[68] F.F. Bruce, 'Qumran and the New Testament', *FT* 90 (1958): pp. 92–102; 'Qumran and the Old Testament', *FT* 91 (1959–60): pp. 9–27, repr. in *A Mind for What Matters* (Grand Rapids, MI: Eerdmans, 1990), pp. 32–48; 'The Gospel of Thomas: Presidential Address, 14 May 1960', *FT* 92 (1961–2): pp. 3–23; 'History and the Gospel', *FT* 93 (1963–4): pp. 121–45, rev. edn in *Jesus of Nazareth: Saviour and Lord* (ed. C.F.H. Henry; Grand Rapids, MI: Eerdmans/London: Tyndale Press, 1966), pp. 89–107.

[69] F.F. Bruce, 'Annual Address: The Victoria Institute and the Bible', *JTVI* 86 (1954): pp. 75-81.

interests to the journal which he edits. If an objective assessor found that in the last thirty years or so the *Quarterly* has contained less systematic and apologetic theology and more exegetical material, I should not be surprised.'[70] The periodical had its roots within the Scottish Reformed tradition, and for the first few years of his editorship continued to advertise itself as devoted to the exposition of 'the Reformed faith',[71] but whilst Bruce was sympathetic to that outlook[72] and understood it well by virtue of his background and education, he broadened the journal's outlook and scope significantly.

A landmark in the gradual metamorphosis of the *Quarterly* was the controversy which blew up in 1955 over an article which Bruce had accepted for publication; he would later describe this as 'the most unpleasant experience I have had in my whole literary career'.[73] He was deeply attached to the journal, later explaining 'other editorships have not been part of me as this one has been', hence the impact on him.[74] The article was by H.L. Ellison (1903–83), a lecturer at London Bible College, and it appeared in the October 1954 issue. It used the same term – inspiration – for the Holy Spirit's activity in illuminating the readers as it did of his inspiration of the original writers. Ellison was therefore accused of advancing views similar to those of Karl Barth.[75] The *Monthly Record of the Free Church of Scotland* criticized the article as 'in its main thesis a definite, if cautious, presentation of the well-known positions of the Reconstructed Liberalism of To-day'.[76]

---

[70] *IR*, p. 186.

[71] Through the 1970s, contributors were allowed 'reasonable liberty in the exposition of the Reformed Faith'.

[72] Cf. the welcome he gave to the *Banner of Truth*: *EQ* 28 (1956): pp. 67–8.

[73] *IR*, p. 187.

[74] *IR*, p. 184.

[75] At the risk of oversimplifying Barth's thought, we may say that for him the word of God existed in three related forms: as revealed in Christ, as written in Scripture, and as preached. The second and third were witnesses to the first, and as such they were limited and fallible. Only in the event of God speaking to human beings through these witnesses could they be identified with the word of God. Inspiration was not only a matter of the words used by the original writers, but also of the Spirit's using those fallible words to speak to modern hearers: Klaas Runia, *Karl Barth and the Word of God* (Leicester: Theological Students' Fellowship, n.d.), Lecture II.

[76] Anon., 'Towards Barthianism: Is "The Evangelical Quarterly" Softening the Ground?', *Monthly Record of the Free Church of Scotland*, February 1955, pp. 29–31, at p. 29.

The timing of its appearance was unfortunate since London Bible College had adopted a strengthened doctrinal basis the year before, explicitly distancing itself from any understanding of the Bible as merely *becoming*, rather than *being*, the word of God, and the principal, Ernest Kevan, was under pressure to explain to Ellison the untenability of his position.[77] Ellison was effectively forced to resign.

Ellison's article did not only cause problems for the college, but also for the IVF, who in 1954 had taken over from James Clarke as publisher of the *Quarterly*.[78] The IVF was committed to a doctrinal statement upholding the divine authority and infallibility of Scripture, and was increasingly sensitive to the issue of Barthian teaching, which had been a factor in the disaffiliation of the Christian Union at Edinburgh University a year or two earlier.[79] Small wonder that IVF speedily sold the periodical, which from 1956 was published by Paternoster; at the same time, Martyn Lloyd-Jones appears to have ceased his involvement with the journal (he had chaired its supervisory committee since 1944), although it is not clear whether Ellison's article influenced his decision.[80] Bruce stated that its growing financial viability made the move possible, though he reckoned that the IVF would have been relieved to have passed on responsibility for it.[81] He was likewise relieved once the periodical moved to Paternoster, reassuring a contributor who had warned

---

[77] Ian Randall, *Educating Evangelicalism: The Origins, Development and Impact of London Bible College* (Carlisle: Paternoster, 2000), pp. 86–8.

[78] *EQ* 26 (1954): p. 1; *IR*, p. 186.

[79] Noble, *Tyndale*, pp. 77–8; the Christian Union was led by students who had been taught by T.F. Torrance, who was becoming a leading mediator of Barth's thought to the English-speaking world; the immediate issue, however, appears to have been their desire to co-operate with the SCM. Bruce would much later describe Torrance as 'an evangelical of evangelicals' in his theology: 'Evangelical Theology Today', *Life of Faith*, February 1978, pp. 16–17, at p. 16.

[80] Iain H. Murray, *D. Martyn Lloyd-Jones: The Fight of Faith 1939–1981* (Edinburgh: Banner of Truth, 1990), p. 237; *EQ* 63 (1991): p. 70 (Bruce's review of this volume). Although Bruce was careful to give no public hint of it, he appears to have fallen out of sympathy with Lloyd-Jones's outlook and approach: cf. Dubuque, IA, Emmaus Bible College Library, Howard Mudditt to Bruce, 2 May 1955.

[81] *IR*, pp. 186, 188; this is confirmed by the *Monthly Record of the Free Church of Scotland*, September 1955, pp. 178–9, where it was stated (prematurely, Bruce asserted) that *EQ* would cease publication at the end of the year if financial arrangements were not made to continue it; even such a rigorously Reformed publication could still pay tribute to Bruce as being 'in whole-hearted sympathy with its aims and objects'.

that his article might be seen as controversial that 'I have a much freer hand now that the EQ is no longer the property of the IVP.'[82]

Given the alleged Barthian overtones of Ellison's article (and I do not think the charge was as wide of the mark as Bruce asserted), why did Bruce not foresee that controversy would break out? Was it, as has been claimed, because he was not as astute theologically as he was exegetically?[83] Was it because in the Reformed teaching which permeated his Scottish background, the illuminating ministry of the Holy Spirit had traditionally been given prominence in the doctrine of Scripture set forth in the Westminster Confession? Or was it because as an academic he was used to enjoying freedom to air and debate differing views without any need to uphold a particular standpoint, and to journals in which this was done in print? Whatever the explanation, and all these factors are germane, the impact on him was profound; at the time, he wryly expressed agreement with a former editor of *The Witness*, J.B. Watson, who said that 'being an editor is one of the quickest ways of losing one's friends'.[84] To the Victoria Institute Bruce recalled the positive impact Barth had made on him as a student, and described himself and others as 'gravely perturbed' at attempts to cast Barth as a heretic and his theology as 'a new modernism'. He went on:

> One particularly disquieting instance of this tendency affects a member of the Council of the Institute, who has been publicly attacked because of an excellent paper which he published lately on this very subject of Biblical inspiration. His approach has been classified as 'Barthian' (which it is not) and condemned out of hand on this ground. Even if it had been Barthian, instead of being much more adequate and objective than Barth's approach, there would have been no excuse for this reaction.[85]

---

[82] Madrid, Comisión de Biblioteca y Archivos, Centro Evangélico de Formación Bíblica en Madrid, Bruce to Ernest H. Trenchard, 5 January 1957. In the first editorial of 1956, he described it as an 'enfant terrible' to IVF, speaking out of turn on issues such as inspiration and sanctification (in 1955 an article by J.I. Packer had appeared which roundly criticized Keswick teaching regarding sanctification): *EQ* 28 (1956): p. 3.

[83] Roger Shuff, *Searching for the True Church: Brethren and Evangelicals in Mid-Twentieth-Century England* (Carlisle: Paternoster, 2005), p. 93.

[84] F.F. Bruce, 'J.B. Watson: His Writings', *W* 85 (1955): p. 199.

[85] *JTVI* 87 (1955): p. 140. *The New Modernism* was the title of a book by the Reformed theologian Cornelius van Til of Westminster Theological Seminary, Philadelphia. Published in 1946, it was strongly opposed to Barth's theology.

The following year he returned to Ellison's defence in a written comment on the latter's paper to the Institute on 'Some Major Modern Trends in Old Testament Study': Bruce thought it

> deplorable that people in this country who call themselves 'conservative Evangelicals' so signally fail to realize what a tower of strength they have in Mr. Ellison or to appreciate properly his outstanding qualities of Christian scholarship. Conservative Evangelicals in some other countries would long since have provided a man of his caliber with a secure position in which he could have full opportunity to develop his gifts and make significant contributions to Biblical study. Is our professed devotion to unfettered Biblical study much more than lip-service?[86]

Two decades later, he continued to reject the claim that the article was Barthian, and expressed severe criticism of the ethical standards of Ellison's attackers:

> When a man's standing in the constituency which he serves, not to speak of his livelihood, depends on his reputation for fidelity to the truth of Scripture, it is a very serious matter for anyone else to broadcast doubts about his fidelity or orthodoxy. If he himself statedly renounces something which is of the essence of the historic Christian faith, he will be prepared for the consequences, but he should not be held responsible for the inferences which other people may draw from his statements. Most deplorable of all is the launching of a whispering campaign.[87]

---

[86] *JTVI* 88 (1956): pp. 157–8. Bruce is recalled by one who worked with him during the 1950s as having once commented that whilst Ellison believed in the unity of Isaiah and yet was deemed heretical, he himself believed in three Isaiahs and was counted orthodox: Andrew Walls, interview, 18 February 2010. His reference was to Ellison's book on the Old Testament prophets, *Men Spake from God* (London: Paternoster, 1952; for Isaiah, see ch. 6), in the preparation of which Bruce had played a part, encouraging Ellison to deal with the minor as well as the major prophets: ibid. p. 10.

[87] *IR*, pp. 188–9. One wonders whether the strength of Bruce's reaction also owed something to the loss of support apparently suffered by his father. In 1964, Bruce expressed support for another LBC lecturer, Ralph Martin, who had published articles deemed to be too positive towards Barth and Bonhoeffer; another supporter was a Brethren member of the college's board, Derek Warren, who feared the loss of scholars from the faculty if others were to be so treated: Randall, *Educating*

Discussion of this controversy leads us to consider Bruce's own doctrine of Scripture as it was developing during this period. His conservative credentials were impeccable: he was a member of the Bible League council,[88] and when it was mooted that the word 'infallible' be removed from the article in the IVF doctrinal basis, he assured Johnson that the suggestion would get no support from him.[89] Nobody would have taken exception to his statement that 'Biblical inspiration is that special control exercised by the Spirit of God over the writers of Holy Scripture, by reason of which their words adequately express the Word of God'.[90] A useful elaboration of this, however, was his article on 'The Scriptures' in a 1952 symposium on doctrine by Brethren writers, *The Faith*.[91] It begins with three quotations from the Westminster Shorter Catechism (which would have endeared him to many Scottish Brethren); together they set out 'the chief end of man', the status of the word of God as the sole rule for achieving this, and its main teaching. In line with the thinking of the Biblical Theology movement, Bruce stresses the role of Scripture as a record of salvation-history. Following the Dutch Calvinist Abraham Kuyper (1837–1920), he described the Holy Spirit as its primary and perpetual author. Since it possessed divine authority, it must be self-authenticating to the reader, for there could not be any external authority for God to rely on to authenticate his word. This self-authentication happened by means of the inward witness of the Holy Spirit to the divine authority of Scripture; here Bruce's thought parallels Calvin's *Institutes of the Christian Religion* and the Westminster tradition.[92] In the individual, this led to a conviction that the Scriptures were indeed from God; in the church, it had resulted in the recognition of those writings deemed to form part of the

---

Evangelicalism, p. 129. A third member of the LBC faculty, Leslie Allen (also a member of the Brethren), provoked controversy in the late 1970s by a commentary on Jonah which cast doubt on its historicity: ibid. pp. 206, 226. In all three cases, Brethren openness to 'unfettered scholarship' played a significant role in one way or another.

[88] UCCF archives, Bruce to Douglas Johnson, 18 June 1944. The Bible League was founded in 1892 'To promote the Reverent Study of the Holy Scriptures, and to resist the varied attacks made upon their Inspiration, Infallibility and Sole Sufficiency as the Word of God': http://www.bibleleaguetrust.org (accessed 4 May 2010).

[89] UCCF archives, Bruce to Johnson, 29 July 1944.

[90] *H* 37 (1958): p. 171: Q. 725.

[91] F.F. Bruce, 'The Scriptures', in *The Faith: A Symposium* (ed. F.A. Tatford; London: Pickering & Inglis, 1952), pp. 13-26.

[92] His earliest statement of this argument appeared in 'Some Aspects of Gospel Introduction', *EQ* 15 (1943): pp. 3-20, at p. 19, originally read to an IVF Theological

biblical canon. Bruce was no fundamentalist, however; he insisted that the Bible's inspiration and infallibility must be understood in the light of its intended purpose, which was to make wise to salvation and to train in godliness. Was it therefore immaterial whether or not the Bible was accurate regarding matters on which it only touched incidentally? He discussed its account of creation, the astonishing degree to which historical research confirmed the reliability of the text, and the fact that if the resurrection could be proved to be unhistorical, the fabric of Christian faith would be destroyed; but he did not answer the question with an unambiguous affirmation of its accuracy in every historical detail.[93] The article concludes with a lengthy quotation from chapters 24 to 26 of the Westminster Confession, in Bruce's view the best summary ever written of the doctrine of Scripture.[94]

A theologian whom Bruce quoted from time to time regarding the authority was Robertson Smith, whose writings probably helped Bruce as a student wrestling with the implications of biblical criticism for faith. Smith had asserted:

> If I am asked why I receive Scripture as the Word of God and as the only perfect rule of faith and life, I answer with all the fathers of the

---

Students' Conference in December 1941. In that paper Bruce was urging a positive attitude to critical scholarship on the basis that discovering the truth about such matters as the origin of the gospels could never contradict the truth which Christians have come to know by means of the Spirit's testimony. Cf. 'The End of the Second Gospel', *EQ* 17 (1945): pp. 169-81, at p. 177, where he described the Spirit's witness as the one proof of biblical inspiration, quoting the Westminster Confession in support.

[93] A few years earlier, however, he had done so: Oakes, 'Bruce', p. 111, citing *JTVI* 78 (1946): p. 124. Responding to questions after a lecture to the Victoria Institute on 6 May 1946 on the theme 'What Do We Mean by Biblical Inspiration?', Bruce had rejected the use of the term 'verbal inspiration' as a test of orthodoxy, although he was prepared to assent to it with the clarification that he did not accept any kind of dictation theory regarding the origin of the Scriptures: *JTVI* 78 (1946): p. 137; for the lecture, see ibid. pp. 121–8. In a letter to Douglas Johnson on 9 July 1944, he also intimated that he did not regard 'infallibility' as a synonym for 'inerrancy'. In an interview on 7 April 2009, J.I. Packer paralleled Bruce with the Scottish theologian James Orr (1844–1913) in this respect, Orr likewise distinguishing between the divine teaching given through Scripture and specific incidental details (on which he did not affirm the Bible's complete reliability).

[94] He still thought so many years later: J.D. Douglas, 'A Man of Unchanging Faith', *CT*, 10 October 1980, pp. 16–18, at p. 17.

Protestant Church: Because the Bible is the only record of the redeeming love of God, because in the Bible alone I find God drawing near to
man in Christ Jesus, and declaring to us, in Him, His will for our salvation. And this record I know to be true by the witness of His Spirit in
my heart, whereby I am assured that none other than God Himself is
able to speak such words to my soul.[95]

A distinction should be drawn, however, between Smith's argument
that the Bible was to be received as the word of God because of the
inward testimony of the Spirit, and that of the Presbyterian theologians associated with Princeton Seminary in the USA, whose best-
known representative was B.B. Warfield (1851–1921). As expressed
by John Murray (1898-1975), they emphasized that the Bible
possessed divine authority 'antecedently and objectively' apart
from this testimony.[96] Murray interpreted the Westminster
Confession as teaching that the authority of the Bible derived from
its being the word of God and its having been given by divine inspiration; what the testimony of the Holy Spirit did was to convince
individuals of these things.[97]

Bruce's approach to the doctrine of Scripture differs somewhat
from that espoused by the Princetonians. Whilst they would have
affirmed the role of the Holy Spirit in connection with the inspiration of Scripture, Bruce laid more stress than they appear to have
done on the illumination of the Spirit as the final proof to the
believer of the divine inspiration and consequent authority of
Scripture, and (unlike them) had little to say during this period
regarding biblical inerrancy. He preferred to derive his doctrine of
Scripture from close study of the text and insisted that problem passages should not be forced to fit into an *a priori* understanding of
the nature of Scripture, whereas the Princetonians argued that the
doctrine of inerrancy should not be modified to take account of

[95] W. Robertson Smith, *Answer to the Form of Libel before the Free Presbytery of
Aberdeen* (Edinburgh: David Douglas, 1878), p. 21, quoted in Anon., 'Biblical
Inspiration and Authority', *TB*, *OS*, July 1946, pp. 1–4, at p. 1 (this article reviewed
Bruce's lecture to the Victoria Institute referred to in n. 93 above).

[96] John Murray, 'The Attestation of Scripture', in *The Infallible Word: A Symposium by
the Members of the Faculty of Westminster Theological Seminary* (ed. [N.B. Stonehouse
and Paul Woolley]; Philadelphia, PA: Presbyterian Guardian Publishing
Association, 1946), pp. 1–52, at pp. 41–2.

[97] Ibid. pp. 43–4.

particular problems.[98] Many British writers had, like Bruce, affirmed the reliability of Scripture without affirming inerrancy, an approach which David Wright has contrasted with that of Packer (whose influential *Fundamentalism and the Word of God* was published by IVF in 1958) and Warfield, in which 'the nature of Scripture is no longer established in dialogue with biblical criticism but determined deductively, a priori, dogmatically'.[99] To a student who was wrestling with just this issue, Bruce wrote: 'I usually advise my students not to approach the Scriptures with a theory of inspiration derived from some other source, because then they will have unnecessary trouble trying to accommodate the Scriptures to their theory; whereas if they base their theory of inspiration on the actual claims and phenomena of Scripture . . . they will be spared much trouble.'[100] And in a later letter to the same student, he explained:

> the final and only really valid proof of biblical inspiration is the inward witness of the Holy Spirit in the heart . . . The witness of Scripture is validated by the witness of the Spirit within . . . my faith in Christ is a matter of a personal relationship with a living Person, which cannot be punctured by questions of literary or historical criticism. Naturally these are not questions which can be settled by the inward witness of the Spirit, and for that very reason they are peripheral to the central authority of Scripture.[101]

It is easy to see why Ellison's article struck a chord in his own thinking. In subsequent chapters we shall explore Bruce's views further, and see how his approach to Scripture developed against the background of (and sometimes in apparent reaction against) increasing elaboration of the Princeton approach by other evangelicals.

---

[98] Cf. Gary Dorrien, *The Remaking of Evangelical Theology* (Louisville, KY: Westminster John Knox, 1998), p. 18.

[99] David F. Wright, 'Soundings in the Doctrine of Scripture in British Evangelicalism in the First Half of the Twentieth Century', *TB* 31 (1980): pp. 87–106; quotation at p. 103.

[100] Bruce to Leslie Allen, 20 December 1958.

[101] Bruce to Leslie Allen, 15 August 1959. It should also be noted that Bruce's views on the person and work of the Holy Spirit owed much to the Reformed tradition; he described the nineteenth-century Scot George Smeaton's work on the topic, reprinted by Banner of Truth, as 'one of the best treatments of the subject known to me': CBA, Box 11 (11g), Bruce to Ian S. Davidson, 16 January 1986.

◆   ◆   ◆

As an editor, Bruce found himself writing many more book reviews than before. These have been described as 'literary models of the Golden Rule':[102] if a book was so bad that he could find nothing good to say about it, he preferred to leave it unreviewed and to send it back to the publisher; this, he is recalled as saying, was why he had made so few enemies during his long career.[103] Certainly I only found one review which could be described as negative in tone. That said, he believed it quite possible to express disagreement with a book without resorting to criticism of its author. Ultimately he saw himself, like all Christians, as accountable to God for the way in which he judged others, citing Matthew 7:2 to explain this.[104]

It is clear that he was able to grasp the contents of a book with remarkable facility – hence his astonishing output. On one occasion, a scholar came up to him at a meeting of the SOTS; 'You owe me a book review', he said. Bruce immediately took a sheet of paper and dashed off a review, commenting 'I've read the book'.[105] At other times, he was known to write reviews on pages torn out of university examination books. All told, it is reckoned that he wrote over two thousand reviews, many of them for *Evangelical Quarterly*. Some were signed; others appeared with the initials 'R.P.' for 'Rylands Professor'.[106] About fifty appeared in the *Journal of Semitic Studies*, and others in the *Palestine Exploration Quarterly* or various evangelical periodicals; when his specialist knowledge made him the obvious person to approach, he would occasionally review for periodicals outside these constituencies, such as the interdisciplinary European periodical *Erasmus*. Often the reviews simply summarized the contents of a book and explained why its appearance was to be welcomed; for the most part Bruce did not engage in extended critique of the main ideas. If he had little to say, it was not unknown for him to add a humorous anecdote, of which he had an enormous store.[107] His reviews of Bible translations, however, form an exception to this, as they usually included

---

[102] Harris, 'Bruce', p. 219.

[103] *IR*, p. 281; Vancouver, Regent College, faculty discussion, 8 April 2009.

[104] *IR*, pp. 300–04.

[105] Vancouver, Regent College, faculty discussion, 8 April 2009.

[106] Alan Millard, quoted in Oakes, 'Bruce', p. 118.

[107] A[lan]. R. Millard, 'Frederick Fyvie Bruce 1910–1990', *JSS* 36/1 (Spring 1991): pp. 1–6, at p. 1.

incisive extended analyses of the translators' work. It is remarkable to observe in them his facility for tailoring his comments for various publications according to the readership of each.[108]

◆   ◆   ◆

Perhaps the chief way in which Bruce exercised leadership among Brethren during the 1950s was through his 'Answers to Questions' column, which appeared each month in *The Harvester*.[109] Because Brethren lacked centralized structures and institutions, magazines fulfilled a vital role among them, helping them to maintain coherence by disseminating news and providing sound teaching. Question and answer columns enabled editors (and writers chosen by them) to give definitive rulings on any issue which readers might wish to raise, and it is noticeable how many questions actually wanted such a clear-cut ruling. Bruce must have disappointed a good number of them, but many more probably turned to his page first when they picked up their *Harvester* each month. He took over the column on the death of H.P. Barker in 1952, only laying down the responsibility with the two thousandth question in 1975. A selection was brought together on the initiative of Clive Rawlins and published, virtually unedited, by Paternoster as *Answers to Questions* in 1972. That they could appear in book form testifies to the unique importance of this mode of teaching among Brethren; one cannot imagine such a book having sold in other denominational circles.[110] Moreover, they led to his dealing with questions sent him privately, requiring him to exercise 'a ministry of pastoral counselling by post'.[111]

---

[108]For example, his reviews of the Revised Standard Version: 'Revised Standard Version of the Holy Bible', *Life of Faith*, 8 October 1952, pp. 691, 694; 'The Revised Standard Version of the Holy Bible', *The Christian*, 24 October 1952; 'The Revised Standard Version', *Knowing the Scriptures* 10/123 (March–April 1953): pp. 93–4; 'A British Scholar Looks at the RSV Old Testament', *Eternity* (May 1954): pp. 12–13, 42–7.

[109]On *The Harvester*, which was published by Paternoster, see Grass, *Gathering*, esp. pp. 314, 399–406.

[110]Bruce fulfilled a similar role in the 'Christian Workers' Forum' of the interdenominational periodical *Life of Faith* from 1954 until early in 1957, after he became editor of *PEQ*, but he was not the only person dealing with the questions, and the feature was not as prominent in this magazine. Occasional answers from him also appeared in *The Witness*.

[111]F.F. Bruce, foreword to *Answers to Questions* (Exeter: Paternoster, 1972).

Some of Bruce's answers displayed a marked tendency to the Delphic. This is partly because he was fully aware that some of his views were rather 'advanced' for more traditionally minded Brethren, and therefore needed to be couched in suitable terms; indeed, they were often as noteworthy for what they did not say as for what they did say.[112] In some cases, he was aware that his views would differ from those of the editor, Frederick Tatford; of an answer to a question on the partial rapture (the teaching that only some Christians would be raptured) which might look like a deliberate evasion, Bruce explained to Lang that 'In view of the official *Harvester* position on prophecy, it is wise to approach these questions with some attention to tactics.'[113] In addition, he shied away from giving answers which were too clearly prescriptive because of his preference for outlining the options and leaving the reader to make up their own mind, something which reflected his academic setting. Even in the family setting, he would follow this approach.[114] He also considered that he could only deal with questions arising from local situations by outlining general principles; he did not have the specific local knowledge required, and it was 'not the function of this column to usurp the responsibility of the elders of a particular church'.[115] When questioners tried to draw him on some controversial issue, he would play a straight bat, as when he was asked to express an opinion on Ellison's article on inspiration; choosing his words carefully, he commended it for stressing that the Spirit's work in relation to Scripture did not end with inspiration but was continued in Christian experience, so that the Bible was not only the word of God in an objective sense but became so in subjective experience.[116]

Nevertheless, he was quite prepared to say something provocative if he felt the topic justified it; indeed, on looking back he thought it

---

[112] Cf. a letter which he wrote to the editor of *The Believer's Magazine* on 7 April 1966, in which he referred to the idea that the Pastoral Epistles had been edited after Paul's death, a theory which some of its readers had evidently found unacceptable: 'The theory of posthumous editorship was mentioned for the benefit of "those who find it difficult to accept all three in their present form as letters written or dictated directly by Paul"; readers of THE BELIEVER'S MAGAZINE find no such difficulty and therefore have no need of such a theory.' He avoids giving any indication of whether he is to be numbered among them.

[113] CBA, Box 64, Bruce to Lang, 17 July 1953.

[114] Sheila Lukabyo, interview, 2 September 2009.

[115] *H* 34 (1955): p. 171: Q. 400.

[116] *H* 34 (1955): p. 139: Q. 380.

possible that he had been too prone in the earlier years of his tenure to stick his neck out.[117] Thus, on the topic of women participating audibly in assembly gatherings, he expressed the view that 1 Corinthians 14:34 was not to be interpreted as prohibiting women from praying at prayer meetings.[118] A little later, he asserted that women as well as men could serve as deacons.[119] He would also take issue with certain cherished Brethren traditions and interpretations. One example was provided by the concept of the leading of the Holy Spirit, which was commonly applied primarily to the Breaking of Bread, which in traditional Brethren worship was completely unscripted (in such a context, the Spirit's leading seems to have been regarded as some kind of inward impulse leading one brother or another to pray, read a passage of Scripture or give out a hymn). Bruce argued on the basis of Scripture that this leading was in fact something which should be evident in all areas of life, not just the 'morning meeting', and that the supreme test of this leading in ministry was not the speaker's inward feelings but the listeners' edification.[120]

Another was the practice of issuing letters of commendation; these were written by the leading brethren in one assembly in order to commend the bearer to another as a fit recipient of its fellowship. Bruce recalled being given a letter of commendation by Henry Pickering, then editor of *The Witness*, when he went to Vienna as a postgraduate student, which was addressed 'to all the Lord's people everywhere'. It proved very useful, but he still felt that such letters should not be insisted on legalistically, and that the printed forms issued by some Brethren publishers for elders to fill in the blanks did not count as proper letters.[121]

Furthermore, he made it clear that he had no time for the sectarian type of Brethrenism which was widespread outside the south-east of England: commenting on a statement in the 1938 report *Doctrine in the Church of England*, he said: 'If I were compelled to use the term "schism" of any true believers in Christ, I should restrict it to those who draw narrower frontiers of fellowship than those which Christ

---

[117] *IR*, p. 273.

[118] *H* 34 (1955), p. 187: Q. 410. On one occasion during this period he was invited to conduct a communion service at a Baptist church in Dronfield, and was delighted when its deaconesses gave thanks for the bread and the wine: *IR*, p. 155.

[119] *H* 36 (1957): p. 123: Q. 607; cf. 37 (1958): p. 27: Q. 649.

[120] *H* 31 (1952): p. 40: QQ. 42–3.

[121] *H* 38 (1959): p. 131: Q. 804; cf. *IR*, p. 89.

has drawn, and who refuse inter-communion with Christians who do not toe their party line.'[122] Elsewhere he denied that the injunction in 2 Corinthians 6:17 to 'come out from among them, and be ye separate' had any reference (as many Brethren thought it did) to leaving denominations and joining an assembly; it was, he insisted, about separating from idolatry.[123] Yet for all that, he could also raise the possibility that at heart he was 'just an old-fashioned Brother of the traditional school'.[124] The next two chapters will shed light on the extent to which such a self-assessment was justified.

---

[122] *H* 34 (1955): p. 155: Q. 394.
[123] *H* 41 (1962): p. 139: Q. 1051.
[124] *H* 33 (1954): p. 56: Q. 227.

7

Rylands Professor: Manchester (1959–78)

The opening for Bruce to move to Manchester, where his reputation would really be made, came out of the blue. The Rylands Professor of Biblical Criticism and Exegesis, T.W. Manson, had died in office during the summer of 1958, and the appointment process for his successor was becoming a protracted saga, partly because earlier candidates for the post had not secured sufficient support from the search committee.[1] Bruce's name was on a list of candidates by July 1958, but others were approached first and he was not contacted about the post until May 1959. As he wrote, 'it might be inferred that by that time they had begun to scrape the bottom of the barrel'.[2] Although he thought it would be interesting to accept the committee's invitation to meet them for a conversation about the position (it was not intended as a formal interview, and no commitment was implied on either side), he was happy at Sheffield and not looking to move as he had been at Leeds.

On the way back to the station after the meeting, however, a committee member caught him up and informed him of the committee's unanimous decision to recommend that he be offered the post. He spent the ensuing weekend thinking about the offer and ministering at a Brethren conference in Banbury, before intimating his acceptance of the offer. Two months later he wrote to a friend, the Brethren missionary Ernest Trenchard, that he was really surprised to be offered the chair, as he would have thought his IVF and Brethren associations too much for the committee to accept.[3] He may have had some justification

---

[1] One person to be offered the chair had been Bruce's friend George Beasley-Murray, early in 1959: Paul Beasley-Murray, *Fearless for Truth: A Personal Portrait of the Life of George Raymond Beasley-Murray* (Carlisle: Paternoster, 2002), pp. 94–5.

[2] *IR*, p. 202.

[3] Madrid, Comisión de Biblioteca y Archivos, Centro Evangélico de Formación Bíblica en Madrid, Bruce to Ernest H. Trenchard, 11 July 1959.

for this; a testimonial from a renowned New Testament scholar had described him as having been 'at one time a near "Fundamentalist"' but as having broadened rapidly in his position; this would be consonant with his having written earlier in his career for conservative Brethren magazines such as *The Believer's Magazine* and *Precious Seed*. There is a story that, when some on the committee had expressed apprehension about him (presumably at some point before Bruce was invited to meet them), H.H. Rowley, then Professor of Old Testament, reputedly drew their attention to Bruce's commentary on the Greek text of Acts which lay on the table and said that he wanted to secure the appointment of somebody who was capable of producing such work, even if they should be a Jehovah's Witness.[4] Bruce was apprehensive about his lack of experience in theological colleges, but the vice-chancellor assured him that such anxiety sprang from a misunderstanding of the relationship of such colleges with the university.[5]

The relationship was, in fact, a complex one. It was at Manchester that the first non-denominational faculty of theology in Britain was founded, in the belief that theology could best be restored to an honoured position by being taught in the growing universities rather than in the Anglican faculties in older institutions, or in the dissenting colleges.[6] The more vocational and denominationally specific courses were taught in those colleges (and Manchester had training colleges for all the main Nonconformist denominations), as also initially were doctrine and ecclesiastical history, but other subjects were taught under the auspices of the university on a non-denominational basis. The Rylands Chair in Biblical Criticism and Exegesis, which dated back to the founding of the university as an independent institution in 1904, was the first chair of theology or biblical studies in a British university which did not impose a religious test on its occupant. Its occupants were required to demonstrate equal competence in Old and New Testaments, and the first three had all been committed Nonconformists: A.S. Peake (1904–29), C.H. Dodd (1929–35) and T.W. Manson (1935–58).

---

[4] J. Julius Scott Jr, telephone conversation, 11 June 2009.
[5] Manchester, University of Manchester, Vice-Chancellor's Office, appointment file. I am grateful to Lynda McKean for tracking down this file and enabling me to consult it.
[6] Timothy Larsen, 'Introduction', *BJRL* 86/3 (Autumn 2004): pp. 5–8, at p. 6; J.W. Rogerson, 'The Manchester Faculty of Theology 1904: Beginnings and Background', ibid. pp. 9–22, at pp. 18–19. For this section, see also *IR*, ch. 25.

By the time of Bruce's arrival a variety of courses were on offer. The Department of Biblical Studies was, for the first part of his time at least, separate from the Faculty of Theology (although most of its BA degree was taught by members of the latter), a fact which made it more acceptable to evangelical students concerned at what they saw as the liberal outlook of the latter.[7] By 1959 the department was beginning to expand, thanks to the inauguration of a new honours school in Biblical Studies the previous year, a development which paralleled that at Sheffield. A BD degree was offered by the Faculty of Theology, intended primarily for graduates who were ministerial candidates at the denominational colleges. From 1966, it became possible to do a MA in Theology, and from 1969 an honours BA in Religious Studies. The three first degrees were unified in 1976 as a BA taught in the theology faculty. Over this period there was a marked drop in the proportion of students planning to enter the pastoral ministry; this necessitated changes in the way that certain subjects were taught. For example, when Bruce served as dean of the Faculty of Theology for two years (1963–4), he made representations for the establishment of a university chair in the history of doctrine, a subject which had hitherto been taught in the denominational colleges, because an increasing number of students were not ministerial candidates and thus were not registered in these colleges. The faculty was a large one, numbering around thirty academic members of staff by the mid-1960s, and in addition to them there were the theological college tutors whose lecture courses were recognized by the faculty.[8]

Throughout his tenure, he maintained a full teaching load.[9] By contrast with the situation at Sheffield, he inherited an existing set of courses, but the expectation that he would pursue his own interests allowed him to major on the New Testament, although he did also

---

[7] Pam Harrison, interview, 25 April 2009. It appears to have acquired a dual status, as both a department in the Faculty of Theology and a department in the Faculty of Arts; this complicated working relationships with other departments in the Faculty of Theology: David Pailin to the author, 7 May 2010.

[8] *IR*, p. 215; Ronald H. Preston, 'The Faculty of Theology in the University of Manchester: The First Seventy-Five Years', in *University of Manchester, Faculty of Theology: Seventy-Fifth Anniversary Papers 1979* (ed. David A. Pailin; Manchester: Victoria University of Manchester, 1980), pp. 1–24; David Pailin to the author, 7 May 2010.

[9] Murray J. Harris, 'Frederick Fyvie Bruce', in *Bible Interpreters of the 20th Century: A Selection of Evangelical Voices* (ed. Walter A. Elwell and J.D. Weaver; Grand Rapids, MI: Baker, 1999), pp. 216–27, at p. 218.

teach courses on Daniel and on the text and canon of the Old Testament.[10] Only two prospectuses have been traced from the period of his professorship, for 1959–60 and 1964–5, but the picture they give is probably typical, if partial, since it has not been possible to establish what courses he taught for the Faculty of Arts. He began Thursdays (the only day of the week for which full details seem to be available) by lecturing on the text and canon of the Old or New Testament, the lectures eventually forming the basis of his last major book.[11] The two testaments were covered in alternate years. The second half of Thursday mornings was given over to studying the New Testament in Greek (jointly with another member of staff); set texts were the Gospel of John one year and Romans and 1 John the next; student recollections indicate that other books were studied in other courses. Thursday afternoons saw him teaching New Testament history, theology and 'Introduction' (again jointly) over two sessions, alternating between the apostolic age and the life and teaching of Jesus. Many of his male students took the theology degree in preparation for pastoral ministry with various denominations, while many of the women took the biblical studies degree and went into school teaching, worked with para-church agencies or (as Bruce explained to one external examiner) married the male students and presumably wrote their sermons for them![12] Bruce was also a student himself, attending an elementary Coptic class in 1962–3.[13]

As Rylands professor, it was expected that he would deliver public lectures as part of the library's wider educational remit; this he did annually from 1960 until 1986, his lectures usually being the first and the best attended of each session. Former students who had become teachers would on occasion bring groups of sixth-formers to hear him.[14] All of his lectures appear to have been published in the *Bulletin of the John Rylands Library*. The topics can be ascertained from the bibliography; here we simply note that most formed series (except when specific topics were in the public eye) on Paul in Rome, Galatians, Paul's theology, and Paul in Macedonia; many were recycled to form part of commentary introductions or his major work on Paul.

---

[10] *IR*, p. 206.

[11] F.F. Bruce, *The Canon of Scripture* (Glasgow: Chapter House, 1988), p. 9.

[12] *IR*, pp. 229–30.

[13] Northwood, LST, J.D. Douglas papers, Bruce to Douglas, 25 December 1962.

[14] R.H. Preston, memorial tribute, Thanksgiving Service, Manchester University Chaplaincy, 13 March 1991; Adrian Curtis, interview, 28 January 2010.

Although he was expected to possess equal competence in Old and New Testaments, only the first lecture focused on an Old Testament subject.

Some students from North America were caught out by the more relaxed attitudes in British evangelical circles to many issues, and it is said that on occasion a disapproving student would walk out of one of Bruce's lectures. Most, however, would have had a more practical reason for discontent: Bruce usually read his lectures in a monotone, and often did so from the proofs of one of his books. Thus he is recalled as more or less reading his commentary when lecturing on Romans.[15] An undergraduate from the 1970s recalls a little man in a black gown, reading notes in tiny handwriting on the backs of envelopes in a quiet voice which could lull students to sleep, with the risk that in succumbing some gem might be missed.[16] This was not, however, a judgement on the worth of the content: one student recalled that 'Prof's lectures were quite dry and there were the times I escaped to play hockey when I should have been at a double lecture', yet when she had to revise for examinations the notes came to life and she was excited at the intellectual and practical helpfulness of the material.[17]

The focus of postgraduate life in the department was the weekly seminar which Bruce conducted jointly with the Bishop Fraser Senior Lecturer in Ecclesiastical History, Dr Arnold Ehrhardt (it was named the Ehrhardt Seminar following his death in 1965) on Thursdays at 11 a.m.[18] One speaker recalled Bruce as bringing his tea and biscuits into the room and appearing absorbed in marking essays or correcting proofs, but belying appearances by his ability to engage in a penetrating manner with the arguments put forward.[19]

On several occasions Bruce expressed a degree of wariness, even scepticism, concerning the research doctorate. In 1944, he had argued that German critical radicalism was due not to the national character,

---

[15] Kent Brower, interview, 30 May 2008; cf. the story of a Free Church ministerial candidate who had been preaching at the weekend and fell asleep in a Monday morning lecture on Romans, and was advised by Bruce 'in the kindest of tones, simply to read his Commentary': obituary in the *Daily Telegraph*, 20 September 1990.

[16] Isabelle McGarahan, interview, 1 September 2009.

[17] Joan Wragg to the author, 3 June 2009, 31 August 2010.

[18] *IR*, p. 213; Loveday Alexander, interview, 30 May 2008. The seminar still meets today, but at a different time.

[19] Adrian Curtis, interview, 28 January 2010.

as evangelical apologists had frequently alleged, but to the doctoral dissertation system:

> As, generation after generation, German students submit dissertations for the doctorate of their faculty, they have the choice of confirming old views or presenting new ones. Naturally, more 'kudos' attaches to the publication of a new theory than to the re-establishment of an old one, and the most brilliant and ambitious students will seek to put forth 'some new thing.' In some faculties the results of this tendency are wholly beneficial, but in such subjects as classical literature or biblical theology this is not always so. The number of *probable* hypotheses in these realms is limited, and as these have long ago been exhausted, the chances are that *improbable* hypotheses will multiply.

The practice of dissecting literary documents had begun with the classicists but, he claimed, it persisted in the field of biblical studies long after other disciplines had abandoned it.[20]

Nevertheless, analysis of the relevant minute books indicates that he supervised around fifty doctoral students while at Manchester, said to be more than any other British supervisor in the field had ever coped with.[21] Three-fifths of them were from overseas, many from North America, which gives some weight to his humorous comment that 'the PhD was invented so that Americans could take an advanced degree home with them when they came to the UK for further study'.[22] His standing with transatlantic evangelicals presented him with a problem, and his erstwhile colleague Robert Kraft recalls

> a rare conversation with him in his office, at his request, when he expressed concern about American conservatives (I think Dallas Seminary may have been mentioned, among other such contexts) wanting to send him graduate students with the intention that the students would avoid exposure to 'liberal' scholarship. He asked how he might escape or avoid or respond to such requests. I don't remember what I said, but I suppose it was to emphasize that any such candidates be qualified and open to learning, wherever it might lead. I don't think

---

[20] F.F. Bruce, 'True and False Criticism', *Theological Notes*, July–October 1944, pp. 5–7, at p. 6.

[21] J.I. Packer, foreword to *IR*, p. xi.

[22] Laurel and Ward Gasque, 'Frederick Fyvie Bruce: An Appreciation', *H* 69/11 (November 1990): pp. 1–6, at p. 2.

FFB quite understood the deep differences between his British conservatism, with its openness, and radical American conservatism, with its very closed attitudes to certain key issues. He found himself caught in the middle, I think, and certainly did not want to be a pawn of the latter.[23]

A number of his postgraduate students later became well known as scholars in their own right. Apart from those mentioned in this chapter, they included Ronald Fung, Ward Gasque, Robert Gundry, Don Hagner, Murray Harris, Morna Hooker, Seyoon Kim, René Padilla and David Wenham. Almost all focused on some aspect of New Testament studies, many of them on Paul; only one worked primarily on the Dead Sea Scrolls, and none majored on the Old Testament. A few became members of staff for a time, helping to create the ethos which Bruce saw as desirable. Among these were Colin Hemer and Clark Pinnock.

Several of these students came from the Church of the Nazarene, a small denomination in the Wesleyan holiness tradition.[24] Doubtless Bruce's concern for holiness and his familiarity with Methodism in Scotland helped them to sense a kindred spirit, and he had also reviewed kindly a history of the denomination by his friend Jack Ford, *In the Steps of John Wesley*.[25] The Nazarenes warmed to Bruce's understanding of holiness, and were doubtless influenced by him.[26] He also did much to help the denomination's college in Manchester, notably in expanding its library, and would become its first Didsbury lecturer in 1978.[27]

Other students came from the Seventh-Day Adventist Church in Australia, at a time when evangelicals generally were highly suspicious of Adventism. They included Desmond Ford and Norman Young, both of whom were sympathetic to Wesleyan and Reformational thinking about justification by grace alone through faith. Their desire to study under his supervision, and to engage in critical assessment of certain

---

[23] Robert H. Kraft to the author, 14 August 2009.
[24] They included Alex Deasley and Kent Brower.
[25] *EQ* 41 (1969): pp. 184–5.
[26] Kent Brower, interview, 30 May 2008.
[27] He was chosen to inaugurate other lectures, too, thus putting them on a respectable academic footing: the Rendle Short Memorial Lectures of the Bristol Library for Biblical Research (1962), the Laing Lectures at LBC (1971), and the Finlayson Lectures of the Scottish Evangelical Theological Society (1981).

significant themes in Adventist teaching, was not well received by their denomination, which is understandable given that Bruce had expressed himself forcefully in print regarding what he saw as Adventist errors, the chief of which were the insistence on observing the Saturday Sabbath and aspects of Adventist teaching regarding the saving work of Christ.[28] In the late 1970s Ford in particular was to become embroiled in a controversy regarding justification which resulted in his losing ministerial standing in the church. Bruce, however, continued warmly to support him, doubtless in the expectation that he would prove to be an agent for evangelical renewal in Adventist circles; thanking Ford for a brochure he had been sent, he wrote: 'It is always refreshing to see the central message of the gospel emphasized so plainly as it is here, and in every issue of GNU [*Good News Unlimited*, Ford's evangelical paper]. You have made great contributions to the cause of Christ, and you are still making them, but none of them is so valuable as this broadcasting of the essence of the good news.'[29]

Bruce's approach as a supervisor was fairly 'hands off'. John Drane, who worked on Paul and Gnosticism, described him as a great supervisor for self-starters; he would not initiate contact, but when approached would readily give up half a day for a supervision session.[30] Another former student, Paul Beasley-Murray, explained:

> I was one of FF Bruce's doctoral students 1967–1970. Bruce was of the 'old school' in that he basically left his students to their own devices. I would normally see him once a term – but the supervision largely consisted of engaging in evangelical gossip rather than of discussing the developing thesis. In the course of such a supervision I remember his saying: 'Theology is like millinery. It has its fashions!'[31]

Where assessment of written material was necessary, Bruce would offer corrections and challenges humbly and kindly, often beginning with points of detail. One student, J. Julius Scott Jr, who had been attracted by Bruce's competence in both New Testament and early

---

[28] *W* 87 (1957): p. 106: Q. 2727.
[29] Bruce to Desmond and Gill Ford, 18 December 1984. Doubtless with the Ellison affair in his mind, he had written to the Fords on 8 August 1980: 'I have always felt a special sympathy for colleagues in other schools whose tenure may be at risk if they speak their minds freely.'
[30] John Drane, telephone conversation, 20 October 2009.
[31] Paul Beasley-Murray to the author, 2 February 2008.

church history, explained at their first meeting that he wished to work on a topic in the overlap between these disciplines. This was evidently welcome news to Bruce, who is recalled as having claimed that he had enough approaches from students wanting to write on Paul's view of sin. He set Scott to read his colleague S.G.F. Brandon's controversial book, *The Fall of Jerusalem and the Christian Church*, and suggested that he discuss the work with its author, whose office adjoined Bruce's. When they met again, Scott offered about thirty questions which had come to his mind while reading; Bruce then suggested that an attempt to answer these questions would form an excellent research project.[32]

Bruce was equally economical when it came to the process of final examination. One student recalls having expressed worries that he would be required to resubmit his doctoral thesis; Bruce reassured him that if he had not considered that the student was ready to submit, he would have said so.[33] Another, worried about whether she had passed a rather challenging oral examination, was relieved to receive a laconic postcard on which was written 'O.K. FFB.'[34]

As well as his supervisory responsibilities, he served as internal examiner for several doctoral theses each year, mostly by students whom he had supervised. He served in that capacity for theses presented at Aberdeen,[35] and at other places too; students regarded it as a privilege to have him.

◆   ◆   ◆

At a social level, most of his postgraduates were invited to his house at some point, but rarely did any deep friendship develop, especially once he had a large number of students to supervise, although there is some anecdotal evidence that those from a Brethren background had a greater degree of social contact with him. Yet the most striking thing to have emerged during research for this book was the esteem in which Bruce is still held by many who had studied under him. One reason for this must be his interest in young people. Whereas many

---

[32] J. Julius Scott Jr, telephone conversation, 11 June 2009; Scott to the author, 3 August 2010.

[33] Kent Brower, interview, 30 May 2008.

[34] Margaret Curtis to the author, 2 December 2009.

[35] Howard Marshall, tribute prepared for memorial service, Brinnington Evangelical Church, 27 October 1990.

academics and others might wish to compare current students and young people unfavourably with those of earlier generations, Bruce took the opposite view. Asked on one occasion whether young Christians encouraged him or made him despair, he expressed an optimism grounded in his belief that 'they seem to be so much better in many ways than my contemporaries and I were at the same age'.[36] When the *Living Bible*, a paraphrase intended for young people, was first published in 1971, he provided this advertising blurb for it: 'The strength of the *Living Bible* lies particularly in its ability to communicate to young people. They are a class for which I have a special concern, and I am glad it has met their needs so effectively.'[37] This was a continuation of the outlook which had made him 'part of the furniture' at the young people's holiday conferences where, in his cardigan and slippers, he had been a valued contributor to informal sessions and 'Brains Trusts'.[38] Drily informing his readers that 'gospel pop groups' were not his musical idiom, he was nevertheless honoured to be invited to become a prayer partner for one group.[39] More generally, Brethren seeking good teachers to speak to their young people's groups found him very ready to oblige. As he would later explain, 'I have always had a special sympathy for young people brought up in the Brethren or similar evangelical traditions who were finding their horizons widened – after all, I was once in that position myself – and I have tried to show them how to get rid of the bath-water without losing the baby.'[40]

This interest in young people made him a useful school governor. From 1956 until the early 1970s he served as a governor of an evangelical boarding school, Clarendon, then based at Abergele in North Wales, on one occasion taking a school group round a Dead Sea Scrolls exhibition in Manchester.[41] Other schools which he served included Scarisbrick Hall, Ormskirk, founded by a fellow member of the Brethren, Charles Oxley; and Cavendish Girls' Grammar School,

---

[36] *H* 48 (1969): p. 107: Q. 1645.
[37] Harris, 'Bruce', p. 221.
[38] Anne Russell, undated memorandum; Bruce would happily chat to, and play with, children present.
[39] *H* 48 (1969): p. 191: Q. 1672.
[40] Bruce to Jean Angell, 7 May 1987.
[41] Caroline Smith to the author, 2 June 2008; Roland Symons to the author, 10 June 2008. The exhibition was mounted in March 1966, during which Bruce delivered a lecture on 'The Dead Sea Scrolls and Early Christianity': *BJRL* 49 (1966-7): pp. 69–90.

Buxton. He was also a governor of what was then known as Chester College of Education.[42]

In the academic world, this neat man, dressed in a suit and sporting a conventional haircut[43] was not the most obvious figure for students to warm to, especially in the unsettled atmosphere of the late 1960s and 1970s, but they appear to have sensed his commitment to them. He and Betty were recalled as having often been present at student occasions. Although he did not often speak at its meetings, he maintained an interest in the activities of the Christian Union at Manchester (as he did for its counterpart at Sheffield), and in his contributions to the Cambridge Prayer Fellowship newsletters often mentioned their missions as matters for prayer. Oliver Barclay recalls Bruce's readiness to support and to speak to Christian Union groups at a time when this was not a popular thing for academics to do.[44] It is not surprising, then, that he should have been asked to participate in the inductions or weddings of former students. One, whose marriage was conducted by Bruce in a Glasgow Brethren hall, recollects that the officiant kissed the bride before the groom did.[45] Yet he was by no means lax in his approach to matters of lifestyle and ethics along the lines of the 'New Morality' of the 1960s; indeed, he considered it a time for tightening ethical standards, not relaxing them.[46] Such conservatism was not defensive at all; during his first year at Manchester he preached a sermon at a student evensong which challenged Christian students to tackle the implications of contemporary issues for Christian faith.[47]

Not only was he interested in young people, but as a university teacher he regarded himself as accountable – firstly to the university, secondly to his students as 'the most vulnerable section of the university community', and only after that to his colleagues. Ultimately, of course, he regarded himself as accountable to God.[48] Here was no

---

[42] G.C.D. Howley, 'Frederick Fyvie Bruce: An Appreciation', in *Apostolic History and the Gospel: Biblical and Historical Essays Presented to F.F. Bruce on His 60th Birthday* (ed. W. Ward Gasque and Ralph P. Martin; Paternoster, 1970), pp. 15–19, at p. 15.

[43] One interviewee stated that while in Vancouver Bruce had his hair cut each week, presumably a reflection of his habits at home: Ward Gasque, 4 April 2009.

[44] Oliver R. Barclay to the author, 20 August 2009.

[45] David Payne, interview, 2 May 2009.

[46] *H* 49 (1970): p. 10: Q. 1677.

[47] Preston, memorial tribute.

[48] F. F. Bruce, 'Accountability in University Life', *Spectrum* 12/1 (September 1979): pp. 10–11.

self-serving scholar looking simply to further his own career; and it was, paradoxically, because he rejected that way that he was to achieve a far greater degree of influence.

Another reason for the esteem in which he was held was undoubtedly his helpfulness. Peter Oakes has remarked on his willingness to give large amounts of time to answering questions, whether by correspondence or through the pages of *The Harvester*, as the most striking practical expression of Bruce's Christianity.[49] People who had not even known him would write with their queries, and he would respond promptly and in detail, often offering valuable suggestions for further reading. One Scottish teenager received detailed suggestions of helpful commentaries and doctrinal works, as well as careful answers to queries about interpretation of particular Bible passages, in a correspondence stretching over several years during the early 1970s.[50] Bruce wrote forewords for a wide range of books, Brethren and non-Brethren, academic and popular, even for books with whose argument he disagreed. Many former students received such a favour from him, doubtless hoping that such endorsement would boost the work's sales. For their part, publishers often consulted Bruce about manuscripts submitted to them, and were glad to listen when he wrote to recommend that they publish works by younger scholars; one editor, commenting that such writers 'would play the Bruce card', also recalled his firm's confidence that Bruce's students would be their kind of author.[51]

Within the university, Bruce seems to have been highly respected for his fairness and integrity, able to relate well to his colleagues and on occasion to act as a bridge builder. He was able to distinguish between academic disagreement and personal antagonism in a way that scholars have not always done. With some, notably the Methodists Benjamin Drewery and Gordon Rupp, he felt a sense of evangelical kinship; with others, a good relationship developed in spite of their controversial opinions.[52] Of S.G.F. Brandon (1907–71), the Professor of Comparative Religion, he said that their relationship was marked by mutual respect in spite of their holding opposing views on

---

[49] Oakes, 'Bruce', p. 104.
[50] Bruce to Kenneth Roxburgh, between 1970 and 1974.
[51] Jon Pott, interview, 31 March 2009.
[52] On Bruce's colleagues at Manchester, see *IR*, ch. 26. Sadly, lack of space, and the desire to avoid repeating what he has written there, preclude any discussion of them in this book.

certain topics, and he offered a heartfelt tribute at Brandon's memori-
al service, yet such respect did not hinder Bruce from opposing in his
New Testament History Brandon's controversial thesis that Jesus was a
Zealot revolutionary, or from contributing to a work which was
designed as a refutation of it, *Jesus and the Politics of His Day*.[53]
   Another controversial figure until his departure in 1970 was John
M. Allegro, who from the early 1950s had been one of the foremost
scholars active in translating and publishing the Dead Sea Scrolls.
Allegro's assessment of the debt of Jesus' teaching to Essene thought,
not to mention his later linking of early Christian insights with a cul-
tus which included drug taking, secured for him equal measures of
media attention and academic opprobrium. The storm had burst after
three BBC broadcasts in January 1956, in which he claimed that the
New Testament portrayal of Jesus was modelled on the Teacher of
Righteousness at Qumran. Five scholars wrote to *The Times* to disso-
ciate themselves from his views, and Rowley publicly criticized
Allegro's work.[54] During the early 1960s Bruce solved a disagreement
in the Department of Near Eastern Studies by inviting Allegro to
move to that of Biblical Criticism and Exegesis and teach courses on
the Old Testament and the intertestamental literature.[55] Some in the
university refused to work with him, but Bruce was willing to do so,
although he did not give in to Allegro's more eccentric demands. A
student who heard Bruce speak at the Oxford Union during the late
1960s recalls Bruce's courtesy towards Allegro:

> It was about the time when John Allegro . . . was creating a stir with his
> theory about Jesus and the 'Magic Mushroom'. A very earnest student
> stood up and, his voice dripping with sarcasm, asked Bruce what he
> thought of 'this character John Allegro' – with 'character' heavily
> accented. There was a pause while Bruce gathered his thoughts for a
> reply, and then, in very measured and quiet tones, he said, 'I am very

---

[53] F.F. Bruce, 'History and the Gospel', *FT* 93 (1963–4): pp. 121–45, at p. 139 n. 3, where
he stated that he had learned more from Brandon than from many with whom he
was in much closer agreement; Oakes, 'Bruce', p. 123; Stephen Neill and Tom
Wright, *The Interpretation of the New Testament 1861–1986* (Oxford: OUP, 2nd edn,
1988), p. 380 n. Bruce's articles were 'The Date and Character of Mark' and 'Render
to Caesar', in *Jesus and the Politics of His Day* (ed. Ernst Bammel and C.F.D. Moule;
Cambridge: CUP, 1984), pp. 69–89, 249–63.

[54] Anon., 'Religion: Allegro under Fire', *Time*, 2 April 1956 http://www.time.com/
time/magazine/article/0,9171,862089-2,00.html (accessed 9 October 2009).

[55] Oakes, 'Bruce', p. 123.

interested that you should want to ask me a question about my friend and colleague John Allegro' – with all the emphasis on the words 'friend' and 'colleague'.[56]

Again, his support for Allegro did not prevent him from assisting Christian leaders who sought to counter the man's more outrageous claims, nor from rejecting Allegro's theories as 'the most incredible fantasy from beginning to end' which would do great harm to their author's scholarly reputation.[57]

Bruce's writing output owed much to his secretaries, notably Margaret Hogg, who from 1963 until he retired typed manuscripts, read the proofs and compiled indexes with enviable accuracy; often thanking her and her sister June (who had preceded her) in his books, his relationship with them remained formal, however, as it did with most faculty and staff. Margaret is recalled as having been able to decipher notes Bruce wrote on the backs of envelopes during train journeys – no mean feat.[58]

In 1970, Bruce received the honour of a *Festschrift* edited by a former student, Ward Gasque, and a former colleague, Ralph Martin: *Apostolic History and the Gospel*.[59] On 7 October a dinner was held in the Midland Hotel in Manchester to mark the occasion. After Bruce had spoken, C.F.D. Moule, a renowned Cambridge New Testament scholar, in proposing the toast told how on a bus trip to Caesarea Philippi Bruce had been asked at short notice to talk about the site while they were there, and had proceeded to offer a first-rate unscripted lecture. The book was a watershed for Paternoster, rescuing the firm from financial problems and strengthening its academic credibility.[60] In addition, a special issue of the *Journal of the Christian Brethren Research Fellowship* appeared the following year. The

---

[56] Colin Sedgwick to the author, 22 May 2008, 2 August 2010.

[57] Dubuque, IA, Emmaus Bible College Library, Bruce to Mr Flanagan, 27 May 1971.

[58] Sheila Lukabyo to the author, undated.

[59] W. Ward Gasque and Ralph P. Martin, eds, *Apostolic History and the Gospel: Biblical and Historical Essays Presented to F.F. Bruce on His 60th Birthday* (Exeter: Paternoster, 1970). The project had first been broached in 1966; there was some initial debate as to whether it should appear under the imprint of a recognized academic publisher in order to secure contributions from continental scholars of standing, but eventually Eerdmans and Paternoster were settled on: Grand Rapids, Eerdmans, correspondence file relating to *Apostolic History and the Gospel*.

[60] B. Howard Mudditt, 'The Paternoster Story (4): "The End of the Beginning" ', *H* 64/9 (September 1985): pp. 5–7, at p. 6; Jeremy Mudditt, telephone conversation, 4 March 2009.

brainchild of his former student and close friend Ward Gasque, it was composed of tributes from various figures in the Brethren and evangelical worlds to Bruce as a person and to various aspects of his influence. A bound and inscribed edition was presented to him.[61]

Academic recognition came in other forms too. In 1965 he served as president of the SOTS.[62] He was elected a Fellow of the British Academy in 1973, an award made to those who have achieved distinction in the humanities or social sciences; since he did not like London, however, he did not attend its meetings.[63] Finally, in 1975 he became president of the SNTS, thus becoming only the second person to have presided over both societies. His presidential address, delivered at Aberdeen, was on the subject of 'The New Testament and Classical Studies'. In it he contended that classicists were uniquely placed to study the New Testament because it was part of the cultural world which was their field and because the skills required to do so were those which they used in studying ancient writings. As a case study he took the writings of Luke, and especially the book of Acts, arguing controversially for the essential historicity of the speeches recorded in it. His conclusion was that 'the Graeco-Roman contribution to early Christianity should not be depreciated as though it were an alien accretion upon the pure gospel'.[64] It was the only occasion on which Gasque had seen him nervous. Bruce was probably well aware that his emphasis on the importance of the classical background and his attempt to achieve objectivity in his handling of the text would run counter to the more conceptually orientated and philosophically committed approach of many continental scholars, and that his lay status would not be approved of by some clerical scholars present, but his lecture was the best Gasque had ever heard him give, 'bearing witness to his convictions as a scholar and as a disciple'. Ernst Käsemann, a distinguished if sometimes combative German scholar, was seen to grow redder as the lecture progressed, but it may be a mark of his respect for Bruce that he does not appear to have entered into debate with him at the conference. On a more relaxed note,

---

[61] Manchester, CBA, Box 4, Bruce to Roy Coad, 19 September 1972.

[62] His presidential address was published as 'Josephus and Daniel', *Annual of the Swedish Theological Institute* 4 (1965): pp. 148–62.

[63] J.P. Kane, 'Obituary: F.F. Bruce', *PEQ* 123 (1991): pp. 2–3.

[64] F.F. Bruce, 'The New Testament and Classical Studies: Society for New Testament Studies Presidential Address, 1975', *New Testament Studies* 22 (1975–6): pp. 229–42 (quotation at p. 241), repr. in F.F. Bruce, *A Mind for What Matters* (Grand Rapids, MI: Eerdmans, 1990), pp. 3–16.

Howard Marshall arranged an informal gathering of friends and former students, at which Bruce's speech (sadly not recorded) referred
systematically to each one present.[65]

◆   ◆   ◆

As a recognized scholar, Bruce found himself being invited to give
series of lectures at a number of North American institutions repre-
senting various denominations.[66] In 1961 he crossed the Atlantic by
sea to teach on Acts and the Dead Sea Scrolls at a summer school of
theology at Winona Lake, Indiana, conducted under the auspices of
Fuller Theological Seminary (itself based in Pasadena, California).
While there, he and Betty celebrated their silver wedding anniversary
in modest fashion, taking a walk round the lake and going out to dinner.

Given his international status and wide network of contacts, it is
surprising that few attempts were made to lure him away from
Manchester; doubtless his commitment to that university and his con-
tentment in his post were understood. Perhaps the most serious possibility was that of joining the faculty of Regent College, Vancouver, a
venture which was the brainchild of several local Brethren in an area
whose assemblies were known for being progressive in outlook. Late
in 1965 the project was made public, and in time James Houston was
appointed the first principal. Houston was an Oxford geography lecturer who was already developing an influential ministry among
younger Open Brethren which came to focus on Christian spirituality; he had worked closely with Bruce and others in the Young Men's
Bible Teaching Conferences. It was Houston who would influence the
planners away from a Bible college model, intended to train Brethren
workers, towards the vision of a college based on a university cam-
pus, offering graduate level instruction, and equipping students to

---

[65]Laurel and Ward Gasque, 'An Appreciation', pp. 3–5; Laurel and Ward Gasque,
interview, 6 April 2009. That Käsemann was capable of reacting audibly to papers
of which he disapproved is confirmed by John K. Riches, *A Century of New
Testament Study* (Cambridge: Lutterworth, 1993), pp. 202–3. Riches recalls him contending that a presentation at the 1978 SNTS conference lacked a sense of 'address'
because it focused on what texts said about the first-century Mediterranean world
instead of a word from God which demanded a response. He would probably have
felt the same about what Bruce said.
[66]See *IR*, pp. 239–44.

engage as Christians with the world of work and culture.[67] Houston recalls asking Bruce to join the faculty, but Bruce indicated that he had no wish to leave Manchester.[68]

His support for the new institution was nonetheless warm. He joined the college's council of reference, helping to give it academic credibility in the face of some hostility from local theological colleges, and lectured at its summer schools in 1970, 1973 and 1976. With Betty, he visited Vancouver on the way home from New Zealand in August 1966 for what he later described as 'two days of energetic fellowship with brethren', especially those who were involved with the new venture.[69] The main purpose of his meeting with the college's prime movers was to give them some input; in a meeting over dinner at a restaurant, he spoke about theological education and answered their questions. He also spoke at two evening meetings in Granville Chapel, a Brethren assembly, audiences at which totalled 1,300. His topics were 'Faith and Life' from 1 John, and 'Jesus Christ the Same Today' (from Hebrews).[70] Over two hundred heard him speak on the Dead Sea Scrolls and the reliability of the New Testament documents, and at least eighty women attended a coffee hour with Betty.[71]

As was the case on occasion elsewhere, his lecturing at Regent appears to have amounted to reading from one of his books, and on one occasion when he paused to take a glass of water, a student jumped up and began to carry on from the point where he had left off, momentarily disconcerting him. Gasque later tried to assign him topics on which he did not appear to have written, and took the precaution of advising

---

[67] John G. Stackhouse Jr, *Canadian Evangelicalism in the Twentieth Century: An Introduction to Its Character* (Toronto: University of Toronto Press, 1993), pp. 155–7.

[68] Ibid. p. 280 n. 9; James Houston, interview, 6 April 2009. It has been suggested that Bruce had been approached, either formally or informally, about the principalship: Kenneth V. Botton, 'Regent College: An Experiment in Theological Education', PhD thesis, Trinity International University, 2004, pp. 9–10, 48–9, 171–80; cf. Alister McGrath, *To Know and Serve God: A Biography of James I. Packer* (London: Hodder & Stoughton, 1997), pp. 227–8. However, the varying recollections of the period which I have encountered cannot be reconciled and I have found no firm evidence that he was so approached.

[69] Madrid, Comisión de Biblioteca y Archivos, Centro Evangélico de Formación Bíblica en Madrid, Bruce to Ernest H. Trenchard, 5 January 1967.

[70] For the first, he was probably reusing a talk he had given in New Zealand; the second was published in a local Brethren magazine: 'Jesus Christ the Same', *Calling* 9/2 (Summer 1967): pp. 18–23.

[71] E. Marshall Sheppard and Wemyss Reid (Vancouver), letter in *W* 96 (1966): p. 388.

him that half the lecture time was to be given to answering questions; students who after the first half of the session were wanting their money back were thus completely won over by the end.[72]

A number of other North American institutions invited Bruce to give special lectures. In February and March of 1968 he delivered the Payton Lectures at Fuller, which was a flagship of the 'New Evangelicalism' in the USA and as such noted (and criticized) for its progressive stance on a range of issues to do with biblical interpretation,[73] and the Norton Lectures on Religion and Science in the Southern Baptist seminary at Louisville, Kentucky. The former were published in 1968 as *This Is That: The New Testament Development of Some Old Testament Themes*, and the latter in 1970 as *Tradition Old and New*.[74] 1970 saw him making two more trips to the USA. In April he gave the Smyth Lectures at Columbia Theological Seminary, Decatur, Georgia, on 'Pillars for a Life of Jesus Today' and the Earle Lectures on Biblical Literature at the Nazarene Theological Seminary, Kansas City, on 'Jesus and His Contemporaries'. Neither set was published, although at one point he hoped to incorporate them into a larger work. A third set of lectures followed in November, the Nils W. Lund Memorial Lectures at North Park Seminary, Chicago, on 'The Beginnings of Bible Interpretation'. Again, these remained unpublished.

Ontario was Bruce's destination during the Easter vacation of 1973. As on other trips, he combined academic and church engagements. On the Sunday, he spoke at the morning Breaking of Bread at Bethany Chapel, Hamilton; a talk that evening on 'The Reliability of the New Testament Documents' and a question session drew a large audience including Anglicans and 'tight' Brethren. Recordings are extant of both evening sessions. The question session lasted well over an hour and ranged over a wide field. Bruce was clearly at home in such a context and his assured handling of the evidence would have done a great deal to boost his hearers' confidence in the reliability of the Scriptures. He prefaced it by explaining that his more dogmatic statements were to be interpreted as him saying 'it appears to me', and warning that if he should inadvertently contradict what individuals

---

[72] Ward Gasque, 'Frederick Fyvie Bruce (1910–1990): An Unhyphenated Evangelical', *Crux* 43/4 (Winter 2007): pp. 21–30; group discussion, Vancouver, 5 April 2009.

[73] See George M. Marsden, *Reforming Fundamentalism: Fuller Seminary and the New Evangelicalism* (Grand Rapids, MI: Eerdmans, 1987).

[74] For discussion of them, see ch. 8.

would have been told by their elders, nothing he said was to be used as a stick to beat them with; whilst this demonstrated his sense of Christian diplomacy, he could not have been unaware that his exegetical comments would in time generate an impetus for change. At McMaster University, a seminar organized by the Department of Religious Studies attracted a full house, but his main business was to give the Thomas F. Staley Lectures at what was then Ontario Bible College (later Ontario Theological Seminary). These were published as *Paul and Jesus*, and we shall return to them later. The end of December saw him at Wheaton, Illinois, lecturing at a conference of the Evangelical Theological Society on 'New Light on the Origins of the New Testament Canon'.[75]

As a guest lecturer, Bruce often drew large audiences, although they were probably somewhat disappointed by his dull style (this helps to explain why he was not often invited to conferences at which a more lively form of presentation was deemed necessary). An anecdote from Charles Price relating to his visit to Australia in 1977 indicates that he may well have been aware of this:

> I remember him once saying that he was not a good public speaker, and preferred writing. He said he was to speak at Sydney Anglican Cathedral in Australia on one occasion, and as he was driven to the cathedral they found people lined up round the building waiting for entrance (such was his reputation). He said that he commented to his driver, 'My, these people will be disappointed', and then he paused, and added to me, 'And they were!'[76]

He was not inaudible, for he spoke clearly and coherently, with hardly a word out of place, but he did not often vary his tone or pace, or appear to depart from his manuscript. If transcribed, his lectures would lack much of the oral feel which often has to be removed when preparing such material for publication. Although 'dull' represents the general opinion of his lecturing, it may be less than fair to him; the recordings to which I have listened are easy to follow because of the clarity of content, and enlivened by unscripted asides which, to judge by the audible audience response, helped to keep his hearers with him. For example, a

---

[75] F.F. Bruce, 'New Light on the Origins of the New Testament Canon', in *New Dimensions in New Testament Study* (ed. Richard N. Longenecker and Merrill C. Tenney; Grand Rapids, MI: Zondervan, 1974), pp. 3–18.

[76] Charles Price to the author, 27 January 2008.

lecture he gave at Regent College on the book of Revelation begins with an anecdote about a new Bible reader encountering the book and describing it as science fiction.[77] Moreover, plenty of informants have testified that they found themselves captivated by the content and clarity of his lectures. I suspect that, as Gasque guessed, his lecturing was much more successful when he was not simply reading a published text.

What compensated, however, was when he took questions, often after a lecture. After each question, there would be a pause, and he might take off his glasses and appear to be mentally scrolling the text before offering his response. If quoting the Bible, he would refer to original Hebrew or Greek if talking to an academic audience, to a contemporary translation when dealing with students, and when speaking to church people he would use a translation familiar to most of them, such as the King James Version or later the Revised Standard or New International Version.[78] Questions would flow thick and fast, and his answers were remarkable for their combination of brevity, clarity and coherence. Audiences might be invited to submit questions in advance, as on one occasion in Seattle when he took a Sunday night question session in a church. Into the pulpit he took about fifty of the index cards on which questions had been written, and he proceeded to work his way through them. This was one of several occasions there and in Vancouver where the Gasques arranged for him to do this in place of a normal Sunday evening sermon, and the reception was always enthusiastic.[79]

Such sessions would have been attractive to audiences not just because of his academic competence, but also because of the way in which evangelicals looked for individuals who could function as oracles, offering authoritative and credible answers to the intellectual and exegetical difficulties which they encountered. In many ways, these question sessions are reminiscent of his 'Answers to Questions' page in *The Harvester*, in which he was constantly being pressed for oracular rulings on difficult points. That said, he was not willing to be drawn on certain divisive issues affecting the Brethren or evangelicals

---

[77] F.F. Bruce, 'The Book of Revelation', Regent College, Vancouver (ref. 607), 1976.
[78] Laurel and Ward Gasque, interview, 6 April 2009; W. Ward Gasque, 'Bruce, F(rederick) F(yvie) (1910-1991)', in *Dictionary of Major Biblical Interpreters* (ed. Donald K. McKim; Downers Grove, IL: IVP, 2007), pp. 237–42, at p. 239.
[79] Laurel and Ward Gasque, 'An Appreciation', p. 3; Group discussion, Vancouver, 5 April 2009.

generally; if he sensed that he was being tested to see whether his views were 'sound', he could refuse to answer the question, perhaps in the words of Proverbs 1:17: 'in vain the net is spread in the sight of any bird'.[80]

As a visiting lecturer, he was often the recipient of hospitality in the homes of local Christians. Socially speaking, he was not an extrovert, although people found it quite easy to engage him in conversation where they shared common acquaintances or interests, especially in Brethren circles. Many wives were apprehensive about hosting him, especially given his reputation for a lack of small talk. Others were less daunted, however: one couple who had been defeated in the attempt to get a conversation going were amazed to come downstairs the following morning to find their young daughter chatting happily to him.[81] There are stories of him playing games with his hosts' children, making them daisy chains, and even giving them piggybacks. One former student invited Bruce to give a guest lecture at his university and to spend the day with him and his family. His eldest son was about 4 at the time, which stimulated Bruce to recall taking his own family to the zoo when they were young and telling them what each animal was called; 'I felt like Adam in the Garden of Eden, naming all the animals.'[82] One wife asked Betty what he liked for lunch, and was informed that a palatable wine would assist his conversational skills.[83] He was also delighted to be introduced to cheese fondue, which became a popular dinner-party dish in the 1970s (partly because it requires a high degree of sociability to enjoy dipping pieces of bread into a pot of melted cheese in the middle of the table) and was usually accompanied by wine.[84] At academic conferences he would often sit quietly, speaking only when spoken to, but once an approach had been made he often proved a good listener and conversationalist.

◆   ◆   ◆

---

[80] He had cited this verse when first taking over the page: *H* 31/7 (July 1952): p. 80.

[81] Jim and Ruth Nyquist, interview, 2 April 2009.

[82] John Drane, telephone conversation, 20 October 2009.

[83] Carl Armerding, interview, 3 April 2009. To set this in context, it should be noted that Fred and Betty did not drink alcohol at home until their children were grown up, and that by the early 1970s wine was perfectly acceptable in most British evangelical circles as an accompaniment to a meal.

[84] Ward Gasque, in conversation, 3 April 2009.

In March 1960 the family moved to Buxton, a modestly sized town about twenty-five miles south-east of Manchester, high up in the Peak District. It had been a well-known watering place in the nineteenth century, and evidences of its status still remain, as does an air of quiet gentility. Sheila had a friend who lived there, whose parents convinced the Bruces that this was the place for them.[85] So it proved to be; they would not move house again. The Crossways was a large detached house built in the 1920s and surrounded by gardens, on a road junction about fifteen minutes' walk from the station; Fred considered that he got his daily exercise by walking to and from the station at each end of his journey.

His workload demanded rigorous organization and application; in his pocketbook he used to carry a list of current projects with their deadlines, on which each was ticked off as it was completed.[86] One of the rare occasions when family members saw him ruffled was when, after moving to Buxton, he mislaid his five-year diary. Asked at a holiday conference how he could read and listen at once, he explained 'I don't read with my ears.'[87] The same research could be put to productive use in books and articles as well as lectures, which helps to explain why anyone who reads much of Bruce's output is likely sooner or later to come away feeling that they have read a certain paragraph before; it is not so much that he has consciously reused it wholesale as that his thoughts on the matter have not fundamentally changed and that they were based on the same evidence. Much of his work was done on the train, and he never learned to drive because he saw it as a waste of time which could be used to work.[88] Several people recollect that if he was on the same train as they were, he would greet them and talk briefly before getting out his work and occupying himself with it for the rest of the journey. Even the daily journey between Buxton and Manchester (about an hour each way) could be put to good use: he proofread the *Theological Dictionary of the New Testament*, a ten-volume English translation of a German reference work, on that line between 1963 and 1973, and he read each volume in proof not once but twice.[89] Such an achievement on

---

[85] *IR*, pp. 219–21.

[86] *IR*, p. 300.

[87] Alastair Rossetter, interview, 23 August 2008; Rossetter to the author, 1 September 2010.

[88] Sheila Lukabyo, interview, 2 September 2009.

[89] G.W. Bromiley, translator's foreword to *Theological Dictionary of the New Testament* (10 vols; ed. Gerhard Kittel; Grand Rapids, MI: Eerdmans, 1964–74), 1:ix; W 96

a crowded commuter train was little short of heroic. One winter night, though, the train was held up by a snowstorm, and he did not arrive home until 3.35 a.m. Even this did not worry him; asked what he had done to pass the time, he explained calmly that he had been marking.[90] At home, the centre of operations was the study, which extended from front to back of the house and was lined with books from floor to ceiling, as well as free-standing bookcases. There was also a book-lined room next to the kitchen, and to Betty's dismay further books overflowed to an upstairs corridor and a top cupboard in the kitchen. They included a large number of books on local history, especially on his native Morayshire, as well as many acquired during their travels. Offprints of articles sent to him by their authors were kept in a dresser in the pantry.

Each evening Fred and Betty did the newspaper crossword together. For relaxation, he also read detective novels and often took them on holiday, notably those of Agatha Christie (he read the entire canon), Dorothy Sayers and Carter Dickson (John Dickson Carr).[91] Occasionally, he would take Betty away for a weekend at a hotel nearby, from where they would explore the Peak District on foot. Going out for meals was, as with most people then, something one only did on birthdays and wedding anniversaries. Other relaxations were few; probably his family and friends provided sufficient relaxation, for he enjoyed his work immensely. When they entertained, Betty as a 'professional housewife' liked to have a full tea-table ready. Lunch was simpler, often comprising soup made with leftover vegetables followed by yoghurt.[92]

(1966): p. 389; Harris, 'Bruce', p. 220. On Kittel, see Neill and Wright, *Interpretation of the New Testament*, pp. 371–2. Bruce also helped with reading and advising on the *New International Dictionary of New Testament Theology*: *W* 106 (1976): p. 108. He agreed to proofread the multi-volume Old Testament counterpart to Kittel, *Theological Dictionary of the Old Testament* (edited by G. Johannes Botterweck and Helmer Ringgren: Eerdmans), correspondence file, F.F. Bruce 1967–77, Bruce to W.B. Eerdmans Jr, 20 December 1972.

[90] Sheila Lukabyo, interview, 2 September 2009. He is even recalled as correcting proofs on flights to and from Israel: Robert H. Kraft to the author, 14 August 2009.

[91] Andrew Walls remembers Fred on overnight train journeys during the austere early 1950s, wrapped up in overcoat and woolly hat and reading detective stories: interview, 18 February 2010.

[92] *IR*, pp. 219–20; Ward and Laurel Gasque, 'F.F. Bruce – Layman and Scholar', *H* 68/8 (August 1989): pp. 10–11, at p. 11; Alan and Margaret Millard, interview, 29 May 2008; Group discussion, Vancouver, 5 April 2009; Sheila Lukabyo, interview, 2 September 2009.

Both children emigrated in 1963.[93] Iain, who had already married Pam, became a lecturer in classics at the Memorial University of Newfoundland, and would spend his entire academic career there, emulating his father as both classicist and effective administrator.[94] In 1965 Sheila married a Ugandan whom she met while lecturing at a teacher training college there, James Lukabyo. Fred considered the Christmas he and Betty spent with them that year as 'one of the most enjoyable holidays ever'.[95] He considered their marriage an example of Christian freedom, and did not share the popular suspicion of interracial marriages.[96] The children being mixed-race, Fred liked to keep photographs of them prominently visible on top of the piano, and would watch to see how visitors reacted. He and Betty visited both growing families as often as they could, usually in alternate years and until late in his life combining this with lecturing and meeting academic colleagues.

Fred described becoming a grandfather as 'the greatest honour that has come my way', and he was certainly not a distant or uninvolved grandparent. Between 1969 and 1971 Sheila and her family lived with her parents while James studied for a master's degree in Plant Pathology at the University of California. Fred paid for the children to attend a small private school in Buxton, as he was concerned at how they might be treated in a larger establishment. For many grandparents it would have been a shock to the system to have a house full of children, but the Bruces evidently relished the experience. Fred's experience of helping to bring up his younger siblings may have been a factor in his lifelong ability to relate to children. At any rate, he delighted to spend time with his grandchildren (though they were often put to bed before he arrived home from work): he read them Dr

---

[93] *IR*, pp. 237–9.

[94] Iain was conscious of the debt he owed to his parents, dedicating to them the publication of which his doctoral thesis was the basis: I.A.F. Bruce, *An Historical Commentary on the Hellenica Oxyrhynchia* (Cambridge: CUP, 1967). It is worth noting that there appear to be similarities between his and his father's approaches to commentary writing.

[95] Madrid, Comisión de Biblioteca y Archivos, Centro Evangélico de Formación Bíblica en Madrid, Bruce to Ernest H. Trenchard, 30 January 1966.

[96] In 1961 he had described the Bible as 'totally hostile' to apartheid, then in the news following events in South Africa during the previous year; his strong condemnation extended to the 'colour bar' which was widely if not always consciously practised in Britain: *H* 40 (1961): p. 11: Q. 913. No body practising it could claim to be a New Testament church: *H* 42 (1963): p. 91: Q. 1109.

Seuss books and played board games with them, and they knew that they were welcome to enter the study, even when he was working. When the family left, one of the grandchildren commented: 'Poor Granny hasn't got any children left, only one big boy called Papa.' It was during this period that a television finally arrived at The Crossways. Fred appears to have taken to children's cartoons, *Top Cat* being a favourite. Thereafter, Betty enjoyed watching cricket (Fred did not share her interest), and she is even recalled as staying up to watch the Eurovision Song Contest in 1974. Another innovation greeted with enthusiasm was the 'teasmade', which appeared in the late 1960s.[97]

Whilst Fred was very much a home body, he thoroughly enjoyed travelling, and he was known in the family for always packing his own suitcase.[98] In 1974 the Lukabyo family were forced to leave Uganda and made their home in Australia, following which Fred and Betty made a number of visits there. Betty also accompanied him to conferences of the SOTS and SNTS, as did other spouses. They visited the Holy Land in 1969 and 1979, and Rome in 1968 and 1973.[99] But Mediterranean destinations seem to have been particularly attractive, and they would take a cruise together as late as 1989.

◆   ◆   ◆

The assembly at Buxton, where the Bruces lived, had closed in 1957 due to declining membership, and so they made their home at one in Crescent Road, Stockport, where Fred already knew people from the young people's Easter house parties.[100] This was accessible by train both from Buxton on Sundays and from Manchester during the week. The Bruces would travel to Stockport each Sunday morning, being collected from the station or getting a taxi, and arriving in time for the

---

[97] Bruce to Alan Millard, 21 June 1969; CPF 1934 newsletter, June 1971; Alastair and Jane Rossetter, interview, 23 August 2008; Sheila Lukabyo to the author, undated; Alan Millard to Ward Gasque, 11 April 2009; Sheila Lukabyo and Lesley Young, interview, 2 September 2009; Lesley Young to the author, 9 August 2010.

[98] Alastair Rossetter, interview, 23 August 2008.

[99] *IR*, chs 31–2. He once claimed that it was possible to learn more from a trip to the British Museum than a tour of the Holy Land (Carl Armerding, interview, 3 April 2009), but perhaps this was hyperbolic.

[100] On the assembly, see David Brady and Fred J. Evans, *Christian Brethren in Manchester and District: A History* (London: Heritage Publications, 1997), pp. 161–2; Fred Evans, *A Christian Witness in Stockport 1910–1985* (n.pl.: n.p., [1985]).

Breaking of Bread; frequently they would have lunch with Douglas and Betty Buckley, with whom they developed a firm friendship, before returning home late in the afternoon in time to listen to *Gardeners' Question Time*.

Fred's first visit appears to have been on 21 February 1960, when he conducted a service which was broadcast on BBC Radio's North of England Home Service.[101] He was attracted to the ethos of the assembly, which was one of freedom, and just two years after his first visit he was made an elder, gaining a reputation as an efficient chairman of meetings. In the capacity of teaching elder, he gave a series of mid-week studies each winter, complete with handouts, to which members of other local assemblies were welcomed. (At that time it was rare among Brethren for teaching to be planned weeks in advance as these addresses were.) Within a few years, planned ministry had been introduced to follow the Breaking of Bread every other Sunday morning, and he played a major role in this. Members must have been amused when *Answers to Questions* appeared in 1972, dedicated 'To the members of Crescent Road Church Stockport, who ask their share of questions'.

But his church involvement was not confined to teaching. At the Breaking of Bread the singing was traditionally unaccompanied, and he would sometimes be responsible for raising the tune. He was also known for his pastoral heart, and could sometimes be seen standing at the back of the hall after a meeting, with his finger to his mouth, gently asking 'I wonder if you've thought of it this way.' Even though he stood down from the eldership in 1983, he was called back six years later to deal with a crisis. In the assembly he was long known simply as 'Prof', although he eventually persuaded people to address him by his Christian name. Some were overawed by him but not all: a trained chemist who was converted to Christ as an adult recalls Bruce's willingness to listen to his perplexities as he sought to understand the Christian faith; Bruce preached at his baptism and in time approached him about joining the eldership.

Fred became close friends with a fellow elder, Arnold Pickering (1908–84), with whom he shared in leading the Easter house parties; they both believed that freedom should mark the life of a local assembly, and held views on the public ministry of women which were

---

[101] A recording survives, and the talk was published as 'The Son of Man Came', *H* 39 (1960): pp. 54–5. It was a straight exposition of Scripture, with little explicit linkage to the twentieth century, but avoiding theological or evangelical jargon.

much more egalitarian than those of their fellow elders. In his obituary of Pickering, he testified: 'I owe him a greater spiritual debt than I owe to any other man of my age-group.'[102] In 1974 the assembly moved to a former Methodist building at Brinnington, a large council estate on the outskirts of Stockport with poor transport links; Bruce ceremonially received the keys to the building from the circuit superintendent at the last Methodist communion. Sadly, the congregation eventually disbanded in 2007, partly because it had never established a base of local members.

In 1966 about twenty members left Crescent Road to form a new congregation in the nearby town of Marple; apparently they allowed more freedom for women to take part, and this may have been a factor in the division, although they left on good terms; it has been suggested to me that Bruce played a significant role in keeping the relationship positive, with his ability to pour oil on troubled waters.

Locally, the council of churches in Buxton asked Bruce to give a series of Lent talks on two occasions, and he often spoke to local auxiliaries of the British and Foreign Bible Society, an agency in which Brethren have always had a special interest. In his view, Christian unity was best pursued not as an end in itself but as a by-product of co-operation in such activities.[103]

He was also active in the Christian community in Manchester, as when he gave a series of Lent talks in the city centre church of St Ann's on the theme 'Jesus Christ: Who is He?' In the late 1970s, the Christian World Centre opened in Deansgate, offering what was then an innovative combination of Christian bookshop and resource centre and coffee shop. Bruce would often come in for a cup of tea as it was near the John Rylands Library; he would entertain postgraduate students there for supervisions, or take a cup of tea to the homeless people who came in. Even after his retirement, he remained concerned about the city; when riots in Moss Side, a deprived area just to the

---

[102] F.F. Bruce, 'Arnold Pickering (1908–1984)', *H* 64/1 (January 1985): p. 7.

[103] For the previous paragraphs, see *IR*, pp. 221–7; Arnold Pickering, 'F.F. Bruce as a Fellow-Elder', *JCBRF*, no. 22 (November 1971), pp. 16–17; Betty Buckley, interview, 28 May 2008; Alan and Margaret Millard, interview, 29 May 2008; Barry Hale, interview, 30 May 2008; Mr and Mrs A.W. Headley to the author, 11 September 2008. Betty appears to have been of a more conservative disposition, continuing to prefer the Authorized Version (one was kept for her at church); unlike Fred, she did not take communion when they attended Sheila's family's Anglican church: Sheila Lukabyo, interview, 2 September 2009.

south-west of the main university site in Oxford Road, made the
national news in 1981, he would talk with an acquaintance who had
grown up in the area, trying to understand the factors at work, and
when the area was mentioned on the news he would telephone to see
how things were.[104] From the late 1960s he took an interest in the city's
fledgling Chinese church, as some of his postgraduates attended it
and were involved in teaching and preaching. He used his offices to
ensure that they were able to invite good-quality speakers.[105]

In the Greater Manchester area, he would occasionally speak at
Saturday evening meetings during the 1950s and 1960s.[106] Further
afield, it is noteworthy that he was not often asked to speak at assemblies in the north-east of Scotland. When he spoke at the centenary of
the annual Aberdeen Conference in 1973, he commented that the last
time he had done so was as a bachelor, and now he was a grandfather.
It is likely that his eschatological views, as well as his progressive
stance on other issues, would have made his ministry less than welcome.[107] He did, however, speak at a rather unusual event, a 'memorial conference' at Elgin on 2 April 1966. His mother had died the year
before, and it appears to have been arranged as a tribute to her and
her husband. The afternoon was for people to share recollections of
them, and the evening for comments and ministry by Fred. He also
preached at the opening of the Elgin assembly's new hall in 1983,
when he presented them with a family Bible for pulpit use. That
weekend he also preached at the university service in King's College
Chapel, and lectured the following day on the Dead Sea Scrolls.[108]

When he preached at gospel meetings, his sermons would be
expositions of some biblical passage, sometimes written out in full
and at other times in note form on the backs of old envelopes; they
were delivered in an undemonstrative fashion and not long-winded.
Even those who valued his ministry sometimes wondered whether it
would appeal to non-Christian attenders. On the other hand, a fellow
member of the assembly, Betty Buckley, conducted a male voice choir
for many years, and when they sang at a special evening service at
Brinnington she invited Fred to preach as she knew that he would

---

[104] Kevin McGarahan, interview, 1 September 2009.
[105] Alan Hewerdine, in conversation, 10 December 2009.
[106] Personal information.
[107] Sandy Stewart, interview, 22 August 2008; Alastair and Jane Rossetter, interview, 23
     August 2008.
[108] 'Elgin Prof. back in N.E.', *Aberdeen Press & Journal*, 3 June 1971.

not 'have a go' at them as was the manner of some Brethren preachers.[109]

If we consider his language as opposed to his delivery, it is clear and straightforward, and he possessed a remarkable facility for explaining complex issues in a comprehensible and non-patronizing manner. This clarity reflected his convictions about the language of Scripture. Commenting on the discovery late in the nineteenth century of large quantities of letters and documents written by ordinary people, in Greek which turned out to be strikingly similar to that of their contemporaries, the New Testament writers, he asserted: 'The "language of the Holy Ghost" turned out to be the language of the common people – which is just what we should expect. (One still finds good people, all the same, who imagine that he has a decided preference for Elizabethan or Jacobean English!)'[110] Furthermore, this clarity made his ministry accessible to all. The story is told of 'a Building site worker who joined the fellowship after his conversion and who was confronted by his work-mates with difficult questions about his new-found faith. He returned with the most excellent and well-informed answers until at last his work-mates asked him where all his answers came from. "O well," he said, "there's an old fellow at our church called Fred. He seems to know all about these things."'[111]

Not only was his ministry accessible, but all agreed that he was easy to entertain as a visiting preacher. One couple occasionally entertained the Bruces in Oldham, doubtless when he was preaching locally, and an informant wrote: 'She worked in the mills for years until her marriage, as did her husband. She said Dr Bruce was a very quiet man but enjoyed his Sunday lunches with them! There was clearly no awkwardness in terms of differences in class or education.'[112]

◆   ◆   ◆

---

[109] Betty Buckley and Peter Tait, interview, 28 May 2008; Alan Millard, interview, 29 May 2008; Alan Dixon, telephone conversation, 5 October 2009.

[110] F.F. Bruce, *The Books and the Parchments* (Old Tappan, NJ: Fleming H. Revell, 4th edn, 1984), p. 55. That said, his recorded prayers are characterized by continued use of 'Thee' and 'Thou' when addressing God.

[111] The story was told by Mr A.W. Headley, an elder at Brinnington, at the Service of Thanksgiving on 27 October 1990, but the quotation comes from Tom Noble's tribute in the *Tyndale Fellowship Newsletter* 49 (March 1991); cf. I. Howard Marshall, 'Frederick Fyvie Bruce 1910–1990', *Proceedings of the British Academy* 80 (1991): pp. 245–60, at p. 260.

[112] Eiluned Parry to the author, 4 February 2008, 18 May 2008.

Many outside the Brethren movement were by now wondering why Bruce remained in it, given its reputation for fundamentalism (a reputation which was not totally deserved, it must be said). In 1965 the *Journal of the Christian Brethren Research Fellowship* ran a special issue featuring testimonies from a number of writers as to 'Why I Have Stayed with the Brethren', following from an earlier issue which had addressed the theme of 'Why I Left the Brethren'. That they felt this worth doing is indicative of the leakage from assemblies which had already begun and which was to gather strength later on. Bruce was one of those included in the article. Having disposed first of the difficulty of answering the question (because he belonged only to the universal church and to a local congregation meeting at Crescent Road Hall, Stockport), he admitted that one reason for not moving was inertia. It had never occurred to him to leave them, and like most Christians at that time he stayed in the tradition where he was brought up. However, he felt no disadvantage from doing so; indeed, he was grateful for the early training he had received among them. And they encouraged him to recognize his membership in the universal church by welcoming all believers and not setting up any smaller circle of fellowship as the primary focus of allegiance. He looked for two things in a church, which he found among assemblies: faithfulness to the gospel, and commitment to maintaining Christian freedom. He minimized the power of their traditions, which to some appeared even more binding than creedal subscription, and defended Brethren against the charge of anti-intellectualism. Given his temperament as a 'persistent layman', the assemblies with their rejection of ordination provided an ideal environment in which to serve.[113] As he explained in a letter to *Christianity Today*, 'I am "unordained" not merely because I belong to a fellowship in which the distinction between clergy and laity is not recognized. My vocation, as I am conscious of it, is to a lay ministry, and, so far as I can judge, I should have

---

[113] F.F. Bruce, 'Why I Have Stayed with the Brethren', *JCBRF*, no. 10 (December 1965): pp. 5–6; cf. *H* 44 (1965): p. 139: Q. 1305; *IR*, ch. 35. For his 'persistent' lay status, see *H* 49 (1970): p. 90: Q. 1711: 'I rarely bestir myself to correct public statements which (as I think) misrepresent me, but I do repeatedly find it necessary to insist on my lay status.' One reason for this was that he wished to avoid being accused of saying certain things because the church had told him to: Ward and Laurel Gasque, 'F.F. Bruce – Layman and Scholar', *H* 68/8 (August 1989): pp. 10–11, at p. 10. He was free as an academic to say what he wanted, and wished to make clear that he spoke under no external constraint.

remained a layman no matter what my ecclesiastical attachment had been.'[114]

For Bruce, one of the great benefits of associating with the Brethren was the free inquiry which allowed him to approach the Scriptures without any restrictive framework of interpretation:

> It is part of our heritage that we are encouraged to study the Bible for ourselves and reach our own conclusions about its teaching, without undue deference to one particular school of thought; we are encouraged, in other words, to cultivate a spirit of free inquiry. This free inquiry is the counterpart, in the religious realm, of that free inquiry which has been mentioned already as indispensable to academic life. The Christian acceptance of the Bible as God's word written does not in the least inhibit the unfettered study of its contents and setting; on the contrary, it acts as an incentive to their most detailed and comprehensive investigation.[115]

Had he lived elsewhere, he might have been less sanguine, but as it was he felt profoundly thankful to belong to a community in which his church activity and his academic work could form a seamless whole. As he testified,

> I am sometimes asked if I am aware of a tension between my academic study of the Bible and my approach to the Bible in personal or church life. I am bound to say that I am aware of no such tension. Throughout my career as a university teacher I have also discharged a teaching ministry in my local church and occasionally in other churches. Naturally, when I discharge a teaching ministry in church I avoid the technicalities of academic discourse and I apply the message of Scripture in a more practical way. But there is no conflict between my critical or exegetical activity in a university context and my Bible exposition in church; the former makes a substantial contribution to the latter. At the same time, membership in a local church, involvement in the activities of a worshipping community, helps the academic theologian to remember what his subject is all about, and keeps his studies properly 'earthed'.[116]

---

[114] F.F. Bruce, 'Matter of Call' [letter], *CT*, 26 March 1965, p. 38.
[115] *IR*, p. 144. This paralleled the freedom which he enjoyed in the academic sphere: *H* 40 (1961): p. 122: Q. 966.
[116] *IR*, pp. 143–4.

But who or what, for Bruce, were the Brethren? His pamphlet *Who Are the Brethren?* first appeared as an article in *The Witness* during 1961.[117] Aimed at non-Brethren, and an example of a popular genre of literature in the movement, the intent was to supply information and remove misconceptions. So he explained how the movement originated, why it had divided into Open and Exclusive, and praised its commitment to overseas mission. It was not to be distinguished from other Christian traditions on account of its doctrines, which were those of the evangelical movement, but on account of its practices, most notably the Breaking of Bread service and the lack of any ordained ministry. As he explained elsewhere, he did not accept the argument sometimes put forward that Brethren were not a denomination but simply 'New Testament gatherings of believers'.

> If the sum total of the people called Brethren do not constitute an ecclesiastical community, at least we share a historical identity (the Brethren movement is an important phase of nineteenth century church history) and (whether we realize it or not) we constitute a sociological entity. Invite any sociologist to have a look at us, and he will have no doubt on this score. Our local churches have (mercifully) no ecclesiastical superstructure but they are securely underpinned by a sociological infrastructure.[118]

Bruce's Brethren allegiance was evident in his writing. He continued to interact with Brethren writers, expressing appreciation of their insights,[119] using their commentaries in his own[120] and on occasion taking

---

[117] W 91 (1961): pp. 406–7. It was reprinted as a booklet by Pickering & Inglis the following year; included as an appendix to vol. 1 of F.A. Tatford's history of Echoes of Service, *That the World May Know* (Bath: Echoes of Service, 1982); as an appendix to *In Retrospect*; and finally reprinted in *Harvester/Aware* 69 (June 1990): pp. 4–5. Very similar in wording were his articles on 'Plymouth Brethren Worship', 'Baptism 13: Plymouth Brethren', and 'Liturgies 13: Plymouth Brethren', in *A Dictionary of Liturgy and Worship* (ed. J.G. Davies; London: SCM, 1972).

[118] *IR*, p. 287.

[119] e.g. a 1954 series of articles by Andrew Borland (editor of *BM*) on baptism: F.F. Bruce, *The Epistle to the Ephesians: A Verse-by-Verse Exposition* (London: Pickering and Inglis, 1983; first publ. 1961), p. 116 n, cf. p. 80 n; idem, *The Epistles to the Colossians, to Philemon and to the Ephesians*, NICNT (Grand Rapids, MI: Eerdmans, 1984), p. 389 (both on Eph. 5:26).

[120] e.g. in F.F. Bruce, *The Epistle to the Hebrews*, NLCNT (London: Marshall, Morgan & Scott, 1965): he made use of G.H. Lang, whom he considered was almost unrivalled when it came to practical application, J.N. Darby, William Kelly, William Lincoln and W.E. Vine.

issue with their more idiosyncratic interpretations.[121] An important instance of this is his paper to the CBRF in 1971 on Brethren thinking about 'The Humanity of Jesus Christ'. Sending it to the editor, Roy Coad, for publication, he expressed the hope that it was 'not too inflammatory'.[122] It was not; but it was hard-hitting, for it claimed that 'a weakness on the doctrine of our Lord's humanity, verging at times on Docetism, has been endemic in certain phases of the Brethren movement',[123] and that the biblicism of nineteenth-century Brethren which saw no value in the mainstream Christian theological tradition had resulted in their repeating all the main Christological heresies of four centuries of early Christian thought in just seven decades. As so often, for a concise concluding statement of a sound Christology, Bruce turned to the Westminster Shorter Catechism.

Adherence to the Brethren did not mean adopting a fixed theological standpoint but carried with it a continuing openness to Spirit-led change. As a result, it was essential to guard against the perennial tendency of renewal movements to become fossilized, to change from being pioneers to being settlers. It is difficult to avoid seeing a reference to the Brethren in the conclusion of his commentary on Hebrews:

> The faith once for all delivered to the saints is not something which can be caught and tamed; it continually leads the saints forth to new ventures in the cause of Christ, as God calls afresh . . . To stay at the point to which some revered teacher of the past has brought us, out of a mistaken sense of loyalty to him; to continue to follow a certain pattern of religious activity or attitude just because it was good enough for our fathers and grandfathers – these and the like are temptations which make the message of Hebrews a necessary and salutary one for us to listen to. Every fresh movement of the Spirit of God tends to become stereotyped in the next generation, and what we have heard with our ears, what our fathers have told us, becomes a tenacious tradition

---

[121] e.g. by the nineteenth-century Exclusive writer C.E. Stuart: *Hebrews*, p. 201 n. 82, where Bruce warned against basing doctrine on typological interpretations, something to which Brethren had been prone at various points in their history.

[122] CBA, Box 5A, Bruce to Roy Coad, 6 March 1972.

[123] F.F. Bruce, 'The Humanity of Jesus Christ', *JCBRF*, no. 24 (September 1973): pp. 5–15, at p. 5. Cf. his later assertion: 'If there is one cardinal doctrine of the Christian faith on which Brethren have sometimes been shaky, it is the real manhood of our Lord Jesus Christ': 'Thoughts from My Study: Creeds or No Creeds?', *Calling* 11/4 (Winter 1969): pp. 16–18, at p. 18. He excepted those Exclusive Brethren who had followed William Kelly and W.J. Lowe.

encroaching on the allegiance which ought to be accorded only to the living and active word of God.[124]

One aspect of assembly life in which he believed that the fossilizing tendency was at work was that of worship, which for Brethren meant primarily the 'morning meeting', the Lord's Supper or Breaking of Bread.

> There was probably a time in the early days of the Brethren movement when, with the conscious abandonment of a fixed liturgy, one never knew in the course of a meeting for worship what was going to happen next. Nowadays, with the fixation in many places of another (albeit unwritten) liturgy, one often knows only too well what is going to happen next. Some of us may think that our familiar order of worship provides adequate room for the liberty of the Spirit, but by use and wont we have come to expect the Spirit to move in well-recognized ways.[125]

The article from which the quotation above was taken offers a striking insight into Bruce's developed understanding of the nature of the church. 'Lessons from the Early Church' formed part of a volume of essays on ecclesiology in honour of G.C.D. Howley, editor until 1977 of *The Witness* and Bruce's close friend and kindred spirit.[126] In 1945 Bruce had referred in a book review to 'the Scriptural order of church government by elders'.[127] Now, however, rejecting the idea that the

---

[124] Bruce, *Hebrews*, p. 416.

[125] F.F. Bruce, 'Lessons from the Early Church', in *In God's Community: Essays on the Church and Its Ministry* (ed. David J. Ellis and W. Ward Gasque; Wheaton, IL: Harold Shaw, 1979), pp. 153–68, at p. 159. Bruce was by no means alone in this criticism: Grass, *Gathering*, pp. 444–8. On the significance of the 'morning meeting' among Brethren, see Neil Dickson, ' "Shut in with Thee": The Morning Meeting among Scottish Brethren, 1830s–1960s', in *Continuity and Change in Christian Worship*, Studies in Church History 35 (ed. R.N. Swanson; Woodbridge: Boydell & Brewer, 1999), pp. 275–88.

[126] Ellis and Gasque, eds, *In God's Community*, pp. 153–68. For Bruce's tribute to their friendship, see 'George Cecil Douglas Howley: An Appreciation', ibid. pp. ix–xiii. Bruce first encountered Howley during the 1930s, and soon recognized that they shared a similar approach to biblical interpretation which set them apart from most Brethren: 'He was concerned to bring out the plain meaning of the words in their literary and historical context, leaving typology and allegorization to others (and we had more of those "others" then than we have now)': ibid. p. ix.

[127] *EQ* 17 (1945): p. 80.

New Testament laid down one blueprint to be followed by all local congregations if they wished to be considered 'biblical', he argued that in the New Testament there were diverse patterns of church order, the common feature being a flexibility which allowed the Holy Spirit to provide for their needs as necessary. He even claimed a respected Brethren writer in support – Henry Craik, in his *New Testament Church Order* (1863). Within the New Testament there was evidence of development in this area, and unlike G.H. Lang Bruce did not believe that all development was departure; rather, it could represent the unfolding of what was already there in the bud.[128] The criterion for assessing the legitimacy of such development was whether it helped the church to discharge her proper functions of worship, fellowship and witness.[129] It is no surprise that he admitted having learned many lessons since contributing to the 1949 volume on *The Church*.[130]

We see, then, that Bruce was increasingly wary of attempts to find in the New Testament some kind of divine and unchanging blueprint for church life. His preference was for an approach which looked for the principle underlying particular injunctions or prohibitions, which he regarded as working out such commands in a particular cultural context, which was not that of believers in the twentieth century. As a teenager, a book by Lang had convinced him that whenever a group tries to reproduce the pattern of first-century Christianity, its successors always reproduce the Christianity of the second century, which to Brethren represented a sharp declension from the divine ideal.[131] He set out his thinking in a Bloomsbury address on 6 November 1976 on 'The Local Church: Pattern or Principle?'[132] In it he argued that principles were more fundamental than patterns, but also more flexible. The New Testament provided principles, but patterns may change as cultural contexts change. His examples included head covering in 1 Corinthians 11 and the order of worship in 1 Corinthians 14. Once

---

[128] Ellis and Gasque, eds, *In God's Community*, pp. 157–8, cf. p. 154.

[129] Ibid. p. 168.

[130] Ibid. p. 153.

[131] 'Professor Bruce Asks', *H* 58 (1979): p. 357.

[132] This only appeared in print much later, after G.W. Robson had the recording transcribed and sent to the editor of *The Harvester*: CBA, Box 138, Bloomsbury Committee papers, F.F. Bruce, 'The Church: Pattern or Principle?', typescript; 'Practice or Principle', *H* 68/1 (January 1989): pp. 12–13; 68/2 (February 1989): pp. 6–8.

again, he quoted Henry Craik to the effect that the New Testament provided precedents for all main varieties of church order.[133]

Sometimes his views on church life were expressed in terms which made the hearers sit up and think. To a young people's conference at a Salford assembly, he asserted that God was more interested in what a woman had in her head than on it, which would have shocked those Brethren who believed that the wearing of a head covering by a woman was mandatory for corporate worship.[134] And when asked at a house party what he would do if a young woman came to the Breaking of Bread wearing a miniskirt, he replied that he probably would not notice.[135]

For some, his continued presence among Brethren, and his willingness to express his convictions forthrightly, undoubtedly made it possible for them to remain where they were. Others, however, feared the incursion of unacceptable theological views and the erosion of traditional assembly distinctives. They had some grounds for this; he welcomed the prospect of Brethren being subsumed into a wider evangelicalism as the two communities faced similar problems, and he raised the possibility that Brethrenism might need to disappear for the sake of the continuing practice of New Testament principles.[136] Small wonder that in some circles, therefore, he was regarded as 'the leader of the apostasy among the Brethren'.[137]

One topic on which this was so was biblical prophecy. He regarded the book of Revelation as written primarily for the benefit of first-century readers and its symbols and visions as having first-century references. This is evident in his contribution on the book to *A New Testament Commentary*, which was written by members of the Brethren;[138] in his opinion, although scrappy, 'it will at least stimulate

---

[133] Bruce, 'The Church: Pattern or Principle?'

[134] Brian Maiden, telephone conversation, 23 January 2009.

[135] Dennis Angell to the author, 15 July 2008; cf. a similar response in *H* 47 (1968): p. 26: Q. 1524, in which he made the point that older believers should try to understand the matter from the viewpoint of young people, and to guard against giving the impression that Christ did not welcome them. He was delighted when the Christian youth magazine *Buzz* awarded him its badge of honour for this answer; cf. *H* 47 (1968): p. 199: Q. 1604.

[136] *IR*, p. 289; cf. 'Professor Bruce Asks', *H* 52 (1973): p. 47; 'Replies to Professor Bruce', *H* 52 (1973): p. 95.

[137] 'Professor Bruce Asks', *H* 59 (1980): p. 74.

[138] G.C.D. Howley, ed., *A New Testament Commentary: Based on the Revised Standard Version* (London: Pickering & Inglis, 1969), pp. 629–66. A valuable overview of the book, which is very different from his commentary, was given as a lecture at Regent College in 1976, and the recording is still available from Regent College Bookstore: 'The Book of Revelation', (ref. 607).

questions and raise eyebrows!'[139] The disquiet aroused by the book was often because its tone and idiom were not that of traditional Brethren expositions; particularly in North America, concern was also expressed at the lack of a consistent dispensationalist standpoint.[140] Bruce's exegetically orientated approach meant that he did not align himself with any one prophetic school of thinking; 'It says something, I feel, that a person can write a whole commentary on Revelation, and you don't know, at the end, what millenial position he is taking!'[141]

Another area in which he was seen as having a corroding influence was that of attitudes towards other Christian traditions. A feature of his outlook which became very evident during this period was his catholicity. As one reporter expressed it: 'He does not restrict the term "Christian" to those who think as he does or belong to his own tradition. "If a man professes 'Jesus is Lord', unless I know of very good reasons to the contrary, that man is a Christian."'[142] One of the things Bruce most welcomed about *Apostolic History and the Gospel* was that the contributors were drawn from a wide range of traditions.[143] His catholic outlook sometimes found pointed expression; at the opening of a gospel hall in Doncaster in 1975, he commented that he could have fellowship with the Pope and Ian Paisley, though preferably not at the same time![144] Asked at one Easter conference what he would do if the Pope turned up at his assembly one Sunday morning, he said: 'I would ask if he loved the Lord and wished to remember him in his death. If he said "Yes", I would give a warm welcome to the "corresponding brother from the assembly of the Lord's people in Rome"'.[145] At the other end of the spectrum, he could answer the question 'Is it proper for a good assembly man to have fellowship with Dr. Billy Graham?' with the one-word response 'Yes'.[146] Each assertion would have been unacceptable to conservative Brethren.

---

[139] CBA, Box 64, Bruce to J.A. Green, 10 March 1969.

[140] *IR*, p. 272.

[141] Brian Davies to the author, 22 October 2008.

[142] John Capon, 'From Scotland with Scholarship', *Crusade*, April 1976.

[143] Alastair and Jane Rossetter, interview, 23 August 2008; Alastair Rossetter to the author, 1 September 2010.

[144] Personal information.

[145] Peter Tait, interview, 28 May 2008; 'corresponding brother' was a Brethren term for the secretary of a local assembly, and it was customary to welcome Christian visitors by name at the beginning of the Breaking of Bread.

[146] *H* 40 (1961): p. 154: Q. 979. Bruce later joined Graham's council of reference: *H* 45 (1966): p. 59: Q. 1348.

Bruce's breadth of sympathy owed something to the revivalist strain in his own background, but it found ready expression in the interconfessional nature of his work as a biblical scholar. The dedication of *In Retrospect* to 'My Companions on the Way' is followed by Psalm 122:8 from the Jerusalem Bible, a Roman Catholic translation: 'Since all are my brothers and friends, I say "PEACE BE WITH YOU!"' His outlook differed, however, from the approach which characterized the ecumenical movement during the 1960s, which laid much more stress on institutional unity. Asked whether evangelicals should be more positive towards the World Council of Churches with its newly strengthened doctrinal basis, he admitted in response that he was not keen on another layer of bureaucracy, but 'let the evangelical contribution to the World council [*sic*] consist one hundred per cent of undiluted evangelical witness, and the outcome need not be feared'. With all his reservations, he applauded its decision to meet at the heart of non-Christian Asia and to take as the theme for its meeting 'Jesus Christ the Light of the World'. Brethren congregations, however, were independent, so there was no question of associating with the WCC through any denominational structure, but at the local level councils of churches could include assemblies, and it was up to each to decide for itself whether or not to join.[147] Catholicity did not mean, then, that he bought into contemporary enthusiasm for institutional ecumenism. This is evident from his contribution to the 1964 Swanwick Conference of Brethren, which was devoted to the theme of 'Christian Unity'; the gathering provoked widespread disquiet among Brethren, made worse by the presence of a representative of the British Council of Churches.[148] But Bruce was no institutional ecumenist and had little time for the grandiose schemes for visible church unity being dreamed up at that time. Rather, he saw unity as a by-product of co-operation in work such as that of the British and

---

[147] *H* 41 (1962): p. 74: Q. 1032. In 1961, the WCC strengthened its doctrinal basis to emphasize that its membership comprised churches which confessed Jesus Christ as 'God and Saviour according to the Scriptures' and which sought to fulfil their common calling together 'to the glory of one God, Father, Son and Holy Spirit', thus introducing explicit references to the Bible and the Trinity. Its assembly that year met in New Delhi.

[148] *IR*, pp. 160–61. He had earlier explained why, in his view, Brethren could not even join a fundamentalist counterpart to the WCC, the International Council of Christian Churches; they had no mechanism for acting as a denomination, and in any case if they resisted federation among their own churches they would be all the more reluctant to join any wider federation: *H* 34 (1955): p. 43: Q. 316.

Foreign Bible Society, for which he frequently spoke, and academic societies for biblical study.

Bruce's influence among Brethren was also evident outside the United Kingdom. From the late 1950s he developed a warm friendship with Ernest Trenchard (1902–72), a fellow member of the Tyndale Fellowship who was a Brethren missionary in Spain. Trenchard's expertise was, like Bruce's, exegetical, and he sought to provide sound and scholarly literature for the use of evangelicals in a country where there was still considerable religious persecution; Bruce read Trenchard's manuscripts and offered feedback. Their correspondence is marked by mutual respect, but that did not stop Trenchard from graciously challenging Bruce on points where they disagreed. A longstanding Brethren worker notes that Trenchard nurtured a team of Bible teachers who in their turn learned from Bruce through his writings.[149] Bruce's interest in Spain may have owed something not only to the nature of the work in which Trenchard was engaged but also to the fact that his father had at one point contemplated becoming a missionary to the country, although *In Retrospect* does not mention this.[150]

We have already noted Bruce's involvement with Regent College, Vancouver, and another striking instance of this overseas influence is his trip to New Zealand in July and August 1966.[151] He had been invited by the Wellington Area Research Fellowship (WARF; founded by Brethren in 1961 and supported by him, and the model for the British CBRF) and the national IVF. Together they arranged a packed itinerary in which he spoke seventy-eight times in thirty-six days to students, Brethren leaders, and ministers' conferences.[152] The WARF annual report for 1966 noted that its conference in Auckland had been its biggest so far, and featured Bruce introducing selected New

---

[149] Terry Wickham to the author, 7 December 2008, 25 February 2009.

[150] In the books detailing inquiries about missionary service held by Echoes of Service, the main Brethren mission agency, there is the following entry regarding a Mr Bruce (evidently Peter from the details given): 'Mentioned by Mr. D. McNab, Oct.23.'06, as desiring to go to Spain. Is known & esteemed by brethren in the N. of Scotland. Has had some 7 years of experience in moving about with the Gospel in this land, & the Lord has blessed His word through him, since he was brought to the Lord some 15 years ago. He is studying Spanish': Bath, Echoes of Service, Candidates' Book 4, fol. 368.

[151] *IR*, ch. 30.

[152] Madrid, Comisión de Biblioteca y Archivos, Centro Evangélico de Formación Bíblica en Madrid, Bruce to Ernest H. Trenchard, 5 January 1967.

Testament books.[153] He also spoke at several day conferences and assembly meetings, and to another WARF conference at Marton on Ephesians.[154] Overall, his visit had been a highlight for assemblies, although 'There is a danger that having achieved a degree of recognition and respectability through the visit of Professor Bruce, the Fellowship might cease to prove relevant to young enthusiasts like those who formed it.'

The WARF report for the following year reflected that the visit had come at a time when the views of a conservative biblical scholar had needed to be heard in the country.[155] Nonetheless, it is clear that some of what he said came as a shock to the systems of some Brethren. One instance was his address on 'The Sources of the Synoptic Gospels', which concluded: 'I am well aware, Mr. Chairman, that source criticism is not everyones [sic] "cup of tea", but as you have pointed out at the beginning, this is what you asked for and therefore you've got it.'[156] The chairman opened the succeeding discussion by asserting that talk about gospel sources was inconsistent with the 'doctrine' that the Holy Spirit dictated the gospels in the form that we have them; he hoped that someone would ask what practical use this knowledge was, and how it related to the theory of inspiration. In response, Bruce explained that source criticism showed that the gospels were not written decades later 'out of the blue' as was sometimes claimed but were the result of reliable transmission of material. He also distinguished inspiration from dictation, affirming the variety of methods which had been used in the production of the biblical books, such as Luke's patient historical research.

Some wanted to draw him out on issues which were already proving controversial among assemblies. At the time, the charismatic movement was being hotly debated, and Dr W.H. Pettit, who was strongly opposed to it, put a question to Bruce to see where he stood.

[153] F.F. Bruce, 'The Sources of the Synoptic Gospels', 'John's Gospel', 'The First Epistle of John', 'The General Epistles', *Wellington Assembly Research Fellowship*, no. 30 (July 1967). He also gave papers on the Pauline Epistles and on Hebrews, thus covering the whole New Testament apart from Acts and Revelation, no mean feat for a weekend conference.

[154] F.F. Bruce, 'The Broken Wall', and 'Principalities and Powers', *Wellington Assembly Research Fellowship*, no. 28 (April 1967): pp. 1–11, 12–22.

[155] CBA, Box 8. The background to the final comment is that in 1966 a Presbyterian theologian named Lloyd Geering had denied the historicity of the resurrection and provoked a storm which was fully covered by national news media.

[156] Bruce, 'Sources of the Synoptic Gospels', p. 13.

To no avail; the response was a laconic: 'In vain the net is spread in the sight of the bird. Next question please.'[157]

◆   ◆   ◆

A few years before retiring, Bruce was struck by the recognition that he had attained every professional ambition which he could have expected to do,[158] a circumstance which brought its own temptations, on which he had been reflecting.[159] In December 1977, he wrote that advertisements for a new occupant for the Rylands chair had brought home to him more sharply the prospect of retirement; indeed, a friend described this as 'traumatic' for him.[160] He would miss student contact especially, but would be glad to be free of administration and com-mittees.[161] With a string of writing projects lined up, he was looking forward to having time for uninterrupted research and writing. Before reviewing his post-retirement output, in the next chapter we shall look at some significant aspects of his writing career during his time at Manchester.

---

[157] Peter McKenzie, 'A Tribute to Professor F.F. Bruce', *CBRF Journal*, no. 123 (January 1991): p. 6.

[158] *IR*, p. 308, cf. the original version: 'Remembrance of Things Past (36): In Conclusion – for the Time Being', *W* 106 (1976): pp. 443–5, at p. 444.

[159] CPF 1934 newsletter, December 1974.

[160] Northwood, LST, J.D. Douglas papers, Douglas to Carl Henry, 14 November 1977.

[161] CPF 1934 newsletter, December 1977.

8

Books and the Book (1959–78)

During the 1960s Bruce consolidated his reputation, then somewhat unusual, as an evangelical writer whose work was acceptable to readers of all persuasions. In this chapter, I want to revisit his thinking on the doctrine of Scripture and his books about the Scriptures. This provides a background against which to examine his other books.[1] Following that, we shall continue our examination of his editorial activities and his answering of questions.

◆　◆　◆

It was C.H. Dodd who suggested Bruce as the author of a book on the English Bible to appear at the same time as the New Testament of the New English Bible.[2] The result was his *History of the Bible in English* (1961). It had been completed under pressure, having been promised to the publisher for the end of 1959; for his first term at Manchester, he was teaching at Sheffield two days a week as well as settling into a new post.[3] Nevertheless, the manuscript was delivered to the publisher on time, and it became a standard work which is still in print half a century later. A second edition appeared in 1970, and a third (which was almost the same apart from the addition of a chapter bringing it up to date) in 1979.

Bruce took readers on a comprehensive survey of English-language versions from Wyclif onwards, enlivening the narrative with anecdotes and flashes of humour. Perhaps more than English writers

---

[1] See also *IR*, ch. 34.

[2] T.C. Mitchell, 'Professor Frederick Fyvie Bruce, D.D. F.B.A.', *FT* 117 (1991): pp. 2–5, at p. 4.

[3] *IR*, pp. 204–5. The approach to write the book must have come somewhat earlier, as he referred to the project in mid-1958: *H* 37 (1958): p. 138: Q. 706.

traversing the same territory, he drew anecdotes and illustrations from Scottish history.[4] He also offered full and positive coverage of the Geneva Bible (1560), Calvinistic notes and all, which remained the preferred version among Puritans and Scots long after the Authorized Version appeared in 1611; the former, he considered, helped to make Protestantism 'the strongly vertebrate movement that it was'.[5] Yet he also discussed Roman Catholic versions sympathetically, and few Brethren hearts could have failed to be moved when he quoted from the Douai version a note on Revelation 22 expressing a deep longing for Christ to return.[6] In the present day, he believed, 'There could be no more important or welcome manifestation of the ecumenical spirit than co-operation in the production and study of the Bible and in the receiving and practising of its message.'[7] His approval of up-to-date versions was balanced by his warm appreciation of the Authorized Version on account of its style: his classical training had given him a feel for the rhythms of prose and poetry, and this led him on occasion to be critical of less felicitous modern renderings (even the Revised Version, of which he otherwise approved highly). Those who criticized the Authorized Version as archaic lacked 'the literary equipment to appreciate it'.[8] So, while praising the Brethren leader J.N. Darby's translation for its sound textual basis, he nevertheless considered that it 'falls short in regard to English style – which would surprise no one acquainted with Darby's voluminous prose writings'.[9] Having learned by experience to deal leniently with translators because of the difficulty of their task, he expressed his preference for the approach known as 'dynamic equivalence', which aimed at producing the same impact as the original did on those who first read or heard it, rather than a literal word-for-word rendition.[10] Throughout, he insisted on the need to face difficulties honestly and not to gloss over them, whether they concerned the original manuscripts or the most appropriate rendition into English. The existence of variations

---

[4] F.F. Bruce, *History of the Bible in English, from the Earliest Versions* (Guildford: Lutterworth, 1979), pp. 2, 91–2, 100; cf. the pairing at the end of the preface of a quotation from the Westminster Shorter Catechism with the Prayer Book collect for the Second Sunday in Advent: ibid. p. xii.

[5] Ibid. p. 90.

[6] Ibid. p. 123–4.

[7] Ibid. p. 219.

[8] Ibid. p. 109–12; quotation at p. 111–12.

[9] Ibid. p. 132.

[10] Ibid. p. ix.

between manuscripts should surprise nobody.[11] Furthermore, the faith was not well served by dogmatic attitudes towards those who did not accept the authenticity of Mark 16:9–20 or by deploying weak arguments to defend the retention of passages such as 1 John 5:7.[12]

Such views would not have engendered any controversy, except among those who were opposed to all modern translations, but during the 1970s evangelicalism was affected by vigorous debates regarding biblical authority and infallibility; Bruce expressed apprehension at certain developments, and aspects of his thinking would not have commended themselves in certain quarters, which is why further consideration is appropriate here.[13]

We begin with the relationship between his views on Scripture and the apparent cooling in his attitude towards the IVF. This was not in respect of its evangelistic and pastoral work among students; he always supported this warmly, writing to encourage elders to commend young people going up to university to the appropriate Christian Union.[14] Rather, it appears to have concerned the way in which the organization sought to ensure that books published under its imprint maintained its distinctive theological stance. He published no new books with Inter-Varsity Press after 1963, and his occasional references to it in correspondence criticize it as difficult to please.[15] I wonder whether this was partly a consequence of the movement's rapid growth from the 1950s onwards; gone were the days when it was held together largely through a network of personal relationships and the IVF's secretary, Douglas Johnson, could address Bruce informally in letters as 'My dear F₂'. With the inevitable weakening of such relationships, the scope for misinterpretation and even suspicion may have increased. Bruce also told one acquaintance that he felt marginalized in IVF circles; that could have been true, given that in London Lloyd-Jones and John Stott, who both ministered in the city, were the

---

[11] Ibid. p. 140.
[12] Ibid. pp. 149 n. 1, 142 respectively.
[13] For another discussion of Bruce's views on Scripture, see Peter Oakes, 'F.F. Bruce and the Development of Evangelical Biblical Scholarship', *BJRL* 86/3 (Autumn 2004): pp. 99–124, esp. pp. 108–13.
[14] For example, *W* 101 (1971): p. 347 (with W.M. Capper); 102 (1972): p. 305; 103 (1973): p. 307; 104 (1974): pp. 308–9; 105 (1975): pp. 349–50; cf. *BM* 67 (1957): p. 227.
[15] For instance, 'the IVF Literature Committee are a sticky crowd to deal with': Madrid, Comisión de Biblioteca y Archivos, Centro Evangélico de Formación Bíblica en Madrid, Bruce to Ernest H. Trenchard, 30 November 1964; cf. Bruce to Desmond Ford, 25 December 1983.

primary theological influences on evangelical students during the 1960s.[16] I do not think that Bruce's views on Scripture changed to any significant degree; what did change, however, was the background against which he maintained them, and such change was reflected in the discussions which would take in Tyndale Fellowship circles during the 1970s, as we shall see.

In 1959 Bruce was one of several Tyndale Fellowship committee members who were asked to attend meetings more frequently.[17] Active during the 1960s, he began to scale down his involvement thereafter, offering to resign from the committee in 1974 on the ground that he remained unable to attend meetings.[18] However, given that he continued to make attendance at certain other gatherings such as those of the SOTS and SNTS a priority, one wonders whether pressure of work was only part of the reason, and that he would have been more regular if he had found the meetings more congenial and a more strategic use of his time. In particular, he was not in sympathy with moves to tighten the doctrinal basis of the fellowship.

In 1971, an invitation to one member (Graham Stanton), then Lecturer in New Testament at King's College London, to write a commentary on Matthew in the Tyndale series (replacing that by R.V.G. Tasker) had been withdrawn. The following year Stanton introduced a discussion in the Tyndale Fellowship committee regarding publication policy, urging the Tyndale Press to broaden its appeal (and presumably the range of views deemed acceptable in its publications). Ronald Inchley's response as publications secretary of IVP was, naturally enough, that it could not contemplate publishing anything which was not consistent with the IVF doctrinal basis.[19] Discussion continued for some years regarding the extent to which contributors could be allowed freedom to express views which might be deemed incompatible with the doctrinal basis, whether in the annual study groups or in publications.

---

[16] Malcolm Harrison, interview, 25 April 2009.

[17] T.A. Noble, *Tyndale House and Fellowship: The First Sixty Years* (Leicester: IVP, 2006), p. 108; cf. BRC minutes, 29 March 1960.

[18] Noble, *Tyndale*, p. 162. To Alan Millard he wrote on 22 May 1974 that it was time he made way for someone younger. His offer was unanimously refused, although a subsequent request to be allowed to stand down from the Tyndale House council was agreed to: BRC minutes, 17 July 1974, 14 April 1976. Thereafter he joined the Tyndale House council of reference: Noble, *Tyndale*, p. 169 n. 17.

[19] Noble, *Tyndale*, p. 148.

A memorandum drafted by Howard Marshall in 1973 and distrib-
uted to study group speakers laid down that the fellowship defined
its premises – acceptance of the position set out in the doctrinal basis,
and in particular Christ's view of Scripture as normative – but not the
conclusions which scholars were expected to reach.[20] However, the
issue rumbled on, and the *bona fides* of some who signed the doctrinal
basis were called into question, especially among the undergraduate
students who made up the bulk of the membership of the Theological
Students' Fellowship; this was also affiliated to IVF and underwent
something of a resurgence during the decade. Discussions between it
and the Tyndale Fellowship indicate that the former consistently took
a more conservative line on many issues of biblical interpretation and
that there were some among it who were suspicious of the more academic body and feared that it was drifting from its moorings. This led
them to call for a tighter approach to the question of subscription to
the doctrinal basis.

In 1975 Bruce favoured the fellowship committee with a forthright
memorandum opposing any action aimed at uncovering members
whose orthodoxy was suspect. In his view, 'We who are members of
the TF are members of a fellowship dedicated to the evangelical faith.
We express that dedication when we join the TF, and we ought to have
sufficient confidence in one another to accept the good faith in which
that dedication is expressed without raising niggling questions.' The
fellowship's existence had demonstrated that academic freedom and
evangelical faith were not mutually exclusive, as his own career illustrated: 'My own career in biblical studies has been due mainly to the
influence of the BRC and TF, turning me from a teacher of classics into
what I have now become.' Tightening the conditions of membership
would give occasion for opponents to assert that an evangelical body
such as the IVF could never allow real academic freedom, and introducing the requirement of subscription to the doctrinal basis 'without
any mental reservations' carried the implication that some members
were at present acting dishonestly. He also pointed out that as a life
member, he could only be removed by a formal vote![21] However, from
1976 Tyndale Fellowship members were required to indicate their

---

[20] For the memorandum, see Noble, *Tyndale*, p. 153; cf. Derek Tidball, 'Post-War
Evangelical Theology: A Generational Perspective', *EQ* 81 (2009): pp. 145–60, at p.
155.

[21] Cambridge, Tyndale House, Box 31, memorandum of 2 May 1975 concerning
'Item 9'.

Bruce's birthplace
12 Rose Place, Elgin

Elgin Academy

The Caledonian Bible Carriage at Johnstone, c.1904: Peter Bruce is standing to the left of the carriage

Fred's Aberdeen graduation photograph

Fred and Betty before marriage

Wedding photograph

Postcard of Lossiemouth beach from the late 1940s; the Bruce
family can be seen walking down the path

Tyndale House,
Cambridge

79 Bower Road,
Sheffield

Bruce in his Aberdeen doctoral robes, 1957

'The Crossways',
Buxton

A group of conference speakers; to the right of Bruce is his friend
Arnold Pickering

The former Crescent Road Hall,
Stockport

F.F. Bruce at his portable typewriter (from *Christianity Today*,
10 October 1980, 16)

Fred and Betty after the conferral of an honorary doctorate from Sheffield, 18 March 1988

Fred and Betty in the garden at 'The Crossways'

agreement with its doctrinal basis rather than merely signing a declaration of personal faith in Christ (the practice in Christian Unions).[22] Some may interpret Bruce's approach to the issue as evidence of incipient liberalism, but this would be to misunderstand him: as a lifelong member of the Open Brethren community, he would have been ill at ease with too much emphasis on creedal subscription. He felt that creeds and confessions 'can enshrine the wisdom of the past and the insight of the present but . . . cannot accommodate that further illumination which coming generations will discover in Scripture. This means that confessional affirmations . . . should never become the standard by which Biblical exposition and belief are to be measured.'[23] That included the IVF doctrinal basis. Furthermore, whilst it was acceptable to subscribe to confessions such as this which used time-honoured language, he objected to being asked to adopt somebody else's choice of non-technical language when they were deemed insufficiently clear by themselves. Doubtless he had in mind the growing insistence of some at that time on using terms such as 'inerrancy' to define who was or was not truly evangelical and to explicate the meaning of the doctrinal basis.[24] This development arose because talk of biblical 'infallibility' was no longer seen as sufficiently clear to exclude certain views associated with more liberal approaches to Scripture. And he openly expressed his preference for the pre-war version of the doctrinal basis, which he saw as offering a more moderate and less tightly defined view of biblical infallibility.[25] The New Testament Study Group, in which Bruce exercised something of a patriarchal influence, was more moderate in its approach than its Old Testament counterpart.[26] Finally, it is clear that he viewed the matter not simply in doctrinal terms but as a question of personal integrity.

---

[22] Noble, *Tyndale*, pp. 163–4.

[23] F.F. Bruce, 'The Lausanne Covenant – 2: The Authority and Power of the Bible', *H* 55 (1976): pp. 320–23, at p. 323.

[24] *IR*, pp. 310–11; the original of this chapter first appeared in December 1976. In 1977 the TSF dismayed many in the TF by adding a paragraph to their constitution asserting that infallibility extended to all affirmations made by the Scriptures, including those on matters of history or cosmology: Noble, *Tyndale*, pp. 164–6. This was an assertion often made by thoroughgoing upholders of the inerrancy of Scripture.

[25] Oakes, 'Bruce', p. 104; cf. David F. Wright, 'Soundings in the Doctrine of Scripture in British Evangelicalism in the First Half of the Twentieth Century', *TB* 31 (1980): pp. 87–106, at p. 105 n. 51.

[26] David Payne, interview, 2 May 2009.

Tension appears to have continued through the late 1970s, and to complicate matters a vigorous literary debate was getting under way on the topic of biblical inerrancy in evangelical circles more generally. Yet Bruce continued to support the vision of the Tyndale Fellowship and Tyndale House. In 1973 he had asserted the strategic significance of Tyndale House when a committee of businessmen associated with IVF had mooted its closure in order to release funds for postgraduate research at universities; in a confidential memorandum, he was quoted as saying:

> I can conceive of nothing that would be a greater disservice to this cause than the closure or dispersal of the library . . . better that the library should never have been founded than that it should at this time of day be dismantled. That such a thing should ever be contemplated or implied would be evidence of the subordinating of long-term strategy to short-term tactics.[27]

The then warden of Tyndale House, R.T. France, noted the influence during this period of the early article in which Bruce set out the Tyndale Fellowship vision: 'When I was Warden of Tyndale House there was lengthy debate about the limits of what was acceptable within the scope of "evangelical" scholarship, culminating in a sort of Tyndale Fellowship "summit" held at St Giles-in-the-Fields (March 1979). Bruce's 1947 article was a key influence in the discussion, and helped to avoid an inappropriately restrictive outcome.'[28]

So it seems clear that Bruce saw himself as maintaining the vision for a renewed evangelical scholarship which would influence not only the ecclesiastical world but wider culture and society. It may be, though I am not sure that it can be demonstrated, that he resisted attempts to tighten things up out of a fear that the result would be a retreat of evangelicals into a ghetto from which he had seen them emerge during the 1940s.

Having looked at how Bruce maintained his position, we need to spell out a little more fully what that position was. The first point to make is that he did not regard a particular concept of inspiration as foreclosing discussion on issues of biblical interpretation; indeed, he

---

[27] Tyndale House, Box 13, memorandum from the BRC to the IVF Business Advisory Committee, [1973]; cf. Noble, *Tyndale*, pp. 155–60.
[28] R.T. France to the author, 16 July 2008; cf. Noble, *Tyndale*, p. 180. From that point, members were expected to indicate their acceptance of the doctrinal basis annually.

believed that one should seek to avoid coming to the biblical text with preconceived ideas about what it said.[29] Thus he was able to accept views on certain contentious issues which were not those of the evangelical tradition. For example, he came to believe that the book of Daniel had in fact been compiled in the second century BC, although it was a recension of sixth-century material.[30] The Matthaean version of the Lord's Prayer, which was fuller than that found in Luke, was, he considered, a first-century adaptation for church use of what Jesus had actually taught the disciples.[31] He was also increasingly reluctant to affirm the Pauline authorship of the Pastoral Epistles, preferring to regard them as including fragments of material from Paul but compiled after his death.[32] It was this expressed willingness to follow where the evidence led that commended Bruce to his colleague at Manchester from 1965 to 1977, James Barr, who exempted Bruce from his claim that evangelical scholars adopted positions which made them unable or unwilling to follow the evidence for fear of 'letting the side down'.[33] As evidence, he cited Bruce's account of a talk to a group of evangelical theological students, who felt that he was letting the side down by accepting, on the basis of the evidence and without contradicting any statement in Scripture or evangelical belief, that Isaiah 40 – 55 were not from the same hand as chapters 1 – 39.

Secondly, Bruce's understanding of biblical inspiration was clarified as he studied the text, rather than being something which he brought to the text.

---

[29] *IR*, p. 311.

[30] J.D. Douglas, 'A Man of Unchanging Faith', *CT*, 10 October 1980, pp. 16–18, at p. 17. Bruce was apparently influenced in his thinking by a conservative Old Testament scholar and apologist, Robert Dick Wilson (1856–1930).

[31] *Encyclopedia International* (19 vols; New York: Grolier, 1966), 'Lord's Prayer, The'.

[32] I. Howard Marshall, 'F.F. Bruce as a Biblical Scholar', *JCBRF*, no. 22 (Nov. 1971): pp. 5–12, at p. 11. As he later explained: 'while I have written commentaries on all the other Pauline letters, I have never tackled the Pastorals. While on the theological level, I respect their canonicity, I do not find in them the same note of authority as I recognize in the capital letters – but that is a purely subjective reaction. On the critical level I take a position somewhere between the fragmentary and secretarial hypotheses: that is to say, I think of them as literary composites embodying disiecta membra of the apostle – parts of letters, notes of teaching, etc., shaped together into their present form by an editorial hand (Luke's?)': Manchester, CBA, Box 11 (11), Bruce to Alan G. Padgett, 1 May 1984.

[33] James Barr, *Escaping from Fundamentalism* (London: SCM, 1984), pp. 156, 185 n. 1, citing F.F. Bruce, *Tradition Old and New* (Exeter: Paternoster, 1970), p. 15; my thanks to Peter Williams for this reference. Bruce did not state in his book which part of the

Occasionally, when I have expounded the meaning of some biblical passage in a particular way, I have been asked, 'But how does that square with inspiration?' But inspiration is not a concept of which I have a clear understanding before I come to the study of the text, so that I know in advance what limits are placed on the meaning of the text by the requirements of inspiration. On the contrary, it is by the patient study of the text that I come to understand better not only what the text itself means but also what is involved in biblical inspiration. My doctrine of Scripture is based on my study of Scripture, not *vice versa*.[34]

And that made him chary of attempts to harmonize apparent discrepancies (then frequently undertaken by evangelical writers) because they often savoured of special pleading or were marked by inadequate exegesis.[35] One of Bruce's postgraduate students summarized his mentor's approach as 'do your work and the trustworthiness of Scripture will become evident', an approach which was contrasted with arguing the case on dogmatic grounds.[36] In this, he was at one with his predecessor A.S. Peake, who likewise adopted an inductive approach to biblical inspiration and drew on Calvin and the Westminster Confession to support his emphasis on the self-authenticating nature of Scripture and the inner witness of the Spirit.[37]

Bible he had been speaking of, but authorized Barr by letter to say that it was Isaiah. Barr had become notorious in evangelical circles for an earlier book, *Fundamentalism*, published in 1977, which offered an excoriating critique of contemporary evangelicalism. Bruce had commented on it: 'my first impression was that he was getting something out of his system. I share many of his earlier experiences, but I have reacted differently to them': Douglas, 'A Man of Unchanging Faith', p. 17. Elsewhere, he wrote that Barr 'has described some of the attitudes to which he himself appears to have been exposed in his earlier years, but a visit to a Tyndale Fellowship study group would reveal a very different approach today': 'Evangelical Theology Today', *Life of Faith*, February 1978, pp. 16–17, at p. 16. Like Bruce, Barr was passionately concerned to assert the primacy of faith in a person, and feared that sections of contemporary evangelicalism were losing a sense of the gospel's liberating power: James Barr, 'The Problem of Fundamentalism Today', *Explorations in Theology* 7 (London: SCM, 1980), pp. 63–90, esp. pp. 81–2. However, he came to be much more critical of both Barth and the Biblical Theology movement than Bruce had done, and his version of the gospel was by no means identical to Bruce's.

[34] *IR*, p. 311.

[35] *IR*, pp. 311–12.

[36] David Wenham, telephone conversation, 25 September 2009.

[37] Timothy Larsen, 'A.S. Peake, the Free Churches and Modern Biblical Criticism', *BJRL* 86/3 (Autumn 2004): pp. 23–53, at p. 46.

That brings us to the third point, which concerns the emphasis on the Spirit's inner testimony which we have already noted. Bruce concluded his reminiscences by expressing the conviction that once believers learned to listen to God speaking to them in Scripture (and it was the Holy Spirit who enabled them to hear him), the precise terms used to express their understanding of the nature and authority of the Bible were relatively unimportant.[38] In this light we can understand why he valued the theology of someone like Barth; it would be because he saw in such people a reverent submission to God speaking to them through the Scriptures. The difference between Bruce's view and that of J.I. Packer and the Princeton theologians could be construed as one of emphasis rather than as a contradiction; he did not explicitly reject the notion of biblical inerrancy (though he saw it as bound up with a deductive and defensive approach to the doctrine of Scripture which he did not follow, and had never seen inerrancy as synonymous with infallibility) so much as stress other aspects of the doctrine of Scripture which he considered more important.

For at least some evangelicals, however, Bruce's view of inspiration was not strong enough. We have already noted that the 1970s saw a widespread discussion of the doctrine of Scripture, with attempts in various quarters to tighten up definitions in order to guard against what were seen as dangerous concessions to liberal thinking. Harold Lindsell was an American evangelical who wrote two widely read books, *The Battle for the Bible* and *The Bible in the Balance*, outlining what he saw as a widespread and potentially fatal declension on the part of many of his fellow academics from the affirmation of biblical inerrancy. A primary target was Fuller Seminary,[39] but other scholars in his sights included Bruce, who had written a foreword to a book by Dewey M. Beegle on *Biblical Inspiration* (of which Lindsell offered a lengthy critique) in which he referred to inerrancy as the product of a 'Maginot-line mentality'.[40] More recently, Iain Murray has claimed that Bruce's position on Scripture was suspect: he allegedly tolerated

---

[38] *IR*, p. 312.

[39] Fuller faculty had set out their position on the doctrine of Scripture in *Biblical Authority* (ed. Jack Rogers; Waco, TX: Word Books, 1977). Like Bruce, they preferred to stress the inward testimony of the Spirit as the ground on which we are convinced of biblical authority; they regarded the insistence on the term 'inerrancy' as bound up with a rationalistic approach to Scripture.

[40] Harold Lindsell, *The Battle for the Bible* (Grand Rapids, MI: Zondervan, 1977), p. 171.

rather than upheld the IVF doctrinal basis, and disapproved of evangelical intolerance of Barthian theology. The latter is certainly true (though it is debatable whether this provides sufficient grounds for asserting that Bruce's view of Scripture was suspect), but the former charge is wide of the mark: his problem was not so much with the doctrinal basis, which he happily continued to sign, but with the attempts of some to hedge it round with clarificatory terminology and to monitor subscription to it.[41]

A by-product of the debates about biblical inspiration and inerrancy was a desire on the part of many to clarify just what was meant by the term 'evangelical'. Bruce refused to couple the term 'conservative' with 'evangelical', on the grounds that it implied caution or timidity.[42] He insisted on remaining an 'unhyphenated Evangelical'.[43] And 'evangelical' included 'every one who believes in the God who justifies the ungodly'.[44] To be an evangelical was therefore about the evangel, the gospel, and did not entail adopting particular positions on issues of biblical interpretation. This led him to see some surprising people as fellow travellers:

> When I try to review as objectively as possible the movement of my mind over the years, one thing that impresses me is the increasing clarity with which I see as fundamental to my thought and life the justifying grace of God, brought near to mankind in the vicarious sacrifice of Christ and offered for acceptance by faith. I cannot remember a time when I did not hold this to be the essence of the gospel, but questions which attached themselves to it in earlier days have apparently resolved themselves out of existence. It is for this reason that I am always happy to be called an evangelical, although I insist on being an unqualified evangelical. I do not willingly answer, for example, to such a designation as 'conservative evangelical'. (Many of my positions are indeed conservative; but I hold them not because they are conservative – still less because I myself am conservative – but because I believe they

---

[41] Iain H. Murray, *Evangelicalism Divided: A Record of Crucial Change in the Years 1950 to 2000* (Edinburgh: Banner of Truth, 2000), p. 181 n.

[42] *EQ* 30 (1958): p. 131.

[43] *H* 46 (1967): p. 74: Q. 1459.

[44] *H* 58 (1979): p. 93, and elsewhere. In his view, non-evangelicals had a defective understanding of salvation and of the sovereignty of God's grace; this included any view which was expressed in terms of merit or human achievement: Ward and Laurel Gasque, 'F.F. Bruce – the Apostle Paul and the Evangelical Heritage', *H* 68/7 (July 1989): pp. 10–12, at p. 10.

are the positions to which the evidence leads.) To believe in the God who justifies the ungodly is to be evangelical. On many points of New Testament criticism I find myself differing from such post-Bultmannians as Ernst Käsemann and Günther Bornkamm, but critical differences become insignificant in the light of their firm understanding and eloquent exposition of the Pauline gospel of justification by faith, which is the very heart of evangelical Christianity. I deplore the misuse of the noble word 'evangelical' in a party sense.[45]

Bruce also manifested a remarkable degree of sympathy for the German theologian Rudolf Bultmann (1884–1976), whose name, he thought, 'ought never to be mentioned without profound respect'.[46] His nuanced understanding of Bultmann's views was evident in an article he wrote for theological students in 1966: in his view, Bultmann in his programme of 'demythologization', which sought to remove the obstacles presented to Christian faith by the mythological concepts in which the New Testament message was clothed, was not (as some claimed) trying to remove the offence of the cross, but simply to clear away that which he believed to obscure it.[47] Bruce was well aware that aspects of Bultmann's teaching could have an unhelpful effect: 'Bultmann's personal faith in the word made flesh secures his own Christian position, but for all his eagerness to enable others to share his personal faith . . . the effect of his teaching on those who have not this vital relationship with Christ can be that they are left with nothing that is distinctively Christian'.[48] His classical background and pastoral concern commended themselves to Bruce, even if the latter felt constrained to disagree with the condemnation of interest in the historical Jesus as amounting to a form of justification by works, to adopt a much more positive estimate of the historicity of the New Testament portrait of Jesus, and to draw from Bultmann's thought the moral that we need to recognize the presuppositions with which we approach the text of Scripture in order to ensure that they

---

[45] *IR*, pp. 309–10. Cf. Bruce's comment, in a letter to Bill Eerdmans Jr of 19 August 1974, that Käsemann's main fault was that he was 'more Pauline than Paul', although he 'finds his centre of gravity at the heart of the evangelical faith': Grand Rapids, Eerdmans, correspondence file, F.F. Bruce 1967–77.

[46] F.F. Bruce, *The Canon of Scripture* (Glasgow: Chapter House, 1988), p. 332.

[47] F.F. Bruce, 'Myth and the New Testament', *TSF Bulletin*, no. 44 (Spring 1966): pp. 10–15.

[48] *JTVI* 86 (1954): p. 129.

do not exercise undue influence on our understanding.[49] And so he penned an appreciative obituary of the German scholar for *The Witness*, noting that Bultmann's negative attitude to the historical evidence had led some sceptics to wonder why 'he bore firm witness to Jesus as the Word became (*sic*) flesh. The reason was not far to seek: he knew whom he had believed.'[50] What some readers would have made of the inclusion of such a figure in the magazine's obituary columns can only be guessed.

So for Bruce, an evangelical was one who embraced the grace of God offered in the gospel. But what was the gospel? He answered this most fully in an early Rylands lecture, 'When Is a Gospel Not a Gospel?'[51] In it he differentiated between true and false gospels, as Paul on occasion had to do. On the one hand he distinguished the reliable accounts of the life of Jesus found in the canonical gospels from non-canonical documents bearing the title 'Gospel' such as the *Gospel of Thomas*, which some argued offered alternative sources for understanding the life and teaching of Jesus. On the other hand he argued that a distinction between true and false gospels could be made with reference to the way in which hearers were said to benefit from the events proclaimed in them: 'The gospel which was no gospel probably did not differ from Paul's gospel with regard to the basic recital of saving events. Where it differed was with regard to the terms on which the benefits accruing from the saving events might be enjoyed.'[52] In Bruce's understanding of the New Testament evidence, a gospel was not a gospel when (i) it became detached from the Jesus of history; (ii) it gave little or no place to the passion of Christ; (iii) it exalted human achievement rather than the grace of God; (iv) it added other conditions to what God required; and (v) it treated righteousness and purity as things which those who were spiritual had outgrown. It was a gospel when (i) it maintained contact with the Jesus of history; (ii) it embraced 'the offence of the cross'; (iii) it extended grace to human beings for their acceptance by faith; (iv) it relied on the Holy Spirit to make its preaching effective to hearers;

---

[49] For a comparison of Bruce and Bultmann, see Anthony R. Cross, 'A Critical Comparison of Professor F.F. Bruce and Professor Rudolf Bultmann on the Historical Reliability of the New Testament', BA dissertation, Bristol University, 1985; idem, 'Historical Methodology and New Testament Study', *Themelios* 22/3 (April 1997): pp. 28–51.

[50] F.F. Bruce, 'Rudolf Bultmann (1884–1976)', W 107 (1977): pp. 19, 21.

[51] F.F. Bruce, 'When Is a Gospel Not a Gospel?', *BJRL* 45 (1962-3): pp. 319–39.

[52] Ibid. p. 334.

and (v) it issued in a righteous life sustained and directed by the love of God.[53]

At the heart of the Scriptures, and giving them their internal unity, was the gospel message of Jesus Christ. Bruce's fullest treatment of the way in which the Old Testament bore witness to this appeared in *This Is That*, delivered (as we saw) as a course of lectures at Fuller Seminary in 1968. As in several other volumes of his lectures, it is marked by a greater readiness to refer to, and to engage with, other scholarly perspectives in the text rather than confining such discussion to footnotes; it also shares with them the lack of a satisfactory conclusion. But it brings together a good deal of important material bearing on the topic, and takes up a theme which was to be of recurrent interest to him: the way in which the Old Testament writings were interpreted, whether by later Old Testament writers, among the Qumran community, or in the New Testament.[54] Such a theme would

---

[53] Ibid. pp. 338–9.

[54] Among his writings on this theme, see *The Sure Mercies of David: A Study in the Fulfilment of Messianic Prophecy* (London: Evangelical Library, [1954]); *The Christian Approach to the Old Testament* (London: IVF, 1955); *Biblical Exegesis in the Qumran Texts*, Exegetica 3.1 (Den Haag: Van Keulen, 1959); 'Qumran and the Old Testament', *FT* 91 (1959–60): pp. 9–27; repr. in *A Mind for What Matters* (Grand Rapids, MI: Eerdmans, 1990), pp. 32–48; 'The Book of Zechariah and the Passion Narrative', *BJRL* 43 (1960–61): pp. 336–53; 'Preparation in the Wilderness: At Qumran and in the New Testament', *Interpretation* 16 (1962): pp. 280–91, repr. in *A Mind for What Matters*, pp. 65–76; 'Promise and Fulfilment in Paul's Presentation of Jesus', in *Promise and Fulfilment: Essays Presented to Professor S.H. Hooke in Celebration of His Ninetieth Birthday . . . by Members of the Society for Old Testament Study and Others* (ed. F.F. Bruce; Edinburgh: T&T Clark, 1963), pp. 36–50; 'The Book of Daniel and the Qumran Community', in *Neotestamentica et Semitica: Essays in Honour of Matthew Black* (ed. E.E. Ellis and M. Wilcox; Edinburgh: T&T Clark, 1969), pp. 221–35; 'The Earliest Old Testament Interpretation', *Oudtestamentische Studiën* 17 (1972): pp. 37–52; 'New Wine in Old Wineskins: III. The Corner Stone', *ExT* 84 (1972–3): pp. 231–5; 'The Davidic Messiah in Luke-Acts', in *Biblical and Near Eastern Studies: Essays in Honor of William Sanford LaSor* (ed. Gary A. Tuttle; Grand Rapids, MI: Eerdmans, 1978), pp. 7–17; 'Prophetic Interpretation in the Septuagint', *Bulletin of the International Organization for Septuagint and Cognate Studies*, no. 12 (Fall 1979): pp. 17–26; repr. in *This Place Is Too Small for Us: The Israelite Prophets in Recent Scholarship* (ed. Robert P. Gordon; Winona Lake, IN: Eisenbrauns, 1995), pp. 539–46; 'The Theology and Interpretation of the Old Testament', in *Tradition and Interpretation: Essays by Members of the Society for Old Testament Study* (ed. G.W. Anderson; Oxford: Clarendon, 1979), pp. 385–416; 'The Background to the Son of Man Sayings', in *Christ the Lord: Studies in Christology Presented to Donald Guthrie*

have been of absorbing interest to Brethren, who delighted to see Christ everywhere, but what struck me when reading the book was the world of difference between his approach and the traditional Brethren or dispensationalist typological treatment of the Old Testament. Indeed, one reviewer from such a perspective described the work as 'destructive of simple faith in the Bible', alleging that the author had missed an opportunity to bear witness to the Bible as God's word.[55] Bruce explained in an essay on 'The Old Testament and the Christian' that the unity of the two testaments was not to be established by fanciful typology, but by discerning the recurring pattern of divine action and human response. And 'if the ceremonial law has been abolished in Christ we need not spend time in allegorizing its details so as to find in them some adumbration of His redemptive work'.[56]

Bruce's belief in the essential unity of the Bible and in the work of the Spirit illuminating its message led him to distinguish between the primary and plenary senses of Scripture. The primary sense was what it meant to its original writers and readers; the plenary sense was what Scripture has come to mean in the experience of God's people.[57] Thus he had an instinctive sympathy with anyone who saw the gospel as running through the whole of Scripture. In his foreword to the evangelical Adventist Desmond Ford's commentary on Daniel, Bruce wrote: 'because he strikes such an evangelical note, I am not much concerned that some aspects of his interpretation differ from mine . . . The gospel which he proclaims is the gospel which I acknowledge: may it continue to speed on and triumph!'[58]

The accumulated experience of the people of God, especially as it concerned the interpretation of Scripture, therefore lay at the heart of what Bruce understood by the concept of tradition. And he had seen enough of Brethren life to be well aware that tradition operated even in communities which claimed not to have any traditions. With his

---

(ed. Harold H. Rowdon; Leicester: IVP, 1982), pp. 50–70; 'Biblical Exposition at Qumran', in *Gospel Perspectives III: Studies in Midrash and Historiography* (ed. R.T. France and D. Wenham; Sheffield: JSOT Press, 1983), pp. 77–98.

[55] I.R. Williams, review in *BibSac* 127 (1970): pp. 270–72, at p. 272.

[56] F.F. Bruce, 'The Old Testament and the Christian', in A *Bible Commentary for Today* (ed. G.C.D. Howley et al.; Glasgow: Pickering & Inglis, 1979), pp. 19–26, at p. 23.

[57] *H* 49 (1970): p. 106: Q. 1718; cf. 'Primary Sense and Plenary Sense', *Epworth Review* 4 (1977): pp. 94–109, repr. in *The Canon of Scripture*, pp. 316–34.

[58] Foreword to Desmond Ford, *Daniel* (Nashville, TN: Southern Publishing Association, 1978), p. 6.

colleague Gordon Rupp, Bruce had edited a colloquium on the topic in 1967 and found it 'a valuable and educative exercise' which had done much to awaken his interest. To it Bruce contributed an essay on 'Scripture and Tradition in the New Testament', in which he welcomed closer Jewish-Christian co-operation arising from a shared acceptance of grammatico-historical methods of exegesis, but defended the validity of a distinctively Christian *sensus plenior* (fuller meaning) which would have grown up during centuries of reflection on the text by the Christian community.[59] He had also had his thinking stimulated by working on the epistles of John, presumably for his commentary.[60]

The theme of tradition represents a counterpoint to another topic which interested him, that of Christian liberty, and in *Tradition Old and New* he explored it at length. According to the publisher, the book did not sell well but it was influential.[61] However, it shared the main fault of most of his published lectures: he did not really draw the threads together or synthesize his judgements on specific points and so the reader does not easily gain an overview of the theme.[62]

Among the reasons he adduced for selecting this topic were current ecumenical interest,[63] the need for any teacher of biblical studies to deal with the traditionary process which produced and interpreted the canonical documents, and 'the prevalence of tradition in churches and religious movements which believed themselves to be free from its influence'.[64] Where subordinate standards governing the interpretation

---

[59] F.F. Bruce, 'Scripture and Tradition in the New Testament', in *Holy Book and Holy Tradition: International Colloquium held in the Faculty of Theology, University of Manchester* (ed. idem and E.G. Rupp; Manchester: Manchester University Press [1968]), pp. 68–93. Other writings on the topic of tradition include a series for the Canadian Brethren journal *Calling* from 1969 to 1971, and a later piece on 'Scripture in Relation to Tradition and Reason', in *Scripture, Tradition and Reason: Essays in Honour of Richard P.C. Hanson* (ed. R. Bauckham and B. Drewery; Edinburgh: T&T Clark, 1988), pp. 35–65.

[60] F.F. Bruce, 'Thoughts from My Study', *Calling* 13/1 (Spring 1971): pp. 9–11, at p. 9.

[61] Jeremy Mudditt, telephone conversation, 4 March 2009.

[62] D.J.A. Clines, review of *Tradition Old and New* in *EQ* 44 (1972): pp. 113–16, at p. 114.

[63] As evidenced in the decrees of the Second Vatican Council (1962–5) and the ecumenical Faith and Order conference at Montreal in 1963 which produced an important report on the topic: *The Fourth World Conference on Faith and Order: Montreal 1963*, Faith and Order Paper 42 (ed. P.C. Rodger and L. Vischer; London: SCM, 1964).

[64] Bruce, *Tradition Old and New*, p. v.

of the Bible were not formally recognized, they might be overlooked because they were not written down, but it was still likely that they were there in practice if not in theory. 'Indeed, in some more enclosed traditions the authority of Scripture will be identified with the authority of the accepted interpretation and application, because it has never occurred to those inside the enclosure that Scripture could be interpreted or applied otherwise.' Quoting F.W. Newman's comment that for J.N. Darby submission to the Bible amounted to submission to his interpretation of it, Bruce claimed that 'The history of the spiritual successors of the "Irish clergyman" provides an adequate commentary on the consequences of such submission.'[65] From personal experience he adduced an example which would have been equally contentious in the wider evangelical world: speaking to theological students who accepted his arguments regarding the structure, date and authorship of a particular part of the Bible, he was surprised to be informed that accepting his view would mean letting the side down. Bruce was sorry that their attitude should be called evangelical, and 'glad for my own sake that I had been brought up to subordinate tradition to evidence'.[66]

The rest of the book was less controversial. Bruce explained how the New Testament documents could be regarded as apostolic tradition in written form, and outlined the process, context and objectives of such tradition. He then looked at how interpretative tradition could arise, focusing on the development of distinct Jewish and Christian traditions of interpreting the same Hebrew Scriptures. Non-canonical traditions received suitable criteria for assessment, and the development of tradition during the early Christian centuries was analyzed. In his closing chapter, he stressed the continuity between authentic tradition and the ministry and teaching of Jesus: 'The tradition which is maintained in life by the risen Lord through the agency of His Spirit is the tradition which originates with the historical Jesus.'[67]

The development of the tradition of New Testament interpretation received attention in an essay on 'The History of New Testament Study'. His survey covers a great deal of material, majoring on the

---

[65] Ibid. p. 14. Bruce had the Exclusive Brethren, and particular those led by Jim Taylor Jr, in his sights; he often referred to them during the mid-1960s when they were attracting considerable hostile media attention.
[66] Ibid. p. 15.
[67] Ibid. p. 175.

sixteenth-century Reformers and their heirs, and he is capable of a sympathetic assessment of some surprising figures, among them Pelagius, the fifth-century opponent of Augustine, who 'has a firm grasp of the principle of justification by grace through faith' and F.C. Baur (1792–1860), often a *bête noire* of evangelical interpreters because of his imposition of a pattern of thesis, antithesis and synthesis as an interpretative framework for reading the New Testament.[68]

A more straightforward and popular presentation was 'The Bible and the Faith', originally given at a Free Church conference in Eastbourne on 23 March 1976. In this Bruce defined tradition simply as the church's family memory. In practice, he warned, allegiance to *sola scriptura* (which for the Reformers designated Scripture as supreme authority in matters of faith and practice) had all too often meant allegiance to Scripture as our tradition has interpreted it, but Scripture was a living oracle and the Spirit could well have something fresh to say from it. He suggested that the essential principle of canonicity was witness to Christ; this was what gave the biblical documents their unity. And since the Spirit's task was to bear witness to Christ, the supreme evidence for the authority of the Bible was the inner witness of the Spirit.[69]

◆   ◆   ◆

We turn now to examine some of Bruce's surveys and works on Bible background and history. An early example is *Israel and the Nations* (1963), described by Howard Mudditt as 'one of the finest books we have ever published'. But it almost failed to be published at all. It had originally been written for another publisher who rejected it as unsound. Once it was submitted to Paternoster, Mudditt mislaid the manuscript; he was steeling himself to confess to the author when he found it in a toolbox.[70] The book was based on two Sheffield lecture courses, a short one covering the period from Exodus to the Exile, and a longer one on the period from the Exile onwards, and is noteworthy for giving as much space to the intertestamental period as to that

---

[68] F.F. Bruce, 'The History of New Testament Study', in *New Testament Interpretation: Essays on Principles and Methods* (ed. I. Howard Marshall; Exeter: Paternoster/ Grand Rapids, MI: Eerdmans, 1977), pp. 21–59; quotation at p. 27. The essays in this volume originated as conference papers at Tyndale House.

[69] F.F. Bruce, 'The Bible and the Faith', *Free Church Chronicle* 31/4 (Winter 1976): pp. 8–16.

[70] B. Howard Mudditt, 'The Paternoster Story (4): "The End of the Beginnning" ', *H* 64/9 (September 1985): pp. 5–7, at p. 5; Jeremy Mudditt, telephone conversation, 4 March 2009.

covered by the Old Testament. Publication came at the request of a group of teachers of what was then known as 'Scripture' in schools, but the work was intended to serve as a prolegomenon to the Paternoster Church History series, of which Bruce was the general editor.[71] His readiness to accept the historical accuracy of the Old Testament documents provides a noticeable contrast with some other works on this area. John Bright, himself the author of a standard *History of Israel* (1959), commended the work highly; it was 'as good a thing of its scope as is available'.[72] However, one American reviewer feared that Bruce was bending over too far to be fair to liberal viewpoints, instancing his apparent acceptance of the idea that there was more than one Isaiah and of a second-century BC date for Daniel.[73]

A counterpart to *Israel and the Nations* was Bruce's *New Testament History* (1969), although this appeared from a different publisher. He dedicated the work to his colleagues in the Faculty of Theology, one of whom (H.H. Rowley) had invited him to write it. He wrote as a historian, believing that the theological implications of the documents stood out more clearly when a sound historical basis had been laid.[74] Once again, Bruce offered no challenge to the historicity or accuracy of the New Testament writings, and the footnotes are remarkable for the predominance of references to primary rather than secondary sources. Judged with hindsight, the treatment is patchy, perhaps reflecting contemporary scholarly emphases: one scholar alleged that its extensive coverage of the Jewish background contrasted with the brevity of the account of contemporary philosophical schools and the lack of discussion of pagan religion; Bruce's 1975 SNTS presidential address, he believed, 'equally fails to engage the subject'.[75] As a classicist, Bruce would have been well enough informed to do justice to

---

[71] F.F. Bruce, *Israel and the Nations from the Exodus to the Fall of the Second Temple* (Exeter: Paternoster, 1963), p. 7.

[72] John Bright to William B. Eerdmans, 6 May 1963, in the CBA copy of the American edition.

[73] Hugh J. Blair, review in *Blue Banner Faith & Life* 19/3 (July–September 1964), in the CBA copy of the 1969 illustrated reprint.

[74] F.F. Bruce, *New Testament History*, Nelson's Library of Theology (London: Oliphants, 1971), p. ix.

[75] Abraham J. Malherbe, 'Greco-Roman Religion and Philosophy and the New Testament', in *The New Testament and Its Modern Interpreters* (ed. Eldon Jay Epp and George W. MacRae; Philadelphia, PA: Fortress Press/Atlanta, GA: Scholars Press, 1989), pp. 1–26, at p. 7 n. Malherbe's approach has since become much more influential: I. Howard Marshall to the author, 8 December 2009.

the aspects which Malherbe picked up, and one assumes that he deliberately chose not to do so. Perhaps more serious was Marshall's criticism as a fellow evangelical that Bruce's writing on the New Testament did not engage enough with those who found its evidence inconsistent, loaded or less straightforward than Bruce himself did.[76]

At a more popular level, another book to emerge from the Glossop conferences was *The Message of the New Testament* (1972), which Bruce dedicated to 'the members past and present of the North Midlands Young People's Holiday Conference' as a fitting conclusion to almost thirty years' association with the gathering.[77] Intended as a complement to H.L. Ellison's *The Message of the Old Testament*, it offered a straightforward evangelical presentation of the New Testament message. Along the way Bruce pointed out the key themes and issues of interpretation for each book or group of books. It is noteworthy that his exposition was thoroughly theological in nature, a contrast to some of his commentaries.

A more apologetic work was his *Jesus and Christian Origins outside the New Testament*, which first appeared in 1974 as a volume in the 'Jesus Library' published by Hodder & Stoughton. Once again, Bruce approached the subject as a historian, arguing for the credibility of the gospels and rejecting the claim that as products of the Christian community their evidence concerning Christian origins was inadmissible. His classical background stood him in good stead as he surveyed the non-canonical literary and archaeological evidence for Jesus and the early church, and a claim to objectivity is implied by his assertion that he was not trying to prove any particular case, simply to survey the material.[78] Nevertheless, the preface, because it was answering an apologetic challenge, was perhaps more direct in its tone than much of his writing.[79] The book demonstrated that he had not lost his concern to commend the gospels (and the gospel) to non-Christians.

The most influential of Bruce's works on the Bible, however, was probably his *magnum opus, Paul* (1977). This had been twenty years in the making, much of the material having been presented piecemeal in lectures and articles over the years, a number in the *Bulletin of the John*

---

[76] Marshall, 'Bruce', p. 9; I. Howard Marshall, 'Frederick Fyvie Bruce 1910–1990', *Proceedings of the British Academy* 80 (1991): pp. 245–60, at p. 254.

[77] F.F. Bruce, *The Message of the New Testament* (Exeter: Paternoster, 1972), p. 9.

[78] F.F. Bruce, *Jesus and Christian Origins outside the New Testament*, The Jesus Library (London: Hodder & Stoughton, repr. 1984), p. 203.

[79] Ibid. pp. 13–18.

Rylands Library. The nucleus, however, was a series of lectures which formed part of the syllabus at Manchester on 'The Missionary Career of Paul in Its Historical Setting', a course which he described as 'specially congenial'. The book was thus built round a narrative approach to the subject. It did not claim to offer a systematic outline of Paul's teaching, but in the course of discussing each of his letters against their biographical and historical background Bruce sought to treat the main themes as they occurred.[80] Extensive and clear coverage of the classical, Jewish and local background was kept readable by confining the scholars' names and debates to footnotes. Bruce's adaptability is evident in the fact that he produced the chapter on Paul's personality in just a few weeks, after Peter Cousins, the editor at Paternoster, noted the absence of such a discussion. The work had wide sales, and in North America it was awarded the Evangelical Christian Publishers' Association gold medal for biography and autobiography in 1979. As with others of his books, the British and American editions came out with different covers; North American students were known to write for copies of the British dust jacket, which featured a yacht on the open sea, for use as a poster in their rooms.[81] The two editions also came out with different subtitles. In Britain, it was subtitled *Apostle of the Free Spirit*, which was the author's preference; however, the American publisher felt that this could be misunderstood because most people there would have understood 'free spirit' as a designation for a hippy or a brand of gasoline, and so it was given the subtitle *Apostle of the Heart Set Free*.[82] Tom Wright, recommending *Paul* as an introductory text, commented that it was: 'A classic biography of Paul. Clear, well laid out, with all the details you wanted to know and lots you hadn't thought of before. Only faults: somewhat unexciting, and sometimes theologically naïve.'[83] Both those have been seen as marking other works by Bruce; yet didactically speaking there is a place for solid, clear presentations such as this one. In a review for *Faith and Thought*, John Drane, while commending the book highly, nevertheless felt that the incorporation of earlier lectures made parts of it read like a volume of

---

[80] F.F. Bruce, *Paul: Apostle of the Free Spirit* (Exeter: Paternoster, rev. edn, 1980), p. 11.
[81] Jeremy Mudditt, telephone conversation, 4 March 2009.
[82] *IR*, p. 244 n. 1. When a reviewer criticized this as using the term 'heart' in an unPauline sense, Bruce consoled himself by reflecting that it had not been his doing!
[83] Tom Wright, *What Saint Paul Really Said* (Oxford: Lion, 1997), p. 186.

essays, that it lacked an overall argument, and that it failed to consider Paul's significance for the development of Christian theology.[84] John Wenham referred to an IVF reviewer as criticizing the book for its lack of detailed consideration of doctrines such as atonement, election, Scripture and apostolic authority. It presented Paul's teaching as the developing thought of an apostle which arose from his experience of Christ, rather than as divinely inspired truth, and tended to reach conservative conclusions on liberal assumptions.[85] I think many of these issues resulted from Bruce's choice of a narrative framework; certainly they should not necessarily be extrapolated to his thought or his writing as a whole. More serious criticisms, however, were the claim that Bruce was too negative in his discussion of Paul and the law, and the weakness of the book's coverage of life in the Spirit.[86] The latter is especially surprising, given Bruce's wish to give full place to other aspects of the Spirit's work, such as the inspiration and illumination of Scripture.

If Bruce could have written only one book, it would have been this one. He began the introduction by explaining why he found Paul so fascinating:

> No excuse is offered for the publication of yet another book on Paul save the excuse offered by the second-century author of the *Acts of Paul*: it was written *amore Pauli*, for love of Paul. For half a century and more I have been a student and teacher of ancient literature, and to no other writer of antiquity have I devoted so much time and attention as to Paul. Nor can I think of any other writer, ancient or modern, whose study is so richly rewarding as his. This is due to several aspects of his many-faceted character: the attractive warmth of his personality, his intellectual stature, the exhilarating release effected by his gospel of redeeming grace, the dynamism with which he propagated that gospel throughout the world, devoting himself single mindedly to fulfilling

---

[84] *FT* 105 (1978): pp. 140–3.

[85] John Wenham, *Facing Hell: An Autobiography 1913–1996* (Carlisle: Paternoster, 1998), pp. 195–6.

[86] David H. Campbell, review of *Paul* in *Themelios* 4 (1978–9): pp. 78–9. On Bruce, Paul and the law, see Greg A. Couser, 'The Law in Galatians: A Comparison of Bruce and Paul', MA dissertation, Liberty University, Lynchburg, VA, 1988 http://digital-commons.liberty.edu/cgi/viewcontent.cgi?article=1034&context=masters (accessed 3 December 2009). Couser's main argument is that Bruce's commentary on Galatians (on which see ch. 9) is unduly negative in its treatment of Paul and the law.

the commission entrusted to him on the Damascus road ('this one thing I do') and labouring more abundantly than all his fellow-apostles – 'yet not I, but the grace of God which was with me'. My purpose in writing this book, then, is to share with others something of the rich reward which I myself have reaped from the study of Paul.[87]

A clue to the perspective offered is provided by the quotation on the title page: 'Where the Spirit of the Lord is, there the heart is free' (2 Cor. 3:17, Basic English Version).[88] For Bruce, Paul was pre-eminently the apostle of liberty: 'Time and again, when the gospel has been in danger of being fettered and disabled in the bonds of legalism or out-worn tradition, it has been the words of Paul that have broken the bonds and set the gospel free to exert its emancipating power once more in the life of mankind.'[89] Small wonder that, as in his Romans commentary, he included a section on figures in church history who had been influenced by Paul.[90] Indeed, he even asserted that the sec-ond-century heretic Marcion had grasped the heart of Paul's gospel of free grace in a way that his more orthodox opponents had not.[91] Bruce's emphasis on liberty and flexibility in church life, then, sprang not from some kind of woolly liberalism but from the way in which he had been gripped by the message of Paul, who 'was persuaded that the freedom of the Spirit was a more powerful incentive to the good life than all the ordinances or decrees in the world'.[92]

---

[87] Bruce, *Paul*, p.15.

[88] He had quoted this translation of the verse as long ago as 1955: *H* 34 (1955): pp. 90–91. The theme of Christian freedom was the one he chose for his University Sermon at the Church of St Mary the Virgin in Oxford on 18 February 1979, his text being Gal. 5:1.

[89] Bruce, *Paul*, p. 470.

[90] Ibid. pp. 470–74.

[91] Ibid. p. 20. Because of his belief that the gospel was one of love to the exclusion of anything which savoured of law, Marcion had rejected the Old Testament (and the God portrayed by it) and all of the New except for Paul's letters (apart from the Pastorals) and an edited version of Luke.

[92] Ibid. p. 187. One of Bruce's earliest expositions of this theme was a little-known article in a periodical edited by G.H. Lang: 'Children of God and Sons of God', *The Disciple* 3 (1956–7): pp. 162–5 (photographic reprint, Miami Springs, FL: Conley & Schoettle, 1984). There he argued that 'children of God' referred to relationship, and 'sons of God' to status. Many children of God, he asserted, did not enjoy con-sciousness of their sonship or experience the ongoing leading of the Spirit, living instead by rules and regulations. 'Those who are children of God by the new birth,

That being so, Bruce had no time for the caricature of Paul, found in some scholars and popularizers of the day, as the one who turned the religion of Jesus into a set of rules and regulations and founded the institutional church. For him, Paul and Jesus were in the closest continuity, a conviction which he expounded in *Paul and Jesus* (1974).

> The authentic Paul is Paul the preacher of emancipation, Paul who announced the replacement of the yoke of legal bondage by the freedom of the Spirit, Paul who proclaimed that men had come of age in Christ and refused to let religion be treated any more as a matter of rules and regulations such as befitted the apron-string stage of their spiritual development, Paul whose insistence that in Christ there is neither male nor female entitles him to be recognized as the patron-saint of women's liberation, Paul the author of that great hymn in praise of love, Paul whose 'genius for friendship' has become a proverb – almost a cliché.[93]

This emphasis explains two of his favourite quotations. One was from the Scottish lay theologian Thomas Erskine (1788–1870): 'In the New Testament, religion is grace and ethics is gratitude'.[94] The other was from Martin Luther's *Freedom of a Christian Man*: 'A Christian is a most free lord of all, subject to none; a Christian is a most dutiful servant of all, subject to all.'[95]

Two contentious issues in particular surfaced in *Paul*, whose wide circulation brought these to the attention of some readers for the first time.[96] It so happened that both were deemed important in Brethren

---

and consequently possess eternal life, are also sons of God ideally (in terms of God's purpose for them). It is for them to become sons of God in reality, by accepting and standing fast in the freedom with which Christ has set them free, and by following the daily leading of His Spirit': ibid. p. 165.

[93] F.F. Bruce, *Paul and Jesus* (London: SPCK, 1977), p. 12.

[94] Bruce, *Message of the New Testament*, p. 31; *1 and 2 Corinthians*, New Century Bible (London: Oliphants, 1971), p. 198; *Paul and Jesus*, p. 54; *Paul*, p. 19; *1 & 2 Thessalonians*, Word Biblical Commentary, vol. 45 (Waco, TX: Word, 1982), p. 127; *The Epistles to the Colossians, Philemon and Ephesians*, NICNT (Grand Rapids, MI: Eerdmans, 1984), p. 49.

[95] Bruce, *1 and 2 Corinthians*, p. 86; *Paul*, p. 202.

[96] Oddly enough, a third issue appears not to have been noticed: Bruce considered that Paul's attitude to his opponents had mellowed appreciably between 2 Cor. 10:1 and Phil. 1:15–18, and at least implied that Paul's earlier outlook was reprehensible: *Paul*, pp. 390–91.

circles. One was that of women and ministry, which we shall consider later; he claimed that 'The mainstream churches of
Christendom, as they inch along towards a worthier recognition of
the ministry of women, have some way to go yet before they come
abreast of Paul.'[97] The other concerned Bruce's suggestion that Paul
changed his views on the imminence of the Second Coming, early
writings being marked by a belief that it was likely to occur within a
few years, and later ones by a more agnostic outlook on that particular question. Paul's change of mind occurred between writing 1 and 2
Corinthians, after facing what looked like the prospect of certain
death; hence his consideration of the intermediate state in 2
Corinthians 5 and his conclusion that believers would receive their
resurrection body then rather than at the Second Coming.[98] Bruce saw
no problem with this; he was not saying that Paul had made any erroneous statements, nor was his view inherently contradictory to a view
of Scripture such as that enshrined in the UCCF (formerly IVF) doctrinal basis. As he explained elsewhere:

> Because the resurrection hope, for Paul, was grounded in the saving
> work of Christ, the question *when* it would be realized was of secondary
> importance. He nowhere claims to know the time of the expected
> Advent of Christ, so he could not know whether he would be alive or
> not when it took place. If, in his earlier letters, he associates himself with
> those who will survive to the great event and, in his later letters, with
> those who will then be raised from the dead, this was a natural shift in
> perspective arising from advancing years and changing circumstances.

[97] Ibid. p. 457.
[98] Ibid. ch. 27, esp. p. 310; for an earlier statement of this argument see his Drew
Lecture on Immortality, 'Paul on Immortality', *Scottish Journal of Theology* 24 (1971):
pp. 457–72. Earlier, however, he had expressed his agreement with the teaching of
the Westminster Shorter Catechism, that the soul was glorified at death and the
body at the final resurrection: *W* 90 (1960): p. 226. When Bruce wrote Paul, it was
widely believed that the early Christians expected the Second Coming imminently
and so they had to account for its delay, with the consequence that increasing
emphasis was given to questions of church order; cf. his 'Exiles in an Alien World',
in *Understanding the Bible: The New Testament*, The Catholic Layman's Library, vol.
2: (ed. John P. Bradley and John Quinlan, Gastonia, NC: Good Will Publishers,
1970), pp. 265–301, at p. 272. Such a view has been challenged in more recent
decades: Neill and Wright, *Interpretation of the New Testament*, pp. 377–8. Bruce himself had rejected it in an early article: 'The Second Coming of Christ', *Supplement to
the I.V.F. Graduates' Fellowship News-Letter*, no. 17 (January 1946).

The shift in perspective involved no change in eschatological faith and no diminution of hope. The so-called 'delay of the parousia' was no problem for Paul.[99]

Bruce's commentaries were rather more straightforward and less provocative in the interpretations they advanced. In them, and the exegetical articles which often appeared as spin-offs, he demonstrated his ability to write in a variety of genres and series, aimed at very different audiences. Yet he insisted that this made little essential difference, for the meaning of the text remained the same whatever the audience.[100] Evidence of his ability to write for a nonspecialist audience is provided by *The Epistle to the Ephesians: A Verse-by-Verse Exposition* (1961). This began life as a series of articles for a Brethren magazine, *Knowing the Scriptures*, beginning in 1955; when it ceased publication, the series was taken over by *The Believer's Magazine*. Based on his beloved Revised Version, the treatment is straightforward and makes more use than some of his more technical commentaries of illustrative material, quoting hymns[101] and using events in Brethren history by way of application.[102] Works quoted or commended include several Puritan classics: the Westminster Shorter Catechism, Henry Scougal's *Life of God in the Soul of Man* (Scougal's connection with Aberdeen may

---

[99] Bruce, *1 & 2 Thessalonians*, p. 105 (on 1 Thess. 4:13–18). Oliver Barclay criticized Bruce on this point, claiming that he considered that Paul had been in error: *Evangelicalism in Britain 1935–1995: A Personal Sketch* (Leicester: IVP, 1997), p. 129. Oakes, however, considers such a charge unfair: 'Bruce', p. 116. Even if Bruce had considered Paul in error, it would have presented no problems for his view of Scripture, which stressed fitness for purpose: as Bruce himself had explained, the delay did not cause Paul to modify his theology significantly but merely affected his personal expectation of being alive when it happened: 'St Paul in Macedonia: 3. The Philippian Correspondence', *BJRL* 63 (1980–81): pp. 260–84, at p. 279.

[100] *IR*, pp. 279–80.

[101] F.F. Bruce, *The Epistle to the Ephesians: A Verse-by-Verse Exposition* (London: Pickering and Inglis, 2nd edn, 1968), pp. 71, 103, 108, 123, 152. This habit marked many of his commentaries and betokened their significance in shaping his personal spirituality. One of his favourite hymnwriters was Charles Wesley, and other eighteenth-century evangelical hymnists also appear in his books. However, he did not show similar appreciation of the Sankey-type gospel hymns which so many assemblies loved to sing, nor did he often quote hymns by Brethren writers.

[102] Ibid. p. 98.

have predisposed Bruce to commend it),[103] William Gurnall's
Christian in Complete Armour, and Bunyan's *Pilgrim's Progress*, as
well as *The Screwtape Letters* by C.S. Lewis. Bruce evidently found
in the Puritans a rich vein of spiritual writing, although there is
less evidence that he utilized their commentaries. His love of
Galatians and Romans, with their stress on the doctrine of justification by faith, is well known; but for him Paul's thought had
another focus as well as that one, the corporate and cosmic dimension of redemption expounded in Colossians and Ephesians.[104]

Another popular exposition was *The Epistles of John: Introduction,
Exposition and Notes* (1970). This also first saw the light of day as a
series of magazine articles, in this case in *The Witness* during 1967–8
(hence its publication by Pickering & Inglis in a companion format to
his volume on Ephesians). In revising them for publication in book
form, Bruce added some notes for degree students, aware that even
they would have recourse to such works as this. Based on the Revised
Version, which he always considered the best English version for
close study of the text, it offered a straightforward exposition of the
text rather than extensive discussion of the secondary literature,
although he was not afraid to recommend works by Schnackenburg
and Bultmann in the bibliography. Although much of the work was
somewhat pedestrian, it came to life in certain places, most strikingly
when Bruce commented on worldliness. In his view, this was a matter of the heart (many Brethren judged – and condemned – by out-
ward appearances); the pietist outlook usually failed to denounce the
sort of worldliness which represented unthinking acquiescence in evil
policies, and needed to be challenged on that score:

> If, in a world where the richer nations tend to become richer and the
> poorer to become poorer, the administration of a richer nation makes fur-
> ther increases in economic prosperity a major plank in its platform, the
> Christian – especially, perhaps, the Christian who prefers to remain as
> detached as possible from political responsibility – must be constantly

---

[103] Scougal (1650–78) was minister of Auchterless, then Professor of Divinity at King's
College, Aberdeen. What Bruce often quoted was his insistence that true religion is
about Christ being formed in us: Henry Scougal, *The Life of God in the Soul of Man*
(Harrisonburg, VA: Sprinkle Publications, 1986), p. 34; cf. F.F. Bruce, *The Gospel of
John* (Basingstoke: Pickering Paperbacks), p. 338 n. (on John 17:22–3).
[104] Bruce, *Ephesians*, p. 15. He made a similar point in a more technical treatment,
Colossians, Philemon and Ephesians, p. 29 n. 119.

vigilant lest his own life reflect the unadmitted assumptions underlying such a policy. To share political, social or economic presuppositions which are inconsistent with the Father's love is one form of worldliness.[105]

John's 'lust of the flesh', 'lust of the eyes' and 'pride of life' amounted, in Bruce's opinion, to straightforward materialism. It is not often that we find such social critique in Bruce's writings, but he knew his audience and his point was well made. Another form of worldliness was, he asserted, the adaptation of the gospel to some contemporary outlook, or identifying God's interests with those of a particular organization.

Pitched at a level between works such as these and the technical commentaries on Acts was Bruce's volume on Romans, which appeared in 1963 as one of the Tyndale New Testament Commentaries. It had earlier been suggested that he be asked to write the commentary on Matthew in the same series, but his name was not taken up at that point because of his other commitments and because of a slight doubt as to whether his style would be appropriate. However, the IVF realized (or were advised) that he could adapt, and so he was added to the list of potential contributors.[106] In spite of his aspirations to objectivity, his love of Paul and of the Pauline message meant that this commentary was marked not so much by objectivity as by a desire that his readers should share Paul's experience of being justified through faith in Christ alone, and he concluded a discussion of 'The Influence of Romans' on various figures in church history with the words:

> There is no telling what may happen when people begin to study the Epistle to the Romans. What happened to Augustine, Luther, Wesley and Barth launched great spiritual movements which have left their mark in world history. But similar things have happened, much more frequently, to very ordinary people as the words of this Epistle came home to them with power. So, let those who have read thus far be prepared for the consequences of reading further: you have been warned![107]

---

[105] F.F. Bruce, *The Epistles of John: Introduction, Exposition and Notes* (London: Pickering & Inglis, 1970), p. 61 (on 1 John 2:15–17).

[106] Tyndale House, Box 19, Correspondence of Andrew F. Walls, Ronald Inchley to Walls, 17 January 1955.

[107] F.F. Bruce, *The Epistle to the Romans*, TNTC (London: Tyndale Press, 1963), p. 60, cf. his appeal to the experience of many believers: ibid. p. 141 (on 6:15–23).

An 'argument' summarized the message of the epistle,[108] and the commentary itself combined close exegesis of the Greek with practical and devotional application, spiced with quotations from hymns.[109] As far as the theology of the epistle is concerned, Bruce's reading of it seems to have been broadly within the Reformed tradition: he stressed the continuity of God's purposes of grace throughout human history, and he turned to the Westminster Shorter Catechism for summary definitions of two key terms, justification and effectual calling.[110] But a hint of a wider perspective is given by his assertion that the created order, as well as humanity, was in need of redemption, and his musing about what the impact of a fully redeemed humanity might be upon creation.[111] Bruce's insistence on liberty did not mean discounting the sensitivities of others and claiming at all costs the right to spiritual self-expression; as he wrote on Romans 14:1–12, 'Never was there a Christian more thoroughly emancipated from un-Christian inhibitions and taboos. So completely emancipated was he from spiritual bondage that he was not even in bondage to his emancipation.'[112]

One of his more influential commentaries was that on Hebrews, which appeared in the New International series (New London in Britain) in 1964. This was the first to appear under Bruce as series editor, and in his dedication and editorial foreword he pays tribute to his predecessor, Ned Stonehouse, who had invited him to work on the epistle as far back as June 1954.[113] The commentary sometimes lacks theological discussion just where one would look for it, e.g. on the humanity of Christ in relation to Hebrews 4:14–16.[114] But his freedom from the interpretative constraints (as he saw them) imposed by most forms of systematic theology meant that at other points he could allow the text to speak for itself, as in his treatment of the warning passages (Hebrews 6:4–6; 10:26–31), in which he

---

[108] Ibid. pp. 60–65.

[109] Ibid. pp. 103, 126, 131, 139, 141, 162, 170, 175.

[110] Ibid. pp. 103, 176.

[111] Ibid. pp. 168–9 (on Rom. 8:18–30).

[112] Ibid. p. 243.

[113] F.F. Bruce, *The Epistle to the Hebrews*, NLCNT (London: Marshall, Morgan & Scott, 1965), pp. xi–xii.

[114] For his articles on the letter's theology, see 'The Kerygma of Hebrews', *Interpretation* 23 (1969): pp. 3–19; 'The Structure and Argument of Hebrews', *Southwestern Journal of Theology* 28/1 (Fall 1985): pp. 6–12.

considered that apostasy was regarded as a real possibility, even for true believers.[115]

A feature of this commentary was the four-page summary of its argument, evidence of his concern to communicate the epistle's essential message.[116] Another manifestation of that concern was his frequent recourse to hymn quotations from a range of the evangelical classics, and the pastoral tone of his comments on Hebrews 6:4–6, a passage which has always been one of the most problematic for evangelicals giving spiritual counsel to troubled souls.[117] A wide range of authors were laid under tribute, from Søren Kierkegaard and Thomas Mann through George Adam Smith and the Westminster Shorter Catechism to Brethren such as Robert Anderson and W.W. Fereday.

Hebrews was an epistle which lay close to Bruce's heart,[118] although perhaps not for quite the same reasons which endeared it to Brethren of a more traditional stamp. They tended to major on its typological significance, showing how it expounded Christ as the one who had fulfilled the types and shadows of the Tabernacle and the Law of Moses. Bruce, however, rejected this as a mode of interpretation:

> There is one interpretative tradition which by allegorization seeks – and finds – analogies in the minutest details of the sacrificial regulations and tabernacle arrangements to the work of Christ on earth and now in heaven. I need mention only Andrew Bonar's *Commentary on Leviticus* or C.H. Mackintosh's *Notes on the Pentateuch* to illustrate what I have in mind. One difficulty I have with this approach is that, in the absence of exegetical controls, it encourages unfettered fantasy. If a preacher chooses to employ some aspect of these prescriptions to illustrate a point he wishes to make in expounding the gospel, good and well. But if he says, or implies, that this was God's intention in giving these instructions to Moses and Aaron, I must part company with him.[119]

---

[115] Cf. Bruce, *Gospel of John*, p. 332 (on 17:11–12), where he saw it as a possibility even for those given by the Father to the Son – Judas being the prime example.

[116] Bruce, *Hebrews*, pp. xix–xxii.

[117] Ibid. pp. 118–19, 122, 124.

[118] He had already contributed an exposition of the epistle to *Peake's Commentary on the Bible* (ed. Matthew Black and H.H. Rowley; London: Thomas Nelson, 1962), pp. 1008–19.

[119] F.F. Bruce, *The Time is Fulfilled: Five Aspects of the Fulfilment of the Old Testament in the New* (Exeter: Paternoster, 1978), pp. 87–8. Andrew Bonar was a nineteenth-century Church of Scotland minister whose commentaries were popular among Reformed circles, while C.H. Mackintosh (1820–96) popularized the teaching of J.N. Darby in a series of expository works.

Hebrews, he explained, stressed the contrasts between the old order and that inaugurated by Christ, not the analogies.[120] More congenial to him than such allegorizing was the use of parallels from the Qumran literature to provide illumination concerning the author's meaning.

In *The Apostolic Defence of the Gospel*, he had offered a challenging summary of the letter's contemporary relevance:

> Christians are Christians by virtue of certain acts of God which took place at a definite time in the past, but these acts of God have released a dynamic force which will never allow Christians to stay put or stick in the mud. The faith once for all delivered to the saints is not something which we can catch and tame; it is something which is always leading us forth to new ventures in the cause of Christ, as God calls afresh . . . To stay at the point to which some revered teacher of the past brought us, out of a mistaken sense of loyalty to him; to continue to follow a certain pattern of religious activity just because it was good enough for our fathers and grandfathers – these and the like are temptations which make the message of Hebrews a necessary and salutary one for us to listen to. Every new movement of the Spirit of God tends to become stereotyped in the next generation, and what we have heard with our ears, what our fathers have told us, becomes a tenacious tradition encroaching on the allegiance which ought to be accorded only to the living and active Word of God.[121]

He used almost identical words in the conclusion to his commentary.[122] Furthermore, he argued that 'true religion or the worship of God is not tied to externalities of any kind. Our author is insisting on the inwardness of true religion, on the necessity of a purified conscience'.[123]

As with most Brethren of the time, Pentecostalism had not featured on Bruce's radar, and arguably he never came to terms with the charismatic movement; temperamentally, too, he was disinclined to such non-rational expressions of spirituality.[124] As he commented to one friend, speaking in tongues was 'all right for those who want

---

[120] Bruce, *Message of the New Testament*, p. 91.
[121] F.F. Bruce, *The Apostolic Defence of the Gospel* (London: IVF, 1959), p. 85.
[122] Bruce, *Hebrews*, p. 416.
[123] Ibid. pp. xi–xii, cf. p. 196 (on Heb. 9:9). Elsewhere he had suggested that even the sacraments may have been regarded as externals: 'Hebrews, Epistle to the', in *The Zondervan Pictorial Encyclopedia of the Bible* (5 vols; ed. Merrill C. Tenney; Grand Rapids, MI: Zondervan, 1975).
[124] Cf. *H* 43 (1964): p. 154: Q. 1224.

to do it; I've never felt the need. I'm very happy with the Lord.'[125] His lack of experience of such things helps us to understand his commentary on the letters to the Corinthians, which appeared in the New Century Bible series in 1971. In length (or rather brevity) it is comparable to his work on Romans, but it is slightly more technical. By the time it appeared, the charismatic movement had made quite an impact on British evangelicalism, and so his comments on the gift of tongues would have been of more than ordinary interest. He regarded it as resulting from the stimulation of a certain area in the brain, and thus not supernatural in itself; what mattered was the source of this stimulation and the content of the utterance.[126] Bruce contended that the fruit of the Spirit was more important than the gifts,[127] and he cited the renowned historian of the early church, Henry Chadwick, to the effect that in 1 Corinthians 14 Paul was pouring cold water on the gift although he could not deny that it was supernatural.[128] Modern tongues might give rise to a sense of religious exaltation, but utterances needed to be intelligible in order to edify the mind.[129] Overemphasis on tongues was, Bruce felt, evidence of spiritual immaturity.[130] And to those who held up the Corinthian church as a model to follow (Brethren as well as charismatics), he pointed out that 'The Corinthian church of the first century is a perpetual reminder to us that Christianity in the apostolic age was not marked by ideal unity and purity from which later generations declined.'[131] The commentary was too brief to allow him to do justice to two lengthy epistles, but it proved quite popular and was reprinted on several occasions up to 1996. All the same, the fairly cerebral approach to Christian spirituality which it espoused, and which was not untypical of Brethren during the mid-twentieth century, must have limited his influence among that segment of progressive Brethrenism which was opening up to charismatic phenomena. Bruce always refused to argue a cessationist

---

[125] Betty Buckley, interview, 28 May 2008.

[126] Bruce, *1 and 2 Corinthians*, p. 117 (on 1 Cor. 12:1–2).

[127] Ibid. p. 124 (on 1 Cor. 13).

[128] Ibid. p. 130 (on 1 Cor. 14:5). Chadwick's article, based on a paper given to the *SNTS* in 1954, was one to which he found himself returning time and again in his work on Paul: *IR*, pp. 192–3. Bruce summarized it as making the case that Paul went as far as he could in agreeing with his opponents before offering a qualification which sometimes was so radical as to undercut their entire position.

[129] Ibid. p. 131 (on 1 Cor. 14:13–17).

[130] Ibid. p. 132 (on 1 Cor. 14:20).

[131] Ibid. p. 256 (conclusion).

position, though: back in 1957 he had written that in history such phenomena tended to appear at the beginning of fresh movements of the
Holy Spirit, as when the gospel was brought to an area for the first
time. Tests to apply included what they said of Christ; whether they
served to build up the hearers; and whether their exercise was
marked by decency and order.[132] And in 1964 he had asserted that the
gifts all remained available wherever conditions reproduced those of
the apostolic age.[133] On one occasion he applied Paul's strictures on
uninterpreted tongues more widely: 'The strange sounds need not be
the result of speaking with tongues; they can be the product of our
peculiar jargon which is meaningless to outsiders, and not all that
meaningful to those inside!'[134]

It may be a surprise to some that not all Bruce's writing projects
resulted in publication. One project which failed to see the light of day
was a commentary on Ezekiel, to which Bruce referred during 1960.[135]
He had written on the book in 1951 for the *Scripture Union Bible Study
Notes*, and there exists a notebook in which he pasted and extensively annotated the relevant pages, but his only other writing on it
was the section in *A Bible Commentary for Today*, published in 1979.[136]
Another involved contributions to a history of Jewish biblical exegesis being edited by Raphael Loewe for Cambridge University Press.
During 1970 and 1971 Bruce was working on exegesis in the Dead Sea
Scrolls, the significance of the Septuagint and other Greek versions,
and the interpretation of the Old Testament in the Apocrypha and
pseudepigrapha. Although the book itself never appeared, the work
on the Septuagint at least was recycled in later articles, and some of
the work on the Scrolls may have been also. A third project was a
multi-volume history of Israel, on which he was advising Paternoster
around 1975; only one volume of this ever appeared, David Payne's
Kingdoms of the Lord (1980), although several had been assigned to
contributors. He also contributed to a volume of *Documents from New
Testament Times*, which was under way by 1962 but finally abandoned
three decades later because of the impossibility of securing contributors to deal with one key topic.[137]

---

[132] *H* 36 (1957): p. 27: Q. 551.
[133] *H* 43 (1964): p. 123: Q. 1215.
[134] *Daily Notes*, July–September 1965, for 16 August (on 1 Cor. 14:20–40).
[135] *H* 39 (1960): p. 75: Q. 866.
[136] F. F. Bruce, 'Ezekiel', in Howley et al., eds, *Bible Commentary for Today*.
[137] Noble, *Tyndale*, p. 141; cf. Alan Millard to the author, 1 October 2009.

◆　◆　◆

We turn now to the editorial work which Bruce undertook, and the publications which resulted from it. From 1956 to 1978 he was one of about fifty consulting editors to a fairly new American evangelical periodical, *Christianity Today*, which seems to have been intended as a counterpart to the well-established but theologically liberal *Christian Century*. His post appears to have been rather a nominal one, doubtless intended to lend respectability to the new venture; the magazine's archives showed only that during the early years he answered – in fifty words! – a question put to him each year as one of a panel of religious scholars.[138] The answers may be brief, but they provide further evidence of his concern to see the churches committed to the spread of the gospel. In 1959, asked what the most vital issue facing contemporary Christianity was, he thought it 'the urgent necessity for all who profess and call themselves Christians, in west and east alike, to be <u>real</u> Christians, wholeheartedly committed to the cause of Christ in the world and ready to embrace the conditions which He laid down for those who wished to be His disciples'. Two years later he was asked about the most prevalent false gods in contemporary life; he thought that they were:

> the 'status symbols' cherished by Christians and non-Christians alike. On the personal level some of them may seem harmless enough, but their pursuit absorbs much of the energy which should be devoted to the extension of Christ's kingdom. On the national and international level they are too often the very things that threaten the annihilation of mankind; yet their fatal attraction obscures a proper recognition of the things which belong to our peace.

And in 1962, asked what he saw as the chief obstacle to Christian advance, he responded: 'The chief obstacle is Christian reluctance to advance, to leave the comfortable security of the familiar and traditional for the insecurity of the revolutionary and unknown. If Christians showed half the resolution and dedication in the interests of the Kingdom of God that Communists exhibit in the promotion of their cause, the scale of Christian advance would be transformed out of

---

[138] For the development of *Christianity Today*, see Carl F. H. Henry, *Confessions of a Theologian: An Autobiography* (Waco, TX: Word, 1986).

recognition.'[139] He did, however, contribute essays to three volumes edited by the magazine's editor, Carl Henry, on 'Archaeological Confirmation of the New Testament', 'The Person of Christ: Incarnation and Virgin Birth' and 'History and the Gospel', although the third article had first been delivered as a lecture in 1962 and then appeared in another publication.[140]

Several series of books also had Bruce as an editor. From 1961 to 1965 he served as joint editor with William Barclay for a series of Bible Guides published in Britain by Lutterworth Press. Bruce and Barclay were longstanding friends, and both had been elected to membership of the SNTS in 1948. They shared an evangelical background, a classical training and an extensive wider ministry which included writing. Both sought to communicate the best results of contemporary scholarship to ordinary people. Neither had earned a doctorate.[141] This co-operation earned Bruce public criticism in a sermon by Lloyd-Jones at Westminster Chapel in November 1962, because he had signed the IVF doctrinal basis and yet was prepared to work with one whose views were far different.[142] However, Bruce's view was that 'Willie loves the Lord, and that's enough for me', as he put it to one student around that time.[143] After Barclay's death, Bruce described him as possessing 'some of the essential qualities of sainthood',[144] and in an obituary for *The Witness* he quoted Howard Mudditt's description of Barclay as a liberal who loved the Lord, something some at

---

[139] Wheaton, IL, Archives of the Billy Graham Center, Collection 008 (Christianity Today Archives), Bruce to David E. Kucharsky, 14 September 1959, 25 September 1961 and 5 September 1962.

[140] F.F. Bruce, 'Archaeological Confirmation of the New Testament', in *Revelation and the Bible* (ed. C.F.H. Henry; Grand Rapids, MI: Baker, 1958/London: Tyndale Press, 1959), pp. 317–31; 'The Person of Christ: Incarnation and Virgin Birth', *CT*, 13 October 1961, pp. 30–31, repr. in *Basic Christian Doctrines* (ed. C.F.H. Henry; New York: Holt, Rinehardt & Winston, 1962), pp. 124–30; 'History and the Gospel', *FT* 93 (1964): pp. 121–45, rev. edn in *Jesus of Nazareth: Saviour and Lord* (ed. C.F.H. Henry; Grand Rapids, MI: Eerdmans/London: Tyndale Press, 1966), pp. 89–107.

[141] Clive Rawlins, *William Barclay: The Authorized Biography* (Grand Rapids, MI: Eerdmans, 1984), pp. 349, 553, 760.

[142] Iain H. Murray, *D. Martyn Lloyd-Jones: The Fight of Faith 1939–1981* (Edinburgh: Banner of Truth, 1990), p. 443.

[143] Jean Angell, telephone conversation, 4 July 2008.

[144] Rawlins, *Barclay*, p. 85: Bruce to Rawlins, 15 December 1979. The episode raises the issue of what Bruce would have regarded as the minimum Christological confession necessary for fellowship.

least of his readers would have thought impossible.[145] In any case, the editorship of this series entailed little work, simply the submission of a list of potential writers to the publisher, who produced his own after consulting with the American co-publisher.[146] Bruce also contributed a volume to the series, *Paul and His Converts: 1 and 2 Thessalonians, 1 and 2 Corinthians* (1962). It offered non-technical exposition, section by section, of each book, with a concluding section on their 'power' (i.e. their abiding message). It was reissued in 1985 with an additional chapter covering Philippians.[147]

A major series of commentaries which Bruce edited from 1962 until shortly before his death was the New International Commentaries on the New Testament. As series editor, he commissioned writers and read their manuscripts with close attention to detail.[148] His predecessor, Ned Stonehouse (1902–62), who taught at Westminster Theological Seminary in Philadelphia, had preferred to invite writers from the Reformed traditions, but Bruce broadened things out considerably, inviting such scholars as the Methodist Howard Marshall (on the letters of John) and the Pentecostal Gordon Fee (on 1 Corinthians). In the preface to his commentary on Hebrews, the first to appear during his tenure of the editorship, Bruce assured readers that the aim of the series remained to interpret the New Testament in accordance with the best standards of Reformed scholarship, but as with his editorship of *Evangelical Quarterly* there was a shift to a more exegetical or inductive approach: he insisted that the Bible was to be used as a source for theology rather than interpreted in line with a particular theological system.[149]

A lesser-known series which he edited was the Paternoster Church History;[150] again, it was his responsibility to select and invite writers, and we may surmise that it was because a Scot of Reformed convictions was editing the series that it should have included a volume on the seventeenth-century Covenanters, *Light in the North*, by J.D. Douglas (1964). In his foreword, however, Bruce defended the allocation of a volume to this movement on the grounds that it brought out

---

[145] F.F. Bruce, 'William Barclay (1907–78)', *W* 108 (1978): pp. 114–15.

[146] *IR*, p. 266; Rawlins, *Barclay*, p. 554: Bruce to Rawlins, 15 December 1979.

[147] F.F. Bruce, *Paul and His Converts: How Paul Nurtured the Churches He Planted* (Downers Grove, IL: IVP / Crowborough: Highland Books, 1985).

[148] Cf. the tribute paid by Robert H. Mounce, *The Book of Revelation*, NICNT (Grand Rapids, MI: Eerdmans, 1977), p. 13.

[149] Bruce, *Hebrews*, p. ix.

[150] *IR*, p. 267.

a recurrent issue in church history, the relationship between church and state.[151]

We saw earlier that the first attempt by members of the BRC to produce a Bible dictionary foundered, but by 1957 another attempt was under way, and the *New Bible Dictionary* appeared in 1962 to widespread acclaim. Edited by Douglas, Bruce had been one of four consulting editors. Apart from contributing a number of articles, he had had to read all those on Bible topics as manuscripts and again at the proof stage, checking not only the accuracy and quality of scholarship but also their compatibility with the IVF doctrinal basis.[152] He would also serve as a consulting editor for its successor, the three-volume *Illustrated Bible Dictionary*, which appeared in 1980. Bruce and Douglas worked well together: when it was learned that Douglas's name would not appear on the title page, Bruce wrote to the publisher to insist that it should – and, moreover, that it should be placed first, given the importance of his role in the project; Douglas also recalled that Bruce 'had so often covered up for my ignorance' on biblical topics.[153]

◆   ◆   ◆

In 1975, Bruce reached Question 2000 of his 'Answers to Questions' page, whereupon he demitted his charge. He stopped at that point because it was a good one at which to stop, and because he did not wish to go on and then leave the editor in the lurch (perhaps by dying, as his predecessor had done).[154] He did not always enjoy the work, as he explained to Trenchard: 'the page is a bit of a bind at times; and you wouldn't believe how fierce some brethren's reaction is to anything on the subject of feminine attire (whether headgear or miniskirts) that they disapprove of!'[155] Reflecting on his experience with the column, he noted that some of his questioners were uneasy

---

[151] Foreword to *Light in the North: The Story of the Scottish Covenanters* (Exeter: Paternoster, 1964), pp. 7–9.

[152] *IR*, p. 270; cf. Noble, *Tyndale*, pp. 96, 103, 119.

[153] Northwood, LST, J.D. Douglas papers, Douglas to Bruce, 21 December 1959; Bruce to Douglas, 25 December 1959; J.D. Douglas, 'The Half That Can Be Told' [unpaginated typescript memoir].

[154] *H* 54 (1975): p. 95; *IR*, p. 273.

[155] Madrid, Comisión de Biblioteca y Archivos, Centro Evangélico de Formación Bíblica en Madrid, Bruce to Ernest H. Trenchard, 24 November 1968.

with the notion of Christian liberty and would prefer to be guided by legal rulings, while others majored on minors.[156] But we have seen that it opened the door to a valued private ministry by letter and by personal contact, which he discharged conscientiously.

To my mind, one of the most remarkable features of Bruce's tenure of the column is that he was able to co-operate for so long (until the end of 1972) with an editor whose eschatological views were so different from his own. Tatford's eschatology was very much in the traditional Brethren dispensational mould, and he fired off a succession of popular paperbacks on the biblical prophets. Bruce, on the other hand, confessed that: 'As my readers know, I do not follow the dispensationalist line myself'.[157] Yet, in an obituary of Tatford, Bruce could comment: 'His characteristic courtesy and grace were evident in the fact that he never attempted to censor any expression of opinion on my part which differed radically from his own published judgment'.[158] (Indeed, in 1974 Tatford included two articles by Bruce in another journal which he edited, the *Prophetic Witness*.)[159] And since Bruce believed that he had not changed his views, Tatford must have had some idea of what those views were when approaching him to take up the page.[160] All the same, one wonders what Tatford made of Bruce's answer to the question '*Is there any scriptural support for the idea of a secret rapture of the church?* There may be, but I have yet to find it.'[161] The idea that Christians would be secretly raptured or caught up to heaven before the Great Tribulation was at the heart of Brethren eschatology; his dismissal of it would therefore have scandalized those of a traditional outlook among them. In fact, a little later he had

---

[156] F.F. Bruce, 'Lessons I Have Learned', *H* 54 (1975): pp. 154–5.

[157] *H* 40 (1961): p. 27: Q. 920.

[158] F.F. Bruce, 'Homecall: Frederick Albert Tatford (1901–1986)', *H* 65/8 (August 1986): p. 13.

[159] F.F. Bruce, 'Israel's Future Invaders', *Prophetic Witness* 57 (1974): pp. 251–2; idem, 'Armageddon: Past and Future', *Prophetic Witness* 57 (1974): pp. 262–3. The former had been published as 'The Proper Names in Ezekiel 38', *H* 17 (1940): pp. 130–31, and the latter as 'Armageddon through the Ages', *H* 18 (1941): pp. 23–4. Tatford made no acknowledgement of this.

[160] CBA, Box 11 (11), Bruce to J.A. Green, 10 December 1971.

[161] *H* 43 (1964): p. 55: Q. 1192; cf. 40 (1961): p. 107: Q. 962. Another tactfully expressed divergence from dispensationalism was occasioned by a questioner asking whether there was any difference between the kingdom of God and the kingdom of heaven; Bruce answered 'None that I can see; others, of course, may see more clearly': *H* 49 (1970): p. 42: Q. 1697.

to explain that it was the secrecy he rejected, not the idea that believers would be caught up to meet Christ in the air.[162] More tactfully, when asked about those who would be saved after the rapture, he stated that this 'calls for knowledge which I do not command' without indicating why.[163] And when asked about the possibility of a second chance for those who had rejected the gospel before the rapture, he simply passed the buck, saying that it fell so clearly within the editor's sphere of ministry that he had asked him to comment.[164] Later on, he would occasionally refer to John Henry Newman (which would not have endeared him to conservative Brethren), who asserted that time had run towards the end until the birth of Christ and now ran along its edge until the Second Coming.[165]

We have seen Bruce's caution about setting down his views in public and his refusal to align himself with any of the main schools of thought; as he wrote in a letter:

> My own eschatological views are fluid enough, and I am content for them to remain so. I marvel at the precision with which some brethren have the whole order of end-time events taped, and still more at the dogmatism with which they condemn any deviation from their chosen line. Amillennialism is on the increase among younger brethren – but they are too discreet to trumpet the fact abroad![166]

His lack of adherence to traditional views would by itself have been sufficient to cause some brethren to be concerned, since drifting from premillennialism was seen by them as tantamount to adopting liberal views. His approach to interpreting prophecy would have done little to reassure them, for he approached it from a radically different standpoint to that of most Brethren. His treatment in *Biblical Exegesis in the Qumran Texts* of prophecy and of *pesher* exegesis in the New Testament, whilst it was by no means unevangelical, must have been unfamiliar to Brethren, who were not used to looking at the biblical documents from a literary perspective.

---

[162] *H* 43 (1964): p. 91: Q. 1200.
[163] *H* 46 (1967): p. 90: Q. 1470.
[164] *H* 51 (1972): p. 122: Q. 1860.
[165] e.g. Bruce, *Epistles of John*, p. 65; idem, *The Real Jesus*, The Jesus Library (London: Hodder & Stoughton, 1985), p. 195.
[166] CBA, Box 9 (13), Bruce to Mr Casswell, 5 February 1968.

It would appear that Bruce was probably closer in spirit to post-millennialism than to anything else, because of his expectation of a future period of unparalleled blessing on the preaching of the gospel. He reviewed warmly Iain Murray's work *The Puritan Hope*, regarding such a hope – often called postmillennialism because of the idea that the return of Christ would follow a millennium of such blessing – as more biblical than the expectation of eschatological decline.[167] On the other hand, as he wrote to a correspondent, 'one point that emerges clearly from Murray's book is that what he calls "the Puritan hope" is really independent of any particular stance on the millennium (pre-, post-, a-, or any other), being based primarily on a perfectly reasonable interpretation of Rom. 11'. Question 1000 in *The Harvester* asked, '*Are we right in expecting a millennium?*' His response sidestepped the question, commenting: 'Scripture encourages us to believe that on this earth, the place of His rejection, Jesus will ultimately receive universal and joyful recognition as Lord and King.'[168] Along similar lines was a paper he gave to the Swanwick conference in 1962 on 'The Consummation'; here as in few other places his heart is evident and the motivating force provided by his expectation of the triumph of the gospel and the universal reign of Christ joyfully acknowledged.[169]

Bruce's answers to questions were eagerly received; but there seems to have been less enthusiasm on the part of readers for answering the questions which he put to them. In 1973, he began an occasional feature in *The Harvester*, 'Professor Bruce Asks', intended to provoke his readers to thought and to help them tease out sound principles of biblical interpretation and church practice. This ran until 1984, but it never seems to have lived up to expectations; perhaps by then Brethren were losing their appetite for authoritative pronouncements. Its chief value lies in Bruce's own comments when summarizing responses received.

◆   ◆   ◆

In the summer before his retirement, Bruce commented to a friend: 'at present I am spending the busiest long vacation that I have known for some years, as my research students are all trying to get their pound

---

[167] *W* 106 (1976): p. 432.
[168] *H* 40 (1961): p. 187.
[169] F.F. Bruce, 'The Consummation', in *The Rule of God in the Life of Man: Addresses Given at a Conference of Brethren at Swanwick* (London: G.W. Robson, 1962), pp. 63–80.

of flesh out of me in the way of supervision before September 30'.[170]
As far as his writing output was concerned, however, things were not
going to be much quieter for him after that date, as the next chapter
will demonstrate.

---

[170] Bruce to Alan Millard, 16 August 1978.

9

Productive Retirement (1978–90)

Retirement proved unexpectedly easy for Bruce to adjust to. A room had been placed at his disposal in the university library, so that he did not need to haunt the theology faculty, and he usually visited the library once a week.[1] As he wrote to a friend, 'Retirement is wholly enjoyable. It seems to be just as full of activity as my regular teaching career was, but it is wonderful to be liberated from the tyranny of the timetable.'[2] There was another benefit, too: back from a Nile cruise, he wrote to a friend: 'For the first time since I went to school in 1915 I have been able to take a holiday in January–February!'[3] He continued his annual lectures at the John Rylands Library until November 1986, concluding with several which appear to have been connected with the process of revising his commentaries on Romans and Acts. Given that declining attendances had seen the virtual disappearance of the library's public lecture programme by 1980, in spite of a switch to lunchtimes from 1973, the continuance of Bruce's lectures is evidence of their popularity.[4] During 1985–6 he also chaired the Ehrhardt Seminar, which dealt that session with the place of the law in Israel and early Christianity.[5] His new status did not mean that he ceased to take an interest in the activity of his former students; indeed, having been moved by their tributes when he retired, he could later say that

---

[1] CPF 1934 newsletter, December 1978; Manchester, CBA, Box 323/4/1/3, Bruce to Neil Dickson, 19 March 1987.

[2] Vancouver, Regent College, Bruce to Carl Armerding, 19 November 1979.

[3] Bruce to Timothy Stunt, 10 February 1979.

[4] Peter McNiven, 'The John Rylands Library, 1972–2000', *BJRL* 82/2–3 (Summer–Autumn 2000): pp. 3–79, at p. 24.

[5] He contributed a paper on 'Paul and the Law in Recent Research', in *Law and Religion: Essays on the Place of the Law in Israel and Early Christianity, by Members of the Ehrhardt Seminar of Manchester University* (ed. Barnabas Lindars; Cambridge: James Clarke, 1988), pp. 115–25.

'I take pride in the literary productions of my former pupils' and, alluding to 3 John 4, that 'I have no greater joy than to see my former pupils so actively and fruitfully engaged in biblical exegesis.'[6]

Bruce's seventieth birthday in 1980 was marked by a second *Festschrift*, this time by his former research students, entitled *Pauline Studies*. Few scholars receive two such tributes, and to mark the occasion a meal took place at the Garden House Hotel in Cambridge, although the occasion was more low-key than that in Manchester ten years earlier. Another book produced to mark the anniversary was his autobiography *In Retrospect: Remembrance of Things Past*, a lightly updated version of a series of articles appearing in *The Witness* from 1974–6.[7] A fellow New Testament scholar, Donald Guthrie of London Bible College, summed up the general estimate of the book in his review: 'As a chronicle of events and people which have contributed to the author's life, the book may be said to be comprehensive, but we would like to have discovered more about the man himself.'[8] Modesty was one reason why Bruce said so little of himself. Reserve was another: he was essentially a private man, deeply devoted to his wife and family and brought up in a culture which did not encourage the wearing of one's heart on one's sleeve. This meant that he was reticent about his spiritual experience as well as his family life, concerned to avoid the risk of spiritual exhibitionism.[9] As for his comments on other people, 'some of the juiciest personalia that come to my recollection as I write have to be suppressed!'[10]

Bruce did not regard the original series of articles as his 'last will and testament'.[11] In the wake of his death an updated version was produced, incorporating corrections and bibliographical additions which he had made; the initiative came from North America, although it was also published in Britain. At first the American publisher (Baker) had wanted to excise the Brethren-related material in the book, but Betty and the family considered this integral to what they envisaged as the only, and therefore sufficient, work on Bruce's life. Unfortunately, however, Bruce's own foreword was omitted from the British edition, to the consternation of Betty in particular.[12]

---

[6] Bruce to Norman Young, 31 March 1986, 9 May 1988.

[7] *W* 110 (1980): back cover advertisement in the November issue.

[8] *Themelios* 6/3 (April 1981): p. 35.

[9] *IR*, pp. 304–5, 306–7.

[10] Bruce to Timothy Stunt, 16 July 1975.

[11] Bruce to Robert Gordon, 23 June 1974.

[12] Sheila Lukabyo to the author, undated.

A new venture in which Bruce took a leading role was the establishment of the Christian Brethren Archive in 1979. This was to form part of the John Rylands University Library, which was developing an unrivalled collection of denominational archives and was well able to cope with another, and it was Bruce who concluded an agreement with the librarian, F.W. Ratcliffe, who was a personal friend.[13] Brethren lacked central denominational structures and so there had been no mechanism for preserving the movement's literary output apart from the initiative of individual collectors, whose interests tended to lie more with Exclusive than Open material. The result was that Brethren writings have often been very difficult to locate in libraries, with predictable results for research into them and public perception of them. Sometimes, too, material had been deliberately destroyed.[14] A small library had been formed at Bristol in 1960, but it had never really got off the ground, perhaps because it was not housed in an academic institution, and its holdings were later transferred to the new archive. Bruce wrote to the main Brethren magazines appealing for material for the archive,[15] and once a part-time archivist (David Brady) was appointed he continued to act as advisor and to encourage individuals to consider donating material.

In addition, he was invited to give various series of lectures elsewhere. He lectured annually at a Bible school near Lancaster,

---

[13] David Brady, 'The Cristian [*sic*] Brethren Archive in the John Rylands University Library of Manchester', in *Piero Guicciardini 1808–1886: Un Reformatore Religioso nell'Europa dell'ottocento. Atti del Convegno di Studi, Firenze, 11–12 aprile 1986* (ed. Lorenza Giorgi and Massimo Rubboli; Florence: Leo S. Olschki, 1988), pp. 175–91, at p. 175; McNiven, 'The John Rylands Library, 1972–2000', p. 8. Bruce had got on well with Ratcliffe as deputy chairman of the Library Committee: Cambridge, University Library, shelfmark Cam.b.2007.6, F.W. Ratcliffe, '"Books, Books, Just Miles and Miles of Books": Across the Library Counter, 1950–2000', bound typescript, 2007, p. 137.

[14] Cf. a postscript to a letter to Lang of 9 March 1954: 'P.S. I am sorry to learn about the fate of [the] Bethesda books and papers. Rendle [Short] told me once that he would destroy them sooner than run the risk of their falling into the wrong hands, but I had hoped he might find the right hands to entrust them to': CBA, Box 11(11). Bethesda, Bristol, was one of the earliest Brethren assemblies, founded and initially led by George Müller and Henry Craik. The destruction of archival material relating to it thus represented a serious loss, not only for historians but also for those seeking to establish what constituted early Brethren practice in such matters as reception to fellowship and to the Lord's Table.

[15] *W* 109 (1979): p. 309; cf. *H* (1979): p. 242; *W* 110 (1980): p. 307.

Capernwray Hall, a very different type of institution from those in which he had usually taught. As its former principal, Charles Price, recalls:

> FF Bruce graciously came to Capernwray every year, and in a three day period would give around 6 lectures on a NT book . . . Interestingly, for many of the younger students unfamiliar with the name FF Bruce, he was regarded as a bit dull, but for those who knew this was the man other teachers would frequently quote, it was a privilege to sit at his feet.[16]

A noteworthy engagement was the first annual series of Didsbury Lectures at what was then the British Isles Nazarene College, in 1979. His contribution did much to establish the credibility of the lectures, although it was not freshly prepared: his first three lectures had had an earlier outing at the Faculty of Theology in Cardiff in November 1978, and the fourth was a revision of a lecture delivered at the John Rylands Library in October 1977.[17] They were published as *Men and Movements in the Primitive Church*.[18] Although their author was best known for his work on Paul, he insisted that Paul had recognized the existence of other presentations than his own of the Christian message.[19] Accordingly, Bruce offered straightforward expositions of the presentations given by Peter and the eleven disciples, Stephen and the 'Hellenists' (Greek-speaking Jews), James and the Jerusalem church, and John and those around him. Such a task was all the more important, in his view, because 'A Paulinist (and I myself must be so described) is under a constant temptation to underestimate Peter.'[20] Apparently implying that he had done so, he acknowledged his indebtedness to the argument put forward by James D.G. Dunn that Peter did more than anybody else to hold first-century Christianity together.[21] This would have been surprising enough to some among

---

[16] Charles Price to the author, 23 January 2008.

[17] F.F. Bruce, *Men and Movements in the Primitive Church: Studies in Early Non-Pauline Christianity* (Exeter: Paternoster, 1979), p. 11; the Rylands lecture was published as 'St. John at Ephesus', *BJRL* 60 (1977–8): pp. 339–61.

[18] In North America, *Peter, Stephen, James and John*.

[19] Bruce, *Men and Movements*, p. 13.

[20] Ibid. p. 42.

[21] Ibid. pp. 42–3, following James D.G. Dunn, *Unity and Diversity in the New Testament: An Inquiry into the Character of Earliest Christianity* (London: SCM, 1977), p. 385. Nevertheless, Ellison in a critical review alleged that Bruce had not understood the tensions within the Jerusalem church as well as those within churches of the diaspora, a fault to be expected in a Paulinist: *FT* 108 (1981): pp. 75–6.

the Brethren, but it was not all; Bruce's grasp of the literary background to the New Testament led him to insist that it only enabled us to trace a part of the story of the progress of Christianity.[22] Moreover, he made no appeal to the divine authority of the New Testament documents but confined himself to surveying the evidence which they provided. However, his exposition did assume the historicity of Acts and, while introducing scholarly perspectives into the text, kept more technical discussion to the footnotes. The lectures were notable for the absence of conclusions, coming (as so often) to an abrupt end once all the material had been covered.

During the first part of his retirement, he also undertook several lecture tours, including one to Australia and New Zealand during the early part of 1980. At a CBRF conference at Waikanae in New Zealand, he gave two lectures, one on British Brethren history and the other on the authority of the Bible as a record of divine revelation.[23] The content of the latter is worth outlining because of the reaction it provoked. Bruce began by arguing that when we speak of biblical reliability, we have to ask about the purpose for which the Scriptures are reliable. The Bible is the record of divine revelation in history and human response, and as such it builds up a picture progressively; it is not 'a recital of eternal truths cast in propositional form' or 'arranged in the form of a catechism'. Its reliability may be tested by experience; this is not a wholly subjective test because it depends on the inner witness of the Holy Spirit. As for biblical criticism, which he defends, this has acquired a bad name because some critics operate with 'uncritical presuppositions' regarding such matters as the impossibility of miracles or of predictive prophecy. We accept the Bible as authoritative not only in the form in which it was originally given but also in the final form in which we receive it. As always, he is concerned to minimize the differences between these two forms, explaining how textual criticism has made possible the reconstruction of a text in which believers may place their confidence. However, he explains that it is impossible to recover the original autographs of some writings, for example because Paul dictated his letters and so the earliest written version would be the one taken down by his amanuensis: no written version exists of what Paul himself said.

---

[22] Bruce, *Men and Movements*, pp. 84–5.
[23] CBA, Box 7B, *CBRF Trust Newsletter*, January 1981, pp. 10–12. His latter lecture was published as 'Battle for the Bible: Biblical Criticism and Authority', *CBRF Journal*, no. 89 (April 1981): pp. 7–15.

Whilst Bruce's approach encourages readers to regard the Bible in its present form as the word of God, the admittedly minor disparities between the text as we have it and the text as originally given make it desirable for those who follow it to avoid too much precision in defining what the implications are for such matters as its infallibility on matters of incidental detail. Not surprisingly, then, some with a concern to safeguard inerrancy criticized his approach. A local brother, W.R.G. Turkington, issued a pamphlet entitled *Modernism in the Assemblies! Are We Losing Our Belief in the Authority of the Holy Scriptures?* Its focus was on Bruce, and its intent was to warn assembly leaders against the concessions to 'liberal' thought which Turkington felt were evident in Bruce's lecture on 7 March. Fuelled by the concerns which Lindsell had expressed in his two works, Turkington portrayed Bruce as a spearhead for the incursion of liberalism, and accused him of asserting that the Bible *contained* the word of God (allegedly a Barthian understanding) rather than that it *was* the word of God. Perhaps even more dangerous was the fact that as an academic Bruce was expected to associate and co-operate with 'apostates', an approach which could not but rub off on those influenced by him among assemblies. Bruce thus presented an implicit challenge to separatist Brethrenism. It does not appear that this pamphlet had much influence, but it does illustrate the concerns which were felt in some quarters, in Britain as well as in New Zealand.

Soon after this, CBRF in Britain heard him speak on 7 June on the meaning of the biblical text. A noteworthy feature of his paper, 'What Does It Mean?', was his assertion that the plenary sense of Scripture comprises the primary meaning and the further meaning validly discerned by God's people subsequently, the latter including the sense it acquires in context of the whole Bible. This issue was especially pertinent to his Brethren audience, given their tradition of typological and allegorical exposition undertaken in order to find Christ in all the Scriptures. But not all would have appreciated the conclusion to his discussion of this issue: 'The best advice that can be given to those about to engage in allegorical interpretation of Scripture is: "Don't!"'[24]

Later that year Fred and Betty flew to Canada, where, besides spending a fortnight with Iain and his family in Newfoundland, they attended the SNTS conference in Toronto. He took the opportunity of meeting Gordon Fee to invite him to contribute a replacement

---

[24] F.F. Bruce, 'What Does it Mean?', *CBR* 31–32 (February 1982): pp. 41–52; quotation at p. 51.

commentary on 1 Corinthians to the NICNT series. Sadly, he was unable to accept invitations to return to Regent College for its summer school in 1981 and 1982, partly because of other commitments and partly because he appears to have been trying to scale down his travelling for the sake of his health. This was, it must be said, a slow process. Soon after returning from another trip to Australia, his lecture in November 1982 on 'Two Centuries of New Testament Criticism' drew around eighty to a meeting of the Librarians' Christian Fellowship in Loughborough;[25] that month he also delivered the Griffith Thomas Lectures at Wycliffe Hall, Oxford.[26] These were published at the request of the Theological Students' Fellowship as *Paul and the Mind of Christ*, and formed a coda to his book on Paul, taking their point of departure from its final assertion, with reference to the topic of spiritual liberty: 'In this, as in so many other respects, Paul has remained unsurpassed in his insight into the mind of Christ.'[27] In them he demonstrated that, contrary to some contemporary views, the mind of Christ was to be found in the gospels, and that there was a demonstrable continuity of the teaching of the gospels and Paul's outlook.[28]

The summer of 1983 saw Fred and Betty embark on a coach tour of central Asia Minor, keenly anticipated as it would 'include a visit to some sites long familiar by name to a student of Acts and the Epistles, but hitherto unseen'.[29] Nearer home, he gave the Diamond Jubilee Lecture of the London Baptist Preachers' Association on 18 November, on 'St Paul the Preacher'. At one point he commented on the unimpressive nature of the apostle's oratory, comparing it with that of D.L. Moody; one suspects he might also have had his father's delivery – or even his own – in mind. What made the impact, he argued, was not the preacher's gifts but the power of God. It is noticeable that he focuses on Paul's evangelistic preaching; once again, he was showing himself to be his father's son, thinking about preaching primarily in terms of preaching the gospel.[30] His last major lecturing trip, the same month, was to deliver the Griffith Thomas Lectures (a

---

[25] Graham Hedges to the author, 14 February 2008; the lecture was published in *Christian Librarian*, no. 7 (1983): pp. 5–16.

[26] CPF 1934 newsletter, June and December 1982.

[27] F.F. Bruce, *Paul: Apostle of the Free Spirit* (Exeter: Paternoster, rev. edn, 1980), p. 474.

[28] F.F. Bruce, *Paul and the Mind of Christ*, RTSF Monographs 15 ([Leicester]: RTSF, [1985]).

[29] CPF 1934 newsletter, June 1983.

[30] F.F. Bruce, *St Paul the Preacher: 'Diamond Jubilee' Lecture 1983. Lecture Given to the London Baptist Preachers' Association on Friday 18th November 1983* (London: London Baptist Preachers' Association, [1984]).

different series from those given at Oxford) at Dallas Theological Seminary. He chose to deal with problems in the interpretation of Colossians. Dallas being the foremost centre for dispensationalist scholarship, he hoped that this would keep him 'away from the thin ice'![31] He enjoyed it, but told a correspondent that he was 'getting too old for lecturing trips'.[32] At home, he and Betty were no longer able to walk as they used to, but they continued to enjoy being taken for drives around Derbyshire, and Fred possessed enough geological knowledge to add to appreciation of the scenery.[33] They returned to Australia in October 1984, but this time he seems to have taken few if any speaking engagements.

At a personal level, he continued to keep up to date with his reading; until his death he maintained his subscriptions to a number of theological periodicals, among them *Evangelical Quarterly*, *Evangelical Review of Theology*, *Expository Times*, *Journal of Semitic Studies*, *Journal for the Study of the New Testament*, *Journal for the Study of the Old Testament*, *New Testament Studies*, *Theology*, *Themelios*, *Tyndale Bulletin* and *Westminster Theological Journal*. However, he did not attempt to keep up with every new development in biblical scholarship; structuralism was a case in point, for he considered that in the days remaining to him he had more important things to study.[34] 'My own shying away from structuralism is due to my being too old a dog to learn new tricks – and the same goes for the use of computers, word-processors and other products of the electronic age . . . For my part, I go on practising the same old techniques.'[35] At the heart of his approach was his continuing conviction that a sound classical education offered the best foundation for professional biblical study.[36] He was therefore delighted to be asked to serve as external examiner for a doctoral thesis which investigated Graeco-Roman philosophy of rhetoric and its relation to Paul's preaching problems at Corinth and his response in 1 Corinthians 1 – 4. At the end of the viva, the

---

[31] CBA, Box 64, Bruce to J.A. Green, 23 September 1983.
[32] Bruce to Desmond Ford, 25 December 1983. The lectures appeared in the seminary's journal *Bibliotheca Sacra* during 1984.
[33] Betty Buckley to the author, 19 February 2008.
[34] *IR*, p. 207.
[35] Bruce to Norman and Elisabeth Young, 27 November 1984.
[36] *IR*, p. 145; cf. F.F. Bruce, 'Bishop Westcott and the Classical Tradition', *Spectrum* 11/1 (September 1978): pp. 19–21, in which he treated the famous textual critic as an example of his belief that 'for the exact study of the New Testament nothing can provide a sounder foundation than the old-fashioned classical curriculum'.

successful candidate asked whether it should be published, and received the immediate response: 'Of course; I've been waiting years for somebody to write this.'[37] Such techniques were also congenial to him because they were concerned primarily with elucidating the original meaning of the text, rather than with responses of readers to it.

Taking up his reference to computers, we may well marvel that until the end of his life Bruce continued to produce material on a small portable typewriter. Computers held no interest for him. On one occasion, a young man came to his door selling software which, it was claimed, would help him write his books. The salesman must have been surprised to be told: 'Young man, I fear you are wasting your time; you see, I have no computer!'[38] However, by 1989, although he was resisting encouragement to buy a word processor, he confessed that he was now making liberal use of liquid paper because his fingers were no longer so obedient as they had been.[39] During the last year of his life he did acquire an electric typewriter, but never used it.[40]

◆   ◆   ◆

It was during Bruce's retirement that his views regarding women in church life came to fullest and most outspoken expression. In June 1979, he addressed a CBRF day conference on the topic of 'Women in the Church: A Biblical Survey'. The audience would have been drawn from the more progressive assemblies, and indeed CBRF as a whole had something of a reputation for radicalism and intellectualism, and for sitting lightly to the things which were most surely believed and practised among Brethren. Bruce began by introducing his hearers to the idea of cultural relativity; this would have been unfamiliar to many, who would not have gone very far in treating parts of the Bible as arising from, and primarily applicable to, a particular cultural context (and hence as not applicable in the same way two millennia later). Equally challenging would have been his contrast of two modes of biblical interpretation, the scribal way (which focused on

---

[37] Duane Litfin, telephone conversation, 22 April 2009; Litfin to the author, 31 July 2010. Bruce's classical training and regular preaching would have given him considerable interest in such an interpretative approach.

[38] Sheila Lukabyo, interview, 2 September 2009.

[39] CPF 1934 newsletter, April 1989. At the time, he was writing articles for a new edition of the *Anchor Bible Dictionary*.

[40] Alan Millard to the author, 27 March 2010.

the application of laws originally given in another cultural context)
and the way of Jesus (which involved going back to the underlying
principles, asking for what purpose the laws were given, and how
that purpose could be fulfilled in a changed cultural context).
Moreover, he asserted that the question of the superiority of man to
woman arose only in the context of the Fall, and that Christ's work
involved breaking the consequences of the Fall. Having thus prepared
the ground, he surveyed the New Testament evidence, arguing for
full equality of role for women and men. Central to his argument was
the statement of equality in Galatians 3:28, which he believed was as
revolutionary for the position of women as it was for that of Gentiles
or slaves; it was simply that the implications in each case took time to
work out in practice. The Pauline prohibitions on women's ministry
related to a particular cultural context and not to the modern world.
It was in any case ironic, he asserted, to treat Paul, the apostle of liberty, as a lawgiver. If women were gifted by the Spirit in certain ways,
those gifts were intended to be used. But Bruce gave no encouragement to those who would ride roughshod over others in asserting
their liberty; another New Testament principle was that the unity of
the Spirit must be safeguarded: 'Let those who understand the scriptures along the lines indicated in this paper have liberty to expound
them thus, but let them not force the pace or try to impose their
understanding of the scriptures until that understanding finds general acceptance with the church – and when it does, there will be no
need to impose it.'[41] Speaking to his own constituency, he asserted
that whilst Brethren might consider the contemporary Anglican
debates about priesthood and the ordination of women as something
which did not concern them, in fact assemblies operated with an
implicitly priestly conception of what was done at the Breaking of
Bread. This, he claimed, should be abandoned and the way thus
opened up for women to give thanks for the bread and wine; but
some assemblies, he believed, would allow anything rather than this.
Brethren, in his opinion, had been a male-dominated constituency
because of a high-church outlook and a scribal hermeneutic (in the

---

[41] F.F. Bruce, 'Women in the Church: A Biblical Survey', *CBR* 33 (1982): pp. 7–14, at
p. 12. In 1970 he had written to a teenager: 'On the question of the ministry of
women in the church, there are diversities of judgment among brethren (and
among sisters too) and the best way to avoid division in any company is to accept
the judgment of the elders (providing they are of one mind)': Bruce to Kenneth
Roxburgh, 29 November 1970.

sense given above). That said, he acknowledged the possibility that those arguing the egalitarian case might be influenced by their cultural context, and warned them to guard against taking their cue from women's liberationism rather than from the teaching of Scripture.

From his other writings of this period, it is clear that he believed two issues to be involved: (i) consistency of interpretation of the various distinctions declared in Galatians 3:28 to have been done away with in Christ, this being the starting point for thinking about the issue in his opinion,[42] and (ii) more generally, the way in which Scripture functioned as authoritative in determining church practice. With his stress on liberty, he was never likely to sympathize with any approach which sought to derive a set of binding regulations from the New Testament documents. Indeed, he even elevated freedom to the status of a hermeneutical principle: 'where there are conflicting practical interpretations of a New Testament text, the interpretation which promotes the cause of freedom is most likely to be the right one'.[43]

> To any one who wants to transfer the church order of the Pastorals as it stands to twentieth-century churches I recommend that in each church an order of widows be instituted, with the stipulation that no woman be admitted to it unless she has reached the age of 60 and has 'washed the feet of the saints'. When people ask me to give a ruling on this kind of issue, I regularly say that we shall be most true to Paul (and to his Lord and ours) if we let the cause of gospel freedom prevail. When I claim the authority of Paul for maintaining the liberty of women to exercise their Spirit-bestowed gifts in church, some people think I am not being serious – but I am. Oddly, ten persons know the textually doubtful 1 Cor. 14:34 for one who knows the unambiguous Gal. 3:28.[44]

What mattered was the underlying spirit in which believers sought to work out their practice in such matters. And he was well aware that his approach could be considered subversive. He concluded his Galatians commentary by writing:

---

[42] Here his thinking parallels that of Paul K. Jewett's influential *Man as Male and Female* (Grand Rapids, MI: Eerdmans, 1975), although he would not have accepted Jewett's assertion that there was a contradiction between the egalitarian Paul of Gal. 3:28 and the subordinationist Paul, deploying rabbinic rather than Christian arguments, of 1 Cor. 14:34–5; cf. Gary Dorrien, *The Remaking of Evangelical Theology* (Louisville, KY: Westminster John Knox, 1998), p. 144.

[43] F.F. Bruce, 'The Call to Freedom', *H* 66/12 (December 1987): pp. 21–2.

[44] CBA, Box 11 (11), Bruce to Alan G. Padgett, 20 April 1984.

The religious mind is too prone to subject itself to regulations, the liberating gospel of sovereign grace is too 'dangerous' to be allowed unre-
strained course. As Paul became less a figure of controversy, as his
memory was venerated and his writings canonized, his teaching was
overlaid with a new legalism. When, from time to time, someone
appeared who understood and proclaimed the genuine message of
Galatians, he was liable to be denounced as a subversive character – as,
indeed, Paul was in his own day. But the letter to the Galatians, with its
trumpet-call to Christian freedom, has time and again released the true
gospel from the bonds in which well-meaning but misguided people
have confined it so that it can once more exert its emancipating power
in the life of mankind, empowering those who receive it to stand fast in
the freedom with which Christ has set them free.[45]

In so writing, Bruce was following a line which is arguably consistent
with earlier Brethren thinking in one respect, though I do not suppose
for a moment that he adopted his particular views in order to follow
a certain traditional approach to the question of the place of the law
in the believer's life; in any case, few Brethren would have been
aware by the latter half of the twentieth century that their forebears
had held such views. During the nineteenth century, Brethren had
attracted considerable opprobrium from Presbyterians in Ireland and
Scotland for their principled rejection of the law of Moses as the primary guide for the believer's conduct and that of the church. Bruce
was, then, radical in the sense of returning to Brethren roots. And he
himself pointed to the freedom enjoyed by women during the earliest
days of Brethren in the north-east of Scotland.

By the time of *The Pauline Circle* (1986), he could write with reference
to a variant reading of Acts 18:26 which put Aquila rather than Priscilla
first, that the editor 'may have felt that it was unfitting that a woman
should take the lead in a teaching ministry. Today some would put that
editor down as a male chauvinist.'[46] And of Euodia and Syntyche, Paul's
fellow labourers to whom he appealed in Philippians 4:2–3, he wrote:
'Whatever form these two women's collaboration with Paul in his gospel
ministry may have taken, it was not confined to making tea for him and
his circle – or whatever the first-century equivalent to that activity was.'[47]

---

[45] F.F. Bruce, *The Epistle of Paul to the Galatians: A Commentary on the Greek Text*,
   NIGTC (Exeter: Paternoster, 1982), pp. 277–8.
[46] F.F. Bruce, *The Pauline Circle* (Exeter: Paternoster, 1986), p. 48 n.
[47] Ibid. p. 85.

Of course, those who disagreed with him would have pointed immediately to the passages in which they believed Paul forbade the kind of public ministry Bruce was advocating: 1 Corinthians 14:33–36 and 1 Timothy 2:11–15. By this period, however, he was arguing that the first passage may have been an interpolation in the text, possibly originating as a scribal comment in the margin, but that even if authentic its primary reference was to women publicly questioning the interpretation of prophecies, which were not a feature of the worship of most Brethren assemblies. As for the second passage, whether or not it was by Paul (and he tended to think that it was not), it was simply a statement of practice at that time, probably an expansion of the Corinthians passage, and not a perpetually binding ordinance. If neither passage was from Paul, then, there was no need to try to reconcile them with Galatians 3:28.[48]

Bruce's assertions regarding the full equality of women were borne out by his conduct. Apart from the fact that many of the dedications to his books were to couples, a number of his students have expressed appreciation of the fact that he listened to them and took them seriously on the spiritual and intellectual levels, yet he combined this with old-fashioned courtesy, holding the door open even for the newest undergraduate. Indeed, 'It was even suggested that his main reason for wearing a hat was that he could raise it to all his female acquaintances.'[49] Betty's conservatism, however, meant that she preferred not to take public part in meetings. One scholar remembers a dinner with the Bruces in the early 1980s at which the subject was raised and varying opinions expressed. When his wife asked Fred whether Betty took part in the assembly, with a twinkle in his eye he responded: 'she knows her place'[50] – but the place was one she chose, not one imposed upon her by anybody else. She was happiest filling a traditional housewife's role, cooking, gardening and offering quiet hospitality, yet her husband could not have been anything like as

---

[48] F.F. Bruce, *Paul and His Converts: How Paul Nurtured the Churches He Planted* (Crowborough: Highland Books, 1985), p. 89; idem, 'The Enigma of Paul: Why Did the Early Church's Great Liberator Get a Reputation as an Authoritarian?', *Bible Review* 4 (August 1988): pp. 32–3; Ward and Laurel Gasque, 'F.F. Bruce – The Apostle Paul and the Evangelical Heritage', *H* 68/7 (July 1989): pp. 10–12, at p. 12. His argument regarding 1 Cor. 14 drew on the commentary by Gordon Fee which he had commissioned for the NICNT series.

[49] Anthea Cousins, appreciation in *H* 69/11 (November 1990): p. 6.

[50] Gerald Hawthorne, telephone conversation, 6 May 2009.

productive without her and he clearly respected her intellectual
capacities.

◆   ◆   ◆

Bruce's retirement was marked by a literary productivity which
would have done credit to the working careers of most ordinary
scholars. Remarkably, no less than eighteen of the four dozen books
he wrote appeared after 1978.

At a popular level, he contributed brief articles each quarter from
1979 until the end of 1986 to an evangelistic periodical apparently
intended as a resource for magazine editors, *Release Nationwide*. This
was published from the Manchester offices of Operation Mobiliz-
ation, an interdenominational evangelistic and publishing agency.
Here we see him once again engaging in apologetics, with a focus on
the person and work of Jesus Christ: the series appeared under the
heading 'Is It Really TRUE?' His historical instincts show clearly in
'Who Was Jesus?', which he sent for publication on 26 September
1979:

> I do not believe that there is a cleavage between the Jesus of history and
> the Christ of faith, but if I had to choose between the two, I should
> plump for the Jesus of history. Why? Because the Jesus of history is a
> real live person, but unless the Christ of faith is securely based on his-
> torical fact, he is apt to be a figment of the believer's imagination.[51]

Several fairly popular works on the person and work of Jesus Christ
also appeared during this period, all marked by a resurgence of the
apologetic motive which had run through his first two books. The
first was *I Want to Know What the Bible Says about the Work of Jesus*, published in 1979 by Kingsway, a charismatic publisher which was seeking to broaden its lists to include books with more of a teaching focus.
He felt himself off his home ground in this type of work because of
the style of presentation required (which was not only popular but
also thematic rather than exegetical), but even so he stamped it with
his own approach, which was to look at what individual writers or
groups of writings had to say about the work of Christ, before collat-
ing the evidence. This work was dedicated to his secretary, Margaret

---

[51] He had made the same point more fully in an untitled article for a magazine published by the Bible Society, *The Bible in the World* (Autumn 1970).

Hogg, it being the last manuscript which she had typed for him over a period of fifteen years.

There were two further titles for Hodder & Stoughton's Jesus Library. The first was *Hard Sayings of Jesus* (1983), which looked at a number of the sayings traditionally found difficult to understand or accept. The second, more directly apologetic and even evangelistic in tone, was *The Real Jesus* (1985).[52] In his foreword, Michael Green paid tribute to the three areas of expertise which Bruce demonstrated in this work on the person of Christ: his 'encyclopaedic knowledge of the source material, the ancient background, and modern literature about the gospels'.[53] Once again, much of the book began as series of articles, twelve in *The Harvester* during 1984 on 'The Jesus of History and the Christ of Faith' and five as part of his series in *Release Nationwide* during 1984–5.[54] The book appeared at a time when Jesus was in the media thanks to a controversial British television series, *Jesus: The Evidence*, and the furore surrounding the denial of the bodily resurrection of Christ by the then Bishop of Durham, David Jenkins. It has been claimed that Bruce seemed unaware of the consternation caused by Jenkins,[55] but I think it more likely that he saw nothing new in what Jenkins was saying, having long before encountered similar controversial assertions by E.W. Barnes as Bishop of Birmingham.[56] Bruce's church involvement ensured that he remained in touch with ordinary people, and his hope was that his work would serve as a positive corrective to recently aired views.[57] His response to those who could not accept the resurrection was expressed by Acts 26:8; why should it be thought incredible that God should raise the

---

[52] Published in North America as *Jesus: Lord and Savior*.

[53] F.F. Bruce, *The Real Jesus*, The Jesus Library (London: Hodder & Stoughton, 1985), p. 9.

[54] Ibid. p. 208 n.

[55] Murray J. Harris, 'Frederick Fyvie Bruce', in *Bible Interpreters of the 20th Century: A Selection of Evangelical Voices* (ed. Walter A. Elwell and J.D. Weaver; Grand Rapids, MI: Baker, 1999), pp. 216–27, at p. 221. His unflappability had earlier been manifested when John Robinson, then Bishop of Woolwich, published *Honest to God* in 1963, and was widely condemned for radical unorthodoxy. Bruce wondered what all the fuss was about; the author was taking seriously his teaching responsibility as a bishop, and made clear that he was thinking aloud. Indeed, Bruce agreed that it was possible to have a wrong mental image of God just as it was possible to worship a physical idol: *Essential Christianity* (June 1963): p. 19.

[56] Cf. F.F. Bruce, 'Scientists *Can* Believe the Bible', *Release Nationwide*, sent March 1985.

[57] CPF 1934 newsletter, April 1985.

dead?[58] As well as surveying the historical evidence for such an event, however, he appealed to the consciousness of the indwelling Christ experienced by believers through the ages.[59] He was quite unashamed in asserting that the message of Christ was for all: 'We should not disparage the founders of any of the great world-religions, but it is the simple truth that none of them is entitled to be called the Saviour of the World.'[60]

Another work which began life as a series of magazine articles was *The Pauline Circle* (1986), which first appeared in the 'Exploring the Bible' section of *The Harvester* during 1983. This was dedicated to Jeremy and Margaret Mudditt, evidence of the esteem in which he held his main British publisher. The book looked at Paul's fellow workers mentioned in the New Testament. And at a popular level he also wrote notes to accompany the maps in the *Paternoster Bible History Atlas* (1982) and a shorter *Student's Atlas of the Bible* (1986).

Much of Bruce's work, however, was in the field of biblical commentary; as well as several new ones, he revised a number of his older commentaries. In 1982, a third commentary appeared on the Acts of the Apostles. This one formed part of a new Scripture Union series designed for daily reading.[61] Each day's page of notes offered a concise summary of the biblical passage, but Bruce did not include any application; this was confined to the 'thought' at the bottom of each page (in which he again indulged his love of quoting hymns) and the weekly page of discussion questions (there is no indication whether he or an editor wrote these).

At the heavyweight end of the commentary range was his work on Galatians, published in 1982 as part of the New International Greek Text Commentary series. As early as 1967, Bruce had the writing of a commentary on Galatians slated as a retirement project. At a strategy conference held in January of that year by the BRC he had argued for the production of commentaries on the Greek text, along the lines of those produced late in the nineteenth century by J.B. Lightfoot and others, as one of the best ways of dealing with the issues raised by Bultmann and his school and exploring the significance of those issues for Christian faith.[62] Once again, his preference for an exegetically based approach is evident. Shortly after, there appeared the first

---

[58] Bruce, *Real Jesus*, p. 123.
[59] Ibid. p. 154.
[60] Ibid. p. 182.
[61] F.F. Bruce, *Acts*, Bible Study Commentary (London: Scripture Union, 1982).
[62] BRC minutes; Noble, *Tyndale House*, p. 130.

of a string of articles on the letter.[63] Many were based on public lectures at the John Rylands University Library; invitations to contribute to *Festschriften* allowed him to clarify his thinking on problem areas or to offer overviews of specific themes. As in other cases, some articles amounted to updates of earlier work.

Publication in the NIGTC series came about because Ward Gasque recalled hearing him say that nearly all his writing had been in response to requests. Gasque knew that he was working on an unsolicited commentary on Galatians and that he had never written on Philippians, so invited him to do both, for different series, an invitation Bruce could not refuse.[64] Not surprisingly, writing a commentary on Galatians was for him a labour of love, and he described it as 'a richly rewarding experience'.[65] The Rylands lectures formed the substance of his introduction,[66] in which he maintained his belief that the letter was addressed to churches in South rather than North Galatia; his broad classical background led him to express disquiet that protagonists of the opposing view gave less attention than formerly to

---

[63] F.F. Bruce, 'Galatian Problems: 1. Autobiographical Data', *BJRL* 51 (1968–9): pp. 292–309; 'Galatian Problems: 2. North or South Galatians?', *BJRL* 52 (1969–70): pp. 243–66; 'Galatian Problems: 3. The "Other" Gospel', *BJRL* 53 (1970–71): pp. 253–71; 'Galatian Problems: 4. The Date of the Epistle', *BJRL* 54 (1971–2): pp. 250–67; 'Galatian Problems: 5. Galatians and Christian Origins', *BJRL* 55 (1972–3): pp. 264–84; '"Abraham Had Two Sons": A Study in Pauline Hermeneutics', in *New Testament Studies: Essays in Honor of Ray Summers in His Sixty-Fifth Year* (ed. Huber L. Drumwright and Curtis Vaughan; Waco, TX: Markham, 1975), pp. 71–84; 'Further Thoughts on Paul's Autobiography: Galatians 1:11 – 2:14', in *Jesus und Paulus: Festschrift für Werner Georg Kümmel zum 70. Geburtstag* (ed. E. Earle Ellis and Erich Grässer; Göttingen: Vandenhoeck & Ruprecht, 1975), pp. 21–9; '"Called to Freedom": A Study in Galatians', in *The New Testament Age: Essays in Honor of Bo Reicke* (2 vols; ed. William C. Weinrich; Macon, GA: Mercer University Press, 1984), 1:61–71; 'The Spirit in the Letter to the Galatians', in *Essays on Apostolic Themes: Studies in Honor of Howard M. Ervin Presented to Him by Colleagues and Friends on His Sixty-Fifth Birthday* (ed. Paul Elbert; Peabody, MA: Hendrickson, 1985), pp. 36–48; 'The Conference in Jerusalem: Galatians 2:1–10', in *God Who Is Rich in Mercy: Essays Presented to Dr D.B. Knox* (ed. Peter T. O'Brien and David G. Peterson; Homebush West, NSW: ANZEA, [1986], pp. 195–212).

[64] Laurel and Ward Gasque, 'Frederick Fyvie Bruce: An Appreciation', *H* 69/11 (November 1990): pp. 1–6, at p. 6.

[65] Bruce, *Galatians*, p. xiii.

[66] One reviewer, however, faulted him for not updating this material, and for not engaging with contemporary debate about Paul's thought: John Barclay, in *Themelios* 9/1 (September 1983): pp. 32–3.

issues of historical geography.[67] Once again he defended the view that the doctrine of justification by faith alone is central to Paul's thought, and commended contemporary German theologians who had emphasized this, although his discussion did not take sufficient account of the lively debate which had got under way during the 1970s regarding Paul and the Jewish law.[68] Although a more technical commentary than most which he wrote, he still found space to refer to John Wesley's conversion[69] and to Scougal's stress on the need for Christ to be formed within the believer as the necessary complement to the experience of justification,[70] and to quote all five stanzas of Isaac Watts's meditation on Galatians 6:14, 'When I Survey the Wondrous Cross'.[71] Moreover, whilst the format of this commentary series did not call for application to contemporary life, Bruce's experience of local churches kept his feet on the ground when it came to interpretation: he rejected the idea that Paul's warnings against conceit, competitiveness and envying one another in 5:26 were directed at those in Galatia with Gnostic tendencies, arguing that such tendencies were quite capable of arising anywhere.[72] C.F.D. Moule, reviewing the commentary, commended its combination of objective scholarship and deep but controlled piety.[73]

At the end of 1980 he sent the Galatians manuscript to the publisher, and was free to give his full attention to 1 and 2 Thessalonians, on which he had been contracted to produce a commentary on the Greek text in the Word Biblical Commentary series. This was completed in August 1981 and published in 1982.[74] The format of this series, which involved separate sections for exegesis, exposition and explanation (what we might call application) seems to have caused Bruce some problems, and he provided little application in this work.

---

[67] Bruce, *Galatians*, p. 14.

[68] Ibid. p. 51.

[69] Ibid. p. 200 (on Gal. 4:6).

[70] Ibid. p. 213 (on Gal. 4:19). Justification by faith for Bruce was no 'legal fiction' in which God declares sinners righteous but does nothing to transform them, as it is sometimes caricatured. In another essay, he argued that in Paul's thought it was always coupled with the reception of the Spirit by faith: Bruce, 'The Spirit in the Letter to the Galatians', pp. 36–48.

[71] Bruce, *Galatians*, pp. 272–3.

[72] Ibid. p. 258.

[73] *Journal of Theological Studies* 36 (1985): pp. 209–11.

[74] CPF 1934 newsletter, December 1980; Vancouver, Regent College, Bruce to Carl Armerding, 17 October 1981.

It was not the sort of commentary likely to appeal to traditionally minded Brethren: in his treatment of 1 Thessalonians 4:3–18, the rapture doctrine did not even receive a mention. Moreover, commenting on 2 Thessalonians 2:1 he took issue with the dispensationalist separation of the 'day of the Lord' mentioned there from the events of 1 Thessalonians 4:13–18.[75] And on the subject of the Antichrist, he commended a work by a somewhat idiosyncratic Russian Orthodox thinker, Vladimir Solovyev, as the most powerful modern portrayal.[76] Rather than attempting to locate the Antichrist within history or biblical prophecy, Bruce insisted in an excursus that the primary reference must have been intelligible to the original readers (which would rule out the attempts made by some in more recent times to equate the Antichrist with contemporary political or religious figures) and that it behoved each reader to ask 'Lord, is it I?'[77] In other words, he invited readers to look within rather than around them, an interpretation unheard of among Brethren.

After this, his next books were *Hard Sayings of Jesus* and the commentary on Philippians mentioned above. He found writing this commentary challenging because it had to be based on the text of the Good News Bible, and at points he found it necessary to explain why he preferred a different rendering of the Greek.[78] It appeared in 1983 under the imprint of a mainstream American publisher, Harper & Row, intended for mainstream Protestant and Catholic laity. However, it became apparent that such people did not often buy commentaries, and so the series was transferred to a relatively new evangelical firm, Hendrickson, and the commentary lightly revised so that it was based on the New International Version.[79]

Next on the list of commissions was the revision of several series of magazine articles which he had written over almost thirty years to form a popular commentary on the Gospel of John, published in 1983 by Pickering & Inglis.[80] It provides a good example of his readiness to

[75] F.F. Bruce, *1 & 2 Thessalonians*, Word Biblical Commentary, vol. 45 (Waco, TX: Word, 1982), p. 163.

[76] Ibid. pp. 177–8 (on 2 Thess. 2:1–12); the work is entitled *Short Narrative about the Antichrist.*

[77] Bruce, *1 & 2 Thessalonians*, p. 187.

[78] CPF 1934 newsletter, December 1981, June 1982.

[79] Ward Gasque to the author, 10 November 2009.

[80] F.F. Bruce, 'An Expository Study of St. John's Gospel', *Bible Student* 24–30 (1953–9), on chs 1 – 7; 'St. John's Passion Narrative', *W* 101–2 (1971–2), undertaken to clarify his thinking on certain problems; and 'The Gospel of John', *W* 107–10 (1977–80), continued in *H* 60–61 (1981–2), which commenced with a revised version of the first series.

rework material. The preface stated that the book was aimed at the general reader. Accordingly, he continued to quote hymns, and offered fairly standard devotional application, but he also included transliterated Greek and illustrations from patristic writers. As one reviewer said: 'If this book does not push back the frontiers, it is nevertheless exactly the sort of work one likes to put into the hands of ordinary Christians who want to know their Bible better.'[81]

Another task which occupied a considerable proportion of Bruce's time was the revision of all his scholarly commentaries. The first was his commentary on Colossians (1957), to which he added one on Ephesians, in no way dependent on his earlier and more popular work on the letter, to replace that by E.K. Simpson; the revised volume was published in 1984. Extensive revision was needed of his treatment of Colossians; this had been his first of a Pauline letter but 'Without an intensive study of the earlier Pauline epistles, I was singularly unequipped to tackle Colossians – much more unequipped than I could realize at the time.'[82] Ephesians, he asserted, 'constitutes the crown of Paulinism, gathering up the main themes of the apostle's teaching into a unified presentation *sub specie aeternitatis*'.[83] As such he evidently enjoyed expounding it. Although the commentary has somewhat less by way of application than his earlier works, he continued to refer to Puritan works,[84] and his discussion of the doctrine of election was noteworthy for drawing on a range of writers from various perspectives.[85]

The next commentary to be tackled was that on Romans, which appeared in 1985. The revision has a surprisingly dated feel to it, in that whilst he often updated bibliographical references, the text remained largely unaltered and he does not often appear to have integrated newer perspectives and approaches into his discussion of

---

[81] D.A. Carson, in *EQ* 58 (1986): p. 174.

[82] F.F. Bruce, *The Epistles to the Colossians, to Philemon and to the Ephesians*, NICNT (Grand Rapids, MI: Eerdmans, 1984), p. xi.

[83] Ibid. pp. xi–xii.

[84] Notably in his discussion of the Christian warfare at Eph. 6:17 (ibid. p. 410), where he referred to Bunyan's *Holy War*, Gurnall's *Christian in Complete Armour*, and the multi-volume exposition of Ephesians by Lloyd-Jones then appearing from Banner of Truth (a work which his reviews show that he appreciated).

[85] Bruce, *Colossians, Philemon and Ephesians*, pp. 254–5: he cited Barth, Berkouwer, John Murray, T.F. Torrance, and Ernest Trenchard, who collaborated with a Spanish writer, J.M. Martínez, to produce what Bruce considered a helpful work on the subject, *Escogidos en Christo* (Madrid: Editorial Literatura Bíblica, 1966).

particular issues. For example, on 8:26 he could have discussed the question of tongues, and on 13:1–7 the burgeoning interest in what is nowadays known as 'political theology'. On 10:3–4 he added a brief note on the 'covenantal nomism' of E.P. Sanders, but did not alter the main thrust of his argument; the lack of engagement with such views is surprising given that Sanders's work has been an extremely important catalyst for much recent thinking about the relationship between Paul, the Mosaic law, and the Jewish people (and Bruce had himself reviewed Sanders's *Paul and Palestinian Judaism* a few years earlier).[86] And one might have expected some interaction with N.T. Wright's 1981 doctoral thesis on 'The Messiah and the People of God', which offered extensive discussion of Romans 9 – 11.[87] In the introduction, a footnote dealing with Roman Catholic views on justification by faith was not updated to take the story beyond Hans Küng's *Justification* and G.C. Berkouwer's 1958 critique; one would have expected at least some reference to the Second Vatican Council (1962–5) and the implications of some of its pronouncements for Catholic engagement with Scripture.[88]

By the end of 1984 he was working on both his Acts commentaries. Although he approached their revision as a New Testament scholar rather than as a classicist, which he had been when he began to write on the book, his fundamental perspective remained unchanged: 'A writer may be at one and the same time a sound historian and a capable theologian. The author of Acts was both. The quality of his history naturally varied according to the availability and trustworthiness of his sources, but being a good theologian as well as a good historian, he did not allow his theology to distort his history.'[89] He remained convinced that the speeches in the book were reliable summaries of what was said, and that Luke was not putting his own ideas into the mouths

---

[86] F.F. Bruce, *The Letter of Paul to the Romans: An Introduction and Commentary*, TNTC (Leicester: IVP/Grand Rapids, MI: Eerdmans, 2nd edn, 1985), p. 190, cf. p. 56 n. 1.

[87] N.T. Wright, 'The Messiah and the People of God: A Study in Pauline Theology with Particular Reference to the Argument of the Epistle to the Romans', DPhil thesis, University of Oxford, 1981.

[88] Bruce, *Romans*, 2nd edn, p. 38 n.

[89] F.F. Bruce, 'The Acts of the Apostles: Historical Record or Theological Reconstruction?', in *Aufstieg und Niedergang der Römischen Welt: Geschichte und Kultur Roms im Spiegel der neueren Forschung*, Teil II: *Principat*, Band 25.3 (ed. Hildegard Temporini and Wolfgang Haase; Berlin/New York: Walter de Gruyter, 1985), pp. 2569–603, at p. 2600.

of the speakers. However, Bruce's emphasis on Acts as history meant that he did not feel the need to revise his commentaries to include more theology. That said, his commentaries in the New International series are considered to have lasted better than most.

The revision of his commentary on Hebrews appeared in 1990. He replaced the text of the American Standard Version (1901) with a translation of his own, updated the footnotes to include references to recent works, but made little change to the text. As with his Romans commentary, he took less account than he might have done of recent discussion, although the impact of this is mitigated by the commentary's focus on the text itself rather than on scholarly debate about it, and on linguistic rather than theological aspects of interpretation.

Completing a short commentary on Habakkuk early in 1987, he was pleased to find that his eyesight could still cope with reading the pointing to Hebrew vowels.[90] His activity was to be severely curtailed, however, when in the spring he suffered congestive heart failure and was seriously ill for some weeks. Indeed, at one point he felt that he had only a few weeks to live.[91] His speaking and conference days were suddenly ended, and he now had to confine himself to writing. His walking days were over too, for he had to avoid gradients. One great disappointment was that he could no longer bring in the coal or carry the tea tray for Betty. They had to cancel a Mediterranean cruise planned for July, although they planned to visit Scotland in October. Once he recovered, it was back to work, but by now he was beginning to scale down what he planned to do.

Ill health did not prevent Fred and Betty from continuing to travel to see their family, visiting Australia in October 1988 and Canada in September 1989. Betty enjoyed flying, which meant that Fred was freer to enjoy it himself; Betty once told friends that on a long-distance flight he was like a child in a sweetie shop![92] They also found long- distance travel easier than many shorter journeys as they could get a taxi from home to Manchester Airport, and be met by family at the other end of a direct flight.[93] As well as visiting family, in September 1985 Fred and Betty took a cruise to Antioch on the Orontes and Jerusalem,

[90] CPF 1934 newsletter, April 1987. It was published in *The Minor Prophets* (3 vols; ed. Thomas E. McComiskey; Grand Rapids, MI: Baker, 1992–5), 2:831–96.
[91] CBA, Box 323/4/1/3, Bruce to Neil Dickson, 19 August 1989.
[92] John Drane, telephone conversation, 20 October 2009; Drane to the author, 31 July 2010.
[93] Bruce to Jean Angell, 18 June 1989.

and April 1989 saw them cruising the Mediterranean with Swan Hellenic again.[94] Small wonder, then, that in the final edition of his *Who's Who* entry he could still list his only recreation as foreign travel.

While still recovering from his heart attack, 'I tried to take my mind off myself by writing up my Manchester lecture notes on the Canon of the OT and NT'.[95] This was to be his last major writing project, although he had had in mind the idea of a book on the history of the New Testament canon as far back as 1944; the resulting volume appeared in 1988 as *The Canon of Scripture*.[96] It examined the growth and process of recognition of both the Old Testament and New Testament canons.[97] Given the solidity of its contents, and the fact that this was emphatically not the work of a scholar in his dotage, one might be forgiven for wondering why no major British publisher took it on (in the USA, it was published by IVP). My guess is that Paternoster may not have been in a position to do so, financially speaking, and that it was Bruce's choice to offer it to a new firm, Chapter House, which was headed by the previous director of Pickering & Inglis, Nicholas Gray. Aspects of it may also have been too controversial for other evangelical firms; indeed, given that it did not follow the conservative line too closely, Bruce felt that IVP in North America were running a risk in taking it on.[98] For example, chapter 7, 'Before and After the Reformation', leaves the reader with the clear impression that Bruce was willing to acknowledge a strong case for including the Apocrypha in Protestant editions of the Bible, as he noted with approval the fact that most of them did so until the mid-nineteenth century, when a more precisely defined view of

---

[94] Bruce to Alan Millard, 11 February 1985; CPF 1934 newsletter, April 1989.

[95] Bruce to Ward and Laurel Gasque, Easter Day 1988.

[96] Leicester, UCCF archives, Bruce to Douglas Johnson, 29 July 1944; CBA, Box 11(11g), Bruce to Ian S. Davidson, 28 July 1987; CPF 1934 newsletter, Autumn 1987; Sheila Lukabyo to the author, undated.

[97] Originally the focus had been intended to be the New Testament only: F.F. Bruce, 'Some Thoughts on the Beginning of the New Testament Canon', *BJRL* 65/2 (Spring 1983): pp. 37–60, at p. 37. Other writings on the canon include 'New Light on the Origins of the New Testament Canon', in *New Dimensions in New Testament Study* (ed. Richard N. Longenecker and Merrill C. Tenney; Grand Rapids, MI: Zondervan, 1974), pp. 3–18; 'Canon', in *Dictionary of Jesus and the Gospels* (ed. Joel B. Green, Scot McKnight and I. Howard Marshall; Downers Grove and Leicester: IVP, 1992).

[98] Cf. Bruce to Ward and Laurel Gasque, Easter Day 1988.

biblical inspiration began to gain or regain ground.[99] In this respect his views had changed since 1954, when he had dismissed the Apocrypha, without any comment on the value of its circulation, on the straightforward grounds that Christ and his apostles showed no signs of accepting it as authoritative.[100] His apprehensions regarding the book's reception appear to have been largely groundless, however; the work was acclaimed in North America, where it won the Evangelical Christian Publishers' Association Gold Medallion Award for 1989 and two Christianity Today Awards in 1990: Readers' Choice and Critics' Choice (in both cases winning first place in the section for books on theology and doctrine).

On a related theme was a remarkable and provocative essay in a *Festschrift* for a former colleague, R.P.C. Hanson, 'Scripture in Relation to Tradition and Reason', also published in 1988. Its interest lies in the positive estimate by an evangelical of the comprehensive understanding of tradition in Eastern Orthodoxy, in which Scripture takes a primary place, which Bruce described as 'approximating to its New Testament usage: it embraces practically everything that goes to make up Christian life and thought, and is indistinguishable from the abiding witness of the Spirit'.[101] He saw no tension in the New Testament between written and unwritten tradition, and asserted that we should not think that what survives in writing was uniquely inspired. Pauline tradition was equally authoritative whether delivered orally or in the form of a letter (2 Thessalonians 2:15); it was validated by the Lord, historically (1 Corinthians 11:23), but also because it was authenticated through the Holy Spirit in the church.

Discussion of his thinking about tradition and canon raises again the issues of biblical inspiration and authority, and it is in some letters to a member of the Churches of Christ that we find Bruce's latest thinking on these subjects. He stressed, firstly, that inspiration continued to inhere in the text of Scripture:

---

[99] This would have been associated with such writers as the Scot Robert Haldane and the Swiss Louis Gaussen, whose *Theopneustia* (first published around 1840) offered an important presentation of the doctrine of biblical inerrancy which some have contrasted with less rigid views held by eighteenth-century British evangelicals.

[100] F.F. Bruce, 'The Canon of Scripture', *Inter-Varsity*, Autumn 1954, pp. 19–22.

[101] F.F. Bruce, 'Scripture in Relation to Tradition and Reason', in *Scripture, Tradition and Reason: Essays in Honour of Richard P.C. Hanson* (ed. R. Bauckham and B. Drewery; Edinburgh: T&T Clark, 1988), pp. 35–65, at p. 37.

Biblical inspiration is not an activity which took place once for all, when the words were spoken or written; it is an on-going quality of the Scriptures, as the Spirit continues to impart and maintain life through them, and it includes the work of the Spirit in the reader or hearer of the Scriptures, empowering him to respond to the prophetic invitation: 'Hear, and your soul shall live.'[102]

This dynamic quality was what had gripped the early Protestant reformers; they were the men they were because they heard God's voice in Scripture. To them it was a living book, although their successors too often treated it as a rule book and gave it, rather than the Lord to whom it bears witness, central place. Bruce was a man who loved the Scriptures because he heard God address him through them, but he did not therefore treat them as abstracted from human culture and history; almost at the end of his life he could affirm that his confidence in the Bible had grown deeper over the years, one factor being his involvement in discoveries which had confirmed its historical reliability.[103]

By December 1987 he was beginning to wind down; that month saw the last of his series of exegetical articles for *The Witness* and then *The Harvester* which stretched back to 1971. He had also completed his book on the canon, and soon after had corrected the proofs of his NICNT commentary on Acts. Thereafter, he edited several more commentaries, presumably in the NICNT series, and completed revision of his own on Hebrews and on the Greek text of Acts (this was his last major piece of work).[104] Ward and Laurel Gasque were therefore commissioned by *Christianity Today* to interview him at his home, which they did in August 1988.[105] By now, he could describe himself as feeling stranded by the loss of most of his few close friends.[106] A few years

---

[102] CBA, Box 11(11g), Bruce to Ian S. Davidson, 28 July 1987.

[103] CBA, Box 11(11g), Bruce to Ian S. Davidson, 22 August 1988, 3 July 1990.

[104] Ward and Laurel Gasque, 'F.F. Bruce – "A Tradition of Independent Bible Study"', *H* 68/6 (June 1989): pp. 10–12, at p. 10; I. Howard Marshall, 'Frederick Fyvie Bruce 1910–1990', *Proceedings of the British Academy* 80 (1991): pp. 245–60, at p. 258 n.

[105] Bruce to Laurel Gasque, 20 June 1988; Bruce to Alan Millard, 11 January 1989; Ward Gasque to the author, 11 September 2009. It appeared, abbreviated, as 'F.F. Bruce: A Mind for What Matters', *CT*, 7 April 1989, pp. 22–5. Other versions included 'An Interview with F.F. Bruce', *St Mark's Review*, no. 139 (Spring 1989): pp. 4–10; 'F.F. Bruce – "A Tradition of Independent Bible Study"', *H* 68/6 (June 1989): pp. 10–12; 'F.F. Bruce – The Apostle Paul and the Evangelical Heritage', *H* 68/7 (July 1989): pp. 10–12; 'F.F. Bruce – Layman and Scholar', *H* 68/8 (August 1989): pp. 10–11.

[106] Ward and Laurel Gasque, 'Layman and Scholar', p. 11.

earlier, correcting the proof pages of a revision of the *Bible Commentary for Today*, he had noted that he was the only surviving member of the original editorial team, his friends H.L. Ellison and G.C.D. Howley having died; the revision appeared from Zondervan in the USA under his name alone.[107]

However, over the last two years of his life he did give considerable assistance as a special reviewer to Kenneth N. Taylor, who was producing a revised version of the *Living Bible* which would appear as the *New Living Translation*. And from time to time he would meet individuals in Manchester, often at the Piccadilly Hotel in order to spare Betty the burden of entertaining.[108] He also continued to be active pastorally; although he had stood down from the eldership in 1983, a case of church discipline precipitated a crisis and he was called to chair two meetings to sort things out.[109] Outside his own congregation, during the late 1980s he agreed to meet a Methodist group near Buxton whose highly conservative views of Scripture placed them in tension with others in the circuit and to share his conclusions with the circuit minister.[110]

By the spring of 1990, he was limiting what he took on, as he liked to think he would have a reasonable chance of surviving to complete it. He had completed an article on the canon for a new IVP *Dictionary of Jesus and the Gospels*, and a ten-thousand word one on 'Paul in Acts and Letters' for the companion *Dictionary of Paul and His Letters*.[111] For the same publisher, he had agreed to revise some of his contributions to the *New Bible Commentary*, but it does not appear that he ever did so. Around this time he handed over editorship of the NICNT series to Gordon Fee.[112]

It is in the light of Bruce's consciousness of his mortality, then, that we should view *A Mind for What Matters*. The preface was dated June

---

[107] Bruce to Alan Millard, 28 June 1985; Alan Millard to the author, 27 March 2010.

[108] Carol Stream, IL, Tyndale House Publishers, Bruce to Jack Hywel-Davies, 26 April 1989; Anon., 'New Living Translation' http://en.wikipedia.org/wiki/New_Living_Translation (accessed 24 November 2009); Anon., 'NLT: Meet the Scholars' http://www.newlivingtranslation.com/05discoverthenlt/meetthescholars.asp (accessed 24 November 2009).

[109] Bruce to Harold G. Humphreys, 2 June 1989.

[110] Bob Davies, interview, 28 May 2008.

[111] CPF 1934 newsletter, April 1990; Bruce, 'Canon'; idem, 'Paul in Acts and Letters', in *Dictionary of Paul and His Letters* (ed. Gerald F. Hawthorne and Ralph P. Martin; Downers Grove, IL, and Leicester: IVP, 1993).

[112] Bruce to Alan Lukabyo, 28 June 1990.

1990, so the book was one of his last writing projects. It collected together eighteen previously published essays which he believed to have abiding significance, for the benefit of a wider public than would have seen the originals. He first floated the idea with Eerdmans in August 1988, but its publication appears to have been intended as an eightieth birthday tribute.[113] The essays ranged over early Judaism, the New Testament, the early church, and three topics of relevance to Brethren in particular – the church in the apostolic era, the humanity of Christ, and a survey of the biblical evidence regarding women in the church. The essays received updated bibliographical references but otherwise remained essentially as they were. The compilation was dedicated to the Faculty of Divinity at Aberdeen, as a 'belated thank-offering from an adopted son' (forty-three years after it had conferred an honorary doctorate on him). But the most arresting thing about the whole book was its first footnote, added to his presidential address to the Society for New Testament Studies: 'When this address was delivered, I could not have foreseen, nor would I have believed it possible, that in November 1987 the authorities of Aberdeen University would so repudiate their noble heritage as to decree the axing of the Department of Classics – a sacrifice on the altar of cost-effectiveness.'[114] Given how much he felt he owed to Aberdeen, it is not surprising that he felt this decision deeply.

For some time early in 1990 he had been feeling out of sorts, and a succession of tests eventually revealed a growth in his right kidney; on 15 May he had the kidney removed, being discharged on the 30th.[115] Before the operation he had told Kenneth Taylor that it would be some time before he could resume assisting him with his translation work, 'if ever' (he appears to have squeezed in those words on rereading what he had written). At first he felt drained, mentally as well as physically, but gradually he recovered.[116] The surgeon was pleased with Fred's progress when he went back for a check-up, and

---

[113] Grand Rapids, Eerdmans, correspondence file, F.F. Bruce 1987–90, Bruce to W.B. Eerdmans Jr, 8 August 1988; Marshall, 'Bruce 1910–1990', p. 258.

[114] F.F. Bruce, *A Mind for What Matters: Collected Essays* (Grand Rapids, MI: Eerdmans, 1990), p. 281 n. 1; cf. the dedication of *The Canon of Scripture* 'To the departments of Humanity and Greek in the University of Aberdeen, founded 1497, axed 1987, with gratitude for the past and with hope of their early and vigorous resurrection'.

[115] Bruce to Alan Lukabyo, 23 April 1990; Bruce to Alan and Margaret Millard, 1 June 1990.

[116] Carol Stream, IL, Tyndale House Publishers, Bruce to Kenneth N. Taylor, 4 May 1990.

he and Betty planned a week's holiday at a hotel in Dovedale for early August.[117]

Even in hospital the letters had continued to arrive, and it may have been during the stay just mentioned that the nurse brought them to him with the words, 'Here you are, Fred; more fan mail for you.'[118] A few weeks before his death, though, he told his close friend Alan Millard that he had done all that he wanted to.[119] In each drawer and cupboard at home he had left a list of where to find other important papers.[120] All or almost all his writing projects had been completed.

Tests in August revealed the presence of an inoperable stomach cancer.[121] On the 26th he wrote to Alan Millard that a stomach ulcer had flared up and that he was being admitted to hospital that afternoon for a few days' observation; with the same letter he returned the corrected proof pages of his contribution to an eventually aborted volume, *Documents from New Testament Times*.[122] Even at this period he retained his concern for others; on 4 September he wrote to assure Jeremy Mudditt of his sympathy and prayers after a fire a few weeks earlier had devastated the Carlisle warehouse in which Paternoster's entire stock of publications was stored.[123] Back at home, his pain was kept under control and he appears to have continued doing some work: an editorial footnote to one article stated that he died just days after correcting the galley proofs. But his work ended when he died at home, with Betty and his brother present, on 11 September, a month short of his eightieth birthday.[124]

At Easter 1990, while in hospital, he had told Iain to write Alan Millard's name in his diary as the one to conduct his funeral. Following Scottish tradition, this was held in the drawing room of The Crossways with a couple of dozen family and close friends present, followed by the committal in the local cemetery.[125] Thanksgiving services followed, one at Brinnington on 27 October and another at

---

[117] Bruce to Alan Lukabyo, 28–29 June 1990.

[118] Alastair and Jane Rossetter, interview, 23 August 2008.

[119] Alan Millard, 'Frederick F. Bruce', in *They Finished Their Course in the 90s* (comp. Robert Plant; Kilmarnock: John Ritchie, 2000), pp. 29–34, at pp. 32–3.

[120] Sheila Lukabyo, interview, 2 September 2009.

[121] Sheila Lukabyo to the author, 9 August 2010.

[122] Bruce to Alan Millard, 26 August 1990.

[123] Eerdmans, correspondence file, F.F. Bruce 1987–90.

[124] F.F. Bruce, 'Luke's Presentation of the Spirit in Acts', *Criswell Theological Review* 5 (1990): pp.15–29, at p. 15 n.; Sheila Lukabyo to the author, 9 August 2010.

[125] Alan Millard to the author, 26 October 2006.

the University Chaplaincy in Manchester on 13 March 1991. Warm tributes were paid by representatives of the different circles in which he had moved. It was clear that 'F.F.B.' had left a remarkable legacy behind him, and in the final chapter we shall try to assess it.

10

Legacy and Evaluation

'To hear the voice of God in Holy Scripture oneself, and to help others to hear it, is a worthy cause to which to devote one's resources; to be commissioned to devote them to this cause is a sacred trust, not to be undertaken lightly, not to be refused irresponsibly, but to be fulfilled thankfully.'[1] So runs the concluding sentence of *In Retrospect*. Bruce sought to discharge this trust to the best of his ability throughout a long and productive career; but what was the impact of his work? What legacy did he leave behind him? How did he influence the thinking and practice of others?

Although he was wary of systematic theology, he made no secret of his liking for the discipline of 'Biblical Theology', perhaps because he felt that this could emerge from inductive study of the text of Scripture; it is therefore debatable whether he could have had the same degree of influence if he had emerged as a biblical scholar after the Biblical Theology movement had gone into terminal decline, though his fundamental approach would probably have remained unaltered. Perhaps the high point of his influence in the wider world was during the 1950s and early 1960s; this was an era when conservative outlooks were dominant in various spheres of thought, including religion (the conservatism of the Biblical Theology movement being a case in point), and the public Christian consensus was not challenged on so widespread a front as would later be the case. In addition, he happened to be an expert on topics which caught the public eye, such as the Dead Sea Scrolls. From the mid-1960s, his influence was probably confined more to the academic world, and in particular the evangelical part of it. I want to look, therefore, at his impact on three communities: Brethren, evangelicalism generally, and the world of academic biblical studies.

---

[1] *IR*, p. 312.

✦   ✦   ✦

Among the Brethren, it remains a fairly common if not quite fair opinion that Bruce was an instructive if not an inspiring speaker; it is also generally agreed that he was at his best in informal question and answer sessions, especially when these formed part of residential gatherings. Given the role played by house parties and conferences in shaping the thinking of the emerging generations of Brethren leaders during the 1940s, 1950s and 1960s, it is not difficult to see how he came to exercise considerable influence in assembly circles, especially as such folk would have been likely to buy his books. In addition, he was constantly travelling to conferences and other meetings to preach, and was a frequent contributor to the magazines which did so much to give Brethren a sense of family identity and coherence. Furthermore, this was an era when some Brethren were becoming more open to the wider evangelical world; Bruce's academic respectability made him both an icon and a trailblazer, and it is no coincidence that this era produced a number of Brethren biblical scholars. Others in assemblies who did not become professional biblical scholars nevertheless aspired to academic respectability in the teaching they sought to provide, for which his books and conference talks were an invaluable resource. At a time when some Brethren were seeking to move away from the separatist aspects of their history and also to acclimatize themselves to the burgeoning suburban middle classes, Bruce's presentation of Brethrenism in particular and evangelical Christianity in general proved congenial. (It should be borne in mind that the more conservative assemblies in Britain were, by contrast, often more working-class in their social composition, and suspicious of anything savouring of intellectualism; his influence among them was more limited, except perhaps where he was known personally.)

Brethren early in the twentieth century were noted for their ability to produce self-taught students of the Bible. Such men (and they were all men) rarely undertook any formal course of theological study and often came from a working-class background in which university education was undreamt of (apart from a few who became schoolteachers), but their mastery of Scripture was, to our generation, nothing short of astonishing. It was not at all unknown for them to set about learning the biblical languages, and to deploy their knowledge of these in Bible readings (open discussions of a passage of Scripture) in assemblies and conferences. Scottish Brethren in particular produced a stream of such men, who exercised a ministry of teaching and writing which was influential beyond the British Isles.[2] To some extent Bruce belonged to this tradition for, as far as biblical studies are concerned, he was indeed largely self-taught; furthermore, he related to some of these men on terms of mutual respect.

The independency of Open Brethren would not necessarily have limited his impact to particular localities, for the magazines in which he wrote circulated widely in Britain; his books, too, would have crossed many boundaries, theological as well as geographical, because they did not come across as the products of a particular theological perspective. Overseas, his impact was probably greatest where Brethren were influenced by the work of IVF, since they would be the most likely to value his approach to biblical exegesis. Such people, often holding professional status in their daily lives, found his writings valuable in equipping them to function as lay theologians at the assembly level. The 1950s and 1960s saw a massive expansion of the availability of higher education in various countries, creating a new market for serious books on Christian themes at a time when there were few evangelicals in high academic positions, and thus his writings had few competitors.[3] It is a remarkable fact that of his fifty books, no less than half remain in print in Britain or North America.[4] In more open North American Brethren circles, the writings and ministry of scholarly British leaders (such as Bruce and his friend G.C.D. Howley) helped to move assemblies away from suspicion of higher education towards a more positive attitude.

We should not overstate Bruce's influence on post-war Brethren, however. As far as the dispensationalist consensus is concerned, it may be argued that George Eldon Ladd did more to undermine it by producing a string of works offering systematic expositions of eschatological themes; Bruce's work was primarily exegetical in nature and

---

[2] Cf. Neil Dickson, *Brethren in Scotland 1838–2000: A Social Study of an Evangelical Movement* (Carlisle: Paternoster, 2002). Many such men were recorded in several compilations of obituaries published by the conservative Brethren firm of John Ritchie in Kilmarnock: James Anderson, ed., *They Finished Their Course* (1980); idem, ed., *They Finished Their Course in the Eighties* (1990); Robert Plant, comp., *They Finished Their Course in the 90s* (2000). Bruce was included in the third of these.

[3] Robert Baylis, *My People: The History of Those Christians Sometimes Called Plymouth Brethren* (Port Colborne, ON: Gospel Folio Press, 2006), p. 288; Robert Gordon, interview, 6 August 2008; Mark Noll, interview, 31 March 2009.

[4] At 1 October 2009, publisher's websites listed 11 in print in Britain, and 23 in the United States; some would have been in print in both countries.

he was wary of systematizing.[5] Moreover, Ladd was working in North America, where dispensationalism was most influential, while Bruce in Britain was on its peripheries. It is also worth noting that the area of North America where Bruce was most influential was Western Canada. British Columbia retained strong links with Great Britain, and its evangelicalism was marked by openness to new thinking and a relative freedom from traditional constraints. In assessing his influence on Brethren in various parts of the English-speaking world, then, there is a complex interplay between Brethren ethos, educational background, links with Britain and strength of local traditions.

In some quarters, it seems that Brethren liked the idea of Bruce, but were perhaps less certain about the reality: they were glad to acknowledge him as a renowned biblical scholar, but would not necessarily have approved of his methodology or conclusions. To have 'one of us' in a position of influence is always an encouragement to a minority, and such individuals may well be allowed to write or say things which rank and file members would not. Some of his utterances left the meaning to be decoded by the hearer or reader. Certainly there are occasions when one needs to think carefully about what he is actually saying – or, more often, not saying.

Bruce could be seen as pulling the Brethren movement back to its true focus and away from the sectarianism into which it had slipped.[6] Others, however, would see his influence as leading to the erosion of what they believe to be New Testament patterns of church life, and to the loss of assembly distinctiveness. For all his irenic outlook, therefore, he could be regarded as having had something of a divisive influence, especially when his views were taken up by others who perhaps lacked his fine sense of pastoral tact. Assemblies might function happily enough with a divergence of views among their members on certain issues, but when it came to a divergence of practice, this proved much more difficult to cope with. One example would be his commitment to egalitarianism in church life. He is recalled as returning to his old assembly in Sheffield to speak on the ministry of women after a Sunday evening service; they later allowed women to participate audibly in services, with the resulting loss of a number of

---

[5] Ward Gasque, interview, 6 April 2009. On Ladd and his project, see John A. D'Elia, 'A Place at the Table: George Eldon Ladd and the Rehabilitation of Evangelical Scholarship in America', PhD dissertation, University of Stirling, 2005, since published under the same title (New York: OUP, 2008).
[6] Robert Gordon, interview, 6 August 2008.

members who disagreed with this move.[7] However, it could fairly be argued that any opinion whatever on such a topic is likely to prove divisive when implemented in practice. What must be acknowledged is that Bruce's ministry could be seen as contributing to the growth of alternative views on a range of issues, and that these divergences may have proved impossible to contain in certain contexts. Indeed, the mere fact that he encouraged and modelled the pursuit of academic understanding of the Bible was itself likely to prove divisive in a group of churches which was extensively influenced by fundamentalist attitudes. And indirectly his influence in the Young Men's Bible Teaching Conferences may have been divisive, in that it was from these that the Christian Brethren Research Fellowship drew much of its initial inspiration, and the CBRF as a progressive body willing to take a fresh look at all aspects of Brethren received tradition was never universally approved of among assemblies.[8] On the other hand, many would doubtless have testified to benefiting from his teaching sessions at such conferences, and from the books which they purchased after hearing him speak. Bruce was one of a group of Brethren who saw the need for young leaders to be given a solid grounding in the truths of the faith and in the techniques of handling Scripture.

◆   ◆   ◆

Bruce's impact on English-speaking evangelicalism, especially in Britain, has been more widely acknowledged. He has been called 'evangelicalism's Erasmus, a man of phenomenal knowledge and prodigious literary output, the main stimulus in a revival of biblical scholarship, and one of the most renowned biblical scholars of his time'.[9] His scholarship was respected by evangelicals of most persuasions, and he consistently refused to align himself with any one evangelical tribe, grateful that 'In this country evangelicals generally (and wisely) prefer to be unhyphenated evangelicals.'[10] When his former student and close friend Ward Gasque lectured on Bruce at Manchester's John Rylands University Library in July 2007, he chose

---

[7] Alan Dixon, telephone conversation, 5 October 2009.

[8] Alan Millard, interview, 28 May 2008.

[9] Murray J. Harris, 'Frederick Fyvie Bruce', in *Bible Interpreters of the 20th Century: A Selection of Evangelical Voices* (ed. Walter A. Elwell and J.D. Weaver; Grand Rapids, MI: Baker, 1999), pp. 216–27, at p. 226.

[10] *IR*, p. 278.

to entitle his lecture 'F.F. Bruce – An Unhyphenated Evangelical'. In a letter to his grandson, Bruce struck an authentically evangelical note, expressing the opinion, with reference to the history of the Student Christian Movement, that the point at which a Christian should stick fast and refuse to compromise his or her beliefs 'is reached with the claim that Jesus, and no other, is the Saviour of the world'. Who are Christians to tell others what to believe? Simply those who have received what they feel compelled to share with others.[11] The issues which, for Bruce, were non-negotiable may be summarized as the reliability of the New Testament, the person and work of Christ, the Christian life as one of forgiveness and liberty as befits those who are being led by the Spirit, and the right and duty of every believer to use whatever gifts God has given them.

His influence on the evangelical world has been summarized as twofold: he paved the way for widespread evangelical acceptance of critical methodologies as having a part to play in reverent and submissive biblical study, and for wider academic acceptance of evangelicals as genuine scholars. (In Britain he was perhaps the prime mover in this.) It has been suggested that his scholarship and influence helped to counter the earlier evangelical tendency to withdraw into a narrowly 'devotional' approach to Scripture.[12] Evangelical scholars found him a great encourager; one even called him an 'apostolic individual' because of his support and encouragement to many embarking on biblical research.[13] For many evangelicals, Bruce was 'Exhibit A' as evidence for their claim to have an intellectually credible position.[14] And I think it fair to say that he had something of a 'fan base', people who bought his books as they appeared, and who adopted his approach to exegesis; I have come across more than one person with a collection of Bruce's books and articles. Ministers who were guided by his commentaries would have mediated his influence through their preaching and teaching, and the Tyndale Fellowship (and hence many of its members) has been moulded by the emphasis on painstaking critical study of the biblical text which he shared with W.J. Martin.

At a personal level, his impact on his students was significant and lasting, and many testified to this. To some, he gave confidence to

---

[11] Bruce to Alan Lukabyo, 9 March 1990.

[12] Oliver R. Barclay to the author, 20 August 2009.

[13] Peter H. Davids, *The First Epistle of Peter*, NICNT (Grand Rapids, MI: Eerdmans, 1990), p. ix.

[14] Carl Armerding, interview, 6 April 2009.

express themselves academically; to others, he gave skills which they would use constantly in their future work; to many, he provided the necessary reassurance that it was possible to study the Bible critically without losing their faith or divorcing the intellectual and devotional sides of their lives. Several examples may be given. A Scripture Union volunteer staff worker, now a tutor of Methodist lay preachers, considered that 'my studies with Prof. Bruce gave me all the tools I need for sorting out exegetical or hermeneutical questions'.[15] A nurse recollected how his talks and books had confirmed her faith and strengthened her witness as a Christian believer.[16] A schoolteacher remembered Bruce allaying his fears about academic theological study by saying that all truth is God's truth, and that it therefore cannot lead us astray.[17] As he explained to evangelical graduates, the practice of textual criticism was not a threat to faith but it enabled believers to appreciate the justification for the Westminster Confession's assertion that text of Scripture had been preserved 'by God's singular care and providence'.[18] Another teacher summed up Bruce's influence on her as being:

> to deepen my existing love of Holy Scripture. He was able to demonstrate how one could consider Scripture 'critically' while still maintaining belief in its Divine inspiration and authority. With FFB, to study 'Biblical Criticism and Exegesis' was to deepen one's understanding and appreciation of the spiritual and moral implications of the text – he never reduced it simply to an interesting collection of ancient documents to be analysed. I suppose that one unconsciously absorbed from him an attitude towards scripture; not merely factual information, or techniques for studying ancient literature written in a 'dead language'.
>
> Suffice it to say that when I left Manchester, I went to my first teaching post with confidence that I had a comprehensive knowledge of the Bible and the skills to debate on a wide range of related topics . . . FFB played a real role in giving me that confidence and the debating skills I needed.[19]

[15] Joan Wragg to the author, 3 June 2009.
[16] Janet Hill to the author, 17 October 2008.
[17] Dennis Angell to the author, 15 July 2008.
[18] F.F. Bruce, 'Textual Criticism', CG 6 (1953): pp. 135–9.
[19] Heather Booth to the author, 21 September 2009.

For some at least, the secret of his impact lay primarily in what he was as a person: for the cultural historian Laurel Gasque, he was 'the most genuinely free person I have ever met'.[20] As we have already noted, James Barr, who subjected evangelicalism to a series of passionate critiques which perhaps generated more heat than light, exempted Bruce from the charge that evangelicals shared the same underlying assumptions as fundamentalists and so were not to be considered as objective scholars. This was because Bruce did not only deploy critical scholarship when it supported conservative conclusions, and hence did not 'put conservatism before scholarship'.[21] From a very different standpoint, Oliver Barclay, the erstwhile UCCF general secretary, categorized Bruce as a 'conservative liberal'.[22] Iain Murray would view him in the same light; he argues that post-war evangelicals believed that co-operation with liberal scholars on investigating the human aspects of Scripture was possible, using the standard tools for biblical criticism. Murray believes that they hoped to dispel prejudice by leaving the divine aspects of Scripture on one side in this work and so gain academic credibility and respect. Bruce, he claims, 'meant to approach the authority of Scripture cautiously and indirectly'.[23] It is true that Bruce ruled no conclusions out of court on an *a priori* basis because of his understanding of the nature of biblical inspiration and authority, for he genuinely believed that he was prepared to go wherever the evidence led him. Of course, at this distance and in a climate in which objectivity as an ideal is no longer taken as axiomatic, we may wonder why that evidence so often led him in a conservative direction, and whether he was as objective as he thought he was. This would apply to his apologetic work as well as his biblical commentary. However, Bruce never made any secret of his belief that Scripture was divine as well as human, and he had no need to seek respectability in the scholarly world because he had it already; in this he contrasts with some of the

---

[20] Laurel Gasque, interview, 6 April 2009.

[21] Harriet A. Harris, *Fundamentalism and Evangelicals* (Oxford: Clarendon, 1998), p. 75, cf. p. 73.

[22] Oliver Barclay, *Evangelicalism in Britain 1935–1995: A Personal Sketch* (Leicester: IVP, 1997), p. 129. By contrast, Barclay had earlier described Bruce as a 'powerful influence for good': 'F.F. Bruce and the Inter-Varsity Fellowship', *JCBRF*, no. 22 (November 1971): p. 20; cf. Oakes, 'Bruce', pp. 101–2.

[23] Iain H. Murray, *Evangelicalism Divided: A Record of Crucial Change in the Years 1950 to 2000* (Edinburgh: Banner of Truth, 2000), esp. p. 180.

American scholars of the period who were seeking to gain entrance to the world of academic theology as outsiders teaching in evangelical colleges. In addition, it is right to note his lifelong support for the IVF (later UCCF) and for the Tyndale Fellowship. This was a man who both knew where he stood personally and had a finely developed sense of how to use the 'tools of the trade' in a way which was, in his view, consonant with his faith. And it was precisely that faith, with its belief that all truth should be welcomed, which made him as open-minded as he was.

This openness served him well and enabled him to be at ease in the academic sphere, and several who would no longer claim to be evangelicals nevertheless continue to acknowledge a debt to him as far as their approach to the text is concerned, but it is arguable that it has contributed to a downgrading of the importance of systematic theology in evangelical thinking, especially in England. (Of course, other significant factors have also been at work in this trend, and I am not suggesting that a non-theological approach to exegesis and exposition is necessarily the most important.) How can this, which has (perhaps misleadingly) been put down to theological naivety, be explained? Bruce's background in Scottish Reformed evangelicalism gave him a good doctrinal foundation, since he often referred to works such as the Westminster Shorter Catechism and the Puritan classics. Moreover, he had read with appreciation newer writers in the broader Reformed tradition such as Barth and Berkouwer, neither of whom can be called straightforward to read, and he always saw himself as standing within the broader Reformed tradition.[24] I think that three factors may have given rise to the belief that he was theologically unsophisticated. The first was a Brethren-inspired wariness of too much emphasis on systematic theology at the expense of close exegetical study of Scripture. Where he did speak of theological matters, he preferred to express the truths of the faith in non-technical terms, although he was happy to accept the wording of the IVF doctrinal basis.[25] The second was that he was reacting against what he saw as a widespread tendency on the part of theologians to pronounce verdicts on the historicity or otherwise of material in the gospels; in his opinion, they were not the ones who were qualified to do so and it was for the historians to make such judgements.[26] The third was a particular

---

[24] IR, p. 302.

[25] IR, pp. 310–11.

[26] Anthony R. Cross, 'A Critical Comparison of Professor F.F. Bruce and Professor Rudolf Bultmann on the Historical Reliability of the New Testament', BA dissertation, Bristol University, 1985, p. 27, citing Bruce's essay 'History and the Gospel', in

conception of what was involved in commentary writing, in which the aim was to elucidate and illuminate the ancient text. When in 1943 he began to write his commentary on the Greek text of Acts, a document on which other classical writings could shed plenty of light, he was still a classics lecturer. As such, he insisted that the primary concern of a commentator was to establish what the text actually said and to shed as much background light on it as possible. Exposition and application were not part of commentary proper, although he was capable of them when the format of a particular series demanded. The lack of theology in many of his commentaries could therefore be put down to a conscious decision on his part to focus on the task in hand. This is one reason why his work found acceptance among scholars of radically different persuasions – there were no theological obstacles to their doing so.

Nevertheless, whilst theology was dependent on sound exegesis, which in its turn required accurate grammatical study, he was convinced that 'The Scriptures' chief function is to bear witness of Christ, and the chief end of their study and exegesis is to increase our inward knowledge of him, under the illumination of the Spirit of God.'[27] This raises the question of the presuppositions with which we approach the study of the Bible, and it must be said that not all evangelicals were (or are) at ease with Bruce's methodology or his conclusions. Bruce was such a gracious and humble man that it is easy to overlook his desire to see evangelicalism change, and to do so particularly in its handling of the Scriptures. As Peter Oakes has explained:

> The discomfort of some evangelicals with Bruce's work stems from the fact that he sought to bring about changes in evangelicalism itself. Bruce made such a far-reaching contribution to the development of evangelical biblical scholarship because he led the field in doing two things. His work persuaded academics of all theological colours that worthwhile academic work could be done by a scholar holding evangelical views. Bruce also persuaded evangelicals to use a much wider range of academic methods for study of the Bible, and to be open to results that might differ from views traditionally held by evangelicals.[28]

Jesus of Nazareth: Saviour and Lord (ed. C.F.H. Henry; London: Tyndale Press, 1966), pp. 89–107, at p. 89.

[27] F.F. Bruce, 'W.E. Vine – The Theologian', in *W.E. Vine: His Life and Ministry* (ed. Percy O. Ruoff; London: Oliphants, 1951), pp. 69–85, at pp. 69, 85 (quotation).

[28] Peter Oakes, 'F.F. Bruce and the Development of Evangelical Biblical Scholarship', *BJRL* 86/3 (Autumn 2004): pp. 99–124, at p. 102.

It is not claiming too much to say that nobody else was quite so influential in these respects, certainly in Britain. But not all evangelical scholars were at ease with his influence. It has been suggested that the divergent approaches to biblical scholarship seen in the early history of the Tyndale Fellowship, and which have surfaced since in various intra-evangelical theological debates, derive from two different approaches to the question of biblical authority. On the one hand, there are those who derive this from patient inductive study of the texts ('authority from below'), among whom Bruce and Martin may be numbered. This tradition owes much to the early twentieth-century theologian James Orr, and possesses a considerable degree of continuity with nineteenth-century scholars such as J.B. Lightfoot. The result, according to John Wenham, was 'a neglect of Christ's view of Scripture and a certain liberalizing of the Tyndale Fellowship for Biblical Research'.[29] On the other hand are those who derive biblical authority 'from above', making it a presupposition of their approach to the Scriptures. Such scholars tend to give greater place to systematic theology as an interpretative framework for studying the Bible, and they stand in the Princeton tradition articulated most influentially by B.B. Warfield. Lloyd-Jones saw himself as standing in that tradition, and this may explain why his relationship with Bruce

---

[29] John Wenham, *Facing Hell: An Autobiography 1913–1996* (Carlisle: Paternoster, 1998), p. 196. Ironically, one area in which Wenham himself was seen by some as moving in a liberal direction, that of conditional immortality and the denial that eternal punishment was something consciously experienced, was one on which Bruce may have shared his views. In a letter to John Stott of 26 March 1989, Bruce acknowledged annihilationism (the idea that the unbelieving cease to exist at some point, whether after death or after the Last Judgement) to be an acceptable interpretation of the New Testament evidence, but he remained agnostic on the topic: 'Eternal conscious torment is incompatible with the revealed character of God. I'd like to be a universalist, and Paul sometimes encourages me in this (cf. Rom. 11:32; 1 Cor. 15:22), but only (I fear) when he is read out of context. Our Lord's teaching seems plain enough: there are some who persist irretrievably in impenitence, and refuse to the end the only salvation that is available for them.' Bruce was not afraid of criticism but refused to be more dogmatic than the evidence allowed: Timothy Dudley-Smith, *John Stott: A Global Ministry* (Leicester: IVP, 2001), pp. 354–5. In a foreword to a book on the subject, Bruce appeared to accept the argument that the biblical evidence was ambiguous. He described his views as neither traditionalist nor conditionalist, but in line with those of C.S. Lewis, who like him did not systematize his thinking: E.W. Fudge, *The Fire that Consumes* (Carlisle: Paternoster, 2nd edn, 1994), pp. ix–x.

appears never to have been a warm one, and why more generally the biblical scholars and the systematicians in Tyndale Fellowship circles have not always seen eye to eye.[30]

Answering the question 'Does doctrine really matter?', Bruce expressed the conviction that behaviour is influenced by the doctrine we hold, and that therefore 'the central doctrines of Christianity matter infinitely; but our interpretations and refinements of these doctrines do not matter nearly so much as we think. Or, to put it otherwise, the doctrines which unite Christians are of superlative importance; the doctrines which divide them ought to be examined to see whether in fact they are full-orbed Christian doctrines, or were partial appreciations of them.'[31] He was what we might call a catholic Christian, unconcerned to stress doctrinal niceties and often dubious about their basis in biblical exegesis. Patient study of the text had to have priority over adherence to doctrinal formulations, and one fundamental reason for this was that for him it was the Scripture, rather than any other document or formula, which was divinely revealed and through which the Holy Spirit spoke to his heart.

◆ ◆ ◆

Thirdly, then, we turn to consider Bruce's impact in the academic world. The first thing to say is that he left no 'big idea' such as Bultmann's insistence on the need to demythologize the New Testament; he rarely claimed to be original in his thinking, and he was apprehensive about allowing 'big ideas' to exercise much influence in the realm of exegesis. Oakes therefore asks:

> How did he become a figure who was admired both by the flag-bearers of conservative theology and by the doyens of European biblical scholarship?
>
> . . . If Bruce was uncreative and unoriginal, how did he influence and inspire a generation of people in settings as diverse as Brethren churches in the United Kingdom and Presbyterian colleges in the United States? More pointedly, what kind of man has friends who think that he will not mind being described as uncreative and unoriginal? In any case, do the charges stick?[32]

---

[30] Noble, *Tyndale*, p. 243.
[31] *H* 37 (1958): p. 75: Q. 673.
[32] Oakes, 'Bruce',. pp. 99, 101.

To focus on originality as a criterion of significance does not necessarily lead to a just estimate of any theologian's influence. As Oakes
observes, Bruce's friends were aware that he was not an original
thinker; in any case, Bruce himself did not seek originality. Sixty years
ago the quest for the new was not part of the academic outlook in the
way that it has since become, and it was not necessary to have earned
a doctorate as evidence of engagement in this quest in order to be recognized as an effective university teacher. A testimonial provided
during the Manchester appointment process described him as
'Possibly not over imaginative' but 'nevertheless an exceedingly
learned and reliable biblical scholar and a man of fine integrity'.[33]
Another New Testament scholar, Robert Mounce, summed up why
Bruce was influential:

> It is evident . . . that Bruce lays before us no new and innovative per-
> spectives. Concern for historical accuracy coupled with a high view of
> the Biblical text inevitably restricts [sic] the role of the imagination, that
> prime mover in theological and higher critical 'breakthroughs.' Bruce's
> lasting contribution to Pauline studies is his careful and informed treat-
> ment of the life and letters of Paul in their historical, social, religious
> and cultural setting. The fact that his interpretations are traditional has
> no bearing on the question of their value for Biblical study. We are
> indebted to F.F. Bruce for his lifelong commitment to a balanced and
> biblical interpretation of the life and thought of the apostle Paul.[34]

His obituaries confirmed this estimate, and Howard Marshall's article
for the recent *Oxford Dictionary of National Biography* describes him as
a scholar rather than a researcher.[35] Indeed, his highest ambition
would very probably have been to represent faithfully the proclamation of his beloved Paul, Paul's great aim being to proclaim Christ.
Bruce often quoted Charles Wesley's words:

> 'Tis all my business here below
> To cry, 'Behold the Lamb!'

---

[33] Manchester, University of Manchester, Vice-Chancellor's Office, appointment file.
[34] Robert H. Mounce, 'The Contribution of F.F. Bruce to Pauline Studies: A Review
Article', *Journal of the Evangelical Theological Society* 23 (1980): pp. 67–73, at pp.
72–3.
[35] I. Howard Marshall, 'Bruce, Frederick Fyvie (1910–1990)', in *Oxford Dictionary of
National Biography* http://www.oxforddnb.com (accessed 14 April 2008).

And we have noted his high regard for his father and for the evangelistic gift which his father gave his life to exercising. That said, he was creative in his vision of an evangelicalism which could both play its part in scholarly discourse and in turn be enriched thereby. He had the vision to see what did not yet exist, and the application to work to make it a reality.

But if he was neither original nor a compelling speaker, why was he so influential? I think that the answer must lie in the way he conducted his relationships with others. He was loyal to his colleagues, many of whom counted as his friends, and he was assiduous in the pastoral care of his students, undergraduates as well as postgraduates. It is also clear that he had a gift for what would nowadays be called 'mentoring', a valuable and all-too-rare commodity in a postgraduate supervisor. Although he had never received any formal training in theology, and belonged to a denomination which did not recognize an ordained ministry, he was nevertheless involved in various ways in training others. Apart from mentoring individuals and teaching ministerial students as part of his duties in Manchester, the Young Men's Bible Teaching Conferences were essentially about training men to minister. Bruce was not the kind of scholar who saw such activity as a distraction from what he really wanted to do.

Another factor contributing to his impact was, quite simply, the care with which he did his work. References were meticulous and always checked personally, manuscripts were delivered punctually and in a condition which needed little if any editorial work, and correspondence was dealt with promptly and cheerfully. He was an ideal author as far as publishers were concerned. His productivity was aided considerably by a remarkably retentive memory and an instinctively lucid writing style which meant that his drafts rarely needed much revision. He therefore won respect from the academic community by his painstaking attention to detail, wide reading and consequent mastery of the issues. This he set against a background of competence in a wide range of areas within the disciplines of biblical studies, and behind that was his thorough classical training. His work thus 'set a very high standard of philological study in the classical British tradition of Lightfoot and Ramsay'.[36] As a result he was able to support positions which were not new with arguments which (to many) were.[37] Small

---

[36] Gerald Bray, *Biblical Interpretation Past and Present* (Leicester: Apollos, 1996), p. 544.

[37] Oakes, 'Bruce', p. 107.

wonder that one person described him as 'a great writer of footnotes', which 'often provided interesting avenues of development'.[38] Many of his surveys of current scholarly work betray an ability to assimilate an astonishing amount of material, and to pick out for consideration those items which would in time be recognized as particularly valuable or influential. They show that his faculty of critical evaluation was fully developed, even if his kindly book reviews might lead one to think otherwise.

Bruce's versatility should not be overlooked. A reviewer of *The Growing Day* described him as possessing two different styles, the learned 'Hittite-Tyndale' and 'Reliable Documents – I.V.F.'[39] In the estimation of David Clines, Bruce 'had an enormous range and could write with wit and erudition and above all wonderful clarity on any subject'; his greatest talent, however, was as a biblical exegete, and 'he produced a stream of superb commentaries on the New Testament'.[40] His commentaries alone demonstrate his ability to write for different audiences. Having said that, although Bruce's expositions are always clear, any introduction is usually brief and a conclusion is often lacking, a feature which perhaps parallels his lack of conversational small talk. Material is often used in more than one work, and once one has read a number of Bruce's books, a sense of *déjà vu* is liable to overtake the reader.

Furthermore, in his methodology, he practised a high degree of objectivity at a period when this was still sought and prized as the scholarly ideal. That objectivity was rooted in his conviction that all truth was God's truth, which made him open to receive truth from wherever it came. He did not fit the caricature of the ignorant and narrow-minded fundamentalist which most people expected a member of the Brethren to be, but learned from and related to scholars of all persuasions. As he put it, 'I have sometimes learned most from scholars with whom I have agreed least: they compel one to think, and rethink.'[41] He was the least defensive person imaginable, secure

---

[38] Brian Davies to the author, 22 October 2008.

[39] Review by O.R. J[ohnston], in *CG* 4 (1951–2): pp. 126–7, at p. 126.

[40] David J.A. Clines, 'The Sheffield Department of Biblical Studies: An Intellectual Biography', in *Auguries: The Jubilee Volume of the Sheffield Department of Biblical Studies, Journal for the Study of the Old Testament Supplement Series* 269 (ed. idem and Stephen Moore; Sheffield: Sheffield Academic Press, 1998), pp. 14–89, at p. 16–17.

[41] F.F. Bruce, *The Epistles to the Colossians, to Philemon and to the Ephesians*, NICNT (Grand Rapids, MI: Eerdmans, 1984), p. xii.

in his own faith, never attributing unworthy motives to those with whom he disagreed, and won respect from many for his willingness to argue on the basis of the evidence rather than adopting a party line.[42]

In conclusion, we could view Bruce as a 'believing critic', and his sympathy for William Robertson Smith tends to confirm this.[43] Perhaps too he was a popularizer of scholarly work, in the best sense of the word. But I would suggest that the most important way to regard him is as a teacher who sought to use his gifts to build up the church and to offer a credible account of the sources on which the Christian faith is founded; David Hubbard, who was president of Fuller Seminary, testified to how Bruce's 'blend of learnedness, clarity, diligence, evenhandedness, and devotion to the gospel' had influenced him during the 1960s.[44] And Bruce taught not only by his words and writings, but by his life. For that life many continue to give thanks.

---

[42] *IR*, pp. 172–3; various people have confirmed this to me.
[43] e.g. F.F. Bruce, *The Canon of Scripture* (Glasgow: Chapter House, 1988), p. 273.
[44] David A. Hubbard, 'Evangelicals and Biblical Scholarship, 1945–1992: An Anecdotal Commentary', *Bulletin for Biblical Research* 3 (1993): pp. 1–16 http://www.ibr-bbr.org/IBRBulletin/BBR_1993/BBR-1993_01_Hubbard_Evangelicals.pdf (accessed 2 December 2009).

Chronology of the Life of F.F. Bruce

Sources: *Aberdeen University Review* 37 (1957–8): p. 176; 54 (1991–2): p. 82; John Mackintosh, comp., *Roll of the Graduates of the University of Aberdeen 1926–1955: With Supplement 1860–1925* (Aberdeen: University of Aberdeen, 1960); Donald A. Hagner and Murray J. Harris, eds, *Pauline Studies: Essays Presented to Professor F.F. Bruce on His 70th Birthday* (Exeter: Paternoster/Grand Rapids, MI: Eerdmans, 1980), pp. xxxvii–xxxviii.

1910: born, Elgin, 12 October
1915–21: West End School, Elgin
1921–8: Elgin Academy
1928: enters Aberdeen University
1932: MA with first-class honours; enters Caius College, Cambridge
1934: BA (Cambridge) with first-class honours
1934–5: postgraduate study in Vienna
1935: Assistant in Greek, Edinburgh University
1936, 19 August: marriage to Annie Bertha Davidson
1938: Lecturer in Greek, Leeds University
1942–51: chairman, Biblical Research Committee
1942: associate editor, *Evangelical Quarterly*
1943: assistant editor, *Evangelical Quarterly*
1943: Diploma in Hebrew (Leeds)
1945: MA (Cambridge)
1945–58: editor, *Yorkshire Celtic Studies*
1947: Senior Lecturer in charge of the Department of Biblical History and
    Literature, Sheffield University
1948–50: president, Yorkshire Society for Celtic Studies
1949–57: editor, *Journal of the Transactions of the Victoria Institute*
1949–80: editor, *Evangelical Quarterly*
1953: president, Yorkshire Society of Aberdeen Graduates and Alumni
1955: professor, Sheffield
1955–8: president, Sheffield branch, Classical Association

1956–78: contributing editor, *Christianity Today*
1957: honorary DD, Aberdeen
1957–71: editor, *Palestine Exploration Quarterly*
1958–65: president, Victoria Institute (remained honorary vice-president until his death)
1959–78: Rylands Professor of Biblical Criticism and Exegesis, Manchester University
1961–5: consulting editor, *Eternity*
1963–5: president, Manchester Egyptian and Oriental Society
1962–90: general editor, NLCNT/NICNT
1963: MA (Manchester) in Hebrew language and literature
1963–4: dean of the Faculty of Theology, Manchester
1965: president, Society for Old Testament Study
1966–90: advisory editor, *Tyndale Bulletin*
1970–79: editorial co-operator, *Erasmus*
1973: Fellow of the British Academy
1975: president, Society for New Testament Study
1978: emeritus professor, Manchester University
1979: Burkitt Medal in biblical studies, British Academy
1988: honorary DLitt, Sheffield
1990: dies, 11 September

Bibliography of the Writings of F.F. Bruce

I have sought to list all items which Bruce is known to have written, but some have proved impossible to locate and others may have been overlooked; additions (and corrections) will therefore be welcomed. The items are arranged in chronological order, and under each year I have listed them in the following order: (i) books of which he was sole or joint author; (ii) books which he edited; (iii) articles and papers in books and magazines. Details are given of all editions of books written by Bruce, but not of those edited by him or of reprints of a particular edition (unless by a new publisher). Review articles are included, but not book reviews, of which he wrote over two thousand. Nor have I included forewords to books by other authors, editorials, or published letters. Thanks are due to Rob Bradshaw, whose online bibliography provided a valuable starting point for research towards this one.

The bibliography to *In Retrospect* lists only books, but many of his reviews are listed in three bibliographies compiled by Ward Gasque:

'A Select Bibliography of the Writings of F.F. Bruce.' Pages 21–34 in *Apostolic History and the Gospel* (ed. W. Ward Gasque and Ralph P. Martin; Exeter: Paternoster, 1970).

'A Select Bibliography of the Writings of F.F. Bruce 1970–1979.' Pages xxii–xxxvi in *Pauline Studies: Essays Presented to Professor F.F. Bruce on His 70th Birthday* (ed. Donald A. Hagner and Murray J. Harris; Exeter: Paternoster/Grand Rapids, MI: Eerdmans, 1980).

'A Supplementary Bibliography of the Writings of F.F. Bruce'. *JCBRF*, no. 22 (November 1971): pp. 21–47 [also includes his answers to questions in *The Witness*].

Books and articles

Series editorships

Gen. ed. Paternoster Church History (London: Paternoster, 1961 onwards).
Gen. ed., with William Barclay. Bible Guides (London: Lutterworth/New York and Nashville, TN: Abingdon, 1961–5).
Gen. ed. New International Commentaries on the New Testament (Grand Rapids, MI: Eerdmans, 1962–90).
Consulting ed. Pathway Books (Eerdmans, 1956–60).

Regular features

'Answers to Questions'. *H* 31–54 (1952–75).
'Christian Workers' Forum'. *Life of Faith*, 1954–7.
'Professor Bruce Asks'. *H* 52–63 (1973–84).
Untitled series of short apologetic articles for *Release Nationwide*, 1979–86.

1923

'Sic itur ad astra'. *Elgin Academy Magazine*, December 1923, p. 11.

1924

'Six Visions of a Scottish City'. *Elgin Academy Magazine*, December 1924, p. 9.

1925

'The Antiquity of the Scottish Race'. *Elgin Academy Magazine*, June 1925, p. 8.

1927

'De libertate'. *Elgin Academy Magazine*, June 1927, p. 9.
'School Celebrities. (Number 3.) The Very Reverend Professor James Cooper, M.A., D.D., Litt.D., D.C.L., Ll.D.'. *Elgin Academy Magazine*, December 1927, pp. 14–15.

1932

'The Proof of God's Love'. *Nairnshire Telegraph*, 3 May 1932.
    repr. as tract.

1933

'The Early Church in the Roman Empire'. *Bible Student* (Bangalore), no. 56 (March–April 1933): pp. 30–32; no. 57 (May–June 1933): pp. 55–8.

1934

'The Chester Beatty Papyri'. *H* 11 (1934): pp. 163–4.

1935

'The New Gospel'. *H* 12 (1935): pp. 168–70.

1936

'Early Translations of the Bible'. *H* 15 (1936): pp. 105–6, 128, 151–2, 173, 176, 199–200.
'Latin Participles as Slave Names'. *Glotta* 25 (1936): pp. 42–50.

1937

'The Syriac Bible'. *H* 14 (1937): p. 77.

1938

'The Bible Comes Alive'. *H* 15 (1938): p. 16.
'Bible Versions'. *H* 15 (1938): p. 252.
'The Earliest Latin Commentary on the Apocalypse'. *EQ* 10 (1938): pp. 352–66. repr. in *A Mind for What Matters* (Grand Rapids, MI: Eerdmans, 1990), pp. 198–212.
'The Latin Bible'. *H* 15 (1938): pp. 202–3.
'Some Roman Slave-Names'. *Proceedings of the Leeds Philosophical Society: Literary and Historical Section* 5/1 (1938): pp. 44–60.

1939

'Old Testament Criticism and Modern Discovery'. *BM* 49 (1939): pp. 242–3.
'The Philistines'. *H* 16 (1939): pp. 245–6.

1940

'The Date of the Epistle to the Galatians'. *ExT* 51 (1939–40): pp. 396–7.
'The End of the First Gospel'. *EQ* 12 (1940): pp. 203–14.
'The Proper Names in Ezekiel 38'. *H* 17 (1940): pp. 130–31.

1941

'Armageddon through the Ages'. *H* 18 (1941): pp. 23–4.
'Babylon and Rome'. *EQ* 13 (1941): pp. 241–61.
'More about Ezekiel 38'. *H* 18 (1941): p. 150.

1942

'The Kingdom of God'. *Supplement to the I.V.F. Graduates' Fellowship News-Letter*, no. 5 (January 1942).
'Some Aspects of Gospel Introduction'. *EQ* 14 (1942): pp. 174–97, 264–80; 15 (1943): pp. 3–20.

1943

Are the New Testament Documents Reliable? (London: IVF, 1943/Grand Rapids, MI: Eerdmans, 1945).
> 2nd edn (London, IVF, [1946]).
> 3rd edn (London: IVF/Chicago, IL: Inter-Varsity Christian Fellowship, [1950]).
> 4th edn (London: IVF, 1954).
> 5th edn, [new title] *The New Testament Documents: Are They Reliable?* (London: IVF/Grand Rapids, MI: Eerdmans/Downers Grove, IL: IVP, 1960).
> [with bibliography and appendices] (London: IVF/Grand Rapids, MI: Eerdmans, 1963).
> 6th edn (Leicester: IVP, 1981) [repr. 1982 with note by author].
> new edn (Leicester: IVP/Grand Rapids, MI: Eerdmans, 2000).
> [with foreword by N.T. Wright] (Downers Grove, IL: IVP, 2003).
The Speeches in the Acts of the Apostles (London: Tyndale Press, 1943) [Tyndale New Testament Lecture, 1942].
(ed. and preface) Macintyre, D.M. *Some Notes on the Gospels* (London: IVF, 1943).
'The Kingdom of God: A Biblical Survey'. *EQ* 15 (1943): pp. 263–8.
'The Ministry of Women'. *Supplement to the I.V.F. Graduates' Fellowship News-Letter*, no. 9 (April 1943).
'The Sources of the Gospels'. *JTVI* 75 (1943): pp. 1–11.

1944

'Aramaic in the Early Church', 'Jesus in the Gospels', 'The Church in the New Testament'. *Theological Notes*, January 1944, pp. 1–2, 2–3, 3–4.
'Christology', 'Eschatology and Apocalyptic', 'True and False Criticism', 'Olmstead on Ramsay and Meyer', 'Aramaic Origins'. *Theological Notes*, July/October 1944, pp. 2–3, 3–5, 5–7, 7–8, 8.

'The Judgment Seat of Christ'. *BM* 54 (1944): pp. 42–3.
'The Second Isaiah'. *Theological Notes*, May 1944, p. 3.
'Some Notes on the Fourth Evangelist'. *EQ* 16 (1944): pp. 101–9.

1945

'Ahasuerus'. *TB*, *OS*, October 1945, pp. 4–5.
'Archaeology and Literary Criticism'. *TB*, OS, October 1945, pp. 3–4.
'Did Jesus Speak Aramaic?' *ExT* 56 (1944–5): p. 328.
'Dispensationalism'. *TB*, OS, July 1945, pp. 2–6.
'The End of the Second Gospel'. *EQ* 17 (1945): pp. 169–81.
'Fellowship'. *W* 75 (1945): pp. 49–50.
'The Gospels and the Apostolic Preaching'. *Bible Expositor* (New Zealand) 1 (1945): pp. 64–9, 115–21, 173–7; 2 (1946): pp. 95–104, 142–52; 3 (1947): pp. 42–52, 94–104.
'Mythology'. *TB*, OS, July 1945, pp. 6–7.
'Review of Some Biblical Studies in 1944'. *TB*, OS, January 1945, pp. 2–7.

1946

'"And the Earth was without form and void" – An Enquiry into the Exact Meaning of Genesis 1, 2'. *JTVI* 78 (1946): pp. 21–4, 34–7.
'The Books and the Parchments'. *Believer's Pathway* 67 (1946): pp. 14, 20, 32.
'Futurist Eschatology'. *TB*, OS, January 1946, pp. 3–4.
'Marius Victorinus and His Works'. *EQ* 18 (1946): pp. 132–53.
      repr. in *A Mind for What Matters*, pp. 213–32.
'Notes on the Aramaic Background of the Gospel Text'. *TB*, OS, January 1946, pp. 5–7; April 1946, p. 2; July 1946, p. 5; January 1947, pp. 1–2; July 1947, pp. 1–2; January 1948, pp. 2–4.
'A One-Volume Bible Dictionary'. *TB*, OS, July 1946, p. 8.
'The Second Coming of Christ'. *Supplement to the I.V.F. Graduates' Fellowship News-Letter*, no. 17 (January 1946).
'Solving a Great Problem: A Study of Acts 15'. *W* 76 (1946): pp. 89–90.
'Was Paul Inconsistent?' *The Christian*, 11 April 1946, p. 9.
'What Do We Mean by Biblical Inspiration?' *JTVI* 78 (1946): pp. 121–8.

1947

Archaeology and the New Testament. Church and Life Series no. 7 (London: Church Book Room Press, 1947).
      repr. in *Bible Expositor* 7 (1951–2): pp. 245–56.
'The Background of the Bible Story'. *Sunday School Magazine* 1 (1947): pp. 11–13, 54–6, 100–01.
'The Deity of Christ'. *Precious Seed* 1 (1947–8): p. 80.

rev. and repr. in *Treasury of Bible Doctrine* (ed. J. Heading and C. Hocking; Aberystwyth: Precious Seed, 1977), pp. 148–51.
'Did Moses Write Genesis?' *Sunday School Magazine* 1 (1947): pp. 201–2, 198.
'The Four Gospels and Acts.' Pages 319–50 in *New Bible Handbook* (ed. G.T. Manley; London: IVF, 1947).
'John Nelson Darby'. *H* 24/6 (June 1947): p. 6.
'Methods of Literary Criticism'. *TB*, OS, April 1947, pp. 7–8.
'Trustworthy Documents'. *Precious Seed* 1 (1947–8): p. 109.
'The Tyndale Fellowship for Biblical Research'. *EQ* 19 (1947): pp. 52–61.
   repr. in T.A. Noble, *Tyndale House and Fellowship: The First Sixty Years* (Leicester: IVP, 2006), pp. 314–25.
'Who Wrote Genesis?' *Sunday School Magazine* 1 (1947): pp. 154–5, 246–7.

1948

The Hittites and the Old Testament (London: Tyndale Press, 1948) [Tyndale Old Testament Lecture, 1947].
'Biblical Criticism'. *CG* 1/2 (June 1948): pp. 5–9.
'Bishop Barnes and "The Rise of Christianity"'. *Science and Religion* 1/3 (April–June 1948): pp. 108–13.
'The Crooked Serpent'. *EQ* 20 (1948): pp. 283–8.
'Moses and the Pentateuch'. *Precious Seed* 1 (1947–8): pp. 189–90.
'The Origin of the Alphabet'. *JTVI* 80 (1948): pp. 1–10.
'Studies in Old Testament Introduction'. *CG* 1/1 (March 1948): pp. 15–16; 1/2 (June 1948): pp. 18–19; 1/3 (September 1948): pp. 16–17; 1/4 (December 1948): pp. 21–2; 2 (1949): pp. 53–5, 89–90, 117–20; 3 (1950): pp. 25–6.

1949

'Appendix I. The Geography of Palestine.' Pages 425–7 in *New Bible Handbook* (ed. G.T. Manley; London: IVF, 2nd edn, 1949).
'The Background of the New Testament' [series]. *Senior Teacher's Magazine* 2 (January–December 1949).
'Church History and Its Lessons'. 'Appendix. Note 12. The Council of Jerusalem.' Pages 178–95, 219–20 in *The Church: A Symposium* (ed. J.B. Watson; London: Pickering & Inglis, 1949).
'The Judgment Seat of Christ'. *Bible Expositor* 5 (1949): pp. 66–8.
'2 Kings 2 – 14'. *Scripture Union Bible Study Notes*, July–August 1949, pp. 8–14.
'2 Kings 15 – 20'. *Scripture Union Bible Study Notes*, September–October 1949, pp. 26–30.
'The Living Christ'. *W* 79 (1949): pp. 37–9.
'The Period between the Testaments'. *Bible Student* (Bangalore) 20 (1949): pp. 9–15, 59–64.

1950

The Books and the Parchments: Some Chapters on the Transmission of the Bible
(London: Pickering & Inglis, 1950).
    2nd rev. edn (London: Pickering & Inglis, [1953]/Westwood,
    NJ: Fleming H. Revell, 1955).
    3rd rev. edn (London and Glasgow: Pickering & Inglis/Westwood,
    NJ: Fleming H. Revell, 1963).
    4th edn (Basingstoke: Pickering & Inglis, 1984) = *The Books and the*
    Parchments: How We Got Our English Bible (Old Tappan, NJ:
    Fleming H. Revell, 1984).
    [5th] rev. edn (Basingstoke: Marshall Pickering, 1991).
    extracts publ. as 'The Old Testament in Greek'. *Bible Translator* 4
    (1953): pp. 129–35, 156–62.
The Dawn of Christianity (London: Paternoster, 1950).
'2 Chronicles 1 – 9'. *Scripture Union Bible Study Notes*, September–October
    1950, pp. 16–22.
'2 Chronicles 10 – 36'. *Scripture Union Bible Study Notes*, November– December 1950, pp. 5–20, 25–8.
'Daniel's First Verse'. *Bible League Quarterly*, no. 202 (July–September 1950):
    pp. 5–7.
'Daniel's First Verse'. *Bible Student* 21 (1950): pp. 70–78.
'Daniel's First Verse'. *CG* 3 (1950): pp. 81–4.
    repr. as 'The Chronology of Daniel 1:1', in T.A. Tatford, The
    Climax of the Ages: Studies in the Prophecy of Daniel . . .
    With an Appendix by . . . F.F. Bruce (London and Edinburgh:
    Marshall, Morgan and Scott, 1953 and subsequent edns).
'The Dead Sea Scrolls'. *W* 80 (1950): p. 62.
'Emeritus Professor Walter Manoel Edwards'. *University of Leeds Review* 2/2
    (December 1950): pp. 159–62.
'2 Kings 21 – 23[:30]'. *Scripture Union Bible Study Notes*, January–February
    1950, pp. 34–6.
'2 Kings 23[:31] – 25'. *Scripture Union Bible Study Notes*, March–April 1950,
    pp. 40–42.
    repr. in *Scripture Union Bible Study Notes*, March–April 1960,
    pp. 41–3.
'More Light on Daniel's First Verse'. *Bible League Quarterly*, no. 203
    (October–December 1950): pp. 6–8.
'Recent Discoveries in Biblical Manuscripts'. *JTVI* 82 (1950): pp. 131–44.
'The Recent Finds in Palestine'. *Bible Student* NS 21 (1950): pp. 43–6.
'Recent Literature on the Book of Daniel'. *Bible Expositor* 6 (1950): pp. 46–52.

1951

The Acts of the Apostles: The Greek Text with Introduction and Commentary (London: Tyndale Press, 1951/Grand Rapids, MI: Eerdmans, 1951 / Chicago, IL: IVCF, 1952).
> 2nd edn (London: Tyndale Press/Grand Rapids, MI: Eerdmans, 1952).
> 3rd rev. and enlarged edn (Leicester: Apollos, 1990/Grand Rapids, MI: Eerdmans/IVCF, 1990).
> repr. (Eugene, OR: Wipf & Stock, 1998).

The Growing Day: The Progress of Christianity from the Fall of Jerusalem to the Accession of Constantine, A.D. 70–313 (London: Paternoster, 1951).

'Ezekiel 1 – 8'. *Scripture Union Bible Study Notes*, January–February 1951, pp. 33–9.

'Ezekiel 9 – 48'. *Scripture Union Bible Study Notes*, March–April 1951, pp. 2–26.

'The Life of Faith Bible School: Ecclesiastical Writings' [series]. *Life of Faith*, 25 April – 11 July 1951.

'Recent Studies in Old Testament Introduction'. *Bible Expositor* 7 (1951–2): pp. 90–98.

'Sir William Mitchell Ramsay: A Centenary Tribute'. *The Christian* (9 March 1951): p. 6.

'W.E. Vine: The Theologian.' Pages 69–85 in Percy O. Ruoff, *W.E. Vine: His Life and Ministry* (London: Oliphants, 1951).

'The Wellhausen Theory'. *Senior Teacher's Magazine* 4 (1951): pp. 83–4.

'The Wisdom Literature of the Bible'. *Bible Student* (Bangalore) 22 (1951): pp. 5–8, 76–7, 116–18; 23 (1952): pp. 5–8, 57–60, 99–103, 144–8.

1952

Light in the West: The Progress of Christianity from the Accession of Constantine to the Conversion of the English (London: Paternoster, 1952).

'Exodus 1 – 32', 'Psalms 103 – 105'. *Scripture Union Bible Study Notes*, May–June 1952, pp. 6–17, 26–32.

'Exodus 33 – 40'. *Scripture Union Bible Study Notes*, July–August 1952, pp. 2–4.

'Interpreting the Bible' [series]. *Senior Teacher's Magazine* 5 (February–December 1952).

'Justification by Faith in the Non-Pauline Writings of the New Testament'. *EQ* 24 (1952): pp. 66–77.

'The Revised Standard Version of the Holy Bible'. *The Christian*, 24 October 1952, p. 4.

'Revised Standard Version of the Holy Bible'. *Life of Faith*, 8 October 1952, pp. 691, 694.

'The Scriptures.' Pages 13–26 in *The Faith: A Symposium* (ed. F.A. Tatford; London: Pickering & Inglis, 1952).

'Sir Frederic George Kenyon, G.B.E., K.C.B., D.Litt., LL.D., F.B.A., F.S.A. 1863–1952'. *JTVI* 84 (1952): pp. xv–xvii.
'Some Principles of Biblical Interpretation'. *Senior Teacher's Magazine* 5 (1952): pp. 3–4.

1953

The Spreading Flame: The Rise and Progress of Christianity from Its First Beginnings to the Conversion of the English (Grand Rapids, MI: Eerdmans, 1953) [= *The Dawn of Christianity*, *The Growing Day* and *Light in the West*].
    rev. edn (London: Paternoster/Grand Rapids, MI: Eerdmans, 1958).
    rev. edn (Exeter: Paternoster, 1981).
    repr. (Eugene, OR: Wipf & Stock, 2004).
'Acts [1 – 20]'. *Scripture Union Bible Study Notes*, March–April 1953, pp. 8–24, 29–32.
'Acts 21 – 28'. *Scripture Union Bible Study Notes*, May–June 1953, pp. 20–25.
'The Apostolic Witness'. *W* 83 (1953): pp. 209, 212.
'The Bible Today'. *Bible League Quarterly*, no. 212 (January–March 1953): pp. 5–8.
'An Expository Study of St. John's Gospel' [series]. *Bible Student* 24 (1953) – 30 (1959).
'From Constantine to Luther: A Bird's-Eye View of a Period Little Known to Many'. *The Christian*, 7 August 1953, p. 7; 14 August 1953, p. 7.
'New Bible Translations: A Short Survey'. *Inter-Varsity*, Autumn 1953, pp. 15–19.
'The Poetry of the Old Testament', 'The Wisdom Literature of the Old Testament' [with F. Davidson], 'The Fourfold Gospel', 'Judges', 'The Acts of the Apostles', 'I and II Thessalonians', in *The New Bible Commentary* (ed. F. Davidson, A.M. Stibbs and E.F. Kevan; London: IVF / Grand Rapids, MI: Eerdmans, 1953).
    rev. edn (London: IVF/Grand Rapids, MI: Eerdmans, 1954).
'The Revised Standard Version'. *Knowing the Scriptures* 10/123 (March–April 1953): pp. 93–4.
'Textual Criticism'. *CG* 6 (1953): pp. 135–9.

1954

Commentary on the Book of the Acts: The English Text with Introduction, Exposition, and Notes, NICNT (Grand Rapids, MI: Eerdmans/ NLCNT, London: Marshall, Morgan & Scott, 1954).
    repr. with new preface (London: Marshall, Morgan & Scott, 1972/Grand Rapids, MI: Eerdmans, 1977).
    rev. edn (Grand Rapids, MI: Eerdmans, 1988).

The Sure Mercies of David: A Study in the Fulfilment of Messianic Prophecy (London: Evangelical Library, [1954]) [annual lecture of the Evangelical Library, 1954].

'Annual Address: The Victoria Institute and the Bible'. *JTVI* 86 (1954): pp. 75–81.

'The Bible as the Word of Authority for To-Day'. *Life of Faith*, 13 May 1954, pp. 308, 318.

'A British Scholar Looks at the RSV Old Testament'. *Eternity* 5/5 (May 1954): pp. 12–13, 42–7.

'The Canon of Scripture'. *Inter-Varsity*, Autumn 1954, pp. 19–22.

'Isaiah's Virgin Oracle'. *Reformed Journal* 4 (1954): pp. 5–7.

'The Local Church in the New Testament. Pages 24–41 in *The New Testament Church in the Present Day* (ed. P.O. Ruoff; n.pl.: n.p., 1954).

'Religious Education: Bible Teaching in the Faculty of Arts'. *ExT* 65 (1953–4): pp. 306–7.

'Revelation'. *Scripture Union Bible Study Notes*, May–June 1954, pp. 22–43.

'Seventy Sevens'. *The Christian*, 29 October 1954.

1955

The Christian Approach to the Old Testament (London: IVF, 1955).
2nd edn (London: IVF, 1959).

'The Bible and Evangelism. 1: The Prime Purpose of Revelation'. *Methodist Recorder*, 31 March 1955, p. 11.

'The Bible and Evangelism. 2: Lessons in Witness-Bearing'. *Methodist Recorder*, 7 April 1955, p. 9.

'The Bible and Evangelism. 3: Faith and Repentance'. *Methodist Recorder*, 14 April 1955, p. 9.

'The Canon of Scripture'. *H* 34 (1955): pp. 115–16.

'Census', 'Peter the Apostle', in *Twentieth Century Encyclopedia of Religious Knowledge* (ed. Loetscher, L.A., 2 vols; Grand Rapids, MI: Baker, 1955).

'The Christian Faith and Genesis 1 – 3'. *Senior Teacher's Magazine* 8 (1955): pp. 51–2, 63.

'The Church and Its Ministers.' Pages 44–51 in *A New Testament Church in 1955: High Leigh Conference of Brethren, September 16th to 19th, 1955* (Stanmore: T.I. Wilson, [1955]).

'Exposition of the Epistle of Jude'. *Knowing the Scriptures* 11 (1955): pp. 7–9, 20–22, 31–3, 43–5, 55–7, 67–8.

'Important Words of the Bible'. *Senior Teacher's Magazine* 8 (1955): pp. 19, 35, 47, 69; 9 (1956): pp. 19, 67, 86, 99, 148.

'The Planting of Churches'. *W* 85 (1955): pp. 113–14.

'Qumran and Early Christianity'. *New Testament Studies* 2 (1955–6): pp. 176–90.

'Trends in New Testament Interpretation'. *JTVI* 87 (1955): pp. 37–48.
'J.B. Watson: His Writings'. *W* 85 (1955): p. 199.

1956

Second Thoughts on the Dead Sea Scrolls (London: Paternoster/Grand Rapids, MI: Eerdmans, 1956).
> 2nd edn (London, Paternoster, [1961]).
> 3rd edn (London: Paternoster, [1966]/Grand Rapids, MI: Eerdmans, 1968).
> repr. (Eugene, OR: Wipf & Stock, 2006).
'As Originally Given'. *Terminal Letter of the Theological Students' Fellowship* 'Spring 1956', pp. 2–3.
> repr. in *A Symposium from Past Terminal Letters* (London: TSF, 1960), pp. 7–8.
'The Bible: Book of the Month: The Acts of the Apostles'. *CT*, 10 December 1956, pp. 18–19.
'Children of God and Sons of God'. *The Disciple* 3 (1956–7): pp. 162–5.
'Esther'. *Scripture Union Bible Study Notes*, November–December 1956, pp. 18–25.
'Exposition of the Epistle to the Ephesians' [series]. *Knowing the Scriptures* 11 (1955–7); continued in *BM* 68–9 (1958–9).
> publ. in book form as *The Epistle to the Ephesians: A Verse-by-Verse Exposition* (London: Pickering and Inglis, 1961/Westwood, NJ: Fleming H. Revell, 1962).
> 2nd edn (London, Pickering & Inglis/Westwood, NJ: Fleming H. Revell, [1968]).
'The Greek Language and the Christian Ministry'. *Clifton Theological College Magazine*, Trinity Term 1956, pp. 5–10.
'James'. *Scripture Union Bible Study Notes*, July–August 1956, pp. 2–7.
'Prophetic Interpretation in the Dead Sea Scrolls'. *Morning Star*, no. 1198 (July 1956): p. 7.
'A Second Look at the Dead Sea Scrolls: Messianic Expectations at Qumran'. *Eternity* 7/10 (October 1956), pp. 14–15, 29–30.
'Some Implications of the Dead Sea Scrolls'. *CG* 9 (1956): pp. 127–8.

1957

(with E.K. Simpson) *Commentary on the Epistles to the Ephesians and the Colossians. The English Text with Introduction, Exposition and Notes by E.K. Simpson . . . and F.F. Bruce*, NICNT/NLCMT (Grand Rapids, MI: Eerdmans/London: Marshall, Morgan & Scott, 1957).
New Horizons in Biblical Studies (Sheffield: University of Sheffield, 1957 [inaugural address]).

The Teacher of Righteousness in the Qumran Texts (London: Tyndale Press, 1957 [Tyndale Lecture in Biblical Archaeology, 1956]).

'The Apocrypha, Revised and Introduced'. *Eternity* 8/11 (November 1957): pp. 18–19, 42.

'Biblical Jerusalem'. *University of Leeds Review* 5 (1956–7): pp. 290–99.

'Christian Beginnings in Secular History' [series]. *Essential Christianity*, June 1957 – February 1959.

'Chronicle: Recent Literature on Qumran'. *Terminal Letter of the Theological Students' Fellowship* 'Summer 1957', pp. 6–8.

'Mark 1 – 12'. *Scripture Union Bible Study Notes*, January–February 1957, pp. 24–46.

'Mark 13 – 16'. *Scripture Union Bible Study Notes*, March–April 1957, pp. 3–8.

'Minister of the Word of God [Harold St John]'. *W* 87 (1957): pp. 143–4.

'Modern Scribes on the Judean Scrolls'. *CT*, 4 March 1957, pp. 5–7.

'My Word – Shall Accomplish'. *With Tongue and Pen*, January–March 1957, pp. 3–6, 9.

1958

'Archaeological Confirmation of the New Testament.' Pages 317–31 in *Revelation and the Bible* (ed. C.F.H. Henry; Grand Rapids, MI: Baker, 1958/ London: Tyndale Press, 1959).

'The Dead Sea Habakkuk Scroll'. *Annual of Leeds University Oriental Society* 1 (1958–9): pp. 5–24 [1st Bernard Lyons Lecture].

'Eschatology'. *London Quarterly and Holborn Review* (1958): pp. 99–103.

'The Fourth Gospel in Recent Interpretation'. *Terminal Letter of the Theological Students' Fellowship* 'Spring 1958', pp. 2–6 .

    repr. in *A Symposium from Past Terminal Letters*, pp. 11–14.

'George Henry Lang: Author and Teacher, 1874–1958'. *W* 88 (1958): pp. 253–4.

'Qumran and the New Testament'. *FT* 90 (1958): pp. 92–102.

'Two Emperors'. *Essential Christianity*, December 1958, pp. 7–9.

1959

Antichrist in the Early Church, Aids to Prophetic Study no. 92 (Blackburn: Durham & Sons, 1959).

    repr. in *A Mind for What Matters*, pp. 181–97.

Biblical Exegesis in the Qumran Texts, Exegetica 3/1 (Den Haag: Van Keulen, 1959).

    rev. edn (Grand Rapids, MI: Eerdmans, [1959]/London: Tyndale Press, 1960).

The Defense of the Gospel in the New Testament (Grand Rapids, MI: Eerdmans, 1959 [Calvin Foundation Lectures, 1958]).

= *The Apostolic Defence of the Gospel: Christian Apologetic in the New Testament* (London: IVF, 1959).

2nd edn (London: IVF, 1967).

rev. edn, *First-Century Faith: Christian Witness in the New Testament* (Leicester: IVP, 1977).

= *The Defense of the Gospel in the New Testament* (Grand Rapids, MI: Eerdmans, 1978).

'Archaeological Confirmation of the New Testament' [series]. *Essential Christianity*, April–December 1959.

'Bible Book of the Month: Jude'. *CT*, 25 May 1959, pp. 34–5.

'Biblical Archaeology.' Pages 29–49 in *The Bible Companion* (ed. W. Neil; London: Skeffington, 1959).

'Erich Sauer'. *W* 89 (1959): p. 79.

'Qumran and the Old Testament'. *FT* 91 (1959–60): pp. 9–27.

repr. in *A Mind for What Matters*, pp. 32–48.

'The True Apostolic Succession: Recent Study of the Book of Acts'. *Interpretation* 13 (1959): pp. 131–43.

1960

'Biblical Criticism' [series]. *Essential Christianity*, February 1960 – December 1963.

'Criticism and Faith'. *CT*, 21 November 1960, pp. 9–12.

'The Dead Sea Scrolls'. *Modern Churchman NS* 4 (1960–61): pp. 45–54.

'Dead Sea Scrolls', 'Eschatology', 'Form Criticism', 'Fulness', 'Interpretation (Biblical)', 'Will-worship', in *Baker's Dictionary of Theology* (ed. Everett F. Harrison; Grand Rapids, MI: Baker/London: Pickering & Inglis, 1960).

'The Gospels.' Pages 15–22 in *The Biblical Expositor* (3 vols; ed. Carl F.H. Henry; Philadelphia, PA: A.J. Holman, 1960), vol. 3.

'Recent New Testament Studies'. *CT*, 15 February 1960, pp. 9–12.

'The Scottish Reformation, 1560–1960'. *W* 90 (1960): pp. 366–7.

'The Son of Man Came'. *H* 39 (1960): pp. 54–5.

1961

The English Bible: A History of Translations (London: Lutterworth/New York: Oxford University Press, 1961).

Another edition (London: Methuen, 1963).

rev. edn, *The English Bible: A History of Translations, from the Earliest English Versions to the New English Bible* (London: Lutterworth/New York: Oxford University Press, 1970).

3rd rev. edn, *History of the Bible in English, from the Earliest Versions* (New York: Oxford University Press, 1978/Guildford: Lutterworth, 1979).

slightly altered version of one chapter publ. as *The King James Version: The First 350 Years . . . 1611–1961* (New York: Oxford University Press, 1960).

'The Authorized Version and Others'. *International Review of Missions* 50 (1961): pp. 409–16.

'The Book of Zechariah and the Passion Narrative'. *BJRL* 43 (1960–61): pp. 336–53.

'The Gospel of Thomas: Presidential Address, 14 May 1960'. *FT* 92 (1961–2): pp. 3–23.

'The New English Bible'. *CG* 14 (1961): pp. 55–9.

'The New English Bible'. *CT*, 13 March 1961.

'The New English Bible'. *Essential Christianity*, April 1961, pp. 5–7.

'The New English Bible'. *FT* 92 (1961–2): pp. 47–53.

'New Testament Studies in 1960'. *CT*, 13 February 1961, pp. 8–10.

'The Person of Christ: Incarnation and Virgin Birth'. *CT*, 13 October 1961, pp. 30–31.

> repr. in *Basic Christian Doctrines* (ed. C.F.H. Henry; New York: Holt, Rinehardt & Winston, 1962), pp. 124–30.

'The Significance of the Dead Sea Scrolls'. *Times Literary Supplement*, 27 March 1961, pp. vi–vii.

'The Transfiguration'. *Inter-Varsity*, Summer 1961, pp. 19–21.

'This Bible Year'. *BM* 71 (1961): pp. 107–8, 106.

'Who Are the Brethren?' *W* 91 (1961): pp. 406–7.

> repr. in booklet form (London, Pickering & Inglis, [1962]).
>
> Witness Booklet no.1 (Glasgow: Pickering & Inglis, 1962).
>
> repr. in E.A. Tatford, *That the World May Know*, vol. 1: *The Restless Middle East: Lands of the Great Religions* (Bath: Echoes of Service, 1982), pp. 223–6.
>
> updated edn, *Harvester/Aware* 69/6 (June 1990): pp. 4–5.

1962

Paul and His Converts: 1 and 2 Thessalonians, 1 and 2 Corinthians, Bible Guides 17 (London: Lutterworth / New York and Nashville, TN: Abingdon, 1962).

> rev. edn [incl. Philippians], *Paul and His Converts: How Paul Nurtured the Churches He Planted* (Downers Grove, IL: IVP/ Crowborough: Highland Books, 1985).

(consulting ed.) J.D. Douglas, ed. *The New Bible Dictionary* (London: IVF, 1962); articles on 'Abilene', 'Acts, Book of the', 'Ananias', 'Araunah', 'Areopagus', 'Asiarch', 'Assassins', 'Babylon (NT)', 'Barak', 'Bar-Jesus', 'Beast (Apocalypse)', 'Bible', 'Biblical Criticism', 'Book of Life', 'Calendar' (sections 2 and 3), 'Canaanaean', 'Census', 'Chamberlain', 'Chenoboskion', 'Claudius Lysias', 'Coelesyria', 'Cornelius',

'Corruption', 'Council, Jerusalem', 'Covenant (Book of)', 'Dalmanutha', 'Dan', 'Dead Sea Scrolls', 'Deborah', 'Deputy', 'Derbe', 'Easter', 'Egyptian, The', 'Epaphras', 'Essenes', 'Galatians, Epistle to the', 'Genealogy of Jesus Christ', 'Gospels', 'Hebron', 'Herod', 'Herodias', 'Hittites', 'Hour', 'Interpretation (Biblical)', 'Israel', 'Israel of God', 'Jerahmeel', 'John the Baptist', 'Josephus, Flavius', 'Jude (Epistle of)', 'Kiriath-Arba', 'Lycaonia', 'Lysanias', 'Machaerus', 'Mamre', 'Melchizedek', 'Mene, Mene, Tekel, Upharsin', 'Meroz', 'Messiah: II. In the New Testament', 'Proconsul', 'Procurator', 'Rahab', 'Rufus', 'Salt, City of', 'Sapphira', 'Suburb', 'Synzygus', 'Tahtim-hodshi', 'Theophilus', 'Thessalonians, Epistles to the', 'Theudas', 'Unknown God', 'Zadok', 'Zealot'. All except 'Messiah: II. In the New Testament' repr. in *Illustrated Bible Dictionary* (3 vols, ed. J.D. Douglas; Leicester, IVP, 1980).

'Acceptance', 'Access', 'Comfort', 'Consolation', 'Conversation', 'Corruption', 'Deny', 'Gift, Giving', 'Mark (Goal, Sign)', 'New, Newness', 'Seeing', 'Tribulation', 'Trinity', 'Vain', in *The Interpreter's Dictionary of the Bible* (4 vols; ed. G. A. Buttrick et al.; New York/Nashville, TN: Abingdon, 1962).

'Aeneas', 'Ägypter', 'Damaris', 'Dionysius', 'Eutychus', 'Julius', 'Lasäa', 'Prätorium', 'Rhode', 'Tertullus', 'Theudas', 'Urbanus', in *Biblisch-Historisches Handwörterbuch* (4 vols; ed. Bo Reicke and Leonhard Rost; Göttingen: Vandenhoeck & Ruprecht, 1962–79).

'The Biblical Concept, Particularly in the Ministry of the Lord'; 'The Consummation.' Pages 9–22, 63–80 in *The Rule of God in the Life of Man: Addresses Given at a Conference of Brethren at Swanwick* (London: G.W. Robson, 1962).

'Christianity under Claudius'. *BJRL* 44 (1961–2): pp. 309–26.

'Diversity of Gifts'. *Student World* 55 (1962): pp. 19–28.

'The Epistles of Paul'; 'Hebrews.' Pages 927–39, 1008–19 in *Peake's Commentary on the Bible* (ed. Matthew Black and H.H. Rowley; London: Thomas Nelson, 1962).

'The Gospels and Some Recent Discoveries'. *FT* 92 (1962): pp. 149–67 [1st Rendle Short Memorial Lecture].

'The Identity of Jesus'. *Essential Christianity*, August 1962, pp. 7–10.

'New Light from the Dead Sea Scrolls.' Pages 1171–83 in *Holman Study Bible* [RSV] (Philadelphia, PA: A.J. Holman, 1962).

'New Testament Studies in 1961'. *CT*, 2 February 1962, pp. 6–8.

'Preparation in the Wilderness: At Qumran and in the New Testament'. *Interpretation* 16 (1962): pp. 280–91.

　　　repr. in *A Mind for What Matters*, pp. 65–76.

1963

The Epistle to the Romans, TNTC (London: Tyndale Press/Grand Rapids, MI: Eerdmans, 1963).

2nd edn, *The Letter of Paul to the Romans: An Introduction and Commentary* (Leicester: IVP/Grand Rapids, MI: Eerdmans, 1985).
[reformatted] (Downers Grove, IL and Leicester: IVP, 2008).

Israel and the Nations from the Exodus to the Fall of the Second Temple (Exeter: Paternoster / Grand Rapids, MI: Eerdmans, 1963).
illustrated edn (Exeter: Paternoster, 1969).
rev. edn (Exeter: Paternoster, 1983).
rev. by David F. Payne (Carlisle: Paternoster, 1997/Downers Grove, IL: IVP, 1998).

(ed.) *Promise and Fulfilment: Essays Presented to Professor S.H. Hooke in Celebration of His Ninetieth Birthday . . . by Members of the Society for Old Testament Study and Others* (Edinburgh: T&T Clark, 1963); contributed 'Promise and Fulfilment in Paul's Presentation of Jesus', pp. 36–50.

'Altar', 'Ashdod', 'Ashkelon', 'Azekah', 'Carmel', 'Dog', 'Dragon', 'Dreams', 'Hittites', 'Idolatry', 'Image', 'Makkedah', 'Shittim', 'Siddim, Vale of', 'Tabor, Mount', in *Dictionary of the Bible* (ed. James Hastings; rev. F.C. Grant and H.H. Rowley; Edinburgh: T&T Clark/New York: Charles Scribner's Sons, 1963) [some revisions, some entirely new articles].

'Beatitudes, The', 'Bible, The', 'Biblical Criticism', 'Codex', 'Exegesis', 'Higher Criticism', 'King James Version', 'Lord's Prayer', 'Parables of Jesus', 'Resurrection of Christ, The', 'Revised Version', 'Sermon on the Mount', 'Textual Criticism or Lower Criticism', in *Encyclopedia International* (19 vols; New York: Grolier, 1963).

'Bible: Will Joint Bible Study Bring Fellowship?' *Eternity* 14/1 (January 1963): pp. 27–8.

'The History and Doctrine of the Apostolic Age.' Pages 495–522 in *A Companion to the Bible* (ed. H.H. Rowley; Edinburgh: T&T Clark, 2nd edn, 1963).

'New Testament', in *The Zondervan Pictorial Bible Dictionary* (ed. M.C. Tenney; Grand Rapids, MI: Zondervan/London: Marshall, Morgan & Scott, 1963).

'"Our God and Saviour": A Recurring Biblical Pattern.' Pages 51–66 in *The Saviour God: Essays Presented to Professor E.O. James* (ed. S.G.F. Brandon; Manchester: Manchester University Press, 1963).

'The Pattern of the Poetry', in Gunn G.S. *Singers of Israel*, Bible Guides 10 (London: Lutterworth / Nashville, TN and New York: Abingdon, 1963), pp. 32–6.

'Recent Studies in the Epistle to the Romans'. *TSF Bulletin*, no. 35 (Spring 1963): pp. 8–10.

'Survey of New Testament Literature'. *CT*, 1 February 1963, pp. 8–10.

'"To the Hebrews" or "To the Essenes"?' *New Testament Studies* 9 (1962–3): pp. 217–32.

'When Is a Gospel Not a Gospel?' *BJRL* 45 (1962–3): pp. 319–39.

1964

The Epistle to the Hebrews, NICNT/NLCNT (Grand Rapids, MI: Eerdmans, 1964, London: Marshall, Morgan & Scott, 1965).
　　rev. edn (Grand Rapids, MI: Eerdmans, 1990).
'Acts', 'Colossians', 'Jude', in *Exploring the N.T. Backgrounds* (Washington, DC: Christianity Today, 1964).
'The Baptism of the Spirit'. *Calling* 6/3 (Fall 1964): pp. 7–9.
　　repr. in *W* 95 (1965): pp. 247–9.
(with W.J. M[artin].) 'The Deity of Christ'. *CT*, 18 December 1964, pp. 11–17.
　　repr. as booklet (Manchester: North of England Evangelical Trust, 1964).
'The Easter Event'. *CT*, 27 March 1964, pp. 4–6.
'History and the Gospel'. *FT* 93 (1964): pp. 121–45 [C.J. Cadoux Memorial Lecture, 1962].
　　rev. edn, pages 89–107 in *Jesus of Nazareth: Saviour and Lord* (ed. C.F.H. Henry; Grand Rapids, MI: Eerdmans/London: Tyndale Press, 1966).
'The Last Thirty Years', additional chapter to F.G. Kenyon, *The Story of the Bible: A Popular Account of How It Came to Us* (ed. F.F. Bruce; Grand Rapids, MI: Eerdmans, 2nd edn, 1964), pp. 114–37.
'New Testament Studies: 1963'. *CT*, 14 February 1964, pp. 9–11.
'"One Faith."' Pages 47–57 in *Christian Unity: Papers Given at a Conference of Brethren at Swanwick, Derbyshire, in June, 1964* (Bristol: Evangelical Christian Literature, [1964]).
'The Perils of Exclusivism: 2. The Church of Jerusalem'. *JCBRF*, no. 4 (April 1964): pp. 5–14.
'Romans', 'Psalms 144 – 150', 'Ephesians', 'Psalm 119:81–176', 'Malachi', 'Revelation 4 – 22', 'Luke 1 – 2'. *Daily Notes*, October– December 1964.
'St. Paul in Rome'. *BJRL* 46 (1963–4): pp. 326–45.
'Who Is This Jesus?' [series] *Essential Christianity*, February 1964 – April 1965.

1965

An Expanded Paraphrase of the Epistles of Paul (Exeter: Paternoster, 1965) [first publ. as articles in *EQ* 1957–64].
　　= *The Epistles of Paul: An Expanded Paraphrase* (Grand Rapids, MI: Eerdmans, 1965).
　　repr. under British title (Palm Springs, CA: R.N. Haynes, 1981).
'The Dead Sea Scrolls in London'. *Church of England Newspaper*, 10 December 1965.
'1 Corinthians', 'Exodus', 'Genesis 37 – 50'. *Daily Notes*, July–September 1965.
'Herod Antipas, Tetrarch of Galilee and Peraea'. *Annual of Leeds University Oriental Society* 5 (1963–5): pp. 6–23.

'John the Forerunner'. *FT* 94 (1965): pp. 182–90.
'Josephus and Daniel'. *Annual of the Swedish Theological Institute* 4 (1965): pp. 148–62 [presidential address to the Society for Old Testament Study].
  repr. in *A Mind for What Matters*, pp. 19–31.
'New Testament Studies in 1964'. *CT*, 12 February 1965, pp. 9–11.
'St. Paul in Rome: 2. The Epistle to Philemon'. *BJRL* 48 (1965–6): pp. 81–97.
'Tribute to the Rev. Professor A. Guillaume'. *Annual of Leeds University Oriental Society* 5 (1963–5): pp. 4–5.
'Why I Have Stayed with the Brethren'. *JCBRF*, no. 10 (December 1965): pp. 5–6.

1966

(intro.) *The Epistles of St. John: The Greek Text with Notes, by the Late Brooke Foss Westcott . . . New Introduction (Johannine Studies Since Westcott's Day) by F.F. Bruce* (Appleford: Marcham Manor Press, 1966).
'Charles Harold Dodd.' Pages 239–69 in *Creative Minds in Modern Theology* (ed. Philip Edgcumbe Hughes; Grand Rapids, MI: Eerdmans, 1966).
'The Dead Sea Scrolls and Early Christianity'. *BJRL* 49 (1966–7): pp. 69–90.
  repr. in *A Mind for What Matters*, pp. 49–64.
'Holy Spirit in the Qumran Texts'. *Annual of Leeds University Oriental Society* 6 (1966–8): pp. 49–55.
'The Jesus of History and the Christ of Faith: 4. Jesus and Paul'. *TSF Bulletin*, no. 46 (Autumn 1966): pp. 21–6.
'Myth and the New Testament'. *TSF Bulletin*, no. 44 (Spring 1966): pp. 10–15.
'New Testament Studies in 1965'. *CT*, 4 February 1966, pp. 13–15.
'St. Paul in Rome: 3. The Epistle to the Colossians'. *BJRL* 48 (1965–6): pp. 268–85.
'The Story of the Bible.' Pages 1–7 in *The Bible* [RSV] (London: Lutterworth, 1966) [separately paginated from main text].

1967

(intro.) *William Tyndale's Five Books of Moses called The Pentateuch, Being a Verbatim Reprint of the Edition of M.CCCCC.XXX. Compared with Tyndale's Genesis of 1534, and the Pentateuch in the Vulgate, Luther, and Matthew's Bible, with Various Collations and Prolegomena, by the Rev. J.I. Mombert, D.D. and Newly Introduced by F.F. Bruce, D.D.* (Fontwell: Centaur Press, 1967).
'The Broken Wall', 'Principalities and Powers'. *Wellington Assembly Research Fellowship*, no. 28 (April 1967): pp. 1–11, 12–22.
'The Epistles of John' [series]. *W* 97–98 (1967–8).
  rev. and publ. in book form as *The Epistles of John: Introduction, Exposition and Notes* (London: Pickering & Inglis, 1970/Old Tappan, NJ: Fleming H. Revell, 1971).

repr. (Grand Rapids, MI: Eerdmans, 1979).

repr. with *The Gospel of John* (Grand Rapids, MI: Eerdmans, 1994).

'Faith and Life'. *Calling* 9/1 (Spring 1967): pp. 4–10.

'Jesus Christ the Same'. *Calling* 9/2 (Summer 1967): pp. 18–23.

'Literature and Theology to Gregory the Great'. *Journal of Ecclesiastical History* 18 (1967): pp. 227–31.

'Noteworthy Advances in the New Testament Field'. *CT*, 3 February 1967, pp. 9–10, 12.

'Plymouth Brethren', in *Chambers's Encyclopaedia*, vol. 10 (Oxford: Pergamon, new rev. edn, 1967).

'Plymouth Brethren', in *Encyclopaedia Britannica*, vol. 18 (Chicago, IL: Encyclopaedia Britannica, 14th edn, 1967).

'St. Paul in Rome: 4. The Epistle to the Ephesians'. *BJRL* 49 (1966–7): pp. 303–22.

'The Society for Old Testament Study, 1917–1967'. *ExT* 78 (1966–7): pp. 147–8.

'The Sources of the Synoptic Gospels', 'John's Gospel', 'The First Epistle of John', 'The General Epistles'. *Wellington Assembly Research Fellowship*, no. 30 (July 1967).

'Tell el-Amarna.' Pages 3–20 in *Archaeology and Old Testament Study*, Jubilee Volume of the Society for Old Testament Study (ed. D. Winton Thomas; Oxford: Clarendon, 1967).

'Understanding the Bible' [series]. *H* 46–7 (June 1967 – January 1969).

1968

This Is That: The New Testament Development of Some Old Testament Themes (Exeter: Paternoster, 1968) [Payton Lectures, 1968].

= *The New Testament Development of Old Testament Themes* (Grand Rapids, MI: Eerdmans, 1969/Eugene, OR: Wipf & Stock, 2004).

(ed. with E.G. Rupp) *Holy Book and Holy Tradition: International Colloquium Held in the Faculty of Theology, University of Manchester* (Manchester: Manchester University Press/Grand Rapids, MI: Eerdmans, [1968]); contributed 'Scripture and Tradition in the New Testament', pp. 68–93.

'Alan Rowe'. *PEQ* 100 (1968): pp. 76–7.

'Edward Joseph Young: Obituary'. *FT* 97 (1968): pp. 3–5.

'"Jesus is Lord."' Pages 23–36 in *Soli Deo Gloria: New Testament Essays in Honor of William Childs Robinson* (ed. J. McDowell Richards; Richmond, VA: John Knox, 1968).

'The Literary Background of the New Testament'. *FT* 97 (1968): pp. 15–40.

'Paul and Jerusalem'. *TB* 19 (1968): pp. 3–25.

'St. Paul in Rome: 5. Concluding Observations'. *BJRL* 50 (1967–8): pp. 262–79.

'Samuel Henry Hooke'. *PEQ* 100 (1968): pp. 77–8.

'Samuel Henry Hooke (1874–1968)'. *W* 98 (1968): pp. 101, 107.

1969

New Testament History, Nelson's Library of Theology (London: Thomas Nelson, 1969).
    1st rev. edn (London: Oliphants, 1971).
    [with corrections] (Garden City, NJ: Doubleday, 1971).
    2nd rev. edn (London: Oliphants, 1977).
    [3rd rev. edn] (New York: Doubleday, 1980).
    4th edn (London: Pickering & Inglis, 1982).
(consulting ed.) Howley, G.C.D. *A New Testament Commentary: Based on the Revised Standard Version* (London: Pickering & Inglis, 1969); contributed articles on 'The Fourfold Gospel', 'The General Letters', 'Revelation'.
'The Book of Daniel and the Qumran Community.' Pages 221–35 in *Neotestamentica et Semitica: Essays in Honour of Matthew Black* (ed. E.E. Ellis and M. Wilcox; Edinburgh: T&T Clark, 1969).
'Galatian Problems: 1. Autobiographical Data'. *BJRL* 51 (1968–9): pp. 292–309.
'Harold Henry Rowley'. *PEQ* 101 (1969): p. 134.
'Jesus and the Gospels in the Light of the Scrolls.' Pages 70–82 in *The Scrolls and Christianity*, SPCK Theological Collections 11 (ed. M. Black; London: SPCK, 1969).
'The Kerygma of Hebrews'. *Interpretation* 23 (1969): pp. 3–19.
'The Ministry of Christ', 'The Archaeology of the New Testament' (with E.M. Blaiklock), in *Zondervan Pictorial Bible Atlas* (ed. E.M. Blaiklock; Grand Rapids, MI: Zondervan, 1969).
'The Qumran Discoveries and the Bible'. *Ekklesiastikos Pharos* 51 (1952–69): pp. 49–59.
'Recent Contributions to the Understanding of Hebrews'. *ExT* 80 (1969): pp. 260–64.
'Thoughts from My Study'. *Calling* 11/2 (Summer 1969): pp. 14–16.
'Thoughts from My Study: Creeds or No Creeds?' *Calling* 11/4 (Winter 1969): pp. 16–18.
'Thoughts from My Study: Tradition Good and Bad'. *Calling* 11/3 (Fall 1969): pp. 12–14.

1970

St. Matthew, Scripture Union Bible Study Books (London: Scripture Union, 1970 / Grand Rapids, MI: Eerdmans, 1971).
    repr. (Philadelphia, PA: A.J. Holman, 1978).
    repr. in *The Daily Bible Commentary*, vol. 3, *St Matthew to Acts*. (London: Scripture Union, 1974), pp. 10–103.
Tradition Old and New (Exeter: Paternoster/Grand Rapids, MI: Zondervan, 1970/Eugene, OR: Wipf & Stock, 2006).

pp. 129–50 repr. as 'Tradition and the Canon of Scripture.' Pages
59–84 in *The Authoritative Word: Essays on the Nature of Scripture* (ed.
Donald K. McKim; Grand Rapids, MI: Eerdmans, 1983).
'Between the Testaments.' Pages 59–63 in *New Bible Commentary: Revised* (ed.
D. Guthrie et al.; London: IVP/Grand Rapids, MI: Eerdmans, 1970).
'Dead Sea Scrolls'. *Man, Myth and Magic*, no. 22 ([18 June] 1970): pp. 609–11.
'Exiles in an Alien World.' Pages 265–301 in *The Catholic Layman's Library*, vol.
2, *Understanding the Bible: The New Testament* (ed. John P. Bradley and
John Quinlan; Gastonia, NC: Good Will Publishers, 1970).
'Galatian Problems: 2. North or South Galatians?' *BJRL* 52 (1969–70): pp.
243–66.
'The New English Bible'. *CT*, 30 January 1970, pp. 8–11.
'The Origins of the Witness'. *W* 100 (1970): pp. 7–9.
'Qumran.' Pages 522–5 in *A Dictionary of Comparative Religion* (ed. S.G.F.
Brandon; London: Weidenfeld & Nicolson, 1970).
'Regent College, Vancouver'. *W* 100 (1970): pp. 418–20.
'Texts and Translations.' Pages 1–5 in *Encounters with Books* (ed. H.P.
Merchant; Downers Grove, IL: IVP, 1970), pp. 1–5.
'Thoughts from My Study'. *Calling* 12/1 (Spring 1970): pp. 10–12.
'Thoughts from My Study'. *Calling* 12/2 (Summer 1970): pp. 10–11.
'Thoughts from My Study: Apostolic Tradition'. *Calling* 12/3 (Fall 1970): pp.
10–13.
'Thoughts from My Study: Freedom'. *Calling* 12/4 (Winter 1970): pp. 10–12.
[untitled article], *The Bible in the World* (Autumn 1970): pp. 4–5.

1971

1 and 2 Corinthians, New Century Bible (London: Oliphants, 1971).
          repr. (Grand Rapids, MI: Eerdmans/London: Marshall Morgan and
          Scott, 1980).
(departmental ed. for Dead Sea Scrolls) *Encyclopedia Judaica* (16 vols; ed. Cecil
          Roth and Geoffrey Wigoder; Jerusalem: Encyclopedia Judaica/
          Macmillan, 1971); contributed articles on 'Copper Scroll', 'Dead Sea
          Scrolls', 'Ein Feshkba', 'Kittim', 'Lies, Man of', 'Lies, Prophet of', 'Lion of
          Wrath', 'Murabb'at', 'Pesher', 'Qumran', 'Seekers after Smooth Things',
          'Serekh', 'Shapira Fragments', 'Sons of Light', 'Teacher of Righteous-
          ness', 'War Scroll', 'Wicked Priest', 'Yahad', 'Zadokite Work'.
          many articles repr. and some added in *Encyclopedia Judaica* (22 vols;
          ed. Fred Skolnik and Michael Berenbaum; Farmington Hills, MI:
          Macmillan Reference/Jerusalem: Keter, 2007): 'Asceticism'; 'Cop-
          per Scroll'; 'Damascus, Book of'; '[Damascus,] Covenant of'; 'Dead
          Sea Scrolls'; 'Kittim', 'Lies, Man of', 'Lies, Prophet of', 'Lion of
          Wrath', 'Murabb'at Scrolls', 'Pesher', 'Qumran', 'Seekers after
          Smooth Things', 'Serekh', 'Shapira Fragments', 'Sons of Light',

'Teacher of Righteousness', 'War Scroll', 'Wicked Priest', 'Yahad', 'Zadokites'.

'Galatian Problems: 3. The "Other" Gospel'. *BJRL* 53 (1970–71): pp. 253–71.

'Inter-Testamental Literature. Pages 83–104 in *Preface to Christian Studies* (ed. F.G. Healey; London: Lutterworth, 1971).

'New Light from the Dead Sea Scrolls' (rev. from 1962), 'The Early Manuscripts of the Bible', in *Holman's Family Reference Bible* (Philadelphia, PA: A.J. Holman, 1971).

'Paul on Immortality'. *Scottish Journal of Theology* 24 (1971): pp. 457–72.

'St. John's Passion Narrative' [series]. *W* 101–2 (1971–2).

'Some Thoughts on Paul and Paulinism'. *Vox Evangelica* 7 (1971): pp. 5–16.

'Thoughts from My Study'. *Calling* 13/1 (Spring 1971): pp. 9–11.

'Thoughts from My Study'. *Calling* 13/2 (Summer 1971): pp. 5–7.

1972

Answers to Questions (Exeter: Paternoster, 1972/Grand Rapids, MI: Zondervan, 1973).

The Message of the New Testament (Exeter: Paternoster, 1972/Grand Rapids, MI: Eerdmans, 1973).

'Biblical Authority'. *Reformed Journal* 22/4 (April 1972): pp. 10–12.

'Corinthians, Second Epistle to the', in *The Encyclopedia of Christianity*, vol. 3 (ed. Philip E. Hughes; Marshallton, DE: National Foundation for Christian Education, 1972).

'The Earliest Old Testament Interpretation'. *Oudtestamentische Studiën* 17 (1972): pp. 37–52.

'Galatian Problems: 4. The Date of the Epistle'. *BJRL* 54 (1971–2): pp. 250–67.

'On Dating the New Testament'. *Eternity* 23/6 (June 1972): pp. 32–3.

'Plymouth Brethren Worship', 'Baptism 13: Plymouth Brethren', 'Liturgies 13: Plymouth Brethren', in *A Dictionary of Liturgy and Worship* (ed. J.G. Davies; London: SCM, 1972).

1973

'Are the Gospels Anti-Semitic?' *Eternity* 24/11 (November 1973): pp. 16–18.

'Dr. G.R. Beasley-Murray'. *Spurgeon's College Record*, no. 57 (December 1973): pp. 7–9.

'Bible, The'. Pages 54–7 in *Webster's New World Companion to English and American Literature* (ed. Arthur Pollard; London: Compton Russell/New York: World Publishing, 1973).

'Charles Harold Dodd (1884–1973)'. *W* 103 (1973): pp. 424–5.

'Eschatology in the Apostolic Fathers.' Pages 77–89 in *The Heritage of the Early Church: Essays in Honor of Georges Vasilievich Florovsky on the Occasion of His Eightieth Birthday*, Orientalia Christiana Analecta 195 (ed. David

Neiman and Margaret Schatkin; Rome: Pontificial Institutum Studiorum Orientalium, 1973).

'Evangelism in the New Testament'. *Thrust*, no. 5 (July 1973): pp. 5–7.

'Galatian Problems: 5. Galatians and Christian Origins'. *BJRL* 55 (1972–3): pp. 264–84.

'The Holy Spirit in the Acts of the Apostles'. *Interpretation* 27 (1973): pp. 166–83.

'The Humanity of Jesus Christ'. *JCBRF*, no. 24 (September 1973): pp. 5–15.

    repr. in *A Mind for What Matters*, pp. 248–58.

    repr. in *The Lord of Glory: or, The Person of Christ Historically Considered* (ed. David J. MacLeod; Dubuque, IA: Emmaus Bible College, 2008).

'Jesus, Ethical Teachings'. Pages 348–51 in *Baker Dictionary of Christian Ethics* (ed. Carl F.H. Henry; Grand Rapids, MI: Baker, 1973).

'New Wine in Old Wineskins: III. The Corner Stone'. *ExT* 84 (1972–3): pp. 231–5.

'Salvation History in the New Testament'. Pages 75–90 in *Man and His Salvation: Studies in Memory of S.G.F. Brandon* (ed. E.J. Sharpe and J.R. Hinnells; Manchester: Manchester University Press, 1973).

'The Spirit in the Apocalypse'. Pages 333–44 in *Christ and Spirit in the New Testament: In Honour of Charles Francis Digby Moule* (ed. Stephen S. Smalley and Barnabas Lindars; Cambridge and New York: Cambridge University Press, 1973).

1974

Jesus and Christian Origins outside the New Testament (London: Hodder & Stoughton/Grand Rapids, MI: Eerdmans, 1974).

    new edn (London: Hodder & Stoughton, [1984]).

Paul and Jesus (Grand Rapids, MI: Baker, 1974) [Thomas F. Staley Academic Lecture Series].

    repr. (London: SPCK, 1977).

The 'Secret' Gospel of Mark: The Ethel M. Wood Lecture Delivered before the University of London on 11 February 1974 (London: Athlone Press, 1974).

    repr. in *The Canon of Scripture* (Downers Grove, IL: IVP/Glasgow: Chapter House, 1988), pp. 298–315.

'Acts of the Apostles', 'Bible (English Versions)', 'Epistles, Pauline', 'Jesus Christ', 'Manson, Thomas Walter (1893–1958)', 'Manuscripts of the Bible', 'Rowley, Harold Henry (1890–1969)', in *The New International Dictionary of the Christian Church* (ed. J.D. Douglas; Exeter: Paternoster/Grand Rapids, MI: Zondervan, 1974, 2nd edn, 1978).

'Armageddon: Past and Future'. *Prophetic Witness* 57 (1974): pp. 262–3.

'Exegesis and Hermeneutics, Biblical', in *Encyclopaedia Britannica*, vol. 19 (Chicago, IL: Encyclopaedia Britannica, 15th edn, 1974).

'Israel's Future Invaders'. *Prophetic Witness* 57 (1974): pp. 251–2.
'The Kingdom and the Church'. *Bible Characters and Doctrines* 13 (London: Scripture Union/Grand Rapids, MI: Eerdmans, 1974).
repr. as *God's Kingdom and Church*, Understanding Bible Teaching (London: Scripture Union/Grand Rapids, MI: Eerdmans, 1978).
'New Light on the Origin of the New Testament'. *FT* 101 (1974): pp. 158–62.
'New Light on the Origins of the New Testament Canon'. Pages 3–18 in *New Dimensions in New Testament Study* (ed. Richard N. Longenecker and Merrill C. Tenney; Grand Rapids, MI: Zondervan, 1974).
'Paul and the Historical Jesus'. *BJRL* 56 (1973–4): pp. 317–35.
'Remembrance of Things Past'. *W* 104–6 (1974–6).
publ. in book form as *In Retrospect: Remembrance of Things Past* (London: Pickering & Inglis/Grand Rapids, MI: Baker, 1980).
'In Conclusion' repr. in *Reformed Journal* 40 (1990): pp. 13–16.
rev. edn (London: Marshall Pickering/Grand Rapids, MI: Baker, 1993).
'The Speeches in Acts: Thirty Years After'. Pages 53–68 in *Reconciliation and Hope: New Testament Essays on Atonement and Eschatology Presented to L.L. Morris on His 60th Birthday* (ed. Robert Banks; Exeter: Paternoster/Grand Rapids, MI: Eerdmans, 1974).
(et al.) 'Which Bible Is Best for You'. *Eternity* 25/4 (April 1974): pp. 27–31.

1975

'"Abraham had Two Sons": A Study in Pauline Hermeneutics'. Pages 71–84 in *New Testament Studies: Essays in Honor of Ray Summers in His Sixty-Fifth Year* (ed. Huber L. Drumwright and Curtis Vaughan; Waco, TX: Markham, 1975).
'Apollos in the New Testament'. *Ekklesiastikos Pharos* 57 (1975): pp. 354–66.
'Aquila', 'Barjesus', 'Barnabas', 'Elymas', 'John the Baptist', 'Priscilla', 'Stephen', in *Wycliffe Bible Encyclopedia* (2 vols; ed. C.F. Pfeiffer; Chicago, IL: Moody, 1975).
'Corinthians, First Epistle to the', 'Form Criticism', 'Hebrews, Epistle to the', 'Parable', 'Romans, Epistle to the', in *Zondervan Pictorial Encyclopedia of the Bible* (5 vols; ed. Merrill C. Tenney; Grand Rapids, MI: Zondervan, 1975).
'Further Thoughts on Paul's Autobiography: Galatians 1:11 – 2:14'. Pages 21–9 in *Jesus und Paulus: Festschrift für Werner Georg Kümmel zum 70. Geburtstag* (ed. E. Earle Ellis and Erich Grässer; Göttingen: Vandenhoeck & Ruprecht, 1975).
'Godfrey Rolles Driver (1892–1975)'. *W* 105 (1975): pp. 266–7.
'The Grace of God and the Law of Christ: A Study in Pauline Ethics.' Pages 22–34 in *God and the Good: Essays in Honor of Henry Stob* (ed. Clifton Orlebeke and Lewis Smedes; Grand Rapids, MI: Eerdmans, 1975).

'Introduction'. Pages 9–11 in *Current Issues in Biblical and Patristic Interpretation: Studies in Honor of Merrill C. Tenney, Presented by His Former Students* (ed. G.F. Hawthorne; Grand Rapids, MI: Eerdmans, 1975).
'Lessons I Have Learned'. *H* 54 (1975): pp. 154–5.
'Paul and the Athenians'. *ExT* 88 (1976–7): pp. 8–12.
'Paul and the Law of Moses'. *BJRL* 57 (1974–5): pp. 259–79.
'A Reappraisal of Jewish Apocalyptic Literature'. *Review and Expositor* 72 (1975): pp. 305–15.
'Samuel Prideaux Tregelles'. *H* 54 (1975): pp. 211–12.
'Was Paul a Mystic?' *Reformed Theological Review* 34 (1975): pp. 66–75.

1976

(intro.) *The New Testament, 1526* (trans. William Tyndale, Bristol: David Paradine Developments for Bristol Baptist College, 1976).
'Altar, NT', 'Election, NT', 'Hebrews, Letter to the', in *The Interpreter's Dictionary of the Bible: Supplementary Volume* (ed. Keith Crim et al.; Nashville, TN: Abingdon, 1976).
'The Bible and the Faith'. *Free Church Chronicle* 31/4 (Winter 1976): pp. 8–16.
     repr. in *A Mind for What Matters*, pp. 269–79.
(et al.) 'Image', 'Myth', 'Name', 'Noah', in *The New International Dictionary of New Testament Theology*, vol. 2 (ed. Colin Brown; Exeter: Paternoster/Grand Rapids, MI: Zondervan, 1976).
'Is the Paul of Acts the Real Paul?' *BJRL* 58 (1975–6): pp. 282–305.
'The Lausanne Covenant – 2: The Authority and Power of the Bible'. *H* 55 (1976): pp. 320–23.
'Myth & History'. Pages 79–100 in *History, Criticism & Faith: Four Exploratory Studies* (ed. Colin Brown; Leicester/Downers Grove, IL: IVP, 1976) [= expansion of 'Myth and the New Testament'. *TSF Bulletin*, no. 44 (Spring 1966): pp. 10–15].
     repr. Vancouver: Regent College, 1995.
'The New Testament and Classical Studies: Society for New Testament Studies Presidential Address, 1975'. *New Testament Studies* 22 (1975–6): pp. 229–42.
     repr. in *A Mind for What Matters*, pp. 3–16.
'Some Thoughts on Biblical Inspiration'. *Looking* 5/2 (1976): pp. 26–8.

1977

Paul: Apostle of the Free Spirit (Exeter: Paternoster, 1977).
     = *Paul: Apostle of the Heart Set Free* (Grand Rapids, MI: Eerdmans, 1978).
     rev. edn (Exeter: Paternoster/Grand Rapids, MI: Eerdmans, 1980).
'Christ and Spirit in Paul'. *BJRL* 59 (1976–7): pp. 259–85.
     repr. in *A Mind for What Matters*, pp. 114–32.

'The Early Church's Experiment in Communism'. *Shaft*, no. 18 (December 1977): pp. 6–8.
'The Gospel of John'. *W* 107–10 (1977–80); continued in *H* 60–61 (1981–2).
'The History of New Testament Study'. Pages 21–59 in *New Testament Interpretation: Essays on Principles and Methods* (ed. I. Howard Marshall; Exeter: Paternoster/Grand Rapids, MI: Eerdmans, 1977).
 rev. edn (Exeter: Paternoster, 1979).
'My Father: Peter Fyvie Bruce (1874–1955)'. *BM* 87 (1977): pp. 20–21.
'The Oldest Greek Version of Daniel'. *Oudtestamentiche Studiën* 20 (1977): pp. 22–40.
'Primary Sense and Plenary Sense'. *Epworth Review* 4 (1977): pp. 94–109 [Peake Memorial Lecture].
 repr. in *The Canon of Scripture*, pp. 316–34.
'Rudolf Bultmann (1884–1976)'. *W* 107 (1977): pp. 19, 21.
'Titles and Descriptive Titles of God in the Old Testament', 'Titles and Descriptive Titles of God in the New Testament', 'Our Lord's Incarnation and Virgin Birth.' Pages 62–9, 69–72, 148–51 in *Treasury of Bible Doctrine* (ed. J. Heading and C. Hocking; Aberystwyth: Precious Seed, 1977).

1978

The Time is Fulfilled: Five Aspects of the Fulfilment of the Old Testament in the New (Exeter: Paternoster, 1978/ Grand Rapids, MI: Eerdmans, 1979) [Moore College lectures, 1977].
 repr. (Eugene, OR: Wipf & Stock, 2006).
'All Things to All Men: Diversity in Unity and Other Pauline Tensions'. Pages 82–99 in *Unity and Diversity in New Testament Theology: Essays in Honor of George E. Ladd* (ed. R.A. Guelich; Grand Rapids, MI: Eerdmans, 1978).
'Are the New Testament Document Still Reliable?' *CT*, 20 October 1978, pp. 28–33.
'Are the New Testament Documents Still Reliable?' Pages 49–61 in *Evangelical Roots: A Tribute to Wilbur Smith* (ed. Kenneth S. Kantzer; Nashville, TN: Thomas Nelson, 1978).
'Bishop Westcott and the Classical Tradition'. *Spectrum* 11/1 (September 1978): pp. 19–21.
'Cecil Howley: A Tribute of Friendship'. *W* 108 (1978): pp. 3–4.
'Christian Destiny – 2: Christ our Hope'. *H* 57 (1978): pp. 132–3, 165–8.
'The Davidic Messiah in Luke–Acts'. Pages 7–17 in *Biblical and Near Eastern Studies: Essays in Honor of William Sanford LaSor* (ed. Gary A. Tuttle; Grand Rapids, MI: Eerdmans, 1978).
'Evangelical Theology Today'. *Life of Faith*, February 1978, pp. 16–17.
'The Full Name of the Procurator Felix'. *Journal for the Study of the New Testament*, no. 1 (October 1978): pp. 33–6.

'George Cecil Douglas Howley: An Appreciation', 'Lessons from the Early Church'. Pages ix–xii, 153–68 in *In God's Community: Essays on the Church and Its Ministry* (ed. David J. Ellis and W. Ward Gasque; London: Pickering & Inglis, 1978/Wheaton, IL: Harold Shaw, 1979).
    the latter repr. in *A Mind for What Matters*, pp. 235–47.
'Response' to John A. Buell and O. Quentin Hyder, *Jesus: God, Ghost or Guru?* (Grand Rapids, MI: Zondervan, 1978), pp. 121–3.
'The Romans through Jewish Eyes'. Pages 3–12 in *Paganisme, Judaïsme, Christianisme, Influences et affrontements dans le monde antique: Mélanges offerts à Marcel Simon* (ed. A. Benoit, M. Philonenko and C. Vogel; Paris: Editions E. de Boccard, 1978).
'St. John at Ephesus'. *BJRL* 60 (1977–8): pp. 339–61.
'William Barclay (1907–78)'. *W* 108 (1978): pp. 114–15.

1979

I Want to Know What the Bible Says about the Work of Jesus (Eastbourne: Kingsway, 1979).
    = *What the Bible Teaches about What Jesus Did* (Wheaton, IL, Tyndale House, 1979).
    = *The Work of Jesus* (Eastbourne: Kingsway, 1984).
    = *Jesus Past, Present and Future: The Work of Christ* (Downers Grove, IL: IVP, 1998).
Men and Movements in the Primitive Church: Studies in Early Non-Pauline Christianity (Exeter: Paternoster, 1979).
    = *Peter, Stephen, James, and John: Studies in Early Non-Pauline Christianity* (Grand Rapids, MI: Eerdmans, 1980).
(ed. and intro.) *Vine's Expository Dictionary of Old Testament Words* (London: Oliphants, 1979).
'Accountability in University Life'. *Spectrum* 12/1 (September 1979), pp. 10–11.
'Acts of the Apostles', 'Age', 'Colossians, Epistle to the', 'Criticism', 'Hittites', 'Paul, the Apostle', in *International Standard Bible Encyclopedia* (4 vols; ed. G.W. Bromiley et al.; Grand Rapids, MI: Eerdmans, rev. edn, 1979–88).
'Arthur Samuel Peake: Biblical Scholar'. *Methodist Recorder*, 16 August 1979, p. 29.
'The Gospel Text of Marius Victorinus.' Pages 69–78 in *Text and Interpretation: Studies in the New Testament Presented to Matthew Black* (ed. Ernest Best and R. McL. Wilson; Cambridge: Cambridge University Press, 1979).
'The Main Ideas of the New Testament'. Pages 35–40 in *Introduction to the Bible* (London: Scripture Union, 1978).
'The Old Testament and the Christian', 'Chronology of the Old Testament', 'Introduction to the Poetical Books', 'Introduction to the Wisdom Literature', 'Ezekiel', in *A Bible Commentary for Today* (ed. G.C.D. Howley et al. [including Bruce]; Glasgow: Pickering & Inglis, 1979).

= *The New Layman's Bible Commentary in One Volume* (Grand Rapids, MI: Zondervan, 1979).

= *The Pickering Bible Commentary for Today* (Basingstoke: Marshall Pickering, 1984).

(gen. ed.) rev. edn, *The International Bible Commentary with the New International Version* (Basingstoke: Marshall Pickering/Grand Rapids, MI: Zondervan, 1986).

'Prophetic Interpretation in the Septuagint'. *Bulletin of the International Organization for Septuagint and Cognate Studies*, no. 12 (Fall 1979): pp. 17–26.

repr. in *This Place Is Too Small for Us: The Israelite Prophets in Recent Scholarship* (ed. Robert P. Gordon; Winona Lake, IN: Eisenbrauns, 1995, pp. 539–46).

'St. Paul in Macedonia'. *BJRL* 61 (1978–9): pp. 337–54.

'The Theology and Interpretation of the Old Testament'. Pages 385–416 in *Tradition and Interpretation: Essays by Members of the Society for Old Testament Study* (ed. G.W. Anderson; Oxford: Clarendon, 1979).

'The Transmission and Translation of the Bible'. Pages 37–57 in *The Expositor's Bible Commentary*, vol. 1 (ed. F.E. Gaebelein; Grand Rapids, MI: Zondervan, 1979).

1980

(intro.) Smith, George Adam. *Four Psalms* (New Canaan, CT: Keats, 1980).

'Appeal to Caesar', 'Collection', 'Hellenists', 'Myth, Mythology', in *The Illustrated Bible Dictionary* (3 vols; ed. J.D. Douglas; Leicester: IVP/ Wheaton, IL: Tyndale House, 1980) [also articles from New Bible Dictionary (1962), *q.v.*].

'Charting New Directions for New Testament Studies'. *CT*, 10 October 1980, pp. 19–22.

'St. Paul in Macedonia: 2. The Thessalonian Correspondence'. *BJRL* 62 (1979–80): pp. 328–45.

'The Trial of Jesus in the Fourth Gospel'. Pages 7–20 in *Gospel Perspectives I: Studies of History and Tradition in the Four Gospels* (ed. R.T. France and D. Wenham; Sheffield: JSOT Press, 1980).

1981

Places They Knew: Jesus and Paul (London: Ark, 1981) [comprised 2 vols: *Places Jesus Knew* and *Places Paul Knew*].

= *Jesus and Paul: Places they Knew* (Nashville, TN: Thomas Nelson, 1983).

repr. separately as:

In the Steps of Our Lord (Grand Rapids, MI: Kregel, 1997).

In the Steps of the Apostle Paul (Grand Rapids, MI: Kregel, 1995; [n.pl.]: Candle Books, 2000).
'Anthony Tyrrell Hanson: A Tribute'. *Journal for the Study of the New Testament*, no. 13 (October 1981): pp. 3–8.
'Battle for the Bible: Biblical Criticism and Authority'. *JCBRF*, no. 89 (April 1981): pp. 7–15.
'Commentaries on Acts'. *Epworth Review* 8/3 (September 1981): pp. 82–7.
'St Paul in Macedonia: 3. The Philippian Correspondence'. *BJRL* 63 (1980–81): pp. 260–84.

1982

Acts, Bible Study Commentary (London: Scripture Union / Fort Washington, PA: CLC, 1982).
(consulting ed.) Elrose Hunter and Paul Marsh, eds. *The Book of Bible Knowledge* (London: Scripture Union, [1982]); contributed 'Foreword', 'Translating the Bible'.
  = *Sadlier's Bible Encyclopedia: A Comprehensive Guide to the World of the Bible in Full Color* (Nashville, TN: Thomas Nelson, 1982).
The Epistle of Paul to the Galatians: A Commentary on the Greek Text, NIGTC (Exeter: Paternoster/Grand Rapids, MI: Eerdmans, 1982).
Paternoster Bible History Atlas (Exeter: Paternoster, 1982).
  = *Carta's Bible History Atlas* (Jerusalem: Carta, 1982).
  = *Bible History Atlas* (New York: Crossroad, 1982).
1 & 2 Thessalonians. Word Biblical Commentary, vol. 45 (Waco, TX and London: Word/Nashville, TN: Thomas Nelson, 1982).
'The Acts of the Apostles To-day', *BJRL* 65/1 (Autumn 1982): pp. 36–56.
'The Background to the Son of Man Sayings'. Pages 50–70 in *Christ the Lord: Studies in Christology Presented to Donald Guthrie* (ed. Harold H. Rowdon; Leicester: IVP, 1982).
'The Curse of the Law'. Pages 27–36 in *Paul and Paulinism: Essays in Honour of C.K. Barrett* (ed. M.D. Hooker and S. G. Wilson; London: SPCK, 1982).
'The Romans Debate – Continued'. *BJRL* 64 (1981–2): pp. 334–59 [Manson Memorial Lecture, 1981].
  repr. in *A Mind for What Matters*, pp. 79–97.
'What Does It Mean?' *CBR*, no. 31–32 (1982): pp. 41–52.
'Women in the Church: A Biblical Survey'. *CBR*, no. 33 (1982): pp. 7–14.
  repr. in *A Mind for What Matters*, pp. 259–66.

1983

The Gospel of John (Basingstoke: Pickering Paperbacks/Grand Rapids, MI: Eerdmans, 1983).
  repr. with *The Epistles of John* (Grand Rapids, MI: Eerdmans, 1994).

The Hard Sayings of Jesus (London: Hodder & Stoughton/Downers Grove, IL: IVP, 1983).

    incorp. into Walter C. Kaiser Jr, Peter H. Davids, F.F. Bruce and Manfred T. Brauch, *Hard Sayings of the Bible* (Downers Grove, IL: IVP, 1996).

Philippians, Good News Commentary (San Francisco: Harper & Row, 1983/Basingstoke: Pickering & Inglis, 1984).

    rev. edn, *Philippians*, New International Biblical Commentary, vol. 11 (Carlisle: Paternoster, 1989/Peabody, MA: Hendrickson, 1990, 1995).

'Amarna', 'Amarna Letters', 'Cenchrea', 'Galatia', 'Hierapolis' [with E. M. Blaiklock], 'Maccabees', 'Peter, Tomb of', 'Qumran', 'Solomon's Porch', 'Zeno Papyri', in *New International Dictionary of Biblical Archaeology* (ed. E.M. Blaiklock and R.K. Harrison; Grand Rapids, MI: Zondervan, 1983).

'The Bible and the Environment'. Pages 15–29 in *The Living and Active Word of God: Studies in Honor of Samuel J. Schultz* (ed. Morris Inch and Ronald Youngblood; Winona Lake, IN: Eisenbrauns, 1983).

'Biblical Exposition at Qumran'. Pages 77–98 in *Gospel Perspectives III: Studies in Midrash and Historiography* (ed. R.T. France and D. Wenham; Sheffield: JSOT Press, 1983).

'Henry Leopold Ellison (1903–1983)'. *H* 62/10 (October 1983): pp. 2–3.

'The Pauline Circle' [series]. *H* 62 (1983).

    publ. in book form as *The Pauline Circle* (Grand Rapids, MI: Eerdmans/Exeter: Paternoster, 1986; Eugene, OR: Wipf & Stock, 2006).

'Robertson Smith and "The Prophets of Israel" '. *ExT* 95 (1983–4): pp. 45–9.

'Some Thoughts on the Beginning of the New Testament Canon'. *BJRL* 65/2 (Spring 1983): pp. 37–60.

'Two Centuries of New Testament Criticism'. *Christian Librarian*, no. 7 (1983): pp. 5–16.

1984

Abraham and David: Places They Knew (London: Scripture Union/ Nashville, TN: Thomas Nelson, 1984) [comprised 2 vols: *Places Abraham Knew and Places David Knew*].

The Epistles to the Colossians, to Philemon and to the Ephesians, NICNT (Grand Rapids, MI: Eerdmans, 1984).

St Paul the Preacher: 'Diamond Jubilee' Lecture 1983. Lecture Given to the London Baptist Preachers' Association on Friday 18th November 1983 (London: London Baptist Preachers' Association), [1984].

'"Called to Freedom": A Study in Galatians'. Pages 61–71 in *The New Testament Age: Essays in Honor of Bo Reicke* (2 vols; ed. William C. Weinrich; Macon, GA: Mercer University Press, 1984), vol. 1.

'Colossian Problems. Part 1: Jews and Christians in the Lycus Valley'. *BibSac* 141 (1984): pp. 3–15.
'Colossian Problems. Part 2: The "Christ Hymn" of Colossians 1:15–20'. *BibSac* 141 (1984), pp. 99–111.
'Colossian Problems. Part 3: The Colossian Heresy'. *BibSac* 141 (1984): pp. 195–208.
'Colossian Problems. Part 4: Christ as Conqueror and Reconciler'. *BibSac* 141 (1984): pp. 291–302.
'The Date and Character of Mark', 'Render to Caesar'. Pages 69–89, 249–63 in *Jesus and the Politics of His Day* (ed. Ernst Bammel and C.F.D. Moule; Cambridge: Cambridge University Press, 1984).
'The Jesus of History and the Christ of Faith' [series]. *H* 63 (1984).
'John Wycliffe and the English Bible'. *Churchman* 98 (1984): pp. 294–306.
'The Reliability of the New Testament'. Pages 255–6 in *The Intellectuals Speak Out about God: A Handbook for the Christian Student in a Secular Society* (ed. Roy Abraham Varghese; Chicago, IL: Regnery Gateway, 1984).
'St Paul and "The Powers That Be" '. *BJRL* 66/2 (Spring 1984), pp. 78–96.
    repr. in *A Mind for What Matters*, pp. 98–113.
'Tacitus on Jewish History'. *JSS* 29/1 (Spring 1984): pp. 33–44.

1985

Paul and the Mind of Christ (Leicester: Religious & Theological Studies Fellowship, [1985]).
The Real Jesus: Who Is He? (London: Hodder & Stoughton, 1985).
    = *Jesus: Lord and Savior* (Downers Grove, IL: IVP, 1986).
'The Acts of the Apostles: Historical Record or Theological Reconstruction?' Pages 2569–603 in *Aufstieg und Niedergang der Römischen Welt: Geschichte und Kultur Roms im Spiegel der neueren Forschung*, Teil II: *Principat*, Band 25.3 (ed. Hildegard Temporini and Wolfgang Haase; Berlin and New York: Walter de Gruyter, 1985).
'Arnold Pickering (1908–1984)'. *H* 64/1 (January 1985): p. 7.
'The Church of Jerusalem in the Acts of the Apostles'. *BJRL* 67 (1984–5): pp. 641–61.
    repr. in *A Mind for What Matters*, pp. 150–65.
'The Letter of Jude' [series]. *H* 64 (1985).
'St Luke's Portrait of St Paul'. Pages 181–91 in *Aksum – Thyateira: A Festschrift for Archbishop Methodios of Thyateira and Great Britain* (ed. George Dion Dragas; London and Athens: Thyateira House, 1985).
'The Social Identity of Early Christians'. Pages 38–47 in *Through Christ's Word: A Festschrift for Dr Philip E. Hughes* (ed. W. Robert Godfrey and Jesse L. Boyd; Phillipsburg, NJ: Presbyterian & Reformed, 1985).
'The Spirit in the Letter to the Galatians'. Pages 36–48 in *Essays on Apostolic Themes: Studies in Honor of Howard M. Ervin Presented to Him by Colleagues*

and Friends on His Sixty-Fifth Birthday (ed. Paul Elbert; Peabody, MA: Hendrickson, 1985).
'The Structure and Argument of Hebrews'. *Southwestern Journal of Theology* 28/1 (Fall 1985): pp. 6–12.

1986

Student's Atlas of the Bible ([Exeter]: Paternoster, [1986]).
(consulting ed. and contributor) Herbert Lockyer Sr, ed. *Nelson's Illustrated Bible Dictionary* (Nashville, TN: Nelson, 1986).
= *The Hodder and Stoughton Illustrated Bible Dictionary* ([Sevenoaks]: Hodder & Stoughton, 1986).
'The Apostolic Decree of Acts 15'. Pages 115–24 in *Studien zum Text und zur Ethik des Neuen Testaments: Festschrift zum 80. Geburtstag von Heinrich Greeven*, Beihefte zür Zeitshrift fur die neutestementliche Wissenschaft 47 (ed. Wolfgang Schrage; Berlin: Walter de Gruyter, 1986).
'Baptism 13. Plymouth Brethren', 'Books, Liturgical 13. Plymouth Brethren', 'Burial 12. Plymouth Brethren', 'Liturgies 13. Plymouth Brethren', 'Marriage 12. Plymouth Brethren', 'Plymouth Brethren Worship', in *A New Dictionary of Liturgy and Worship* (ed. J.G. Davies; London: SCM, 1986).
'Chronological Questions in the Acts of the Apostles'. *BJRL* 68 (1985–6): pp. 273–95.
    repr. in *A Mind for What Matters*, pp. 133–49.
'The Conference in Jerusalem: Galatians 2:1–10'. Pages 195–212 in *God Who Is Rich in Mercy: Essays Presented to Dr D.B. Knox* (ed. Peter T. O'Brien and David G. Peterson; Homebush West, NSW: ANZEA, [1986]).
'Homecall: Frederick Albert Tatford (1901–1986)'. *H* 65 (August 1986): p. 13.
'Studies in the Pastoral Epistles' [series]. *H* 65 (1986).

1987

(consulting ed.) J.D. Douglas and Merrill C. Tenney, eds. *The New International Dictionary of the Bible* (Grand Rapids, MI: Zondervan/ Basingstoke: Marshall Pickering, 1987) [= revision of *Zondervan Pictorial Bible Dictionary*].
'Biblical Studies at Sheffield: The Early Days'. Pages 25–7 in *The Bible in Three Dimensions: Essays in Celebration of Forty Years of Biblical Studies in the University of Sheffield, JSOT Supplement Series* 87 (ed. David J.A. Clines, Stephen E. Fowl and Stanley E. Porter; Sheffield: Sheffield Academic Press, 1987).
'The First Church Historian'. Pages 1–14 in *Church, Word and Spirit: Historical and Theological Essays in Honor of Geoffrey W. Bromiley* (ed. James E. Bradley and Richard A. Muller; Grand Rapids, MI: Eerdmans, 1987).

'My View: Faith vs Scientific Study of the Bible'. *Bible Review*, no. 3 (Summer 1987): pp. 4–5.
'Paul's Apologetic and the Purpose of Acts'. *BJRL* 69 (1986–7): pp. 379–93. repr. in *A Mind for What Matters*, pp. 166–78.
'Paul's Use of the Old Testament in Acts'. Pages 71–9 in *Tradition and Interpretation in the New Testament: Essays in Honor of E. Earle Ellis for His 60th Birthday* (ed. Gerald F. Hawthorne with Otto Betz; Grand Rapids, MI: Eerdmans/Tübingen: J.C.B. Mohr [Paul Siebeck], 1987).
'Problem Texts' [series]. *H* 66 (1987).
'Stephen's Apologia'. Pages 37–50 in *Scripture: Meaning and Method: Essays Presented to Anthony Tyrrell Hanson for His Seventieth Birthday* (ed. Barry P. Thompson; Hull: Hull University Press, 1987).
'The Theology of Acts'. *TSF Bulletin*, no. 10 (May–June 1987): pp. 15–17.
'"To the Hebrews": A Document of Roman Christianity'. Pages 3496–521 in *Aufstieg und Niedergang der Römischen Welt: Geschichte und Kultur Roms im Spiegel der neueren Forschung*, Teil II: *Principat*, Band 25.4 (ed. Hildegard Temporini and Wolfgang Haase; Berlin and New York: Walter de Gruyter, 1987).

1988

The Canon of Scripture (Downers Grove, IL: IVP/Glasgow: Chapter House, 1988).
'The Dead Sea Scrolls', in *New Dictionary of Theology* (ed. Sinclair B. Ferguson, David F. Wright and J.I. Packer; Leicester: IVP, 1988).
'The Enigma of Paul: Why Did the Early Church's Great Liberator Get a Reputation as an Authoritarian?' *Bible Review*, no. 4 (August 1988): pp. 32–3.
'Eschatology in Acts'. Pages 51–63 in *Eschatology and the New Testament: Essays in Honor of George Raymond Beasley-Murray* (ed. W. Hulitt Gloer; Peabody, MA: Hendrickson, 1988).
'Fresh and Unpretentious'. *Reformed Journal* 38/12 (December 1988): p. 26.
'Paul and the Law in Recent Research'. Pages 115–25 in *Law and Religion: Essays on the Place of the Law in Israel and Early Christianity, by Members of the Ehrhardt Seminar of Manchester University* (ed. Barnabas Lindars; Cambridge: James Clarke, 1988).
'Scripture in Relation to Tradition and Reason'. Pages 35–65 in *Scripture, Tradition and Reason: Essays in Honour of Richard P.C. Hanson* (ed. R. Bauckham and B. Drewery; Edinburgh: T&T Clark, 1988).

1989

'Commentaries on Acts'. *Bible Translator* 40/3 (July 1989): pp. 315–21.
'Eschatology: Understanding the End of Days'. *Bible Review*, no. 5 (December 1989): pp. 43–4.

'J.B. Lightfoot (died 1889), Commentator and Theologian'. *Evangel* 7/2 (Summer 1989): pp. 10–12.
'The Open Bible in England'. *Churchman* 103 (1989): pp. 117–19.
'Philip and the Ethiopian'. *JSS* 34 (1989), pp. 377–86.
'Practice or Principle'. *H* 68/1 (January 1989): pp. 12–13; 68/2 (February 1989): pp. 6–8.

1990

A Mind for What Matters: Collected Essays (Grand Rapids, MI: Eerdmans, 1990; Exeter: Paternoster, 1992).
'Letter to a Brother'. *H* 69/1 (January 1990): pp. 6–7.
'Luke's Presentation of the Spirit in Acts'. *Criswell Theological Review* 5 (1990): pp. 15–29.
'One in Christ Jesus: Thoughts on Galatians 3:26–29', *CBRF Journal*, no. 122 (August 1990): pp. 7–10.
'The Significance of the Speeches for Interpreting Acts'. *Southwestern Journal of Theology* 33 (1990): pp. 20–28.

1991

Contributions to *New 20th-Century Encyclopedia of Religious Knowledge* (ed. J.D. Douglas; Grand Rapids, MI: Baker, 2nd edn, 1991).

1992

'The Bible', in *The Origin of the Bible* (ed. P.W. Comfort; Wheaton, IL: Tyndale House, 1992), pp. 10–12 [from 2nd edn of *New Bible Dictionary*].
'Canon', in *Dictionary of Jesus and the Gospels* (ed. Joel B. Green, Scot McKnight, and I. Howard Marshall; Downers Grove and Leicester: IVP, 1992).
Contributions to *The Anchor Bible Dictionary* (6 vols; ed. David Noel Freedman; New York: Doubleday, 1992).
Contributions to *A Dictionary of Biblical Tradition in English Literature* (ed. David Lyle Jeffrey; Grand Rapids, MI: Eerdmans, 1992).
'Hebrew Poetry' repr. in *The Psalms: Ancient Poetry of the Spirit* (Oxford: Lion, 1997/New York: St Martin's Press, 2000).
'Habakkuk'. Pages 831–96 in *The Minor Prophets*, vol. 2 (ed. Thomas E. McComiskey; Grand Rapids, MI: Baker, 1993).
'Manson, Thomas Walter'. Pages 63–5 in *Theologische Realenzyklopädie*, Band 22.1 (ed. Gerhard Müller; Berlin and New York: Walter de Gruyter, 1992).
'Textual Problems in the Epistle to the Hebrews'. Pages 27–39 in *Scribes and Scripture: New Testament Essays in Honour of J. Harold Greenlee* (ed. David Alan Black; Winona Lake, IN: Eisenbrauns, 1992).

1993

'Paul in Acts and Letters', in *Dictionary of Paul and His Letters* (ed. Gerald F. Hawthorne and Ralph P. Martin; Downers Grove, IL and Leicester: IVP, 1993).

1995

'One in Christ Jesus: Thoughts on Galatians 3:26–29'. *Stimulus*, no. 3 (August 1995): pp. 9–11 [possibly a reprint of the 1990 *CBRF Journal* article with this title].

Extant manuscript material

Addresses

'Christ in the Old Testament'. Address to Tyndale Fellowship study group, July 1974, typescript.
'Christian Freedom'. University Sermon, St Mary the Virgin, Oxford, 18 February 1979, typescript.
'The Church: Pattern or Principle?' Address at the Bloomsbury meetings, 6 November 1976, typescript.
'Women in the Church: A Biblical Survey'. CBRF Summer Seminar, 9 June 1979, typescript.

Other items

Aberdeen University, MS 2975, 'The Latinity of Gaius Marius Victorinus Afer, with Appendices on His Biblical Text and on the Vocabulary of Candidus the Arian', 1935.
Aberdeen University, Logic examination paper, n.d.
Contributions to Cambridge Prayer Fellowship 1934 newsletters, 1970–90.
'Evangeliarium Mario-Victorinianum', typescript.
Notebooks containing pasted-in and annotated copies of magazine articles.
Paraphrase of Galatians, typescript [1957?].
Typescripts and correspondence relating to a proposed history of Jewish biblical exegesis, ed. Raphael Loewe for Cambridge University Press, 1969–71.

Extant recordings

Broadcast Service, Crescent Road, Stockport, 21 February 1960.
'Evangelism in New Testament Perspective'. Regent College, Vancouver, ref. 312, n.d.

Question and Answer session, Bethany Gospel Chapel, Hamilton, Ontario, March 1973.

'The Reliability of the NT Documents'. Bethany Gospel Chapel, Hamilton, Ontario, March 1973.

Stockport Male Voice Praise, evangelistic service, Brinnington Evangelical Church, 1974.

'The Book of Revelation'. Regent College, Vancouver, ref. 607, 1976.

'Christ and Caesar in the First Century'. Regent College, Vancouver, ref. 306, 1976.

'The Gospel behind the Gospels'. Regent College, Vancouver, ref. 603A, 1976.

'Why Four Gospels?' Regent College, Vancouver, ref. 603B, 1976.

'Mark's Witness to Jesus'. Regent College, Vancouver, ref. 603C, 1976.

'Mark: Date and Purpose'. Regent College, Vancouver, ref. 603D, 1976.

'The Synoptic Question'. Regent College, Vancouver, ref. 603E, 1976.

Select Bibliography of Other Items

Manuscript material

In private hands

Preston, Ronald H. 'Fred Bruce in Manchester' [tribute for Thanksgiving Service, 13 March 1991], typescript.
Prophecy Investigation Society, minute book 1928–62.
Rowdon, Harold, notes on twentieth-century Brethren history.
Stewart, Sandy. 'A Record of Gospel Work. Christian Brethren. Moray and Nairn' [A4 file containing notes, cuttings, photocopies etc.].

Bath, Echoes of Service

Candidates' Book 4.

Cambridge, Tyndale House

Papers and correspondence regarding Tyndale House and the Tyndale Fellowship: Box 13, Biblical Research Committee minutes 1959–77, Tyndale House Committee minutes 1967–75; Box 14, Biblical Research Committee minutes 1942–52; Box 18, Biblical Research Committee minutes; Box 41, Douglas Johnson, unpublished history of Tyndale House [typescript, 1980], with related correspondence and memoranda.

Cambridge, University Library

Ratcliffe, F.W. ' "Books, Books, Just Miles and Miles of Books": Across the Library Counter, 1950–2000', bound typescript, 2007, Shelfmark Camb. 2007.6.

Carol Stream, IL, Tyndale House publishers

Correspondence between F.F. Bruce and Kenneth N. Taylor relating to revision of the Living Bible, 1988–90.

Dubuque, IA, Emmaus Bible College Library

Correspondence between F.F. Bruce and others, 1952–72.

Edinburgh, National Library of Scotland

Acc. 9471, correspondence of /about William Barclay, 1946–79.

Grand Rapids, MI, William B. Eerdmans publishers

Files and correspondence relating to books by Bruce.

Leeds, Brotherton Library, Special Collections

Yorkshire Society for Celtic Studies, minute books, correspondence and notices of meetings.

Leicester, Universities and Colleges Christian Fellowship

Correspondence between Bruce and Paul Woodbridge, 1983–5.
Correspondence, minutes and programmes relating to the Biblical Research Committee and Tyndale House, 1939–59.
IVF Trust, minute book.

London, Palestine Exploration Fund

Minute Book 9, 1935–66; Minute Book 10, 1965–90.

Madrid, Comisión de Biblioteca y Archivos, Centro Evangélico de Formación Bíblica en Madrid

Correspondence between F.F. Bruce and Ernest Trenchard, 1955–71.

Manchester, University of Manchester

Vice-Chancellor's Office, file concerning Bruce's appointment as Rylands Professor.

Manchester, University of Manchester, Special Collections

Faculty of Theology, Minute Books of Proceedings of the Board of Faculty of Theology 2, 3, FTH/1/2, 3.
Faculty of Theology, papers and correspondence, 1959–79, VCA/7/401, folders 1–3.
Faculty of Theology, prospectuses for 1959–60, 1964–5.

Manson Papers, E.I.235, Bruce to T.W. Manson, 24 November 1953; F.IV.15, synopsis of Bruce's paper to SNTS, Bangor, September 1955, 'Qumran and Early Christianity'.
University Archives, General Board of Faculties Arts Section Minutes and Board of Faculty of Arts minutes, 1959–78.

Manchester, University of Manchester, Special Collections, Christian Brethren Archive

Correspondence between Bruce and Ian S. Davidson, Box 11(11g).
Correspondence between Bruce and Neil T.R. Dickson, 1987–9, Box 323/4/1/3.
Correspondence between Bruce and Robbie Orr, 1988, Box 323/4/1/4.
Correspondence file 'B'.
Papers relating to the Christian Brethren Research Fellowship, later Partnership (UK), Boxes 4–7B, 132, 148(1).
Papers relating to the High Leigh and Swanwick conferences, Boxes 106, 108–12.
Papers relating to the Wellington Area Research Fellowship, Box 8.
Papers relating to the Young Men's Bible Teaching Conferences, Boxes 13(2), 138, 147 (1).
Bruce, F.F., letter to J.R. Casswell, 5 February 1968, Box 9(13).
Campbell, W.W. 'A Short History of the Edinburgh Assemblies (3) Bellevue Chapel', photocopy of typescript, n.d., Box 318/2/29/8.
Howarth, E. to Bruce, 31 March 1962, CBA 1987.
Lang, G.H., letters and papers, CBA 241–273, Boxes 11, 26, 64A, 66, 68, 69.
Watson, J.B., letters and papers, Boxes 229–255.

Northwood, Middlesex, London School of Theology

Papers of J.D. Douglas, including unfinished typescript memoir, 'The Half That Can Be Told' and correspondence with F.F. Bruce and others.

Sheffield, University of Sheffield, Staff Centenary History Archives

Potter, G.R., manuscript history of Sheffield University, 1980.

Vancouver, Regent College

Michael Collison collection of papers relating to the history of Regent College.

Wheaton, IL, Wheaton College, Archives of the Billy Graham Center

Papers in collection 008 (Christianity Today).
Papers in collection 192 (Harold Lindsell).

Theses and unpublished papers

Atherstone, Andrew. 'Alan Stibbs (1901–1971): Missionary, Preacher, Theologian', unpublished paper.

Botton, Kenneth V. 'Regent College: An Experiment in Theological Education', PhD thesis, Trinity International University, 2004.

Couser, Greg A. 'The Law in Galatians: A Comparison of Bruce and Paul', MA dissertation, Liberty University, Lynchburg, VA, 1988 http://digital-commons.liberty.edu/cgi/viewcontent.cgi?article=1034&context=masters (accessed 3 December 2009).

Cross, Anthony R. 'A Critical Comparison of Professor F.F. Bruce and Professor Rudolf Bultmann on the Historical Reliability of the New Testament', BA dissertation, Bristol University, 1985.

D'Elia, John A. 'A Place at the Table: George Eldon Ladd and the Rehabilitation of Evangelical Scholarship in America', PhD dissertation, University of Stirling, 2005.

Gasque, Ward. 'Frederick Fyvie Bruce (1910–1990): An Unhyphenated Evangelical', lecture given at the John Rylands University Library, Manchester, July 2007.

Rowdon, Harold. 'Brethren in Britain, 1945–2000: A Personal Sketch', paper delivered at the Brethren Archivists' and Historians' Network Conference, Gloucester, July 2003.

Shuff, Roger Norman. 'Searching for the True Church: Brethren and Evangelicals in mid-Twentieth-Century England', PhD thesis, University of Wales (Spurgeon's College), 2003.

Books and articles

Andrews, John S. 'Haute Vulgarisation'. *Librarians' Christian Fellowship Newsletter*, no. 46 (Winter 1990): pp. 3–4.

Anon. *Aberdeen University Calendar* (Aberdeen: University Press, 1928–32) [issued annually].

Anon. 'Biblical Inspiration and Authority'. *TB*, os, July 1946, pp. 1–4.

Anon. *Sandy Scott's Bible Class* (London: Bliss, Sands & Co., 1897).

Anon. 'Towards Barthianism: Is "The Evangelical Quarterly" Softening the Ground?' *Monthly Record of the Free Church of Scotland*, February 1955, p. 26.

Anon., *Who's Who 1990* (London: A&C Black, 1990).

BTD. 'F.F. Bruce'. *Aware/Harvester* 69/12 (December 1990): p. 26.

Baird, William. *History of New Testament Research*, 2: *From Jonathan Edwards to Rudolf Bultmann* (Minneapolis, MN: Fortress, 2003).

Ballis, Peter H. *Leaving the Adventist Ministry: A Study of the Process of Exiting, Religion in the Age of Transformation* (Westport, CT: Praeger, 1999).

Barclay, Oliver. Evangelicalism in Britain 1935–1995: A Personal Sketch (Leicester: IVP, 1997).
— 'F.F. Bruce and the Inter-Varsity Fellowship'. JCBRF, no. 22 (November 1971): p. 20.
— Whatever Happened to the Jesus Lane Lot? (Leicester: IVP, 1977).
Barr, James. 'The Problem of Fundamentalism Today'. Pages 63–90 in Explorations in Theology 7 (idem; London: SCM, 1980).
Barron, Gordon. West End School: A Celebration of 130 Years, 1875–2005 ([Elgin]: n.p., [2005]).
Baylis, Robert. My People: The History of Those Christians Sometimes Called Plymouth Brethren (Port Colborne, ON: Gospel Folio Press, 2006).
Beasley-Murray, Paul. Fearless for Truth: A Personal Portrait of the Life of George Raymond Beasley-Murray (Carlisle: Paternoster, 2002).
Bebbington, D.W. Evangelicalism in Modern Britain: A History from the 1730s to the 1980s (London: Unwin Hyman, 1989).
Birkinshaw, Robert K. Pilgrims in Lotus Land: Conservative Protestantism in British Columbia 1917–1981 (Montreal: McGill-Queen's University Press, 1995).
Borland, A. Woman's Place in the Assemblies: An Assessment of Bible Teaching (Kilmarnock: John Ritchie, [c. 1970]).
Bosworth, C.E., and S. Strelcyn, eds. Studies in Honour of F.F. Bruce = JSS 23/2 (Autumn 1978).
Bottoms, Avril. 'The Methodist Contribution'. Methodist Recorder, 24 May 1979, pp. 3, 6.
Brady, David. 'The Cristian [sic] Brethren Archive in the John Rylands University Library of Manchester'. Pages 175–91 in Piero Guicciardini 1808–1886: Un Reformatore Religioso nell'Europa dell'ottocento. Atti del Convegno di Studi, Firenze, 11–12 aprile 1986 (ed. Lorenza Giorgi and Massimo Rubboli; Florence: Leo S. Olschki, 1988).
Brady, David and Fred J. Evans. Christian Brethren in Manchester and District: A History (London: Heritage Publications, 1997).
Bray, Gerald. Biblical Interpretation Past and Present (Leicester: Apollos, 1996).
Brencher, John. Martyn Lloyd-Jones (1899–1981) and Twentieth-Century Evangelicalism (Carlisle: Paternoster, 2002).
[Brown, Matthew S.R., et al.]. Aberdeen Christian Conference Centenary 1874–1973 (Aberdeen: Alex P. Reid, 1972).
Bruce, I.A.F. An Historical Commentary on the Hellenica Oxyrhynchia (Cambridge: Cambridge University Press, 1967).
Byatt, Mary. Elgin: A History and Celebration of the Town (Teffont, Salisbury: Francis Frith Collection, 2005).
Capon, John. 'From Scotland with Scholarship'. Crusade, April 1976 [typescript supplied by the author].
Capper, W. Melville and Douglas Johnson. Arthur Rendle Short, Surgeon and Christian (London: Inter-Varsity Fellowship, 1954).

Carson, D.A. and John D. Woodbridge, eds. *Scripture and Truth* (Leicester: IVP, 1983).

Childs, Brevard S. *Biblical Theology in Crisis* (Philadelphia, PA: Westminster, 1970).

— *Introduction to the Old Testament as Scripture* (London: SCM, 1979).

Clements, Ronald E. 'The Biblical Scholarship of H.H. Rowley'. *Baptist Quarterly* 38 (1999): pp. 70–82.

Clines, David J.A. 'The Sheffield Department of Biblical Studies: An Intellectual Biography.' Pages 14–89 in *Auguries: The Jubilee Volume of the Sheffield Department of Biblical Studies, Journal for the Study of the Old Testament Supplement Series* 269 (ed. idem and Stephen Moore; Sheffield: Sheffield Academic Press, 1998).

—, Stephen E. Fowl and Stanley E. Porter, eds. *The Bible in Three Dimensions: Essays in Celebration of Forty Years of Biblical Studies in the University of Sheffield*, JSOT Supplement Series 87 (Sheffield: Sheffield Academic Press, 1990).

Coad, F. Roy. 'F.F. Bruce: His Influence on Brethren in the British Isles'. *JCBRF*, no. 22 (November 1971): pp. 13–14.

— *A History of the Brethren Movement* (Exeter: Paternoster, 2nd edn, 1976).

— *Laing: The Biography of Sir John W. Laing, C.B.E. (1879–1978)* (London: Hodder & Stoughton, 1979).

Coggins, Richard. 'A Future for the Commentary?' Pages 163–75 in *The Open Text: New Directions for Biblical Studies?* (ed. Francis Watson; London: SCM, 1993).

Cordiner, F. *Fragments from the Past: An Account of People and Events in the Assemblies of Northern Scotland* (London: Pickering & Inglis, 1961).

Cross, Anthony R. 'Historical Methodology and New Testament Study'. *Themelios* 22/3 (April 1997): pp. 28–51.

Demarest, Bruce. *A History of Interpretation of Hebrews 7, 1–10 from the Reformation to the Present*, Beiträge zur Geschichte der biblischen Exegese 19 (Tübingen: J.C.B. Mohr [Paul Siebeck], 1976).

Dickson, Neil. ' "Shut in with Thee": The Morning Meeting among Scottish Brethren, 1830s–1960s.' Pages 275–88 in *Continuity and Change in Christian Worship*, Studies in Church History 35 (ed. R.N. Swanson; Woodbridge: Boydell & Brewer, 1999).

— *Brethren in Scotland 1838–2000: A Social Study of an Evangelical Movement* (Carlisle: Paternoster, 2002).

Dillistone, F.W. *C.H. Dodd: Interpreter of the New Testament* (London: Hodder & Stoughton, 1977).

Dorrien, Gary. *The Remaking of Evangelical Theology* (Louisville, KY: Westminster John Knox, 1998).

Douglas, J.D. 'A Man of Unchanging Faith: An Interview with F.F. Bruce'. *CT*, 10 October 1980, pp. 16–18.

Dudley-Smith, Timothy. *John Stott: A Global Ministry* (Leicester: IVP, 2001).

Dunn, James D.G. 'The Authority of Scripture According to Scripture'. *Churchman* 96 (1982): pp. 104–22, 201–25.

Duthie, Charles S. 'F.F. Bruce – Committed to the Substance of Scripture'. *British Weekly*, 6 November 1970.

Edwards, G. Patrick. 'Aberdeen and Its Classical Tradition'. *Aberdeen University Review*, no. 176 (Autumn 1986): pp. 410–26.

Ellison, H.L., *Men Spake from God* (London: Paternoster, 1952).

— 'Some Thoughts on Inspiration'. *EQ* 26 (1954): pp. 210–27.

— *The Household Church* (Exeter: Paternoster, 1963, 2nd edn 1979).

Elwell, Walter A. and J.D. Weaver, eds. *Bible Interpreters of the 20th Century: A Selection of Evangelical Voices* (Grand Rapids, MI: Baker, 1999).

[Evans, Fred]. *A Christian Witness in Stockport 1910–1985* (n.pl.: n.p., [1985]).

Fielder, Geraint. *Lord of the Years* (Leicester: IVP, 1988).

France, R.T. 'Evangelical Disagreements about the Bible'. *Churchman* 96 (1982): pp. 226–40.

— 'James Barr and Evangelical Scholarship'. *Anvil* 8 (1991): pp. 51–64.

Gasque, Laurel and Ward. 'F.F. Bruce (1910–1990): An Appreciation'. *Crux* 26/4 (December 1990): pp. 2, 47.

— 'Frederick Fyvie Bruce: An Appreciation'. *H* 69/11 (November 1990): pp. 1–6.

Gasque, Ward. 'Frederick Fyvie Bruce (1910–1990): An Unhyphenated Evangelical'. *Crux* 43/4 (Winter 2007): pp. 21–30.

— *A History of the Criticism of the Acts of the Apostles* (Tübingen: J.C.B. Mohr [Paul Siebeck], 1975).

— 'The Legacy of F.F. Bruce'. *CT*, 5 November 1990, p. 19.

Gasque, Ward and Laurel. 'An Interview with F.F. Bruce'. *St Mark's Review*, no. 139 (Spring 1989): pp. 4–10.

— 'F.F. Bruce – The Apostle Paul and the Evangelical Heritage'. *H* 68/7 (July 1989): pp. 10–12.

— 'F.F. Bruce – Layman and Scholar'. *H* 68/8 (August 1989): pp. 10–11.

— 'F.F. Bruce: A Mind for What Matters'. *CT*, 7 April 1989, pp. 22–5.

— 'F.F. Bruce – "A Tradition of Independent Bible Study"'. *H* 68/6 (June 1989): pp. 10–12.

Gasque, W. Ward and Ralph P. Martin, eds. *Apostolic History and the Gospel: Biblical and Historical Essays Presented to F.F. Bruce on His 60th Birthday* (Exeter: Paternoster, 1970).

Geisler, Norman L., ed. *Inerrancy* (Grand Rapids, MI: Zondervan, 1980).

Goldingay, John. *Approaches to Old Testament Interpretation* (Leicester: Apollos, updated edn, 1990).

— *Models of Scripture* (Grand Rapids, MI: Eerdmans/Carlisle: Paternoster, 1994).

Goodman, Montague. *An Urgent Call to Christian Unity* (London: Paternoster, 1948).

Gordon, James M. *James Denney (1856–1917): An Intellectual and Contextual Biography* (Bletchley: Paternoster, 2006).

Gordon, Robert P. '"Isaiah's Wild Measure": R.M. McCheyne'. *ExT* 103 (1991–2): pp. 235–7.

Grass, Tim. 'Called to Freedom: The Spirituality of F.F. Bruce'. *Crux* 45/4 (Winter 2009): pp. 10–20.

— *Gathering to His Name: The Story of Open Brethren in Britain and Ireland* (Bletchley: Paternoster, 2006).

Harris, Harriet A. *Fundamentalism and Evangelicals* (Oxford: Clarendon, 1998).

Henry, Carl F.H. *Confessions of a Theologian: An Autobiography* (Waco, TX: Word, 1986).

Houlden, J.L. 'Commentary, New Testament', in *Dictionary of Biblical Interpretation* (ed. R.J. Coggins and J.L. Houlden; London: SCM, 1990).

Howley, G.C.D., ed. *A Bible Commentary for Today* (Glasgow: Pickering & Inglis, 1979).

— 'F.F. Bruce as a Friend'. *JCBRF*, no. 22 (November 1971): pp. 17–18 .

— 'F.F. Bruce – on His Retirement'. *W* 108 (1978): pp. 259–60.

Inchley, Ronald. 'A Milestone in I.V.F. Publishing'. *CG* 15 (1962): pp. 18–20.

Ironside, H.A. *A Historical Sketch of the Brethren Movement* (Grand Rapids, MI: Zondervan, 1942).

Jeffrey, Kenneth S. *When the Lord Walked the Land: The 1858–62 Revival in the North East of Scotland* (Carlisle: Paternoster, 2002).

Jewett, Paul K. *Man as Male and Female: A Study in Sexual Relationships from a Theological Point of View* (Grand Rapids, MI: Eerdmans, 1975).

Johnson, Douglas. *Contending for the Faith: A History of the Evangelical Movement in the Universities and Colleges* (Leicester: IVP, 1979).

Kane, J.P. 'Obituary: F.F. Bruce'. *PEQ* 123 (1991), pp. 2–3.

Kittel, Gerhard, ed. *Theological Dictionary of the New Testament* (10 vols; Grand Rapids, MI: Eerdmans, 1964–74).

Larsen, Timothy, ed. *Biographical Dictionary of Evangelicals* (Leicester: IVP, 2003).

— 'Introduction', 'A.S. Peake, the Free Churches and Modern Biblical Criticism'. *BJRL* 86/3 (Autumn 2004): pp. 5–8, 23–53.

Lindsell, Harold. *The Battle for the Bible* (Grand Rapids, MI: Zondervan, 1977).

McDonald, Lee Martin and James A. Sanders, eds. *The Canon Debate* (Peabody, MA: Hendrickson, 2002).

McGrath, Alister. *To Know and Serve God: A Biography of James I. Packer* (London: Hodder & Stoughton, 1997).

McKendrick, James. *James McKendrick* (repr. Glasgow: Gospel Tract Publications, 1988) [first publ. as *Seen and Heard*].

McKenzie, Peter. 'A Tribute to Professor F.F. Bruce'. *CBRF Journal*, no. 123 (August 1991): p. 6.

McKim, Donald K., ed. *Dictionary of Major Biblical Interpreters* (Downers Grove, IL: IVP, 2007).

Mackintosh, John, comp. *Roll of the Graduates of the University of Aberdeen 1926–1955: With Supplement 1860–1925* (Aberdeen: University of Aberdeen, 1960).

Macnicol, John. *Twentieth Century Prophet* (Eastbourne: Prophetic Witness, 1971).

McNiven, Peter. 'The John Rylands Library, 1972–2000'. *BJRL* 82/2–3 (Summer–Autumn 2000): pp. 3–79.

Macpherson, John. *Life and Labours of Duncan Matheson, the Scottish Evangelist* (Kilmarnock: John Ritchie, n.d).

Malherbe, Abraham J. 'Greco-Roman Religion and Philosophy and the New Testament.' Pages 1–26 in *The New Testament and Its Modern Interpreters* (ed. Eldon Jay Epp and George W. MacRae; Philadelphia, PA: Fortress Press/Atlanta, GA: Scholars Press, 1989).

Marshall, I. Howard. 'F.F. Bruce as a Biblical Scholar'. *JCBRF*, no. 22 (November 1971): pp. 5–12 .

— 'Frederick Fyvie Bruce 1910–1990'. *Proceedings of the British Academy* 80 (1991): pp. 245–60.

Mathers, Helen. *Steel City Scholars: The Centenary History of the University of Sheffield* (London: James & James, 2005).

Metzger, Bruce Manning. *Reminiscences of an Octogenarian* (Peabody, MA: Hendrickson, 1997).

Millard, Alan. 'Frederick F. Bruce.' Pages 29–34 in *They Finished Their Course in the 90s* (comp. Robert Plant; Kilmarnock: John Ritchie, 2000).

— 'Frederick Fyvie Bruce 1910–1990'. *JSS* 36 (1991): pp. 1–6.

Mitchell, T.C. 'Professor Frederick Fyvie Bruce, D.D. F.B.A.'. *FT* 117 (1991): pp. 2–5.

Moody-Stuart, K. *Brownlow North: His Life and Work* (London: Banner of Truth, rev. edn, 1961) [first publ. 1878].

Most, Glenn W., ed. *Commentaries – Kommentare*, Aporemata: Kritische Studien zur Philologiegeschichte, Band 4 (Göttingen: Vandenhoeck & Ruprecht, 1999).

Mounce, Robert H. 'The Contribution of F.F. Bruce to Pauline Studies: A Review Article'. *Journal of the Evangelical Theological Society* 23 (1980): pp. 67–73.

Mudditt, B. Howard. 'The Paternoster Story (4): "The End of the Beginning"'. *H* 64/9 (September 1985): pp. 5–7.

— 'Proving with Hard Questions'. *H* 54 (1975): p. 94.

— 'A Publishing Partnership'. *JCBRF*, no. 22 (November 1971): pp. 19–20.

Murray, Iain H. *Evangelicalism Divided: A Record of Crucial Change in the Years 1950 to 2000* (Edinburgh: Banner of Truth, 2000).

— *D. Martyn Lloyd-Jones: The Fight of Faith 1939–1981* (Edinburgh: Banner of Truth, 1990).

Murray, John. 'The Attestation of Scripture.' Pages 1–52 in *The Infallible Word: A Symposium by the Members of the Faculty of Westminster Theological Seminary* (ed. [N.B. Stonehouse and Paul Woolley]; Philadelphia, PA: Presbyterian Guardian Publishing Association, 1946).

Neill, Stephen and Tom Wright. *The Interpretation of the New Testament 1861–1986* (Oxford: Oxford University Press, 2nd edn, 1988).

Noble, T.A. *Tyndale House and Fellowship: The First Sixty Years* (Leicester: IVP, 2006).

Noll, Mark A. *Between Faith and Criticism: Evangelicals, Scholarship, and the Bible* (Leicester: Apollos, 1991).

Oakes, Peter. 'F.F. Bruce and the Development of Evangelical Biblical Scholarship'. *BJRL* 86/3 (Autumn 2004): pp. 99–124.

Pailin, David A., ed. *University of Manchester, Faculty of Theology: Seventy-Fifth Anniversary Papers 1979* (Manchester: Victoria University of Manchester, 1980).

Payne, David F. 'F.F. Bruce as a Teacher'. *JCBRF*, no. 22 (November 1971): pp. 15–16.

Pickering, Arnold. 'F.F. Bruce as a Fellow-Elder'. *JCBRF*, no. 22 (November 1971): pp. 16–17.

Porter, James, ed. *After Columba – After Calvin: Religious Community in North-East Scotland*, Elphinstone Institute Occasional Publications 1 (Aberdeen: Elphinstone Institute, 1999).

Pullan, Brian with Michelle Abendstern. *A History of the University of Manchester 1951–73* (Manchester: Manchester University Press, 2000).

— *A History of the University of Manchester 1973–90* (Manchester: Manchester University Press, 2004).

Randall, Ian. *Educating Evangelicalism: The Origins, Development and Impact of London Bible College* (Carlisle: Paternoster, 2000).

— and David Hilborn. *One Body in Christ: The History and Significance of the Evangelical Alliance* (Carlisle: Paternoster, 2001).

Rawlins, Clive. *William Barclay: The Authorized Biography* (Grand Rapids, MI: Eerdmans, 1984).

— 'Honour, Where Honour Is Due'. *H* 52 (1973): pp. 249–50.

Rawlyk, George A. and Mark A. Noll. *Amazing Grace: Evangelicalism in Australia, Britain, Canada, and the United States* (Grand Rapids, MI: Baker, 1993).

Riches, John K. *A Century of New Testament Study* (Cambridge: Lutterworth, 1993).

Riesen, Richard Allen. *Criticism and Faith in Late Victorian Scotland: A.B. Davidson, William Robertson Smith and George Adam Smith* (Lanham, MD, and London: University Press of America, 1985).

Rodger, P.C., and L. Vischer, eds. *The Fourth World Conference on Faith and Order: Montreal 1963*, Faith and Order Paper 42 (London: SCM, 1964).

Rogers, Jack. *Scripture in the Westminster Confession: A Problem of Historical Interpretation for American Presbyterianism* (Kampen: J.H. Kok, 1966).

—, ed. *Biblical Authority* (Waco, TX: Word Books, 1977).

Rogerson, J.W. *The Bible and Criticism in Victorian Britain*, JSOT Supplement Series 201 (Sheffield: Sheffield Academic Press, 1995).

— 'The Manchester Faculty of Theology 1904: Beginnings and Background'. *BJRL* 86/3 (Autumn 2004): pp. 9–22.

R[oss]., C.W., ed. *Donald Ross, Pioneer Evangelist of the North of Scotland and the United States of America* (Kilmarnock: John Ritchie, n.d).

Runia, Klaas. *Karl Barth and the Word of God* (Leicester: Theological Students' Fellowship, n.d).

Ruoff, Percy O., ed. W.E. *Vine: His Life and Ministry* (London: Oliphants, 1951).

St John, Patricia. *Harold St. John: A Portrait* (London: Pickering & Inglis, 1961).

Saunders, Ernest W. *Searching the Scriptures: A History of the Society of Biblical Literature 1880–1980*, Biblical Scholarship in North America 8 (Chico, CA: Scholars Press, 1982).

Schwarz, Richard W. and Floyd Greenleaf. *Light Bearers: A History of the Seventh-Day Adventist Church* (Nampa, ID: Pacific Press Publishing Association, rev. edn, 1995).

Scott, J.J., Jr. 'Bruce, Frederick Fyvie (1910–90)', in *Dictionary of Biblical Interpretation* (2 vols; ed. John H. Hayes: Nashville, TN: Abingdon, 1999).

Scougal, Henry. *The Life of God in the Soul of Man* (Harrisonburg, VA: Sprinkle Publications, 1986).

Shaw, Trevor. *E.M. Blaiklock: A Christian Scholar* (London: Hodder & Stoughton, 1986).

Shuff, Roger. *Searching for the True Church: Brethren and Evangelicals in mid-Twentieth-Century England* (Carlisle: Paternoster, 2005).

Silva, Moises. 'Betz and Bruce on Galatians'. *Westminster Theological Journal* 45 (1983): pp. 371–85.

Souter, A., ed. *Novum Testamentum Graece* (Oxford: Oxford University Press, 2nd edn, 1947).

Stackhouse, John G., Jr. *Canadian Evangelicalism in the Twentieth Century: An Introduction to Its Character* (Toronto, ON: University of Toronto Press, 1993).

T., L.R. 'William Thomson Walker'. *British Homeopathic Journal* 72 (1983): pp. 87–9.

Tarling, Lowell R. *The Edges of Seventh-day Adventism: A Study of Separatist Groups Emerging from the Seventh–day Adventist Church (1844–1980)* (Barragga Bay, Bermagui South, NSW: Galilee Publications, 1981).

Thiselton, Anthony C. 'New Testament Interpretation in Historical Perspective.' Pages 10–36 in *Hearing the New Testament: Strategies for Interpretation* (ed. Joel B. Green; Grand Rapids, MI: Eerdmans / Carlisle: Paternoster, 1995).

Thomas, Arthur Dicken, Jr. 'James M. Houston, Pioneering Spiritual Director to Evangelicals: Part One'. *Crux* 29/3 (September 1993): pp. 2–10.

Tidball, Derek, 'Post-War Evangelical Theology: A Generational Perspective'. *EQ* 81 (2009): pp. 145–60.

Turkington, W.R.G. *Modernism in the Assemblies! Are We Losing Our Belief in the Authority of the Holy Scriptures?* (Petone, New Zealand: n.p., [1980]).

Wenham, John. *Facing Hell: An Autobiography 1913–1996* (Carlisle: Paternoster, 1998).

— 'Fifty Years of Evangelical Biblical Research: Retrospect and Prospect'. *Churchman* 103 (1989): pp. 209–18.

Widdowson, John. 'Tribute to Iain Bruce'. *The St David's Connection* (Fall 2007): p. 7.

Wilkins, Michael J. and Terence Paige, eds. *Worship, Theology and Ministry in the Early Church: Essays in Honor of Ralph P. Martin*, Journal for the Study of the New Testament Supplement Series 87 (Sheffield: Sheffield Academic Press, 1992).

Wilkinson, John T. *Arthur Samuel Peake: A Biography* (London: Epworth, 1971).

Wood, A. Skevington. 'The Retiring Editor: A Tribute'. *EQ* 53 (1981): pp. 3–5.

Wright, David F. 'Soundings in the Doctrine of Scripture in British Evangelicalism in the First Half of the Twentieth Century'. *TB* 31 (1980): pp. 87–106.

Wright, Tom. *What Saint Paul Really Said* (Oxford: Lion, 1997).

Young, Edward J. *Thy Word Is Truth: Some Thoughts on the Biblical Doctrine of Inspiration* (London: Banner of Truth, 1963).

Websites

Anon. Bible League Trust website http://www.bibleleaguetrust.org (accessed 4 May 2010).

Anon. 'F.F. Bruce' http://en.wikipedia.org/wiki/F.F._Bruce (accessed 5 January 2008).

Anon. 'F.F. Bruce, Study Archive @ PreteristArchive.com – The Internet's Only Balanced Look at Preterism' http://www.preteristarchive.com/StudyArchive/b/bruce-ff.html (accessed 5 January 2008).

Anon. 'Hebron Evangelical Church: Background' http://www.hebron-church.org.uk (accessed 19 November 2009).

Anon. 'Living Bible' http://en.wikipedia.org/wiki/The_Living_Bible (accessed 24 November 2009).

Anon. 'NLT: Meet the Scholars' http://www.newlivingtranslation.com/05discoverthenlt/meetthescholars.asp (accessed 24 November 2009).

Anon. 'New Living Translation' http://en.wikipedia.org/wiki/New_Living_Translation (accessed 24 November 2009).

Anon. 'Religion: Allegro under Fire'. *Time*, 2 April 1956 http://www.time.com/time/magazine/article/0,9171,862089-2,00.html (downloaded 9 October 2009).

Anon. 'Undiscovered Scotland: Elgin' http://www.undiscoveredscotland.co.uk/elgin/elgin/index.html (accessed 17 November 2009).

Anon. 'Yorkshire Celtic Studies: Table of Contents' http://www.ucc.ie/locus/ycs.pdf (accessed 12 November 2009).

278   *Select Bibliography of Other Items*

Bradshaw, Rob. 'Frederick Fyvie Bruce (1910–1990)' [bibliography] http://www.theologicalstudies.org.uk/theo_bruce.php (accessed 9 January 2008) [a number of Bruce's articles were also accessed via this site].

Clines, David J.A. 'Frederick Fyvie Bruce, 1910–1990: In Memoriam'. *CBRF Journal*, no. 123 (August 1991), pp. 53–4 http://www.shef.ac.uk/bibs/DJACcurrres/Bruce.html (accessed 7 January 2008).

Hubbard, David A. 'Evangelicals and Biblical Scholarship, 1945–1992: An Anecdotal Commentary'. *Bulletin for Biblical Research* 3 (1993), pp. 1–16 http://www.ibr-bbr.org/IBRBulletin/BBR_1993/BBR-1993_01_Hubbard_Evangelicals.pdf (accessed 2 December 2009).

Kummel, Werner. Letter to F.F. Bruce, NT Resources Blog http://ntresources.com/blog/?p=102 (accessed 10 March 2008).

Marshall, I. Howard. 'Bruce, Frederick Fyvie (1910–1990)', in *Oxford Dictionary of National Biography* http://www.oxforddnb.com (accessed 14 April 2008).

Rogerson, John. 'The Society for Old Testament Study, 1917–1992' http://www.sots.ac.uk/historyofsots.html (accessed 5 January 2008).

Telford, W.R. 'SNTS, Its Origins, and Robin McL. Wilson's Contribution to the Society (2006)' https://www.surfgroepen.nl/sites/SNTS/Shared%20Documents (accessed 5 January 2008).

Zytkoskee, Adrian. 'Interview with Desmond Ford'. *Spectrum* 11/2 (October 1980): pp. 53–61 http://spectrummagazine.org/files/archive/archive 11-15/11-2zytkoskee.pdf (downloaded 23 September 2009).

Articles in *Ministry* (October 1980) http://www.adventistarchives.org/docs/MIN/MIN1980-10.pdf (accessed 23 September 2009).

Recording

Service of Thanksgiving, Brinnington Evangelical Church, 27 October 1990.

Index